W9-CFQ-652

FRANCIS BACON AND
THE RHETORIC OF NATURE

Thomas J. Wilson Prize

The Board of Syndics of Harvard University Press has awarded this book the eighteenth annual Thomas J. Wilson Prize, honoring the late director of the Press. The Prize is awarded to the book chosen by the Syndics as the best first book accepted by the Press during the calendar year.

FRANCIS BACON

AND THE

RHETORIC OF NATURE

John C. Briggs

HARVARD UNIVERSITY PRESS
CAMBRIDGE, MASSACHUSETTS
LONDON, ENGLAND
1989

Publication of this book has been aided by a grant from
the Andrew W. Mellon Foundation

This book is printed on acid-free paper, and its binding materials
have been chosen for strength and durability.

Library of Congress Cataloging-in-Publication Data

Briggs, John C.
    Francis Bacon and the rhetoric of nature / John C. Briggs.
        p.   cm.
    Includes index.
    ISBN 0-674-31743-2 (alk. paper)
    1. Bacon, Francis, 1561–1626—Contributions in philosophy of
nature.   2. Bacon, Francis, 1561–1626—Contributions in rhetoric.
3. Philosophy of nature—History.   4. Rhetoric—History.   5. Bacon,
Francis, 1561–1626—Contributions in methodology.   6. Methodology—
History.   I. Title.
B1199.N38B75   1989   89-31279
192—dc20   CIP

For My Parents

PREFACE

This book focuses upon the close relation between Bacon's famous reform of scientific method and his less well known conceptions of rhetoric, nature, and religion. Most present-day analysts of Bacon's works have taken for granted that the first two are connected, though they may disagree in their interpretations of Baconian method and rhetoric. Fewer scholars have attempted to link these two to Bacon's natural philosophy, and almost no one has given serious thought to the place of religion in his project. I intend to discuss Bacon's debt to—and radical adaptation of—the Wisdom Literature, the Pauline Epistles, old philosophies of organic nature, and the ideas of the Greek atomists, which he uses to distinguish the new learning from idolatries. Bacon calls on the authority of Solomon, Moses, Paul, and Democritus to conceive a new persuasion, a way of understanding nature and mankind in terms of a code to be broken and exploited through self-abnegation and an assiduously analytic inquiry undertaken for the sake of charity. This book thus seeks to find the links among Bacon's strange paradoxes: a new natural philosophy that elaborates old views of nature while seeming to discard them; a doctrine of selfless scientific inquiry and civil persuasion that licenses coercion and secrecy; and a postulation of scientific charity that tests the limits of Bacon's idea of charity in religion. I will attempt to clarify the way Bacon pairs science with religion, draws natural magic and cryptology into the empirical discovery of nature, and mixes his discussion of open and specialized communication with his own intimations of a secret, world-transforming revelation.

In his recent, illuminating *Francis Bacon and Modernity,* Charles Whitney has begun to restore the importance of Bacon's profession of Christianity. He has also helpfully analyzed some of the shortcomings of studies assigning Bacon a place among the ancients or the moderns at the expense of an understanding of the troubling, intriguing paradoxicality of his "instauration" of learning. Camps of Bacon's defenders, like his attackers, have tended to disagree over what they praise and blame, without attending to the variety and seriousness of their differences. When Bacon has been treated as a liberal reformer, his defenders have not sufficiently explored the implications of his debt to magic or prophecy; when seen as a traditionalist, he has been separated from his innovative use of tradition.

Whitney's most valuable contribution to Bacon studies is to show how innovation and tradition at times fuse and at other times come into conflict in Bacon's works. He goes so far as to argue that Bacon is an archetypal modern precisely because he is entangled in old patterns of learning that he tentatively transcends. But if a supremely paradoxical interaction between the old and the new is the essence of Bacon's modernity, one must continue to ask what Bacon's master trope tells us about his ends and means. So that his texts do not dissolve into manufactured plays of opposites or false syntheses of real differences, it is now all the more necessary to reread Bacon's works—to continue to assess the purposes, passions, and actions that made them in their own time.

If Whitney is right to draw critical attention to Bacon's paradoxes, as I think he is, interpreters must be especially careful to remember Bacon's warning against reading nature merely as a fascinating riddle: the Sphinx's puzzle tears into the minds of those who work at it without regard for the Sphinx's true nature. Some of the limits and powers of paradox as a heuristic for reading Bacon's ambivalent texts are evident in his invocation of biblical prophecy to declare the prospective restoration of archaic truths freed from idolatrous perception. Setting aside for the moment the question of whether Bacon uses Christianity as a veil, we see that he discusses the renovation of learning as though it were a recovery of the most fundamental ground of science—be it the deepest order of nature hidden in the ancient story of Proteus, or the true temple of Solomon and that great king's pious natural philosophy concealed in a new aphoristic method of scientific inquiry. As Whitney points out in detail, the recovery that the new learning promises therefore seems profoundly restorative, even though it is unprecedented. The paradox is as intriguing as it is problematic: the new discoveries, standing cleansed of misapprehension, would seem to bring back truths that are beyond memory. Though no ancient or modern understands the story of Proteus, a wise reading of the myth is supposed to be possible, and necessary, for the new understanding of matter. Scripture only hints at the meaning of Solomon's comprehensive learning of the flora and fauna of Lebanon, but the new Eden to be created by science would somehow turn its residents-to-be back to their *radix*. They will reinterpret the past and recreate in the present a primordial wisdom that their forebears did not know and could not keep. Some of the dizzying permutations of these paradoxes are Bacon's. The allure of their play of opposites, however, invites riddling interpretation. Readers of Bacon must persist in looking beyond what might be only an ostensible master-trope.

Certain detectable purposes, ideas, and nuances in Bacon's works offer organizing principles for discussing his paradoxes. One is the idea of Providence. Another is the analogy Bacon draws between Providence and scientific progress. Providence, in the context of Bacon's putative Christianity, is a progression of events that affirms what is certain and permanent, through means and agents whose effects and significance are unknown until they are revealed. Analogously, Bacon's true scientific innovation is supposed to discover a permanent order that no anticipation can penetrate. In this sense the paradoxes of Bacon's innovative traditionalism take their place within the unifying idea of God's role in history.

Sacred and secular revelations are akin in a more particular sense: both manifest themselves in a kind of code. God is a code-maker who makes nature decipherable to the "sons of science." For Bacon, it is the nature of the best codes that they resist all explication and indeed suggest misleading meanings until they are broken. The moment of their solution is therefore a revelation of the design of the whole, which by definition offers no essential clues of itself until all becomes clear in an instant. The new learning suggests that a true understanding of this principle confirms the primordial design while affirming the code-breaker's untainted originality—his independence from expectations about what the design might be.

The paradigm of the providential code, as it is woven into Bacon's works, is a guide for understanding another controversial issue in Bacon studies: the nature of the relation between his science and rhetoric. Here too a paradox is at work. Bacon sometimes refers to rhetoric as a theory and practice of communication; it is distinct from science, upon which it reports. The degree to which the idolatrous imagination has misled all rhetoricians and their audiences would seem to make the rational use of rhetoric impossible. Yet Bacon frequently encourages the view that rhetoric is the very means by which the new learning conveys itself to the learned. As a science, rhetoric might even be capable of moving audiences beyond the idols of grammar and vulgar vocabulary, benighted commonplaces, badly learned topics, and self-pleasing conceits. Is this fusion of rhetoric with science a delusion or an insight Bacon shares with the ancients? Or is it an indication of a fundamental renovation? Again, the paradigm of the code offers a thread: as an encryption, Baconian rhetoric might be an attractive coloring or a neutral instrument of reason that searches and touches upon the deepest natures of its subjects and audiences.

But how then does one explain Bacon's persuasiveness? Can his famous rhetorical facility be essentially double, perhaps profoundly duplicitous, and remain persuasive? And how might one come to understand Bacon's encoded discourse (if that is what he writes) as an intimation of its own solution, or as a revelation of something beyond itself? To discuss these questions without becoming lost in a maze, it is necessary to grapple with Bacon's idea of persuasion and to see how it is embodied in his works.

The possibility of a connection between Bacon's rhetoric, cryptology, and natural philosophy is doubly strange to a modern reader who does not entertain the old notion that man's understanding and influencing nature have a bearing upon his understanding and persuasion of human beings. In his own way, Bacon preserves the idea that the natural world harbors immaterial bodies or spirits capable of some form of perception. He approaches the problem of understanding and moving things and audiences at least partly in the light of the complexities that accompany the persuasion of these immaterial bodies. What their nature is, what the means are by which they move and are moved, and what the ends are toward which they tend and are persuaded are all factors in Bacon's advancing of providential and secular codes.

Viewed in these terms, Bacon's endeavor at once mirrors and overturns paradigms of persuasion that pervade England in the early Renaissance. Plato, Aristotle, and Cicero, the ancients Bacon most admires and undermines, offer means of discovery and persuasion drawing out in stages the potentialities of things and of audiences according to their most characteristic perfections. The testimonies of appearances and opinions, however limited in their ultimate significance, take on special force in such contexts as initiators of an inquiry that starts with a modicum of consent and moves toward a veiled reality. What is most startling in Bacon's writings, by contrast, is his use of persuasive rhetoric to insinuate and cover the sciences' power to strip away the world's persuadable potentialities for the sake of revealing whatever persists.

Bacon does seem to join with the three ancients when he sets out various forms and levels of plausible reasoning that might contribute to scientific proficiency and discovery, but he enforces the trying, revelatory mode of scientific inquiry and communication in a manner that parallels his theological precedent. The three ancients tend to coax and restrain the potencies of things by costuming themselves, their subjects, and their audiences in appropriate forms and ideas. Their role-playing as inquirers and persuaders is neither entirely hidden nor fully disclosed. Bacon is also a masterful dramatist, despite his identification of the theater with idolatrous learning, but he seeks to assume an unquestionable humility that is a ready disguise for secret purposes. His charity likewise distinguishes itself, in not being subject to question or discussion. The remote benevolence of the new scientific charity permits the sons of science to manipulate ordinary appearances and understandings—vaguely or misleadingly to the mass of men, explicitly to decoders of nature and society.

Bacon's disavowal and exercise of license in his use of the ancients draws from sources deep within English Renaissance culture: old and reformed ideas of religion, rhetoric, poetical ornamentation, white magic, pedagogy, and even the training of horses. But Bacon ultimately moves these sources to a scientific setting that changes them into surds and signs of an order that only a science of decipherment could follow and manipulate.

Without presuming to define the variety of traditional Renaissance views of nature as a single world-picture from which Bacon departed or took his cue, this book takes seriously the possibility that the study of several normative traditions in Bacon's England can help us draw into view some of the deeper characteristics of his project. Paolo Rossi, in his forceful defense of Bacon's borrowing from the old learning, assumes that the old order was Thomistic and "organic," a setting that encouraged bondage to magic, and which therefore was the undesirable alternative to Bacon's reforms. Yet the suggestiveness of A. N. Whitehead's praise for Bacon's "organic" vision of nature indicates that we ought to continue to discuss the meaning of the term and the degree of the old order's hold on Bacon. In the context of this debate, I have called these normative Renaissance traditions "Timaeic," after the influential Platonic dialogue. Although they did not always depend upon customary opinions, they were widespread and remarkably consistent, despite their many eccentricities. And they managed for centuries to coexist with Christianity, though not without tension. Bacon's care to make the new sciences acceptable to religion, as he dares to use religion for his sciences, acknowledges and severely tests that tradition of coexistence.

A final note is in order concerning my choice of evidence from Bacon's writings. I have relied in most instances upon Bacon's more widely known works, particularly *The Advancement of Learning,* its Latin version (*De Dignitate et Augmentis Scientiarum*), the *Novum Organum, The New Atlantis, De Sapientia Veterum (The Wisdom of the Ancients), The Sacred Meditations,* and of course the essays. I draw less frequently from works attributed to Bacon but published after his death, and I make almost no use of a small group of highly problematical works missing from J. Spedding's edition. These include most notably the privately circulated, satirical attack on the ancients in *Temporis Partus Masculus (The Masculine Birth of Time).* Given the difficulty of assessing Bacon's paradoxical ideas of nature and persuasion, I have chosen to return to the more conventional works, and to prepare for a reading of the esoteric texts from the richly conventional perspective. In their collective magnitude both as public gestures and as texts prepared for the guidance of the sons of science, the more famous works display most fully (and conceal most ingeniously) the character and limits of Bacon's design.

I owe this book to my teachers in a previous decade. Though they took no part in my choice of a subject or in my preparation of this text, I am especially grateful to Janel Mueller, David Bevington, and Michael Murrin of the University of Chicago, to Harvey C. Mansfield, Jr., of Harvard University, and to Paul Cantor of the University of Virginia. I thank James Hartman of the University of Kansas for providing the opportunity to extend my studies in rhetoric. Peter Pesic and the faculty of St. John's College in Santa Fe helped me to present and discuss an early version of the chapter on the *Rhetoric* and the *Phaedrus.* The Regents of the University of California gave their generous support in the form of a Regents' Junior Faculty Fellowship, and a grant for a summer of study at the Berkeley campus. Sharon Tyler supplied invaluable editorial assistance.

CONTENTS

INTRODUCTION   1

I   NATURE ACCORDING TO SCRIPTURE   13

II   THE TIMAEIC TRADITION
IN THE SIXTEENTH CENTURY   41

Cosmology and Rhetoric   41
Persuasion and Ornament   79
Nature and Concealment in Courtly Gesture   118

III   ADVANCEMENTS AND REFORMULATIONS   132

Baconian Nature   132
Bacon and Rhetoric   150

IV   CONTRASTING AND ANTECEDENT
TRADITIONS   175

The Phaedrus *and the* Rhetoric   175
Agricola and Ramus   199

V   THE *ESSAYS*   215

POSTSCRIPT: THE NEW SCIENCES AND
BACON'S TRIAL   249

Notes   257
Index   281

FRANCIS BACON AND
THE RHETORIC OF NATURE

ABBREVIATIONS

Adv	*Of the Proficience and Advancement of Learning Divine and Humane*
De Aug	*De Dignitate et Augmentis Scientiarum* (Augmentation of the *Advancement*)
CGE	*The Colours of Good and Evil*
CN	*Cogitationes De Natura Rerum* (*Thoughts on the Nature of Things*)
DG	*Descriptio Globi Intellectualis* (*Description of the Intellectual Globe*)
E	*The Essays*
FL	*Filum Labyrinthi* (*The Clue to the Maze*)
HRK	*History of the Reign of King Henry VII*
HVM	*Historia Vitae et Mortis* (*History of Life and Death*)
IM	*Instauratio Magna* (*The Great Instauration*)
IN	*De Interpretatione Naturae* (*Of the Interpretation of Nature*)
ITCM	*Inquisitions Touching the Compounding of Metals*
LD	*Letter and Discourse to Sir Henry Savill*
LL	*Letters and Life*
MS	*Meditationes Sacrae* (*Sacred Meditations*)
NA	*The New Atlantis*
NE	*Naturalis et Experimentalis* (*Natural and Experimental History*)
NO	*Novum Organum* (*The New Organon*)
P	*Parasceve* (*Preparative Towards a Natural and Experimental History*)
PO	*De Principiis Atque Originibus* (*On Principles and Origins*)
RCB	*Rawley's Commonplace Book*
SS	*Sylva Sylvarum* (*The Natural History in Ten Centuries*)
SV	*De Sapientia Veterum* (*The Wisdom of the Ancients*)
TC	*Thema Coeli* (*Theory of the Heavens*)
VT	*Valerius Terminus* (*Of the Interpretation of Nature*)

INTRODUCTION

The story of Orpheus, which though so well known has not yet
been in all points perfectly well interpreted, seems meant for a
representation of universal Philosophy. For Orpheus himself,—a
man admirable and truly divine, who being master of all harmony
subdued and drew all things after him by sweet and gentle measures,—may pass by an easy metaphor for philosophy personified.
For as the works of wisdom surpass in dignity and power the works
of strength, so the labours of Orpheus surpass the labours of Hercules.   (*SV* VI.720)

But of the three remedies [for temptation], far the best in every way
is that of Orpheus; who by singing and sounding forth the praises
of the gods confounded the voices of the Sirens and put them aside:
for meditations upon things divine excel the pleasures of the sense,
not in power only, but also in sweetness.   (*SV* VI.764)

Orpheus is Bacon's paradigm for "universal Philosophy" or the
"wisdom" he identifies with the new learning. The new sciences,
which indeed promise to move or persuade "all things"—rocks as
well as beasts and human beings—are to be mastered with religious
care rather than merely Herculean force. In traditional accounts that
Bacon would have found in numerous sixteenth-century editions of
Apollodorus' *Library*[1] and Apollonius Rhodius' *Argonautica,*[2] Orpheus
accompanies Jason in the quest for the Golden Fleece; the purpose of
his singing is to help the Argonauts succeed. For Bacon, the Orphic
victory over the Sirens shadows a pious universal philosophy whose
power and sweetness transcend the strength and pleasure of heroic
triumphs.

   The myth also suggests, in Orpheus' loss of Eurydice and the poet's
demise at the hands of the furious Thracian women, something more

than Orpheus' surrender of reason to passion.[3] The didactic medieval interpretation misses the myth's deeper warning about what happens to Orphic wisdom when it is irresolute or inappropriately realized. In the last words of *The Wisdom of the Ancients,* Bacon suggests that beneath the ancient story of Orphic failure a true Orpheus awaits proper interpretation (*SV* VI.764).[4]

The proliferation of specialized studies of Bacon has mined many of the riches of his work, but has not led to an adequate recognition of the new learning's emulation of Orpheus. This book is an attempt to read the pious, philosophical singer back into Bacon's work. Departing from *The Orphic Voice,* Elizabeth Sewell's study of Bacon's repression of his own Orphic science,[5] the following chapters interpret Bacon's key texts in light of the synthesis of philosophy and religion that he saw embedded in the myth of the ancient poet.

Recent debate over Bacon's role in the birth of modernity has usually kept his conceptions of religion, natural philosophy, and universal philosophy apart. Scholars have analyzed them in isolation from his method and rhetoric, subordinated them to the arts of inquiry and transmission, or left them to the scrutiny of others. A recent attempt to synthesize seventeenth-century ideas of natural science, religion, history, law, and literature categorizes Bacon's comprehensive endeavor as a critique of the old learning, on the authority of the Royal Society's supposed preference for Book I of *The Advancement of Learning* over Book II.[6] Yet Thomas Sprat himself, as spokesman for the young Royal Society that looked to Bacon as its founder, appears to have seen far more in him than a critic of outworn disciplines or a champion of inductive method: Bacon was "one great Man, who had the true Imagination of the whole extent of his Enterprize, as it is now set on foot."[7]

Specialization in Bacon studies is sensible in light of the variety, power, and complexity of that Renaissance man's achievements, but in avoiding the charge of dilettantism, modern scholars, particularly literary critics, have skirted the woods of Bacon's syncretism, to the detriment of an understanding of his place in the transformation of culture attendant upon the passing of Elizabeth. Now the trees we see in Bacon scholarship often diminish the forest—the "forest of forests," as Bacon calls one of his own investigations—that fresh readings suggest is there. The need to return to his texts grows as we lose touch with Bacon's particular ends and means, for his innovation continues to have fundamental significance for an under-standing of the modern advancement of learning, particularly the advancement of ideas about moving and persuading things and human beings according to rhetoric, psychology, and the social and natural sciences. This book therefore seeks to shift the study of Bacon away from the encyclopedic and esoteric and toward his new wisdom of per-suasion, which in many ways reflects and transforms pre-Baconian anal-ogies between natural philosophy, cosmology, and the study of man.

Stanley Fish has forcefully demonstrated the *aporia* in modern readings of the *Essays* that neglect Baconian ideas resonant with meaning for the new learning as a whole: in particular, the Baconian conception of experience.[8] Fish argues that modern commentators inevitably mis-read the essays when they neither detect nor undergo the ambiguous and disruptive sufferings at the center of Bacon's theory and practice of experimental science. In the new learning, experiment is more than a method of discovery; it is an ordeal, a test of its subject's true nature. Ultimately, all experiments work upon the matter and spirit of the created world, including the minds and passions of human beings. The scientific method therefore entails a particular understanding of nature, and of human nature.

Bacon adopts a principle much like one that Plato sets out in the *Phaedrus:* that ideas and practices of persuasion stem from ideas about the nature of the subject matters and souls upon which the persuader works. In an early and important letter to a prospective patron, Bacon testifies to his fundamental attachment to the writings of Anaxagoras, the natural philosopher whom Socrates praises in the *Phaedrus* as the man who taught the great persuader Pericles how to "star-gaze." It was such study of nature and the cosmos early in his career that drew Pericles toward true eloquence.[9]

The arduous experience of reading and inquiry that Fish identifies in the *Essays* is also a consequence of Bacon's adaptation of religion for the purposes of the new sciences. Bacon puts great weight on the idea that the Creator moves his creation cryptically, in a manner that tests man as man tests nature. In its deepest movements God's Prov-idence makes man a Job, or a Jonah like the shipwrecked sailors cast up on the shore of the New Atlantis. Exploring nature and reading wise texts are strikingly similar ordeals, in which Bacon would have the champion of the new learning imitate God's way of vexing the world in order to disclose its true nature. Even though Bacon takes extraordinary measures to prevent the new learning from becoming a direct reflection of traditional theology, the pervasiveness and careful consistency of such analogies tell us a great deal about what the new sciences of inquiry and transmission will be. The *Essays* are themselves constructed in part to test their audiences'dedication to the self-effacing quest of the new sciences, just as they testify to their maker's power to penetrate the subjects of prudential wisdom, religion, and human nature.

It is a commonplace to observe that the new learning involves doctrine as well as method. But critics in literary studies have tended to focus on facility or stylistic power without pursuing the new learning's claim to truth as well as utility. Others have attempted to determine the sources and originality of Bacon's scientific innovation. A formidable recent study of Baconian discourse—by Lisa Jardine—characterizes the new learning in terms of its utility as an instrument of discovery and communication.[10]

In a discussion of newly discovered manuscripts that enlarge the known corpus of Bacon's speculative philosophy, Graham Rees has observed that students of Bacon's method must eventually confront a contradiction in the current view that his project is more practical than philosophical:

> The manuscripts lend their formidable weight to the lively suspicion that the speculative philosophy was in many ways just as important to Bacon as the method itself . . . Putting the matter in a rather extreme form, why did Bacon bother to write the *Novum Organum* at all if he believed he already possessed the makings of a creditable and credible body of positive science?[11]

Method is neither a critique of past learning nor Bacon's whole science; one need not go to the unpublished manuscripts to appreciate the pertinence of Rees's point. The penultimate aphorism of the *Novum Organum,* Book I, claims "to speak the whole truth" about the superiority of contemplation to active endeavors: the new sciences will confirm their essentially contemplative character as what Bacon has just called "pledges of truth" rather than as contributors to "the comforts of life" (*NO* IV.110). "To speak the whole truth," he confides, "the very beholding of the light is itself a more excellent and fairer thing than all the uses of it;—so assuredly the very contemplation of things, as they are, without superstition or imposture, error or confusion, is in itself more worthy than all the fruit of inventions" (*NO* IV.115).[12]

The famous letter to Burghley, which Bacon wrote at the threshold of public life, carefully establishes a similar argument for the precedence of contemplation over action. Even though Bacon is petitioning for a role in public affairs, he confides that "the contemplative planet carrieth me away wholly." His proficiency in "study and meditation," he argues, has prepared him against the vainglories of activity in great households. If he fails to find favor, he will turn undaunted to a life like that of the natural philosopher, Anaxagoras, "who reduced himself with contemplation unto voluntary poverty" so as to be "a true pioneer in that mine of truth" (*LL* VIII.108).

In the scientific works, Bacon does show himself taking pains not to erect "abstract notions" or anything resembling an "entire or universal theory" (*NO* IV.103–104). In his famous summary of the *Instauratio Magna* he promises that the goal of the enterprise is "no mere felicity of speculation, but the real business and fortunes of the human race." He grants to "the active part" of the new sciences the power to mark the shape of a contemplative analogue: "let the active part itself be as the seal which prints and determines the contemplative counterpart" (*NO* IV.121).

It is also true that in the letter to Burghley Bacon's emphasis on contemplation is sometimes ambiguous. Professing one's love for star-gazing may be a useful argument for receiving public favor as a candidate untainted by ambition. Indeed, the language with which Bacon describes the contemplative life seems to welcome action. Calling his philosophical endeavor "vast," he declares "I have taken all knowledge to be my province," and hints at the power of meditative energies that "carrieth me away wholly." His Anaxagoras pursues truth with the energy of a miner. Bacon proposes to subdue the realm of knowledge as if it were an abstract Ireland and he the governor, purging false learners who are bandit "rovers" guilty of having "committed so many spoils." He aspires to an abstract plantation of the disordered province of the old learning, using "grounded conclusions" whose fruit would be "profitable inventions" (*LL* VIII.109).

Despite the stridency of these expressions, the young Bacon, portraying himself as a scourge of deluded learning's marauding desires, paints himself as a thinker, as Adam was before the Fall and God's favorite, the contemplative shepherd Abel, was after it (*Adv* III.295). Bacon's application for patronage is in this sense a remarkably limited concession to the active life. Fallen, Adamic man must live by the sweat of his brow and "labour for use," but his true calling—a contemplative "delight in the experiment"—seems to be his even now to the degree that he focuses on natural philosophy rather than knowledge of good and evil beyond God's commandments (*Adv* III.296).

This argument is harmonious with Bacon's critique of idolatry in the *Instauratio Magna,* which warns against both the indiscriminate embrace of experience and the avoidance of experience altogether. Idolaters either avoid it entirely, or commit themselves to its "waves" without submitting to the rigors of experiment. Superficial, impatient learners have pursued their ends "with premature and unseasonable eagerness." By seeking "experiments of Fruit, not experiments of Light," they have failed to imitate "the divine procedure, which in its first day's work created light only and assigned to it one entire day; on which day it produced no material work" (*IM* IV.17).

Viewed in this light, Bacon's pivotal equation of knowledge with power ("human knowledge and human power meet in one"; *NO* IV.47) is problematic. The statement occurs within an aphoristic passage that emphasizes obedient observation of nature rather than the application of knowledge. Contemplation produces fruit only as it submits to a rigorous abstinence from vain anticipations.

The gloss on the first chapter of Genesis in *The Advancement* offers us an early, crucial development of these ideas. From the beginning, "knowledge and illumination" have been superior to active governance and "domination," the creation of light preceding the formation of the world. Conversely, God's establishment of the Sabbath at the end of the Creation is an argument that "the day wherein God did rest and contemplate his own works, was blessed above all the days wherein he did effect and accomplish them" (*Adv* III.296). God indeed "made" heaven and earth first, but none of his creatures can aspire to "manufacture" matter from nothing (*Adv* III.295–96). Solomonic wisdom, the essence of the new learning, is for the wisest of kings an arduous, sweet contemplation of God's grace rather than a manufacture or enjoyment of pleasure-giving riches. These remarks harmonize with Bacon's key statement in the *Novum Organum* that interpretation is "the natural work of the mind when freed from impediments" (*NO* IV.115).

The new knowledge is by no means merely contemplative (and contemplation is by no means merely passive). Book II of *The Advancement* contains Bacon's famous advocacy of the use of knowledge for the benefit of mankind. The meaning of that argument, however, turns upon Bacon's original defense of contemplation over use. It recognizes, for example, the danger that the application of knowledge will pervert the imaginations of those who use it and those who benefit from innovation. Something is needed to protect the new universal philosophers from the impediments of their fallen natures and shelter those whom they would benefit, as they "sweep away all theories and common notions" (*NO* IV.93) and conceal themselves from the idolatries of the benighted. Given the opportunity to make the world over, adepts of the new learning must not make it into the idol of idols.

Bacon's guiding star for the new learning is charity, a "duty" toward the world rather than toward the "private and particular." The laws of nature and Christianity establish that this good is "engraven upon man." It ought to be, "if he degenerate not, . . . more precious than the conservation of life and being." The law of charity appears to settle "most of the controversies wherein Moral Philosophy is conversant," particularly "the question touching the preferment of the contemplative or active life," which it seems to decide against contemplation. Champions of the new learning must act in order to escape exclusive concern for themselves (*Adv* III.421). But how will charitable action prevent idolatrous abuse of knowledge?

In the deeper course of his argument, Bacon is really talking about "good intentions" and "good conscience," not action as such. Charity is essentially the endurance of temptation and indignity (*Adv* III.423); it is a willingness to sacrifice, rather than a consistent practice of generosity. "Active Good" may in fact be remote from charity and be prompted by the private pursuit of security, of variety that relieves Saturnine despair, and of procreation for the sake of pleasure and the illusion of longevity (*Adv* III.424).

True Baconian charity combines contemplation with action so as to efface private desire and yet promote learning's advancement in a world of desire. It sets out to do two things at once: to follow the meditative Socrates by concentrating on the "clearing of perturbations" from the mind, rather than seizing upon the objects of desire; and to adapt the techniques of Socrates' rivals, the Sophists, to justify obtaining those things one desires as "a shew of advancement" in the service of charity rather than for personal indulgence. The remarkable historical figure that joins these antagonistic principles for the sake of religious charity is King Solomon, the exemplary benefactor who is also an imperturbable partaker of pleasure.

Solomonic charity that endures in the world of action alone rides the "contrary motions" of enjoyment and austerity. Men must force themselves to do likewise, as in Bacon's example of the lutist who "breaketh" his hand to the "strange and hard stops" of lyrical and extemporaneous play rather than apply himself to the easier and less ebullient "ground" (*Adv* III.427). Bacon would have the musician indulge in and propagate lyrical pleasure while the ordeal of his playing wins him serenity.

The conversion of new learners is thus comparable in its arduousness to conversion in religion: "the entrance into the kingdom of man, founded on the sciences, being not much other than the entrance into the kingdom of heaven, whereinto none may enter except as a little child" (*NO* IV.69). The new knowledge rivals religion in being "adverse to common sense" (*FL* III.503). Bacon's writings reflect "everywhere," he says, his own "religious care to eject, repress, and as it were exorcise every kind of phantasm" (*IM* IV.30).

The new knowledge is in this sense esoteric, even apocalyptic (*IM* IV.33); but its revelatory power also makes available a world-moving knowledge without regard for the preparation of those who receive it. The greater the ease with which it is apprehended and applied, the more likely the dissipation of the very wonder and discipline that Bacon insists must test charitable scientific practice and shield it from idolatrous misuse.

The mixing of religion with natural philosophy introduces the risk of heresy, a danger that Bacon in the *Novum Organum* sometimes attributes to the old sciences—especially alchemy. Any attempt to construct a natural philosophy (as alchemists had done) on the basis of Genesis or Job "and other parts of the sacred writings" seeks "for the dead among the living." From this "unwholesome mixture of things human and divine there arises not only a fantastic philosophy but also an heretical religion" (*NO* IV.66). Yet we know that in *The Advancement* and elsewhere Bacon looks forward to the propagation of knowledge, allows that the book of Job is "pregnant and swelling with natural philosophy" (*Adv* III.298), points to Solomon's authority in his knowledge of flora and fauna, and incorporates Platonic and alchemical ideas. How then does he avoid the problem of heresy?

Part of the answer lies in the new learning's secrecy, and in the secrecy it finds in nature. Although Bacon heralds the advancement of knowledge that would benefit everyone, and although he promotes the possibility, especially in *The Advancement,* that Adamic perception of nature's truths is as near as the resolve to learn them, he finds his profoundest model for the inquiry and transmission of the new sciences in the cryptic mode of Solomonic aphorisms. The "broken knowledge" of the Wisdom Literature counters heresy by enforcing or teaching wonder and restraint. God's encryption of the world is an enigma, and its maker is hidden to all but those who can discover the signs of God's wisdom by suffering the scourging of their vanities in the sweet ordeal of Solomonic inquiry. For the transmission of the new learning the aphorism seems eminently accessible, yet it preserves and expands the cryptic ends and means of Solomonic inquiry. The mass of mankind, incapable of carrying out the task, will know the new sciences only by their effects (*NO* IV.42), while the true interpreters of nature, occupied with the code of God's wise formation of the world, will conduct and present themselves in a secret, though seemingly open, manner that controls idolatrous excesses both in themselves and in their beneficiaries.

In this sense the analogies between the new learning and religion are a cover for, and a testimony to, a righteousness as well as a moderation that imitate the Solomonic model. They are used not only as forms of instruction and persuasion, but also as guardians of the new learning's integrity, and as protection against misprision—including perhaps the sectarian and insurrectionary trials that Bacon predicted would soon test England (*IN* III.519).

For these reasons, Fish's observation that Bacon's discourse in the *Essays* is "the reverse of what it seems at every point"[13] becomes doubly pertinent. The benighted do not see the discourse's darker turnings while the true initiates come to know, if belatedly, the wrenching they must undergo to be "sons of science." The reader can at best glimpse Bacon's true subject, Fish continues, only as "the abstraction itself" is viewed through an arduous process of recognizing the reader's distance from it.[14]

Fish only hints at what that abstraction might be, since he presents Bacon's ideas primarily as procedures: the new sciences are at bottom psychological manipulations. Just as the inductive method is a machine that displaces the faculty of choice, the *Essays* in Fish's view ultimately yield debased, mechanical adaptations of the process of purifying self-consumption that leads to higher spiritual planes in Plato and Augustine. Bacon is finally a master of utility. What he is saying about nature and Orphic ends is not, and perhaps cannot be, pursued beyond his mechanism.

Other studies prematurely limiting Bacon's Orphic purposes, by

Vickers, Richter, and Harrison, stress mainly the power of his imaginative prose. Vickers, the leading interpreter of Bacon's stylistics, does vigorously attempt to dovetail Bacon's technique and his vision, but he tends to reduce both to a question of style by separating them from fundamental analogues and tensions between Baconian theory and practice. Farrington, Wallace, and Jardine look much more closely at the Baconian program, but their emphasis on Bacon's rationalism does not lead them to questions of the sort that Fish and Rees ask. Rossi's comprehensive treatment of Bacon's rational incorporation of magic ignores the degree to which theological ideas permeate Bacon's project. For Stephens, Bacon's rationality is really a style, and thus the new learning, as he presents it, is a puissant illustration and concealment of its capacity to mold appearances.[15] The studies by Jardine and Stephens are especially revealing because they are closely allied, despite their different purposes, in their denial of the problematic interaction between Bacon's intentions and the modes of his presentations. Jardine reads the *Essays* as smooth implementations of an art of discourse grounded in the new learning's traditional and innovative principles. Granting that Bacon's methods of presenting his intentions invite the use of deception, she assumes that we should take Bacon at his word when he insists, for example, that rhetoric "should be used responsibly."[16] Since his traditional topics for moral discussion are very close to topics in his natural philosophy, his essays attempt to develop a discourse of "practical precepts" that will reveal the truth of things, not pronounce upon that truth.[17] What might appear as moral arguments in the essays yield, in Bacon's use of them, "no explicit advice."[18] Rather than persuading, Bacon is pointing out the facts or the situations requiring appropriate action. Since these facts are commonplaces, their meaning and its bearing upon his argument are not of interest, except insofar as Bacon makes them seem convincing. Still, one wonders, are not such facts relevant to Bacon's speculations about nature and audiences?

Stephens' Bacon is more canny, a diplomat more than a man of science. His Bacon is intent upon finding ways of teaching the learned without offending the ignorant. But there is nothing Orphic about Bacon's shrewdness. Ignorant readers hold the key to his works if they can devote themselves to numerous rereadings. Bacon freely offers the chance to do "a second reading" so that his readers may "come to his work as converts."[19] Here Bacon's effective practice and his emphasis on utility *are* his philosophy. Although his message raises the prospect of discovering new truths, his discourse—including his invocation of the Orphic myth—is "primarily rhetorical."[20] The herald of the new learning is finally a scientific stylist with "no particular philosophy."[21] He is a seer without a vision. Or rather, his vision is his ability to clear away all philosophies as dross. He sets the stage for discoveries yet to be made or delivered, but what these might be is not nearly as interesting as the prospect of learning's renovation.

Stephens allows for the possibility that Bacon's work is, as Sewell argues, a prophetic and tense interplay of disclosure and concealment. But for Stephens, Bacon's concern for utility is clearly paramount.[22] The new learning perfects Aristotle by making the old rhetoric a respectable tool for a new, more powerful art of ingenious presention and persuasion. It appears that the more Machiavellian Bacon's tactics become, the more they can be justified as components of an enlightened style. Confident of Bacon's own enlightenment, we can supposedly appreciate his cleverness without wondering too much about his elaborate caution and formidable prudence.[23]

Stephens and Jardine boldly identify a number of paradoxes in Bacon's project that Sewell's less systematic overview elides. But if Bacon's purposes in the *Essays* are clearly rational and manipulative, what are we to make of his obscurity, or of his insistence on the strenuousness of the task of breaking nature's code? And what precisely is the power and significance of the Orphic inquirer's rhetoric, method, and science when he appears to make his purposes and techniques relatively explicit, even to the mass of vulgar wits unsuited to be called the "sons of science"?

These recent readings of Bacon testify to a more general tendency among modern critics to attribute immense suasory energy to poetic and rhetorical fictions that criticism then reduces to pale images or subversions of their makers' purposes. Of course, Bacon is preoccupied with a similar paradox: the firm grip of idolatry's hold on the imagination seems vulnerable to persuasion and to scientific analysis. But Bacon works upon this paradox in his own way. Charles Whitney's recent book on Bacon and modernity has begun the process of opening up the paradoxicality of Bacon's project.[24] The chapters that follow, as I explain in the Preface, scrutinize Bacon's paradoxes in light of the need to broaden our understanding of his most characteristic nuances while avoiding post-Baconian critical agendas that sometimes resemble those of their subject but encourage anachronistic interpretation.

Bacon repays the assumption that his works are of a piece, whatever might be said about his doubleness or his growth. This is not to say that he never contradicts himself or does not change his way of handling certain issues as his corpus develops and his mode and immediate purposes change. What matters here is that one not overlook, in a spirit of supposedly sophisticated skepticism, the possibility that Bacon's works are various mirrors of one another, some darker than the rest. Like Fish, R. S. Crane has argued that the coherence of Bacon's complex, life-long project is evident even in the microcosm of his seemingly fragmentary and popular *Essays*.[25] The insight entails its converse: that Bacon's esoteric works shadow the *Essays*.

In the introduction to his history of sixteenth-century English literature, C. S. Lewis suggests that English Renaissance ideas of rhetoric—and hence ideas of persuasion—are invisible to modern readers precisely because they have not taken into account the traditional association of natural philosophy, including magic, with the figures and ends of rhetoric.[26] This is a point upon which literary scholarship, the history of science, and the study of Bacon can converge, by returning to the study of his relatively immediate intellectual circumstances.

In English Renaissance traditions, disciplines as remote as oratory, the ornamentation of poetical subject matters, the training of horses, and the persuasion of matter by means of white magic offer rich analogies between ideas of persuasion and movement in nature. Bacon's own idiom, pervaded by such correspondences, gives to posterity his highly particular version of them. He clothes himself in the language of texts, traditions, and commonplaces that justify and cover the new approach.

In the context of what it imitates, the new learning transforms as well as preserves those correspondences. It seriously weakens—and yet demonstrates the persistence of—Timaeic ideas about persuasion and its uses to perfect the most characteristic tendencies of ensouled beings. It makes more vulnerable Christianity's traditional though precarious assimilation of the ancients, especially of the Aristotelian and Platonic traditions, while it attempts to augment those traditions. It is a Reformationist natural theology that knows the need for ancient ideas of moderation and enigmatic writing to temper its contradictions.[27] And it is an exorcism of falsely coercive magicians, alchemists, and astrologers, which yet seeks to accommodate their modes of persuasion by discovering what are, to Bacon, the deepest, Orphic roots of ancient Pythagoreanism.

~ I ~

NATURE ACCORDING TO SCRIPTURE

The reading of Baconian texts resembles the Baconian reading of nature, for in both the interpreter must discover a clue to a labyrinth. "The very thread of the labyrinth" of nature and scientific practice is a circuitous "course of experiment" through a wood that finally gives way to open ground beyond (*NO* IV.245, 80–81). Bacon designs the perfect garden in his essays ("Of Gardens") much as he understands God's making of his garden of the world, and this is also how he makes his discourses: one must enter them by a special gate, then follow them in their winding ways to a promontory from which the broad heath beyond the garden walls is suddenly revealed (*E* VI.491–92).

I

Finding Baconian clues is supposed to be more difficult than Theseus' task of threading the maze of Minos. Theseus, we remember, received the thread from Ariadne, who loved him. Desire therefore helped guide him, if only from without. But Bacon never glosses Ariadne's role in the story of Theseus despite his interest in interpreting the life of Daedalus, the inventor of the Cretan labyrinth. He does not acknowledge in his interpretation that love or desire has a function in the search for the clue. For Bacon the true meaning of the ancient myth of the labyrinth has to do with the solitary Daedalus, the puzzle's inventor (*SV* VI.734–36). And it is Oedipus rather than Theseus who is the featured conqueror of the monster in the labyrinth of nature. Oedipus' clue is a riddle, a test that has led all those before him to their deaths. The reason for his victory is hidden in a deeper clue: the decoder's experience of having been tortured as an infant.

Oedipus' halting gait on maimed feet (the legacy of his father's deluded attempt to evade a tormenting prophecy) both testifies to his
ordeal and prevents him from rushing into the Sphinx's jaws. His
early maiming gives him an advantage over the Sphinx that whole
men do not have (*SV* VI.755–58). The Orphic interpreter of the new
learning is supposed to imitate the limping, Oedipal hero, his longings
scourged of their readiness so that he might cope with nature's maze
of dead-ends. He must thread his way to the Minotaur and out again
by means of a clue that is merely random, yet somehow all-revealing.

In both the smooth rhetoric of *The Advancement* and the jarring
aphoristic structure of his explicitly scientific works, Bacon trains his
careful readers not to draw conclusions with ease. Like Baconian
induction, the new scientific reading of his texts is ultimately a quest
of abnegation. The reader must give up his attachment to the prox-
imate, and go "to and fro in remote and heterogenous instances, by
which axioms are tried as in the fire" and are forced to follow the
"severe laws and overruling authority" of experiment (*NO* IV.57).
The method of such a reading is similar to the one advocated by one
"R. B.," a contemporary of Bacon who explains how to read true
natural philosophers in order to distinguish them from impostors.
Genuine natural philosophy, "R. B." argues, contains hints of the
writer's intent placed in disparate passages, which can be joined together by an interpreter who forces himself to disregard a desire for
ready clarity in order to decode what reveals the whole: "if in one
place the Author write darkly, in some other place some particular
thyng maie bee found that ioyned with the other may explicate the
meanyng, for they disperse their meaning in seuerall places, to the
ende they would be vnderstode onely of the deligent and painfull
reader and not of the vnworthie."[1]

Although Bacon's most aphoristic texts have a measure of rhetorical
momentum, all of his works are dispersals of deeper intent. They are
meant to resist, and yet submit themselves to, an interpreter's persistent fragmentation of their surfaces. The reader must in fact imitate
the Baconian natural philosopher by moving "to and fro in remote
and heterogenous instances," working a variety of remote and difficult sites rather than seeking a lode: "such knowledge . . . is digged
out of the hard mine of history and experience, and falleth out to be
in the same points as adverse to common sense, or popular reason,
as religion, or more" (*FL* III.503).

The *Filum Labyrinthi,* Bacon's "clue to the maze," offers a perplexing hint of the new learning's mode of progress: those who understand its mission must probe the heart of the world and endure the extraordinarily "adverse" and mundane labors of digging in the "hard mine." In order to search "the inwardness of all secrets" of the world (*Adv* III.265), they must virtually ignore the experiments of their predecessors, even those such as William Gilbert who have since won praise as precursors of modern experimental science. The old, ordinary sciences generally avoid digging and suffering. They "go aside" for comfortable fame (*NO* IV.71). Their experiments, uninformed by the new vision of scientific endeavor, are tinkerers' idolatries (*IM* IV.14–18).

Bacon's mining metaphor in the *Filum Labyrinthi* is typical of his tendency to link the adversity of discovering knowledge with the difficulty of communicating and understanding knowledge once it comes to light. What the new sciences discover and bring to the surface vexes common sense just as it has resisted those who have found it. It runs as counter to men's ordinary judgments about ordinary things as it would if it were an intervening truth of religion— "or more" so. The new knowledge is perhaps more difficult to ponder or accept than religion, for the experience of the mine puts into question everything that commonly pleases.

To advance in learning is to mortify the minds of inquirers so that they see and perform the works of truth. Their humiliation must be an interrogation into the self as well as into external bodies. Advancement is an ordeal of the spirit. Learning cannot advance, nature cannot be known in the new age of science unless its true sons bind themselves and their objects upon a kind of rack (the method figured in the *Novum Organum*) that purges idolatry from the testimony of the senses, and conforms men's minds to the truths that the new method discovers: "if I have made any progress, the way has been opened to me by no other means than the true and legitimate humiliation of the human spirit" (*IM* IV.19). By comparison, the old sciences are mere exercises of thought, selfish invocations of demiurges, or impious quests for oracles (*IM* IV.19).

Both the true inquirer and his object must be stripped of ostentation. They must submit to a correction that frees them from the vanity of anticipations and the accidental ostentation of mere appearances. Whereas the Apostle Paul strove to separate the terrestrial from the spiritual, and the humble soul of the faithful from the vauntings of the philosopher and rhetorician, the new learning would divide

appearances from what is real, and humiliate the strengths and ex-
cellences of the wit so that the mind and senses might deliver themselves faithfully. The humiliation of undergoing one's own nakedness
for the sake of faithful witness is akin to the nakedness of truth itself,
and is a figure for the discourse that presents that nakedness:

> dwelling purely and constantly among the facts of nature, [I] with-
> draw my intellect from them no further than may suffice to let the
> images and rays of natural objects meet in a point, as they do in
> the sense of vision; whence it follows that the strength and excel-
> lency of the wit has but little to do in the matter. And the same
> humility which I use in inventing I employ likewise in teaching.
> For I do not endeavour either by triumphs of confutation, or plead-
> ings of antiquity, or assumption of authority, or even by the veil
> of obscurity, to invest these inventions of mine with any majesty;
> which might easily be done by one who sought to give lustre to
> his own name rather than light to men's minds. I have not sought
> (I say) nor do I seek either to force or ensnare men's judgments,
> but I lead them to things themselves and the concordances of things,
> that they may see for themselves what they have. . . . I so present
> these things naked and open, that my errors can be marked and set
> aside before the mass of knowledge be further infected by them.
> (*IM* IV.19)

Yet it is the very strain and confinement of the inquirer's scientific
initiation that opens the world, and so makes his suffering sweet. In
overturning the vulgar faith in the apparent world, the new sciences
offer a revelation or "apocalypse" of nature (*IM* IV.33). The inquirer
can communicate directly the workings of God's power in nature as
long as he enforces his own naked clarity, which his very intelligence
and aspiration tend to deny him. Through his humiliation nature's
configurations, which have lain long-hidden from his presumptions,
reveal themselves for his contemplation and use. He might then find
himself in Adam's world before the Fall took away his power of
naming. When Solomon says God "*hath placed the world in man's heart
yet cannot man find out the work which God worketh from the beginning to
the end,*" Bacon in *The Advancement* takes his meaning to be supremely
optimistic: God has "framed the mind of man as a mirror or glass
capable of the image of the universal world" (*Adv* III.265).

To understand this optimism, one must see that it depends upon
the thoroughness of the reduction. Adam fell because he preferred
his own desires for knowledge over the rigors of obedience that gave

him the power of naming. God offers knowledge that is "an impression of pleasure in itself" (*Adv* III.266), but that knowledge that is in essence a "*lumen siccum* [dry light]" alien to the least moisture afforded by the humors (*Adv* III.267). The humors and their pleasures must be driven out, or controlled with such power that their enlightened master, like King Solomon in his prime, suffers them with a delight that never comes to rest in himself (*NO* IV.114). Rather than a mirror of the whole, the mind is in this sense "an enchanted glass, full of superstition and imposture." It will always be cloudy "if it be not delivered and reduced" (*Adv* III.395).

Bacon's imitation of Solomon extends to the mode of his discourses. The winnowing power of the ancient king's aphorisms is a model for distinguishing the wise reader from the fool. The fragmented, aphoristic profundity of Proverbs, Ecclesiastes, and The Wisdom of Solomon presents hermeneutical and spiritual tests which Bacon adapts to the ends and means of scientific method. In his well-known explanation of the importance of Solomonic discourse, Bacon argues that since the aphorism casts away all finery of rhetorical illusion, it tests the mettle of its maker and its reader by finding out whether each is "sound and grounded": "Aphorisms, except they should be ridiculous, cannot be made but of the pith and heart of sciences . . . and therefore no man can suffice, nor in reason will attempt, to write Aphorisms, but he that is sound and grounded" (*Adv* III.405).

The formulation and interpretation of aphorisms is an ordeal because the discourse of fragments "gathered here and there from very various and widely displaced facts" surprises the understanding and perplexes the imagination. The effect is "so harsh and out of tune" in respect to "the opinions of the time" that aphoristic discourse operates "much as the mysteries of the faith do" (*NO* IV.51–52). Aphorisms are "broken knowledge" that creates "wonder" (*Adv* III.267). Despite their pithy didacticism, which impresses general audiences, they are seeds of knowledge that grow only on ready ground (*Adv* III.266).

William Tyndale's 1549 translation of Proverbs 1.5–6 includes an interpolation that explicitly distinguishes between merely "hearynge" wisdom and experiencing it: "By hearynge, the wyse man shall come by more wysdom: *and by experience* he shalbe more apt to vnderstand a parable & the interpretacion therof, the wordes of the wyse, and the darcke speaches of the same."[2] Neither the Cranmer Bible nor the King James version adds "experience" to "hearing." It is the more vehement Protestant reformer's version that comes closest to the spirit of Bacon's interpretation of Solomon's writings. Proverbs supports Tyndale, at least to a degree, in passages that seem to insist upon biblical interpretation that is explicitly accountable to faithful witness. Men are ignorant of proverbial wisdom unless wisdom has called them.[3] The faithful must try themselves so as to learn from extraordinary instruction. Hence the second verse's distinction between "a proverb" and "the interpretation," between "the words of the wise" and their "dark sayings."[4] Wisdom comes to those who hearken not just to the proverbs but to their interpretation. Bacon goes further when he turns these commonplaces into codes for the new sciences' arduous witness of nature's dark sayings.

Bacon would have known that the Vulgate's The Wisdom of Solomon clearly associates Solomon's wisdom with a knowledge of the structure of the world: "For it is he [God] who gave me unerring knowledge of what exists, to know the structure of the world and the activity of the elements."[5] Solomon himself studied the flora and fauna of Lebanon. He kept natural histories lost to the modern world,[6] but now secretly preserved, according to Bacon's utopian fiction, on a New Atlantis run by masters of nature. The Wisdom Literature attributed to him is in large measure a testament of God's power to test the elements in much the way God tests men's souls.

In The Wisdom of Solomon, the cataclysmic experience of the faithful extends to an ordeal experienced by the world itself. In the process of purging and preserving, God tests and reduces even the four elements. Fire burns "in the water, which quenches all things," and God withdraws its power to burn "so that it might not consume the creatures sent against the ungodly."[7] Analogously, God wrenches false appearances from men's souls in the process of confirming the godly. He tries the faithful "like gold in the furnace."[8] The truth of the righteous man's words is subjected to the wicked's "insult and torture that [the wicked] may find out how gentle he is, and make trial of his forbearance." The torturers "condemn him to a shameful death, for, according to what he says, he will be protected."[9] Since God's powerful hand creates the world "out of formless matter," all things that endure survive because God wills it. Insofar as the "immortal spirit" is in them,[10] God confirms in preserving them whatever might be imperishable. Their seeming demise is the purification of their lasting parts. Hence the flood effaces everything on earth but a splinter of wood and the righteous Noah who knows how to steer the "paltry" remnant to shore: "When the earth was flooded because of him, wisdom again saved it, steering the righteous man by a paltry piece of wood."[11] Thus Bacon can remind his reader that Plato's pagan Atlantis perished in a cataclysm, while the New Atlantis, which has accepted the new faith and preserved Solomon's wisdom, has persisted through the travail of history (NA III.145).

It is not surprising that Bacon should be interested in the sufferings and powers of the bound god, Prometheus, who in Bacon's interpretation of the ancient myths offers a clue to the paradigm of Solomonic experience. In *De Sapientia Veterum,* the Prometheus myth bears the title "The State of Man." Bacon identifies the sufferings of the divine benefactor with the ordeal of the new learning's charitable champions. The agony of Prometheus initially resembles the infernal writhings of idolatrous scholastics, "wise and fore-thoughtful" men who are vainly busy in their adherence to dogmatism and their subservience to necessity (SV VI.751–52). Prometheus, however, undergoes his torture in the prayerful spirit of the new learning, and eventually gives mankind the warmth and light of fire. Fortitude, in the person of Hercules, enables him to survive his imprisonment and to reveal his true nature as an ally of men's needs. His endurance, thanks to Hercules' strangely handicapped intervention, is "a wonderful correspondency with the mysteries of the Christian faith": "The voyage of Hercules especially, sailing in a pitcher to set Prometheus free, seems to present an image of God the Word hastening in the frail vessel of the flesh to redeem the human race" (SV VI.753). Promethean fortitude is "not natural." It is superhuman and "adventitious," assisted "by help from without." In fact, it is a "blessing" unavailable "except by the help of Hercules," who lends his grace only by risking himself in a frail craft. "Brought to us from the Sun" and from torment and prayer, Promethean fortitude is the means to providential salvation. The myth as a whole shadows—hides and discovers—the workings of Providence (SV VI.752).

Conventionally heroic strength and swiftness are no match for Promethean wisdom. Each wise man tries "his own strength and the chance of his own turn," but not in the old fashioned Herculean manner. Wise suffering submits to Providence. If the sufferer survives, he can give thanks for the new Herculean fortification with which he resisted and mastered fortune. His persistence reveals a deeper significance in the Senecan aphorism that Bacon approves in

De Sapientia Veterum: "It is true greatness to have in one the frailty of man and the security of God" (*SV* VI.752).

Solomonic fortitude, says Bacon quoting Juvenal in the companion passage of *De Augmentis,* gives to man a soul "which can grim death defy / And counts it Nature's privilege to die" (*De Aug* V.14). Thomas Middleton's paraphrase of The Wisdom of Solomon, dated 1597, found in these themes an opportunity to exploit his patron's interest in piety as well as ambition. Dedicated to the Earl of Essex, the man to whom Bacon's brother proffered the first edition of the *Essays* in the same year, Middleton's free adaptation includes an apocalyptic prayer that suits the new scientific contemplation as well as Essex's brooding over his practical, political destiny:

> Oh make my sinfull bodies world anew,
> Erect new elements, new aires, new skies,
> The time I haue is fraile, the course vntrue,
> The globe vnconstant, like ill fortunes eies:
> First make the world, which doth my soule contain,
> And next my wisedome, in whose power I raigne.[12]

From the Solomonic perspective, the most extreme transgression of wise experience is the worship of idols, because men who make them have denied the importance of perfective suffering. According to the Wisdom Literature, they have made a god of perishable child, and so have denied the rigors of death by fabricating the living thing to comfort their hopes.[13] Their sin, like the delusions of idol worship that Bacon detects everywhere in the old learning, is the root of all evils: "For the worship of idols not to be named is the beginning and cause and end of every evil."[14] "The worshipers either rave in exultation or prophesy lies"; they love false "objects of hope,"[15] much the way Bacon says the idolators of the old learning follow self-flattery, false language, vain disciplines, and the unexamined generalizations of their tribe.

Nevertheless, in order to pluck down idolatry according to Solomonic principles, righteous iconoclasm is not enough. Solomonic enjoyment of the earth's riches also helps to destroy the icons, for that pleasure proves the wise man's pious fortitude. Bacon draws from this teaching in the Wisdom Literature when he calls himself "a true priest of the sense" in the Solomonic mode (*IM* IV.26). Solomon is capable of delighting in the glories "of treasure and magnificent buildings, of shipping and navigation, of service and attendance, of fame and renown," because in his royal pursuit of natural philosophy and the arts of invention he makes "no claim to any of these glories, . . . only to the glory of inquisition of truth" (*Adv* III.299). Solomon "closes his enumeration of the pleasures with which he abounded in these words; *Likewise my wisdom remained with me*" (*SV* VI.764).

The king's glories are signs of God's favor, to be withdrawn if he ever claimed them. Solomon must experience his God-given bounties if he is to confirm his righteousness, indulging in them while freeing himself of their influence. His pleasure must be an ordeal, and his ordeal a pleasure. Enduring "all alterations and extremities," he achieves "that health of mind . . . which can go through the greatest temptations and perturbations" and come to rest in an instant, as might a perfectly broken horse: "So as Diogenes' opinion is to be accepted, who commended not them which abstained, but them which sustained, and could refrain their mind *in praecipitio* [in full career], and could give unto the mind (as is used in horsemanship) the shortest stop or turn" (*Adv* III.423).

Of Solomon's decline into erotic idolatry Bacon makes no mention, though the story would have been well known.[16] But the wise king's later errors, like Orpheus' loss of Eurydice, serve the Promethean purpose of the new learning. The endurance of the Wisdom Literature, in the face of Solomon's not always happy history in 1 Kings, testifies to wisdom's power to overcome Solomon's mortality, just as Orpheus' failure helps prove the persistence of the Orphic powers that Bacon hints will emerge again (*SV* VI.722). The imperturbability of Solomonic wisdom amidst temptation, pleasure, and seeming disgrace seems to be Bacon's precedent when late in life he confesses to Parliament that he partook of bribery in accepting expensive gifts from petitioners. The confession is guarded, and it permits Bacon to protest his innocence to his king (*LL* XIV.242–45).

2

Bacon finds another prominent guide for the new sciences' experiments: the teaching of the Apostle Paul. Paul's preaching offers a means of controlling the possible excesses of contemplative learning by means of his doctrine and practice of charity. In comparison with Paul, the old philosophers in their pursuit of knowledge for its own sake were evading the exacting trials of public charity. The new meditative "sons of science," to prove that their virtue is not precarious and that in their Solomonic pleasures they have seen through the old self-indulgence, must now demonstrate a rigorously charitable intent to alleviate mankind's fallen condition. Active charity thus comes to bear upon contemplation, if only as intent, in order for contemplation to be virtuous (*De Aug* V.8).

It is worth recalling that charity in the Pauline epistles is the bearing and enduring of all things.[17] Paul's most powerful preachings, those parts of the epistles which Augustine features in *De Doctrine* as examples of Christian eloquence, concern the persecutions that confirm the unboasted glories of Paul's fidelity to the Word.[18] When Paul bears witness to the power of God's grace, his preaching recollects the sufferings that tear asunder everything but the living faith: "Most gladly therefore will I rather glory in my infirmities, that the power of Christ may rest upon me. Therefore I take pleasure in infirmities, in reproaches, in necessities, in persecutions, in distresses for Christ's sake; for when I am weak, then am I strong."[19] The persecutions strip him down to his soul. Or rather, they help determine whether his soul can be recognized once it undergoes the severest of tests. To guard against the least appearance of self-righteousness even in tales of his own humiliation, Paul ironically adopts the boasting mode of his adversaries. He proffers the sermon of a fool.[20]

Paul uses his appeal to charity to argue against speaking esoterically in tongues.[21] And yet Paul's parody of the *hubris* of classical rhetorical demonstration is another form of esotericism; it is a way for him to attest to his inner being's invulnerability to wordly persecution or approval. Preaching passes away, but charity "never faileth." In the end all "shall be revealed by fire; and the fire shall try every man's work of what sort it is."[22]

The *locus* of Bacon's doctrine of charity is his invocation of Paul in the introduction to *The Advancement,* in which he tries to show how the Apostle's doctrine and Solomon's overlap. Both warn against "proud knowledge" (*Adv* III.265). Both say that all is vanity. Each teaches that man must never forget his mortality, that he must therefore apply what he learns never to his ambition but to the "repose and contentment" of others. And in the course of justifying the pursuit of knowledge, Solomon and Paul warn against pursuing the mysteries of God's purposes (*Adv* III.266).

From Bacon's perspective, Paul's method and rhetoric have a more than casual resemblance to Solomon's aphoristic wisdom. When Paul preaches that he withholds from false witnesses what they can not truly see, and that he invites the faithful to be witnesses to the word of God, his presentation, like Solomon's, abjures persuasion so that his faithful audience might undergo an inquisition into itself. Likewise, the Pauline discourses test their author. Whereas the holy aphorism proves the substance of its maker by stripping his discourse of rhetorical accoutrement, Paul's preaching sunders its maker's inner being from the character he assumes as a speaker.

Both scriptural modes draw power from their denial of self-aggrandizement. Solomon becomes all the more gnomic, the more his wise fragmentations suggest a wisdom beyond writing or speech. Paul's oratory reaches the faithful largely because the energy with which he disabuses himself of pretension is an exercise of his own adamant reserve of faith.

The gap between the oratorical maker and his discourse is more complete and personal in Paul's writings than in Solomon's. Paul's uprooting of any desire to win his audiences' approval frees him to take all manner of pleasing disguises in order to win at least some of them for his faith: "For though I be free from all men, yet have I made myself servant unto all, that I might gain the more. And unto the Jews I became as a Jew, that I might gain the Jews; . . . I am made all things to all men [Vulgate: *Omnibus omnia factus sum*], that I might by all means save some."[23] Augustine takes up this principle in his discussion of persuasion in *De Doctrine,* where he argues that biblical rhetoric surpasses the accomplishments of the classical rhetoricians. Augustinian preaching not only possesses its own rhetorical decorum; it makes use of the principle that all rhetorical means, whether they proceed from pagan or Apostle, can be appropriate if they allow the message of salvation to make its way into the world.

Bacon approves of the parodic foolishness of Paul's preaching when he seconds Augustine's praise of Paul's ability to preserve his true calling amidst his foolish speech: "St. Paul, when he boasts of himself, he doth oft interlace, *I speak like a fool;* but speaking of his calling, he saith, *magnificabo apostolatum meum* [I will magnify my mission]" (*E* VI.503). Imitated and modified, the Pauline principle of parodic disguise proves essential to the advancement of the new sciences in civil life. In the *Meditationes Sacrae,* appended to the original 1597 edition of the essays, Bacon is drawn to Paul's 1 Corinthians in the course of condemning vainly enthusiastic impostors in religion. Praising those of the faithful who isolate their private worship from their civil conversation, he defines the "true man" as one who is pious in private before God and capable of adjusting with extraordinary flexibility to public company:

> [The true man's] carriage and conversation towards God is full of excess, or zeal, of extasy. . . . His bearing and conversation with men on the contrary is full of mildness and sobriety and appliable demeanour: whence the saying: *I am become all things to all men [Omnia omnibus factus sum]*, and the like. Contrary it is with the hypocrites and impostors: for they in Church and towards the people set themselves on fire.   (*MS* VII.239, 250)

The idea of doubleness from *1 Corinthians* is here more material and routine, as well as more obscure. It raises the question of how the solitary, vehement devotion of Bacon's true man can carry over to his "appliable demeanour" at all, if it must stand so distinctly apart.

The true inquirer, Bacon says, should not hesitate to apparel himself in all manner of stinging infection and pollution so as to penetrate nature's remotest sinks and man's greatest evils. To justify this reversal of the prayer that the faithful not be led into temptation, the *Sacred Meditations* use another part of the New Testament:

> *Be you wise as Serpents, and innocent as Doves.* There are neither teeth nor stings, nor venom, nor wreaths and folds of serpents, which ought not to be all known, and as far as examination doth lead, tried: neither let any man here fear infection or pollution; for the sun entereth into sinks and is not defiled. . . . *God is sufficient to preserve you immaculate and pure.*   (*MS* VII.245)

A similar passage appears in the explicitly scientific *Novum Organum* (*NO* IV.106–07) and in *De Augmentis*, the latter welcoming the training that makes enlightened men "perfectly acquainted with the nature of evil itself" so that they may overcome the wickedness of others:

> [I]t is not possible to join the wisdom of the serpent with the innocence of the dove, except men be perfectly acquainted with the nature of evil itself; for without this, virtue is open and unfenced; nay, a virtuous and honest man can do no good upon those who are wicked, to correct and reclaim them, without first exploring all the depths and recesses of their malice. . . . [A]ccording to the excellent Proverb of Solomon, "The fool receives not the word of the wise, unless thou speakest the very things that are in his heart."
> (*De Aug* V.17–18)

By such means, Bacon's inquirer becomes a kind of inquisitor. He uses his endurance and his separation from others to take on their corruptions and discover the innermost weaknesses and resistances of their nature. It follows that he suceeds if his discovery is total and prior to his conversation. Then he can reveal that he knows the audience's deepest depravity (or the formal principle of his object's foulest qualities) with a swiftness that disables their resistance to correction. It is necessary, therefore, that the interrogation proceed with secret speed, before it can be espied or evaded, so that the revelation can work with disorienting accuracy. The new learning's mastery over idolatry would imitate and surpass the hero's victory over the basilisk: "if he [the basilisk] see you first, you die for it, but if you see him first, he dies; so is it with deceits, impostures, and evil arts, which, if they be first espied, they lose their life, but if they prevent, they endanger" (*De Aug* V.17).

3

The doubleness that accompanies the Baconian idea of experience is more than a useful means to an end. It is a discovery of the truth of things. Cryptic interrogation and manipulation are humbling imitations of the power expressed in God's creation of the world, a power that reveals, if it is understood, laws that are keys to manipulating nature and civil society for charitable purposes.

The workings and ends of God's providential government of the world are secret, but to him "like unto crystal" (*Adv* III.474). He perfects what "great politiques" try to do: he conceals all final causes from their effects: their material and efficient causes. He moves men by exhibiting his power without betraying his intent. His wisdom is "more admirable, when nature intendeth one thing and providence draweth forth another, than if he had communicated to particular creatures and motions the characters and impressions of his providence" (*Adv* III.359). Pan's crooked staff symbolizes the providential code: "while one thing appears to be doing another is doing really" (*De Aug* IV.323).

As we have seen, interpreting the manifestations of divine power is a game that the sons of science must play as though they were children searching for things hidden by God, who "took delight to hide his works, to the end to have them found out" (*Adv* III.299). The *agon* is easy to the degree that the inquisitors, become as children, happen upon the seeds of knowledge without presuming to know what they are. In order to reduce themselves to children, however, they must go through what "man cannot endure." As they resist being children before God, so they find it extremely difficult to walk the path of the new learning, which resembles "a second infancy or childhood" (*Adv* III.387). Except in revelatory moments, God does not disclose his deeper machinations. Miracles are the occasional glimpses of them, but the natural world is the creation, not the image, of its maker.

The dilemma would seem to be insoluble, were it not for God's delight in men's decoding of his devices when they become children weak enough to see what they no longer desire. He has permitted man to know his power by converting the secrets of its workings in "true signatures and marks set upon the works of creation as they are found in nature" (*NO* IV.51). True interpreters can work the puzzle of his second causes rather than his true intent as long as they disavow their mature anticipations of the code's meaning, or the possibility of its more profound connection with God's shaping Providence. But since the device is a code, any clues to the puzzle's solution, once detected by the child, are capable of revealing the whole pattern of God's power, if not of his Providence, in an instant. The "betrayal" of one of the laws of nature's correspondences "in a single instance leads the way (as is evident from all that has been said) to the discovery of it [the law] in all" (*NO* IV.157).

The divine code in nature reveals, to an audience that has submitted to its own reduction, the instrumentality of the world in the hands of its maker. It is a mere device. Yet the very idea that it is God's highly wrought riddle intimates the possibility that it hides divine purpose in nature and history, and therefore offers a glimpse of Providence and the possibility of acting in its favor. History becomes a mirror in which one might spy and take advantage of the direction of divine power the more ingenious one can be in becoming like a child, in disavowing the desire to spy. Thus the first lines of Bacon's biography of Henry VII characterize his subject's pivotal victory over Richard III in terms of God's providential favoring of an exile who wisely (with sagacious reserve) achieved power. In the rigors of his distance from native fields of ambition and his unassuming (never disclosed by Bacon) design, Henry crowned the momentous unfolding of the Wars of the Roses. He won, thanks to "Divine Revenge, favouring the design of an exiled man" (*HRK* VI.27). Because Henry endured apart and yet used the ordeal of separation from England to hatch his plans, his wise interpretation of history seconded Providence in making him king.

In their vanity, men worship idols because they do not notice or appreciate the dominion of God's trope, and so fail to praise his true glory by playing his game. They miss, for example, the meaning of fables, which by Bacon's definition are profound opposites of what they seem. The most nonsensical fables are the most revelatory, permitting "communion between divinity and humanity" (*SV* VI.696). The best rhetorical device imitates the myths by deceiving anticipation, as does the most pleasing trope in music, which "avoid[s] or slide[s] from the close or cadence" (*Adv* III.348–49, *NO* IV.167).

The best code for these purposes of radical reversal would be one that could "make anything signify anything." Thus its name is *"omnia per omnia,"* a philosophical if not literal echo in Bacon's Latin of Paul's description of charitable disguise (*De Aug* I.659; IV.445). The new learner inquires into nature as though it were such a code, and creates a similar cipher for his own communications as he imitates God's concealing and revealing of divine power.

Bacon's most explicit example of this phenomenon is a device he explains in *De Augmentis*. During his years abroad, in the self-imposed exile of a gentleman aware of his foreignness and likely to be interested in gathering intelligence without raising suspicion, Bacon created his own code. His sample of its operation presents a false yet plausible meaning that hides a secret contrary to anticipations: the open statement "Do not go till I come" reduces via the machinery of Bacon's enigma to "Fly!" (*De Aug* IV.446).

The code of Bacon's youth is designed to block the anticipations of sophisticated as well as naive audiences. Even a wise interpreter who possessed the true "table" of conversions would have to decode the code-maker's "external epistle" letter by letter into a second set of symbols, which for the purposes of Bacon's demonstration are in groups of five that are equivalent to a third set of letters forming the secret. The two-step, abecedarian translation's randomness is supposed to be impenetrable to the benighted, and all-revealing (after a grinding, mechanical delay) to favored holders of its key.

The first phase of the decoding process is the simple conversion of letters into "a" or "b," depending on the cursive style in which the individual letters have been written. The system's ease of operation comes from its painstaking lack of reference to any thoughts but those of a calculating wisdom which is unavailable to persons without tables. On the other hand, the simple-mindedness of the operation requires the decoder to labor with unwavering patience until the real message bursts into view. In the same operation that the code tears sign from meaning and anticipation from truth, it offers the wise interpreter a surd that instantly converts, after the ordeal of calculation, to a *nota* of what is.

Since God is the master of *omnia per omnia* encryption, mere eavesdroppers hoping to detect the divine code in nature must fall victim to the false table of their misapprehensions. The code teases out the misinterpretations of presumptuous code-breakers. Those critics of Shakespeare who have concluded that his works are Bacon's, and who have used for proof passages in the plays where no hint of connection seemed possible, are the ridiculous victims of a delusion encouraged by uncritical readings of this Baconian doctrine of encryption.

Once we begin to take seriously Bacon's preoccupation with codes, other similarities among encryption, decipherment, and aphoristic induction come to light. The machinery that moves Bacon's natural scientist from fragment to law gathers instances (the more unexpected the better) and notes similarities, while prohibiting anything more than accidental speculation as to their significance until a generative principle is revealed. Similarities emerge from the winnowing of dissimilarities and from the collections of negative instances. Bacon sometimes refers to the process as though it were a persuasive progression through stages of certainty. At bottom, however, it is incremental and non-teleological. It scourges the desire to ascend, wears down the love of likenesses, and obscures whatever grounds in nature that rhetorical similitudes and methods of inquiry might possess, except as they become tools or cryptic significations of a power that sees into, and is congruent with, nature's most central laws.

The new sciences' aphorisms, like this estranging pattern of inference, are therefore to be read as ciphers that are two things at once: isolated maxims as well as empowering fragments of wisdom. They conform in this sense to the Solomonic wisdom described in Middleton's paraphrase of The Wisdom of Solomon. In addition to teaching moral truths, wisdom ultimately knows the "summe" of "her braines table-books," and the "solution" of "darke sentences."[24] In their guise as quotable guides to virtue, Bacon's *Essays* are similarly ambivalent; they make a certain prudential sense, but they have a deeper meaning that depends upon their marking of the laws of civil behavior in

Bacon's system of sciences. They are supposed not only to fragment and reverse expectations, as Fish's readings have shown, but also to sign forth the shape of human nature.

Bacon's Solomonic essays stretch the biblical paradigm two ways at once. Their didacticism is more in the line of practical advice, while the sums of their table books point toward laws for sounding and controlling human nature and civil conversation. As a consequence, their adaptation of biblical wisdom runs the risk of seeming to toy with moral intentions. The essays are hortatory, but cannot be what they seem. Their moral discourse threatens, even as it attends to, the morale of audiences and inquirers. If the essays are not hortatory, they risk failing to move general audiences; if they succeed, they risk encouraging new idolatries of custom and civility for the sake of sheer usefulness. Their encryption also confronts scientific readers with the danger of embarking upon a double life of assiduous conventionality and arduous spying.

4

Beneath Bacon's famous definition of rhetoric in *The Advancement,* elaborated in *De Augmentis,* there lies the assumption that rhetoric is cryptic as well as charitable and rational. Modern critics, with the notable exception of Fish and Whitney, have tended to resist this conclusion or to accept it without question. Karl Wallace champions Bacon's open rationality—his careful association of rhetoric with the new sciences—as though *The Advancement* clearly renewed an Aristotelian alliance between rhetoric and philosophy.[25] James Stephens, in contrast, defends Bacon's doubleness as though it were Machiavellian, and Machiavelli a rationalist like Bacon who knows what is necessary to the accomplishment of enlightened ends. In this view, the new learning uses codes, but they routinely open themselves to those who take the time to ponder Bacon's methods and doctrines.[26] Neither approach adequately scrutinizes the conspiratorial character of the new charitable rhetoric.

There are important and well-known grounds for Wallace's and Stephens's positions, evidence which must be studied in greater detail in a later chapter. Bacon does make rhetoric reason's agent for persuading the will by means of its operations upon the imagination. He does allow, at least in some parts of *The Advancement,* that the process of persuasion is sympathetic to its audience's aspirations. For example, he states that the unruly affections, which eloquence must overcome in order to maintain the rule of reason, are themselves sympathetic to enlightenment: they "carry ever an appetite to good, as reason doth" (*Adv* III.410–11). In this vein, he defends rhetoric as though it were melioration, not doubleness. He addresses Plato's charge that rhetoric is really a form of cookery that mars and hides "wholesome meats" while presenting unwholesome ones sauced with deceptive delights. Rhetoric, he says, is "much more conversant in adorning that which is good than in colouring that which is evil" (*Adv* III.410). Thus something in the nature of rhetoric, as in the appetites it works upon, seems to have an affinity for the thing toward which reason would persuade it, as though doubleness and force were unnecessary—even irrelevant—to the idea of the new rhetoric.

In the same section of *The Advancement,* this impression gathers a degree of strength from one of the most famous of Bacon's principles for the transmission of scientific discoveries: that "knowledge that is delivered as a thread to be spun on [to be advanced], ought to be delivered and intimated, if it were possible, *in the same method wherein it was invented*" (*Adv* III.404).

Such passages need to be placed in the context of Bacon's discussions of the objects, means, and ends of persuasion. The appetite's sympathy with good, for instance, is affection for the immediate: an inclination that Bacon has already stigmatized in his discussion of idolatry. Preceding his concession to sympathy in the definition of rhetoric is his insistence that the affections' "continual mutinies and seditions" against the reason testify against their pliancy (*Adv* III.410). Baconian persuasion for this reason by-passes the affections, as though their love of immediate good disqualified them from the rational rhetoricians' attention. The famous definition is in this sense highly utilitarian: "The duty and office of Rhetoric is *to apply Reason to Imagination* for the better moving of the will" (*Adv* III.409). Persuasion must go so far as to "contract a confederacy between Reason and Imagination against the Affections." The process, for all its seeming rationality, is conspiratorial. Rhetoric makes a new sedition to combat the disloyalty of the affections, by creating the imagination's "revolt" from the affections to win reason's cause (*Adv* III.409–11).

The imagination might seem capable of moving toward that cause, but rhetoric must be its motive force. Only when rhetoric converts what is rational and remote so that it can "appear as present" is the imagination persuaded. Thus the imagination moves, but only in the sense that it receives a new impression. The impression dominates not because of any imaginative capacity to grasp a remoter good, but because rhetorical machination is at work, "filling the imagination more" than affection does. Persuasion must in other words "practise" upon the imagination, as Bacon observes in the same paragraph. Persuasion comes to resemble the action of a wisely politic counselor in service to kingly reason; it will do all in its power to defend its sovereign's rule.

Bacon's collateral claim that rhetoric is sympathetic to the good is at least as ambivalent. Speech is much more "conversant," he says, in adorning what is good than what is not good. What a speaker does in public conversation, where he "speaketh more honestly than he can do or think," Bacon uses as proof of eloquence's non-cryptic nature—its inherent tendency toward truth. The argument, however, depends more upon tactic than principle: public speakers do not like to create the impression that they are hypocrites. Doers and thinkers, who are not obligated to publish themselves, would not be so bound by shame. Rhetorical virtue is by comparison something technical, another means to escape detection. The following assertion, that "no man can speak fair of courses sordid and base," reduces to a moral imperative the idea that eloquence might be teleological. Whereas the first example depended on the speakers' shame, and recorded the prevalence of shame as a fact of human nature, the second example invokes the moral and scientific inconceivability of any alliance between baseness and beauty in God's creation.

In the final instance, Bacon's argument that the true scientific method can transmit faithfully the process of scientific invention turns immediately upon the qualification that "no man" knows the path of his own discoveries. The goal of transmitting knowledge "in the same method wherein it was invented" turns out to be communication via similitudes (*Adv* III.404), hence a variation upon rhetoric's use of seeming truths to win the imagination for the cause of reason.

The gap between inquiry and language seems to close as inventors of the new knowledge master the art of similitudes to explain the process and matter of their discoveries. But if Bacon's hint were true about the new inquiry's existing essentially apart from its own transmission, then true inquiry could routinely evade the scrutiny of civil conversation, which followed it, however plainly the inventor used similitudes to describe his work. Unfettered inquiry of this kind would always be able to conceal its probings in the guise of communication. If the transmission of knowledge via similitudes is the one true way of inquiry, as Bacon hints in one of his most tortuous essays ("On Simulation and Dissimulation" [*E* VI.389), a powerful and undetected inquiry on the Baconian model could in fact surprise and manipulate the minds of its audiences by opening up their deepest predilections for images of truth.

The Solomonic matter and form of the *Essays* finally demonstrate and recommend the upright and temperate behavior that Shakespeare's Polonius recommends to Laertes, at the same time that they serve the secret purposes of Polonius's spy Reynaldo, whom he teaches how to vex appearances with lies in order to find truth. Frequently, Polonius's advice is comically entertaining. Yet it is ingeniously conventional in a manner that ironically speaks beyond itself, into the workings of the play of the world as it would be decoded and put on by the new learning. Within the advice to Laertes, too, there is, in his call for truth and honesty, the careful counsel to detect other men's characters without betraying one's own: "Give thy thoughts no tongue," "Give every man thine ear, but few thy voice; / Take each man's censure, but reserve thy judgment." To Reynaldo, Polonius is more darkly wise:

> Your bait of falsehood takes this carp of truth,
> And thus do we of wisdom and of reach,
> With windlasses and with assays of bias,
> By indirections find directions out.[27]

The Polonian aspect of Bacon's discourse is finally more like Hamlet's pretension to master the theater of the court in vaunting and yet filial emulation of God's power, seeking to manipulate appearances for the sake of seeing into and purging men's hearts. The telling difference between the new learning's prudent wisdom and the combined voices of Polonius and Hamlet is that the new sciences of practical advice and world transformation would make the purposes and ideas of heroic tragedy obsolete—unless they conformed to Hamlet's rendering of *The Murder of Gonzago* as a kind of trial manipulated so as to drive audiences to confess their true natures for their own good.

5

When Bacon turns his attention toward natural philosophy, he uses his biblical paradigms of experience and code to encompass the matter and forms of nature. A crucial example will serve as an introduction to Bacon's innovation: his identification of natural matter with Proteus. *The Wisdom of the Ancients* is not original in associating the ancients' sea-god Proteus with matter, but the way in which Bacon recounts the myths, and the manner in which he incorporates the Protean principle into his works, tells us something more about the character and ends of the new sciences.

Proteus, a servant of Neptune, is a herder of sea-creatures. He is also a prophet, giving up his knowledge only to those who can capture him. One's apprehension of Proteus depends upon one's ability to seize him, and then to hold on to the writhing god as he takes every conceivable shape. Proteus is the being that Menelaus wrestles in Book IV of the *Odyssey* in his quest for news about his fellow warriors. He is the divine seer whom Virgil's Aristaeus, a shepherd in the *Georgics,* attempts to take prisoner in order to learn the reason for the death of his bees.

According to Bacon, Proteus must be taken captive with mechanical rigor of handcuffs and chains so that the inquirer can discover matter's fundamental self:

> His dwelling was under an immense cave. There it was his custom every day at noon to count his flock of seals and then go to sleep. And if any one wanted his help in any matter, the only way was to secure his hands with handcuffs, and then to bind him with chains. . . . if any skilful Servant of Nature shall bring force to bear on matter, and shall vex it and drive it to extremities as if with the purpose of reducing it to nothing, then will matter (since annihilation or true destruction is not possible except by the omnipotence of God) finding itself in these straits, turn and transform itself into strange shapes, passing from one change to another till it has gone through the whole circle and finished the period; when, if the force be continued, it returns at last to itself.   (*SV* VI.725–26)

Bacon's Menelaus "vexes" (*vexet*) Proteus in order to see "the whole circle" of his transformations, and finally his reduction to himself. His quarry is so much more material than divine that Bacon does not bother to call it a god. The prophecy that he seeks is the complete pattern of matter's changes; from that pattern comes the revelation of matter's nature. Threatened with annihilation, Proteus returns to his primordial self after experiencing—and forcing his captor to suffer—a world of appearances whose "period," or cycle, encodes and returns to his original self.

In the 1537 Latin *Odyssea,* a close translation of Homer by Andrea Divo, we find no reference to mechanical restraints: Menelaus is

guided by a goddess who tells him he must hold Proteus "unflinch-
ingly" (*firmitor tenete*) and that he must "restrain him" (*comprimite*)
until "of his own will he speaks and questions thee" (*quando te ipse
interrogauorit verbis*).[28] In the actual capture, Menelaus and his men
throw their arms about the god;[29] they ride him, without resorting
to mechanical torments. (Comes' mythography supports the Homeric
rendering to the extent that its Menelaus comprehends [*comprehendere*]
Proteus in the act of seizing him.)[30] Homer's Proteus begins with a
question rather than with an instant revelation; Menelaus must respond, ask questions, and prepare himself for what Proteus warns
might be dark news. The god's replies do not give the hero a complete
key to the way home. Menelaus must first follow Proteus' advice to
make amends for neglecting to sacrifice at the beginning of his journey. At almost every turn, the explication of the past and the future
drawn out of Proteus is bounded by Menelaus' desire for news of
specific friends, and qualified by Proteus' warnings not to desire more
knowledge than the hero is able to bear.

Virgil's adaptation of the episode for the *Georgics* permits Aristaeus
to confine Proteus in chains, but not before seizing him in his own
arms (*manibus vinclisque*).[31] His mother stresses the importance of
capturing Proteus with chains and strength together (*vim duram et
vincula capto / Tende*).[32] As in Homer, the divine seer in Virgil reminds
his captor of the need to make a gesture of devotion to the gods. In
this case Proteus reveals that because Aristaeus is partly responsible
for the death of Eurydice, the wrath of Orpheus has brought death
to the shepherd's bees. Here the independent authority of the seer,
which accompanies the cunning of his resistance to arrest, is evident
in his ability to free himself after informing Aristaeus of his transgression. He plunges back into the water, while Aristaeus' mother remains
to tell her son that he must take responsibility for restoring the hive
by sacrificing to the wood-nymphs. Not from Proteus but out of the
carcasses Aristaeus leaves ceremoniously on the nymphs' altars will
come the bees to replenish his vacant hives.

In the mythography of Bacon's contemporary, Abraham Fraunce,
Proteus is the changeable Egyptian king who seems a god. But
Fraunce also pays attention to the Virgilian and Homeric versions of
the myth. He cites Cornelius Gemma's conclusion that Proteus in the
Georgics is "a type of nature," and he offers a complex interpretation
of Proteus in Homer, a gloss that is more Virgilian and Homeric in
spirit than Bacon's. He mentions the use of "bands" and force, but

only in the context of Proteus' resemblance to the intellect as it at-
tentively enforces its own discipline. The bands of the Protean intellect
are not chains, nor are they thrown by an outsider. What the Protean
intellect imposes on itself is its own seriousness in bending toward
truth. It is "enforced," not bound, by itself:

> [U]nles it seriously and attentively bend it selfe to the contemplation
> of things, [the intellect] shall neuer attaine to the truth, as *Proteus*
> would neuer reueale his propheticall knowledge, but first did turne
> and winde himselfe euery way to escape, until with bands he were
> enforced thereunto, as Homer (the first author of this inuention in
> the fourth of his *Odyssea*) discourseth at large.[33]

The comparison treats Proteus as though he were within and of the
self-moving intellect. Although he is eventually put in "bands," the
passive voice ("enforced") maintains the passage's focus on self-bend-
ing rather than capture.

Although Homer's and Virgil's Menelauses have foreknowledge
of the means to activate Proteus' prophetic power, they overpower
him without violating his divinity. Bacon's explicit interpretation of
the myth supports this precedent when he says that Proteus' contor-
tions are emanations of natural forms that bring forth the species of
the natural world "out of matter already duly prepared and predisposed." Still, the lesson that Bacon draws from the myth turns upon
the wise man's power to chain Proteus to the rack so as to force
matter "to extremities, as if with the purpose of reducing it to nothing." To discover the "conditions, affections, and processes of
matter," the skillful servant of nature has license to work upon his
objects as though he intended to obliterate them, humbly assured that
he can not destroy the essence of what God alone creates ("since
annihilation or true destruction is not possible except by the omnipotence of God"). In accepting his utter subordination to God's power,
the experimenter gains the paradoxical privilege of emulating God's
prerogative to purge matter of its transitory forms in order to discover
"the sum and general issue . . . of all things past, present, and to
come" (*SV* VI.726).

Bacon's speculation about the power of the new sciences over Protean matter is somewhat reminiscent of Augustine's longing in *The
Confessions* for a power over men's Protean minds: "If only men's
minds could be seized and held still! They would see how eternity,
in which there is neither past nor future, determines both past and

future time. Could mine be the hand strong enough to seize the minds of men? Could any words of mine have power to achieve so great a task?"[34] For Augustine the idea is interrogative, a renunciation of rhetorical ambition, although it recalls the power of divine revelation. He wonders whether his words might some day force men to open their eyes to their own salvation, to the sight of themselves in eternity. The result of the confinement would be, as it is in Homer's story of Proteus, a revelation of things past and future, this time with eternity removing temporal impediments altogether. Once held, the soul like Proteus would turn prophet, seeing its immortality in the one true faith.

What Augustine wishes for and does not pursue—a power to bind down his audiences' secular natures—Bacon claims for a learning that seeks mastery of the Protean pageant with the aid of experimental humility and conformity to the nature of natural bodies. The course of scientific experiment

> takes off the mask and veil from natural objects, which are commonly concealed and obscured under the variety of shapes and external appearance. Finally, the vexations of art are certainly as the bonds and handcuffs of Proteus, which betray the ultimate struggles and efforts of matter. For bodies will not be destroyed or annihilated; rather than that they will turn themselves into various forms. (*P* IV.257)[35]

All the traditional elements—earth, air, fire, and water—are merely transient under the power of wise experiment, as they are under God's trials in The Wisdom of Solomon. Even atoms pass away when subjected to such rigorous pressures. Although Bacon sometimes approves of the philosophy of Democritus, he declares in the *Novum Organum* that the doctrine of the unchangeableness of matter, a keystone of atomistic theory, has been misunderstood. The new learning would reduce all "only to real particles, such as really exist" (*NO* IV.126) so as to work nature toward the ends of God and purified man. Since "the nature of things betrays itself more readily under the vexations of art than in its natural freedom" (*IM* IV.29), the force and guile necessary to remove the Protean mask is justified by the material prophecies that result: the discovery of true bodies, their various disguises, and the means to generate new appearances of those bodies for charitable purposes.

In the new learning's adaptation of atomism, Bacon gives another clue to his conception of matter in human beings. His version of Virgil's *Georgics,* which he calls the "Georgics of the Mind," reveals the extent to which the new approach to atoms and Protean matter transforms ways of cultivating the mind. On one level, Bacon's prospectus seems to acknowledge the reasonableness of the Aristotelian commonplace that there are some things in the mind's nature that cannot be changed by external cures or by habit (*De Aug* V.19–24). But the deeper argument of the new *Georgics* is that what cannot be changed is "more profound and radical" than any "common inclination" that might have interested the post-Socratics. In order to discover knowledge of the unchangeable things, new sciences must find out what does not change under experimental pressures (*De Aug* V.20–21). Although there is sense in Aristotle's assumption that habit "has no power over those actions which are natural," enlightened habituation can mold character without Aristotelian regard for the bounds of character, except in the few cases in which fundamental natures are involved (*De Aug* V.24–25). "We do not advance much in fortitude" through the old practice of obtaining virtue by means of mere habit and temperance (*De Aug* V.28). The Aristotelian principle fails in all those instances where nature is made to work against itself; Aristotle does not anticipate the power of experiment, which "by use and continuance" can bend a wand "contrary to its natural growth" (*De Aug* V.25). Experiment is a profounder habituation than the ancient training because it can actualize the full range of the wand's metamorphic potential, thereby discovering a more basic nature in it.

The corollary of this idea in Bacon's ethical culture of man is more complicated but essentially similar. Bacon first endorses the imitation of natural processes when he explains how men are effectively persuaded to pursue what is good; but the conception of nature that his doctrine projects to the learned is far from the one which Virgil's gradual husbandry cultivates in the ancient *Georgics.* Once perfected by enlightened habituation, a Baconian mastery of nature allows man to experience an instantaneous conversion into all that is virtuous: his mind shall "mould itself to all virtues at once" (*De Aug* V.28).

The conversion of human beings on the basis of these Proteus-inspired principles discounts the integrity of characters not yet vexed and reduced. The true student of nature is encouraged to use simulation, as Bacon describes the process in the essay "On Simulation and Dissimulation," to "lay asleep" and "surprise" others in order to "discover the mind" of man. The inquirer is both inquisitor and confessor, one whose appearance of trustworthiness and air of confidentiality lure men to "shew themselves adverse" (*E* VI.389). Turning against themselves, Proteus-like, they display their true natures without realizing that their confessor has won the advantage by having gathered their secrets.

In a juxtaposition of maxims, the essay suggests that the confessor's similitude resembles a vexing lie, one that operates in the mode of the new sciences' capture of the sleeping Proteus: "And therefore it is a good shrewd proverb of the Spaniard, *Tell a lie and find a troth.* As if there were no way of discovery but by simulation" (*E* VI.389). The lie is a heuristic form of persuasion that secretly turns its object inside out.

This doctrine Bacon couches in a nest of qualifications. He takes the aphorism second hand, by attributing it to "the Spaniard" (when in a related essay in the 1625 collection he refers to Spaniards' reputation for seeming "wiser than they are" [*E* VI.435]); he interprets the proverb "as if"; and although he uses the discussion to imply that a shrewd willingness to forge lies might be the best way to discover things, he resists turning the idea into a free-standing principle. Still, in the very disclosure of the Spaniard's own imposture, Bacon has made the Spaniard say something that is wiser, from the point of view of the new learning, than he knows.

6

The secret binding of human beings is an abuse of learning that Bacon specifically condemns in the first book of *The Advancement*: "to be speculative into another man, to the end to know how to work him or wind him or govern him, proceedeth from a heart that is double and cloven, and not entire and ingenuous; which as in friendship it is want of integrity, so towards princes or superiors is want of duty" (*Adv* III.280). Bacon's prohibition, however, does not efface his critique of learned men who dare not advance knowledge because they fear to cross "the honest and just bounds of observation" in studying individual persons. Bacon agrees that such limits on "applying" the new learning to a particular man ought not to be violated, but his argument assumes that no violation will occur if enlightened investigators go "no farther but to understand him sufficiently, whereby not to give him offence, or whereby to be able to give him faithful counsel, or whereby to stand upon reasonable guard and caution in respect of a man's self." The inquirer can pursue the new learning's goals as long as he does not provoke his subject's objection, as long as his goal is to give advice for his subject's own good, or as long as he feels threatened by the person he examines. Secrecy, certainty, and self-protection are here the ambivalent guarantors of the inquirer's moderation. The only absolute barriers to such personal investigations are the inviolable hearts of kings, "which the Scripture hath declared to be inscrutable" (*Adv* III.279–80).

It is curious to see this pattern of argument occur again in *The Advancement*, where Bacon praises that power of persuasion which rests upon the consent, rather than the empty obedience, of audiences. According to the principle that "the dignity of the commandment is according to the dignity of the commanded," the ability to sway the will of another ranks above the power to compel people to act. Bacon's elaboration of this notion, however, implies an opposite. The will, as we read elsewhere in Bacon's definition of rhetoric, is controlled by the operations of charitable reason upon the imagination; knowledge and charity "giveth law to the will itself." The reason's true command over the will is a "just and lawful sovereignty" that foreshadows the absolute rule of kingly reason over seditious passions. Here the rule of reason is supposed to resemble something dear to a king who put great stock in his divine right: "the divine rule." That rule commands according to "truth rightly interpreted" (*Adv* III.316–17).

Civil history would seem to be the last place one might find Proteus bound, but Bacon finds in Britain's history since the civil wars a providential and philosophically appropriate winding of the kingdom's will. The distinctive characteristic of English sovereignty after the Wars of the Roses is the extreme variety of its royal regimes, followed by what was thought or hoped to be the exceedingly stable, even permanent rule of James and his offspring. Providence parallels the capture of the sea-god and the subsequent revelation of its essential being. Henry VII inaugurates the history as a providential agent: by means of force and manoeuvre, he is able to ride the sea-like "working and swelling" of history with the "wisdom" of a good pilot. A Protean pageant of strange and impressive monarchies follows him. In Henry VIII's time, there is "an action which seldom cometh upon the stage" of world history: "the alteration" of the ecclesiastical state. In the succeeding rule, the mere child Edward VI takes the throne,

followed by an attempt at usurpation, then by Mary's wedding with
the Spanish king. These prodigies give way to one more: the reign
of a woman, a queen more "masculine" than her rival princes. Finally,
Elizabeth's "solitary and unmarried" state is followed by the fruitful
stability of her successor, King James.

The history's strange parade resembles the series of testing shapes
that Proteus takes on in captivity. Once seized and piloted by Henry
VII, England and its subsequent sovereigns endure what seem to be
all possible extremities of uncertainty and good fortune, their history
concluding with the revelation of the true and unchangeable form of
Britain itself in the perpetual reign of James:

> [A]nd now, last, this most happy and glorious event, that this island
> of Britain, divided from all the world, should be united in itself;
> and that oracle of rest given to Aeneas, *Antiquam exquirite matrem*
> [seek out your ancient mother] should now be performed and ful-
> filled upon the nations of England and Scotland, being now reunited
> in the ancient mother name of Britain, as a full period of all in-
> stability and peregrinations: so that as it cometh to pass in massive
> bodies, that they have certain trepidations and waverings before
> they fix and settle; so it seemeth that by the providence of God this
> monarchy, before it was to settle in your Majesty and your gen-
> erations, (in which I hope it is now established for ever,) it had
> these prelusive changes and varieties.   (*Adv* III.337)

The hopeful and flattering prediction of this masque of history,
though it does not dare to delineate directly the workings of Providence, illustrates the very natural laws of matter that Bacon uses to
illustrate his praise.

In this and other instances, Bacon's flattery of James entails other
secret bindings. He is using the history to urge his king to become
a patron of the new learning, even though he has said that an adviser
to the king must not presume to know the sovereign will. Second,
he is invoking the ubiquitous Baconian analogy between Solomon
and James, which links James's good fortune to the biblical king's
endurance of mutability. Solomon is a self-knowing, self-binding
Proteus capable of ruling the world. As we find out in *The New
Atlantis,* the cryptic sciences need a sovereign protector of such stature, piety, and politic mutability if they are to succeed. The extended
analogy between James and Solomon would have been a deeply prob-
ing model for a scholarly king known for his indulgence in pleasure,
for his pious reputation, and his willingness to insist upon the divine
right of kings.

II

THE TIMAEIC TRADITION
IN THE SIXTEENTH CENTURY

Cosmology and Rhetoric

The divine Providence that vexes souls and bodies is a model for the new sciences' manipulation of Protean matter. In Bacon's project this doctrine is softened somewhat by the new learning's advancement in charity; but the charitable application of the new kind of inquiry is itself a cryptic discipline in imitation of God's wise disposition of the world after creating it *ex nihilo*. There is a purpose behind divine charity which, like the purpose behind the creation itself, cannot be plumbed. Similarly, scientific charity shows itself to the mass of men only through its effects. Its deeper causes and purposes—certainly its modes of penetrating nature's secrets while suffering in their pursuit— are hidden from idolaters, the mass of men who only know something of the new sciences' power to amaze, please, and comfort.

I

The principle of enlightened manipulation, as we have already noted, guides Bacon's interpretation of Paul's evangelism, and his likening of the wise politician to God. The new sons of science, like the faithful, must somehow see through the configuration of things as they are disposed by a politician who makes men "the instruments" of his "ends and desires" and yet "never acquaint[s] them" with his purposes (*De Aug* IV.364). Again, the mixture of secrecy and outward facility is Solomonic. "In a more divine sense," says Bacon, Solomon "elegantly describes" it in an aphorism: "Thy steps shall not be straitened, and when thou runnest thou shalt not stumble." The first verb ambiguously indicates that the most circuitous course, not just the unconstrained one, somehow ensures the greatest liberty of operation: "the ways of wisdom are not much liable either to straitness or obstruction" (*De Aug* IV.363). A similar principle is at work in the new laws of the forms of nature. The true laws of nature, Bacon explains, are metaphysical—beyond traditional laws of physics. Like the operations of God's Providence, they are in fact wholly separate from vernacular ideas of nature, even though they are essential to the instrumentality of physical appearances in the hands of the wise, who know that the visible world is the expression of the power to make appearances.

While the true laws of the forms do not show themselves to the vulgar, the key to their existence is the manifest world. The initiated inquirer obeys nature in order to see the signs of such laws, and so gains the capacity to imitate God's power and control the puzzle of the world in a feat of *omnia per omnia* encryption, which is capable of turning anything into something else:

> [T]his part of Metaphysic . . . enfranchises the power of men to the greatest liberty, and leads it to the widest and most extensive field of operation. For Physic carries men in narrow and restrained ways, imitating the ordinary flexuous courses of Nature; but the ways of the wise are everywhere broad; to wisdom (which was anciently defined to be the knowledge of things divine and human) there is ever abundance and variety of means. For physical causes give light and direction to new inventions in similar matter. But whosoever knows any Form, knows also the utmost possibility of superinducing that nature upon every variety of matter, and so is less restrained and tied in operation.   (*De Aug* IV.362)

Those who possess the laws of the forms wear a new kind of Gyges' ring: they have the power to mold invisibly a world of seeming things.

Ancient atomism offers support for these ideas. According to Bacon the atomists remove "God and Mind" from "the structure of things," and assume that the configuration of nature is determined by the play of "Fate or Fortune" upon the "necessity" of matter (*De Aug* IV.363–64). The atomists are atheists, and so are not fit to be the acknowledged models for the new metaphysics; but their very abandonment of theological speculation prepares for an understanding of God's remoteness from the "essays and proofs of nature" that the divine power imposes upon natural bodies. Bacon's *De Augmentis* frames the argument tentatively, relying upon "fragments and relics," but the critical passage does not entirely conceal Bacon's major point. The atomists' idea of a godless universe fraught by fortune's trials is ultimately more pious than Plato's and Aristotle's because of the insight it affords into God's providential testing of the world. The Creator's very separation and silence reveal what is most resistant to reduction. Thus Plato was wrong to mix theology and physics not only because he had no interest in experiment but because he did not acknowledge the cryptic power of the divine. Aristotle also erred, in finding final causes either too far from nature or too near. He overlooked not only the useful laws, but the signification of remote, all-powerful divinity in the thing itself.

Drawing from the atomists, Bacon asserts that matter is composed of irreducible bodies brought into play by "common principles" that are the laws of the forms (*SV* VI.737). The sweep and simplicity of those laws would create new theaters for the senses with a swiftness that escaped recognition. And they would immediately reformulate, as they manifested themselves, what the wise had discovered of God's code. For this quasi-atomistic conception of how matter takes form, the generation and regeneration witnessed in daily living would have little relevance.

Bacon interprets the apocalyptic myth of Deucalion and Pyrrha as proof of this "secret of nature": as embodiments of the scientific parents of a new age, standing on an earth otherwise devoid of living things, they must resort to throwing stones in accordance with an oracle in order to save nature from its own regenerative mutability (*SV* VI.737). Nothing in Ovid's account of the couple's grief for the destruction of earthly life, or their puzzlement and gradual recognition that the oracle means them to restore the earth to herself, remains in the new interpretation's scourging enlightenment. Deucalion and Pyrrha are a scientific Adam and Eve who make a new world without conjugal generation, from basest stones cast over their shoulders without aim or desire, in accordance only with an order from an otherworldly power. Even the myth of the Phoenix, which Bacon attaches to this text, is no evidence of matter's regeneration from the Phoenix's ashes. Nature emerges only from the remotest purposes, which work upon far more fundamental bodies than the ashes of mortal things.

The birth of Pan, or "Nature" as Bacon interprets it in *The Wisdom of the Ancients,* seems to offer a more general basis for interpreting seminal generation:

About his origin there are and can be but two opinions; for Nature is either the offspring of Mercury—that is of the Divine Word (an opinion which the Scriptures establish beyond question, and which was entertained by all the more divine philosophers); or else of the seeds of things mixed and confused together. For they who derive all things from a single principle, either take that principle to be God, or if they hold it to be a material principle, assert it to be though actually one yet potentially many; so that all difference of opinion on this point is reducible to one or other of these two heads . . .

. . . [T]his Pan, whom we behold and contemplate and worship only too much, is sprung from the Divine Word, through the medium of confused matter (which is itself God's creature).
(*SV* VI.709)

De Augmentis expounds this compromise as a diminishing and scourging of seminal generation. Seminal generation is identified with a myth that degrades natural tendency in matter, making material desires negligible contributors to the formation of the world, or violent and corrupt forces ready to dissolve it. Bacon ranks various philosophers' conceptions of prime matter according to their progression toward the enlightened view. While the atomists are more insightful than others in their belief that the seeds all have the same substance but vary only in the manner of their combination into visible figures, the most accurate traditional philosophers are those who have "represented Matter as entirely despoiled, shapeless, and indifferent to forms." Unformed matter's shapelessness and indifference are primordial appetites insofar as they are conducive to the designs of corrupt suitors. Thus Bacon allows that matter can be seen as "a common harlot" whose "suitors" are the forms (*De Aug* IV.320). In *De Sapientia Veterum,* Bacon presents the story of the suitors differently: Penelope lived much later than the time of Pan's reputed birth, and she was renowned for her "matronly chastity" (*SV* VI.707–08). But here the praise for Penelope is accidental to the degradation of desire in the world of nature.

In *The Wisdom of the Ancients,* Pan's defeat in his fight against Cupid demonstrates that he is "not without" (*non caret*) an "inclination and appetite"; but that inclination drives him "to dissolve the world and fall back into the ancient chaos." His association with superstitious fears shows that he is incapable of holding to a mean, except by violence imposed upon him or by force he imposes on others. "Cupid or Love" must subdue Pan's "malice and violence" (*malitia et impetus* [639]) by means of the "overswaying concord of things" (*SV*

VI.713,639).''[1] Concord is really control, not a seconding of Pan's disposition. Pan's own victory over the giant Typhon, the counterpart of his defeat by Cupid, betrays an essential propensity in nature to erupt and to repress itself violently. Typhonic "swelling" is common in natural things and must be controlled by confinement in "an inextricable net," bound down "as with a chain of adamant" (SV VI.712–13).

We see in Bacon's interpretation of the myth of Cupid, or the atom, that desire in matter must seem for all practical purposes blind and random, a cryptic sign of Providence. Thus the myth of Cupid, in Bacon's embroidering of the mythographers, is an explanation of *"the natural motion of the atom"* that is meant to frustrate the desire to ascend to a knowledge of *eros*.[2] Although the atomic Cupid "constitutes and fashions all things out of matter," his erotic motion is "inexplicable" except in terms of what he does to other things. Man cannot begin to understand the true Cupid's cause, just as he cannot know God as "the cause of causes" (SV VI.729). What we know of the workings of Cupid's desire makes the god almost ridiculous: he "directs his course, like a blind man groping, by whatever he finds nearest." His awkward motion is a perfect encryption of Providence, which contrives from its "peculiarly empty and destitute" subjects ". . . all the order and beauty of the universe" (SV VI.731).

The government of nature, which includes Pan's necessary combat with Typhon, Love's government of Pan, and Providence's "secret" rule over the world, is therefore similar to music that is "somewhat harsh and untunable" (*durum et quasi absonum*; SV VI.713,640). Nature has no true harmony or aspiration toward order other than what violence generates or what Cupid's rule effects. It proceeds in its operations undetected by the vulgar, whose "overweening confidence of human reason" leads them to prefer pleasant, inferior sounds, just as Minos favors Pan's presumptuous pipe over Apollo's lyre. Men's ignorance is complete in the sense that they do not have a hint of what they are missing. Here Bacon bends the Ovidian story of Minos at the point where the reeds whisper Minos' stupidity to the world. Minos is shown in his ignorance, denied the self-knowledge offered by the reeds. The self-flattering king cannot hear with the ass's ears that are his punishment for misjudgment, just as the mass of men, who are idolaters, do not have an inkling that they are apprehending an encoded nature (SV VI.713).

2

Bacon's concentration on the formless mass and the divine prerogative to make and mold the world takes its general precedent from Christian commentary on Genesis, though the new learning departs significantly from that tradition. Bacon finds support in Lucretius, who deserves commendation because he offers a doctrine for the moment most suited to the contemplative power of the new sciences, the moment when "matter without form" existed before the six days' works, awaiting the molding power of God (*SV* VI.723). Along with Democritus, Lucretius bases his atomism "more openly than anyone else" on "the eternity of matter," yet he points toward the instant in *Genesis* when God's power is most reserved and most poised to work all things.

A brief examination of some contemporary commentary on the first chapters of Genesis reveals some useful points of comparison between Bacon's interpretations and the hexaemeral glosses. Calvin's commentary on Genesis offers justification for the Baconian innovation by pointedly condemning speculation upon Genesis 1.24. Matter is indeed "the seede of the whole worlde," but only as it is formed by God's fiat from a single mass.[3] Whales, which God creates on the fifth day, have a kind of pre-existence apart from the maker's will, but only in the sense that they are in "the whole bodie" God created from nothing, to which "the forme onely was added" in order to make everything else.[4] The earth is really "a dead element." God forms the original mass as he wills and declares, in a manner analogous to his creation of the mass *ex nihilo*.[5] Paul's pronouncement in Hebrews 11.3 on the world's nature as a sign, and on the impossibility of its imaging forth rather than encoding the divine purposes, is in Calvin's emphasis the key to understanding Genesis:

> Wee knowe not God, which is inuisible, but by his workes. Therefore the Apostle notably calleth the worlde, things whiche did not appeare. This is the reason why the Lorde, to call us to the knowledge of him, setteth before our eyes the workmanship of heauen and earth, and maketh him selfe after a sorte to be secure in the same. For his eternall Diuinitie also and power, shineth therein, as sayth the Apostle.[6]

God is present is his creation in the sense that he does not leave himself "without witnesse." But the world is really what does *not* appear. Those who desire "to knowe God aright" will see the world as a "schoole" in which they know the Creator by beginning with the

Gospel.[7] True witness of the world concentrates upon God's "workes" as they can be seen in the light of Scripture. God signals to man, yet man must avoid the "double Labyrinth" that awaits him if he "proceede further than the Lorde calleth," more directly into nature itself.[8]

These assertions are not fundamentally inconsistent with Augustine's hexaemeral doctrine, which stipulates in *The City of God* that all wordly things, being changeable, are to be understood as things made, not as things generated from intermediaries or from seeds: "that is to say, they are made, not begotten."[9] His argument against the idea that angels are intermediate creators is a painstaking distinction between seminal generation and the Creator's hidden, all-seeing wisdom of Genesis:

> We do not call farmers "creators" of crops, since we are told, "The planter does not matter, nor does the waterer. It is God who matters, for it is he who makes things grow" [1 Cor. 3.7]. We do not even ascribe creative power to the earth, although it is clearly the fruitful mother of growing things, promoting their growth as they burst out into shoots, and holding them safely by the roots; for we are also told, "God gives to the seed a body of his choosing, its own body to each seed" [1 Cor. 15.38]. We must not attribute to a woman the creation of her child, but instead to him who said to his servant, "I knew you, before I formed you in the womb." [Jer. 1.5].[10]

These arguments provide Augustine with grounds for accommodating seminal paradigms. He is not loathe to dwell upon Genesis 1.24, "Let the earth bring forth the living creature after his kind," interpreting it as the pattern of later creation of the natural world from seeds that are instinct with generative purposes.[11] Calvin too follows up his emphasis on creation by fiat, by exploring the idea that "matter was the seede of the whole worlde" which God forms and furnishes out of chaos.[12] The forms themselves do not restrain the Creator's disposition of matter; but the species or genera of things are in the "whole bodie" of unformed matter, and give generic stability to animals as they multiply and fill the world according to their kind.[13] The six days' creation furnishes the world so that it is "finished and fulfilled"[14] as though an idea of the whole might be coeval with divine purposes in the six days' work. Similarly, Calvin, like Augustine, invokes an idea of the good in his interpretation of God's commendation of the creation.[15] Augustine had found in the very

contradictions of providential history a series of antitheses that enrich
the beauty of the universe the way rhetorical antitheses embroider
speech.[16] Calvin, although he maintains his emphasis on the inscru-
tability of the Creator, ventures the argument that God "hath after
a sorte put vpon him the image of the worlde, therein to offer himselfe
to be seene" of those who do not "by speculation remove and separate
God" from "the causes and natures of thinges."[17]

Moses himself, continues Calvin, frames his revelation "after a
common and grosse manner,"[18] in order to carry out his duty as a
teacher of the ignorant as well as the learned. His purposes are double
but not set in cryptic speech: "Moses doeth not curreously discuss
secret mysteries; but reporteth those things which are knowen euen
to the ruder sorte, and are in common use." The law-giver's various
audiences are more like eager gatherers than austere decoders as they
find "natural" and "civil" profit, as well as religious training, in God's
offer.[19]

The importance given to persuasion and "seminal reasons" in these
two accounts of the six days are characteristic of the hexaemeral
literature, according to James Nohrnberg's compendious study of
Genesis in *The Faerie Queene*'s Garden of Adonis.[20] The hexaemeral
literature acknowledges a tradition that is Timaeic as well as biblical.
Its collection of ideas about first things in part echoes the influential
Platonic dialogue about origins, the text that the Renaissance painter
Raphael puts in Plato's hand.

Although in *The City of God* Augustine takes issue with a number
of Timaeic doctrines, such as the idea of a creation through intermediate deities, he argues that Plato knew Moses' text. The manner
in which the Timaeic elements are combined to make the visible world
is, he says, in remarkable accordance with Genesis, as is the Platonic
doctrine of the mutability of created things.[21] Some Timaeic principles
are at work in the generation of bodies, if not souls,[22] and the *Timaeus*
lends support to the argument that God takes delight in the teeming
beauty of the creation.[23]

The Timaeic tradition that arises from the dialogue is a way of
understanding seminal generation in terms of the persuasion of matter, particularly persuasion that moves potentiality into actuality, or
unactualized matter into being. The Elizabethan translation of a passage from John de Trevisa's *De Proprietatibus Rerum* offers an epitome
of the Timaeic persuasion from within his pious account of God's
creation of matter:

> The vertue of God made & ordained *Primordial* matter, in which as
> it were in a massie thing, the foure Elements were potentially, and
> not distinguished in tale [weight] and number, as they are now: but
> they were muddeled. And that Massa and lumpe Plato calleth *Yle*
> in *Thimeo*. And thereof the wisedome of God made and brought
> forth all the Elements, and all that is made of Elements, & ordayned
> them in their owne qualyties & place.[24]

Here the hexaemeral synthesis attempts to preserve the Creator's
absolute authority while illustrating the Timaeic notion of a beginning
from potentialities. From the seeds of things are brought forth "their
owne qualities & place," their own natures somehow conceived of
in unformed matter's "easie might of breeding."[25]

Guillaume de Salluste du Bartas, in the Elizabethan translation of
Joshuah Sylvester, offers a more explicitly Timaeic summary of the
six days, lending credence to the notion that the Creation completes
or perfects the world and its species according to their kinds:

> Th' eternall Spring of Power and Providence,
> In Forming of this All-circumstance,
> Did not unlike the Bear, which bringeth-forth
> In th' end of thirty dayes a shapelesse birth;
> But after, licking, it in shape she drawes,
> And by degrees she fashions out the pawes,
> The head, and neck, and finally doth bring
> To a perfect Beast that first deformed thing.
> For when his Word in the vast Voyd had brought
> A confus'd heap of Wet-dry-cold-and-Hot,
> In time the high World from the low hee parted,
> And by itselfe, hot unto hot he sorted;
> Hard unto hard, cold unto cold he sent;
> Moist unto moist, as was expedient.
> And so in *Six dayes* form'd, ingeniously,
> All things contain'd in th' UNIVERSITIE.[26]

Here the perfection of kinds taking place over a period of days ex-
emplifies the divine's artful care for man and nature. Du Bartas's own
process of composition does homage to that care: "We should not
heedless-hastily bestow us / In any Work, but patiently proceed /
With ofte re-vises, *Making sober speed* / In dearest business, and observe / That, What is well done, is done soon enough."[27]

A persistent Timaeic influence upon Renaissance understanding of
genesis *ex nihilo* is apparent in the mid-seventeenth century natural

history of Nathaniel Highmore, who adapts Timaeic cosmology in the process of refuting a contemporary Timaeic theorist.[28] Although he condemns those philosophers after Plato who thought that actualizing forms were "potentially in the matter," he describes matter as a seed whose material atoms are "animated and directed by a spiritual form, proper to that species whose the seed is; and given to such matter at the creation, to distinguish it from other matters, and to make it such a Creature as it is."[29] If all generation were to derive from a single, homogenizing power (in this case, heat), that power would blot out "those indeleble Characters fixt by the finger of the Creator on every species; those inscriptions on all his works, the distinct constitution, parts, operations and figures (which are so many Bushes, or Signes hung out, to discover what are the inhabitants within)."[30]

Highmore refers to a divine code, but he puts the weight of his remarks on how atoms act in the Timaeic fashion as animated things, as does the world itself in its generation, according to Plato's dialogue. He describes the growth of the foetus of the chicken in terms similar to the configuration of all the species of things: it matures as its parts "discover themselves what they are," growing up "to their offices in their visible figures" by means of "the due ordering and regulating of the specified soul."[31]

Where we have seen Bacon tending to divide and attenuate the hexaemeral heritage of biblical commentary into a creation *ex nihilo* and a free manipulation of the unformed mass, Du Bartas and Highmore, like Calvin and Augustine, do not force out with Baconian consistency contradictions between Genesis and the hexaemeral tradition's accommodation of Timaeic ideas.

3

Timaeic philosophy grows out of Egyptian learning, which Bacon, like King James, takes pains to condemn. The new learning does acknowledge a debt to the Egyptians' hieroglyphic writing and their tradition of praising inventors, but the core of Egyptian natural philosophy is only rarely acknowledged to be compatible with the new sciences. Suspicion toward the Egyptian heritage characterizes King James's interpretation of Moses' life in Egypt. The chief reader of *The Advancement of Learning* writes in his own *Daemonologie* that the Egyptian magicians created only "false miracles" that were "casten down" by Moses' rod, its holy transformation into a snake being no

false appearance but "so in effect."[32] Moses became learned "in all
the sciences of the Aegyptians," but only because he was taught lawful
sciences, not magic. He could not hear God while he was in Egypt.[33]
The precise manner in which Bacon's natural theology supports King
James's commentary and departs from the hexaemeral accommodation becomes clearer when we look at the story of Isis and Osiris in
Plutarch's *Moralia,* and then take up the *Timaeus* itself.

Plutarch's compendium of Egyptian myth, available in numerous
sixteenth-century editions of the *Moralia,* highlights an erotic relation
between matter and form. In Isis' love for Osiris, natural matter
yearns for its form. The analytic destruction of natural bodies is what
that yearning resists and repairs.[34] In Plutarch's interpretive interjec-
tions, the sunderer of matter from form is the ruthless titanic destroyer, Typhon, whom Isis overcomes as she repeatedly seeks out
and re-assembles the limbs of her lover Osiris. The integrity of the
manifest world, upheld by the lovers' devotion, prevails over Typhon's frequent dissolution of things, and over his argument that
whatever is embodied is corrupt.

Isis "has an innate love for the first and most dominant of all things,
which is identical with the good, and this she yearns for and pursues."[35]
She "inclines always towards the better and offers to it opportunity
to create from her and to impregnate her with effluxes and likenesses
in which she rejoices and is glad." When Typhon destroys the re-
sulting creation, condemning it as corrupt and forcing it to disappear,
she again defeats him by following the principle that Nature takes on
corporeality according to the guidance of the Reason (*logos*) to ensure
"the creation of the world." Thus led, her desire yearns for, effects,
and conforms to the manifestation of the cosmos (*ton kosmon*)[36] in a
series of regenerations. The power of the *logos* in nature is great,
though not absolute. Generation must occur again and again. It eventually cripples Typhon, but does not destroy him, "thereby instruct-
ing us that Reason . . . creates concord out of discordant elements."[37]
The *logos* seeks to harmonize and press back his wrong-doing.

Denying Isis and Osiris places in its pantheon, the new learning
identifies only an abominable Typhon who fights Zeus (*SV* VI.702–
04). Bacon's Pan incarcerates the swelling destroyer indefinitely. Typhon is a rebel whose swelling has its analogue in seditious men and
in eruptions of nature. As an evil aberration rather than a cyclic
mutability, he has nothing to do with harmony; he must simply be
repressed.[38]

Of course, Bacon's suspicions toward Egypt have grounds in bib-

lical teachings. Plutarch's own *Lives of the Noble Grecians and Romans*
supplies for the Renaissance an Isis in the person of Cleopatra. The
Egyptian queen embodies the equivocation of the worm and the tears
of the crocodile—and the haunting beauty of the Egyptian lovers'
regeneration, if one reads Plutarch through Shakespeare's *Antony and
Cleopatra*. The history as Plutarch preserves it recounts Antony's ambiguous embrace of Isis in his death, and it captures—for all to contemplate—Cleopatra's problematic attempt to die as a Roman, only
painlessly. The play draws out a strange, almost nauseating distress
in Antony's efforts to kill himself, as though he were discovering in
his imitation of Osiris a horror in not being able to die. Likewise,
Cleopatra with her mortal secrets attracts the Roman suspicion that
her Isis-like powers of renewal are false entrapments.

The *Timaeus* itself, which incorporates Egyptian learning, warns
against following its archaic account as though it were a sufficient
model for the political and ethical training necessary for founding
and ennobling cities.[39] Nevertheless, a survey of many of the ways
in which Timaeic learning could be accepted and brought into intellectual traditions of Bacon's era helps us to distinguish the outlines
of Bacon's own incorporation of "white magic" into Orpheus' universal philosophy. The new learning's seeming antagonism toward
Egyptian lore amplifies traditional and biblical reservations at the
same time that it adapts Timaeic learning for its own innovative
purposes.

4

The *Timaeus*, along with the work of interpreters such as Chalcidius,
Plutarch (through Le Roy), and Cornelius Agrippa, makes available
in the Renaissance a cosmology that draws from Egyptian learning.
The creator god of the *Timaeus*, for example, is an imitator and
embellisher of matter that is predisposed to take on the form that the
god gives it. Plutarch, whose elaborations were popularized in a
French version by Le Roy in the early sixteenth century, describes
the god's creation of order from chaos as a perfection of matter according to matter's yearning for a characteristic form:

> [T]he glory of the structure belongs to God,—for the frame itself is
> the most beautiful of all masterpieces, and God the most illustrious
> of all causes—but . . . the substance and materials were not created,
> but always ready at the ordering and disposal of the Omnipotent

Builder, to give it form and figure, as near as might be, approaching to his own resemblance. For the creation was not out of nothing, but out of matter wanting beauty and perfection, like the rude materials of a house, a garment, or a statue, lying first in shapeless confusion. For before the creation of the world there was nothing but a confused heap; yet was that confused heap neither without a body, without motion, nor without a soul . . . This was the disorder of a soul not guided by reason . . . [God was] like a person either musical or poetical, who does not make either the voice or the movement, but only reduces the voice with harmony, and graces the movement with the proper measures. . . . [Thus God] disposed, digested, and embellished the confused mass, so that he brought to perfection a most glorious creature.[40]

Plutarch's passage is a trove of the great variety of assumptions that set the *Timaeus* apart from *ex nihilo* interpretations of the creation. Here is the pre-existence of a kind of matter; the maker's operation according to the perfective ideas of harmony; the creation of a universe that imitates the harmonizing actions of its poetical maker; the primordial propensity of unformed matter to take on body, motion, and soul as though it already had some inkling of its disposition in the hands of its poetical maker. The "confused mass" is not a total chaos. Like an untrained human voice it seems capable of undergoing reduction with a harmony that graces and forms its predilections toward certain tonal colors.

It is difficult to miss the links in this passage between cosmology, poetical fashioning, and rhetorical concepts that in the Renaissance frequently glossed poetical theory and practice. One reason for the affinity between embellishment, imitation, ordering, and perfection in the Timaeic cosmology is the deeper assumption that the parts of the universe are microcosms of the whole, which mirror as well as comprise it. In adorning the whole they imitate it, approaching it in harmonious, praising action. They do not simply make up the whole. Timaeus describes the stars as "disposed . . . throughout all the firmament of heaven, to be an adornment [*kosmos*] of it in very truth, wrought in diverse colors over the whole expanse."[41] They take a fiery, spherical form that imitates the whole and displays them best ("likening it to the All [the maker] shaped it like a sphere"). Their fiery nature renders them "Most radiant and fair to behold."[42] Like the stars, all the parts of the universe and the universe itself mirror the idea of the whole. The divine maker conforms to a decorum that

brings to characteristic perfection the matter and idea that are somehow already given, even though the universe and its parts are to
emulate him, "to be like himself."

In the Timaeic cosmology the maker's work is mediated by a host
of agents that resemble and differ from their maker. Their motion
arises from the universal tendency toward imitation that leads to the
analogous development and differentiation of what is human and what
is heavenly. The ambivalence of that tendency—its movement toward
identification with the model in parallel, distinct resemblance—is a
way of preserving the difference between divine and mundane while
greatly multiplying the grounds for their affinity, and for the possibility that lower orders might move through stages toward their
own perfections. Necessity, the "receptacle of becoming," and the
many levels of creatures that bring other creatures into being all are
considered to imitate the idea of the universe as well as the organisms'
own natures. The maker persuades Necessity itself to cooperate, as
though "reasonable persuasion" were more appropriate to his action
than decree. For its part Necessity—like the unformed matter described by Plutarch—demonstrates a capacity to respond to rationality, if only sluggishly, as though the maker's generative power were
not absolute.[43]

Matter, like Necessity, is here neither congruent with the creator
god nor distinct from him. Although to some commentators it appears to have existed on its own apart from the maker, matter is
capable of imitating a higher order. What might seem to be its mimetic
submission is also embryonic aspiration to become more complete,
more fully itself. Plutarch assumes that the creator god "embellished
and adorned the substance of [the soul] with number, proportion,
and harmony; as being a subject capable of receiving the most goodly
form which these ornaments could produce."[44] The Chalcidian commentary on the *Timaeus* follows Aristotle in assuming that matter
desires form as though it somehow already comprehended what it
lacked. Matter "yearns for form," desiring "adornment, just as the
female desires the male, and what is shapeless longs for beauty."[45]
As the universe comes to be, matter has the capacity to be "struck
with amazement by the majesty of its Maker and Creator,"[46] simultaneously displaying independence and submission when it "let[s]
itself be adorned willingly."[47]

The receptacle or "nurse" of the universe is a special kind of matter
whose character is mimetic in similarly ambivalent ways. It resembles

a mother, who—in accordance with a classical notion of procreation—is supposed to have no direct influence on the male form or seed that enters it. But the mother also performs an indispensable, generative function of receiving the male form and then giving forth—making manifest—an offspring: in this case, the universe itself. The receptacle is supposedly without quality, but this very lack in the scheme of the *Timaeus* is accompanied by a power to respond to forms and to nourish them into being.

Many of these principles are at work in the Hermetic account of creation found in the esoteric dialogue, the *Asclepius,* which Frances Yates has called the foundation text for Renaissance students of magic.[48] There matter has first been "prepared by God [*praeparatus est a deo*]"[49] before the visible world comes into being; the Creator works in stages rather than declaring the world in a moment or a series of instants. Once matter is made ready, nature acts as a kind of demiurge "imprinting the forms [*per species imaginans*]" upon it.[50] The earth becomes an intermediary creator, since it "receives into itself all the forms [*genres*] and renders them anew."[51] God governs all in a manner that accords with the nature of things that the intermediaries have helped coax into being: his spirit fills all things—is in fact "inhaled [*inhalata*]" by them "according to their natural capacities."[52] Numerous intermediaries enter in: efficient causes (the four elements) are the means by which forms are imprinted upon the matter, and the forms or genres strongly influence the generation of one created being from another, since "all individuals of one genre follow the form of their genre."[53]

As spokesman for Hermes Trismegistus, Asclepius assumes that matter is possessed of a certain character, indeed is inspirited, before the creator god's activity brings the material world to light. "In the beginning there was God and matter, and spirit was with, in fact in matter" though not as it was in God or the formal causes of his creation.[54] Through intermediary instruments that become causes of other stages of generation, the Hermetic generation thus persuades pre-existent matter, much as the creator god of the *Timaeus* urges the world into being.

5

Egyptian learning, propagated in the Timaeic tradition, has more than Hermetic significance. Many of its principles are clarified and augmented in Aristotelian commonplaces that permeate the Renaissance: for example, Aristotle's proposition in the first book of the *Physics* that coming-to-be is not adequately explained in Parmenides' theory of creation *ex nihilo*.[55] The distinction that Aristotle uses in his rejoinder to Parmenides is well known: coming-to-be is a process in which potency becomes actuality. King Lear's declaration that "nothing will come of nothing" repeats the idea, though his mistaken belief that Cordelia's words are nothing blinds him to the potency of her love.[56]

In the Aristotelian frame, potentiality is *dunamis,* or potency, unfortunately sometimes translated as "matter" even though it is matter unrealized. Actuality is *energeia,* or fulfillment and actualization of potential, sometimes loosely translated as "form" despite Aristotle's tendency to call it a *setting forth* of form and matter in an actualized whole. In the *Metaphysics,* he explains that *dunamis* and *energeia* are each aspects "of the identical reality": "matter [*dunamis*] and the form [*energeia*] are merely two aspects of the identical reality, the one with respect to a thing's capacities, the other with respect to its actual operation."[57] The modern form/content ratio comes misleadingly to mind. Aristotle assumes, as we tend not to, that what has *dunamis* possesses tendency; its yearning toward actualization is an indication of a capacity to possess what it lacks, to imitate it, given the proper conditions, so that its proper potency "comes into being." Actualization changes potency, but the process of change is a perfection and completion, an awakening of the thing to its own being. Thus in his treatise on the generation and corruption of things, Aristotle goes so far as to explain growth as a fulfillment of form rather than a material accretion.[58] Even food acts as a kind of form and matter at once; it "must be potentially that which is growing" so that it contributes to the organism's development.[59]

The very structure of sentences enacts, according to Aristotle's discussion of predication, a similar actualization of a subject's *potentia* in the application of the predicate to its subject. A verb "indicates always that something is said or asserted of something"[60] in the sense that "every proposition and every problem indicates [*deloi:* makes visible or manifest, shows, discloses] either a genus or a peculiarity or an accident" of the sentence's subject.[61] In larger terms "all things whatsoever, save what we call primary substances, are predicates of primary substances, or [are] present in such as their subjects."[62] The predicate (the word as it is preserved in the Latin combines *prae* and *dicere*) speaks forth and in anticipation of its mute subject. It predicts as well as declares, and so shadows forth the qualities of the subject's coming into being. Without its appropriate predicate, the subject's existence is questionable. The predicate without a true subject or primary substance has not come into being.[63] Hence the decorum of their joining is the true predicate's accuracy, its predictive power, and its decorous restraint in its being applied to, rather than identified with, its subject. The world in these terms is a grammar of illustration and shadowing, of coming-to-be and passing away, that juxtaposes matter and attribute while somehow generating or realizing matter by doing fitting tribute to the cosmic order of becoming.

Plotinus embroiders the idea of a relation between *dunamis* and *energeia* in an eloquent passage of the *Enneads*: "[Determining form] confirms the original state [of matter, the receiver] bringing it into actuality, into full effect, as sowing brings out the natural quality of land, or as a female organism impregnated by the male is not defeminized but becomes more decidedly of its sex; the thing becomes more decidedly itself."[64]

Aristotle invests the idea with ethical significance in Book II of the *Ethics,* where *ethos* or character, a potentiality in all persons, is assumed to manifest itself by means of the application of training and habit. Practice and ethical nature, though not identical, are in close relation as they act as predicate and subject:

> The virtues . . . are engendered in us neither by nature nor yet in violation of nature; nature gives us the capacity to receive them, and this capacity is brought to maturity by habit . . . The virtues . . . we acquire by first having actually practised them, just as we do the arts. We learn an art or craft by doing the things that we shall have to do when we have learnt it . . . [W]e become just by doing just acts.[65]

The ethical capacity is a given, but it is not virtue since virtues normally do not come to be by nature alone. A predisposition toward virtuous action must take deeper color from the repeated tincture of habit. Conversely, training does not forcefully extract or create ethical character, because coerced virtue is no virtue at all.[66] Ethical training is a kind of self-training.[67] It succeeds insofar as ethical potency comes into maturity by emulating what it is capable of becoming.

Much as in the *Timaeus,* the process of becoming in the *Ethics* is a partly ambivalent confirmation of matter. Habitual action by its nature is not entirely chosen or understood; nor can it be simply the product of an already fixed and permanent disposition. And since habitual imitation is so important in bringing virtue into being, mere imitation is difficult to distinguish from the manifestation of real virtue. The affectation of virtue, though it does not ensure ethical maturity, typically accompanies and so helps to effect virtue insofar as a person's capacities, ends, and circumstances become harmonious with what he affects.

Here the analogy between Aristotle's *Ethics* and his theory of learning can be of assistance. Insofar as Aristotle makes learning a recollection brought forth by means of imitation, it is supposed to be an actualization and perfection of a certain capacity to learn. The precise status of the gestures and accoutrements of imitation, as of their stages in habitual action, is commonsensical though not necessarily self-evident. In one sense, mimetic actions merely remind; in another, they help complete the intellect. We see some of the complexity of this process in the *Poetics'* invocation of the commonplace that learning is remembering: "the reason of the delight in seeing the picture is that one is at the same time learning—gathering the meaning of things, e.g. that the man there [in the poetic representation] is so-and-so; for if one has not seen the thing before, one's pleasure will not be in the picture as an imitation of it."[68] For Aristotle, the recognition brought on by the poetic artifact involves judgment of character and character type, not only an identification by name or physiognomy. It is a realization of something that may be known but not consciously discerned, something brought to fruition by an artful making and by the picture's imitation of the viewer's memory. The action and reaction need not go to completion to be recognized. As the *Poetics* makes clear, a potency may be only partially manifested in a given *energeia*. Some tragedies are more fully realized than others, depending on the means, manner, and purposes that bring them into being. Poets have succeeded in making various kinds of tragic drama, though tragedy might not yet have come to its fullest actuality in any of them. The *Poetics* dwells upon these emergent forms while glimpsing what they might become.

The work of Aristotle's artful rhetorician, as he is described in the *Rhetoric,* resembles that of the maker of poems in his persuasive but essentially mimetic confirmation of the rational and passionate desires of his audience's souls. The rhetorician imitates commonplaces rather than creating wholly new grounds for agreement. He selects and orders that which is most likely to persuade. In fact, he conforms with and perfects available means of persuasion that include the ready means and conformable types of rhetorical discourse and their appropriate subject matters. In delivering his speech he imitates that which he desires his audience to imitate and hence to recollect, for by their nature the souls of his listeners cannot be genuinely moved by coercion. In keeping with the discussion of the soul in *De Anima,* the best rhetorician would move the soul toward the pleasant and the good, as the soul moved itself. He would have to take account of differences in the virtues and capacities of his audiences, and so in a number of ways cover and declare his intentions in order to elicit response and avoid misconception. The principle of his persuasion, according to the *Rhetoric,* would be to persuade the soul as if it were—in Aristotle's artful metaphor—"settling down into its natural state."[69]

6

Cornelius Agrippa's *De Occulta Philosophia Libri Tres,* a sixteenth-century collection of sometimes esoteric magical lore, is a highly illustrative introduction to commonplace Renaissance adaptations of Timaeic paradigms. Although Agrippa warns that his information must be kept secret, and although his later work, the enigmatic *De Vanitate,* condemns all the arts and sciences of the world, his *De Occulta* publishes a synthesis of esoteric magic and customary opinions about persuasion and persuasive ornamentation, and claims for that synthesis a kinship with biblical religion. Like Ficino, Agrippa defends his synthesis by distinguishing between the wise magician and the sorcerer, whom unnamed persons of "rash ignorance" have identified with the essence of magic.[70]

Agrippa joins Aristotle, Plato, Orpheus, and the Pythagoreans, who he claims share the idea that the world has a soul and partakes of the "divine mind."[71] The assumption that the heavens are alive is the "foundation of all Philosophy," which Agrippa uses to support hexaemeral interpretations of Genesis:

> And if any doubt that the heavens live, saith *Theophrastus,* he is not to be accounted a Philosopher; and he which denyes the heaven to be animated, so that the mover thereof is not the form thereof, destroyes the foundation of all Philosophy; the world therefore lives, hath a soul, and sense; for it gives life to plants, which are not

produced of seed; and it gives sense to Animals, which are not
generated by coition.[72]

Here Agrippa's very insistence upon the insufficiency of mere seed
dovetails with his argument for an astrological, living power that
forms and is the form of the cosmos.

The fact that Agrippa had to submit his writings to church authorities is reason to scrutinize his defense of magical learning, to
determine if he was doing more than merely conforming to ortho-
doxy or ignoring it. We discover that he cites Plato's *Timaeus* in
support of God's role as the "Divine Majesty," who almost always
works his will through intermediaries, as Plato's demiurge does.[73]
Aristotle's doctrine that the passions have influence upon the forms
of bodies is in accord with Jacob's discoloring of the sheep of Laban.[74]
Partly in the spirit of Pico, Agrippa writes as though Plato and Aristotle agreed with one another and with the biblical tradition on all
essential points. Take, for example, his synthesis of *Genesis,* the *Timaeus,* and the play in Aristotle's work between potentiality and *energeia:*

> For God in the first place is the end, and beginning of all Vertues,
> he gives the seal of the *Ideas* to his servants the Intelligencies; who
> as faithfull offers sign all things intrusted to them with an Ideall
> Vertue, the Heavens, and Stars, as instruments, disposing the matter
> in the mean while for the receiving of those forms which reside in
> Divine Majesty (as saith *Plato* in *Timeus*) and to be conveyed by
> Stars; and the Giver of forms distributes them by the Ministery of
> his Intelligencies, then from the aspects of the Heavens disposing,
> and lastly from the tempers of the Elements disposed, answering
> the influencies of the Heavens, by which the Elements themselves
> are ordered, or disposed.[75]

Rather than focusing on the idea of a creation *ex nihilo,* Agrippa
observes God's operation through numerous subordinates, including
sidereal influences, which are busy "disposing the matter in the mean
[-]while for the receiving of those forms" that originate from God.
The forms reside in God but are "conveyed by the Stars." Once
properly disposed, matter and the virtues answer the heavens that
form them.

Agrippa explains form's animation of matter in Aristotelian terms
mixed with practical observation:

[A]lthough things have some vertues, such as we speak of, yet those vertues do so ly hid that there is seldom any effect produced by them: but as in a grain of Mustardseed bruised, the sharpness which lay hid is stirred up: and as the heat of the fire doth make letters apparently seen, which before could not be read, that were writ with the juice of an Onion or milk: and letters wrote upon a stone with the fat of a Goat, and altogether unperceived, when the stone is put into Vinegar, appear and shew themselves. And as a blow with a stick stirs up the madness of a Dog, which before lay asleep, so doth the Celestiall harmony disclose vertues lying in the water, stirs them up, strengtheneth them, and makes them manifest [*prodit, excitat, corroborat*].[76]

Virtue manifests itself by answering to a form, since "every thing moves, and turns it self to its like, and inclines to it self with all its might."[77] The seeming contradiction of a thing moving toward itself is in reality a statement of matter's yearning for something higher that might make it more complete. In the soul's contemplative preparation for apprehending higher things, it is supposed to "convert itself into it self."[78] Once brought into being, the virtue of a thing similarly attracts or calls out other things, as salt makes salty things it has long been in contact with: "for every agent, when it hath begun to act, doth not attempt to make a thing inferior to it self, but as much as may be, like, and suitable [*consentaneum*] to it self."[79] Here the forming agent imitates itself in an exercise and experience of persuasion: as an enhancement of the taste of things, the salt forms and is formed by the substance it makes suitable to itself.

It might seem, Agrippa concedes, that all things simply thirst for God, "for there is nothing of such transcending vertues which being destitute of Divine assistance, is content with the nature of itself."[80] But Agrippa conceives of a transcendence contingent upon the configuration of intermediaries, and the disposition toward activity in the aspirant:

[A]ll the *Ideas* in God indeed are but one form: but in the Soul of the world they are many. They are placed in the minds of all other things, whether they be joyned to the body, or separated from the body, by a certain participation, and now by degrees are distinguished more, and more. They place them in nature, as certain small seed or forms infused by the *Ideas,* and lastly they place them in matter, as shadows.[81]

The participation expresses "a wonderfull power of operating," since "every species hath its Celestiall shape or figure that is suitable to it . . . which proper gift it receives from its own *Idea,* through the Seminal forms [*rerum seminales*] of the Soul of the world."[82]

An uncritical tolerance of such statements is not enough to draw out Agrippa's meaning. Here his attention to the decorum of the idea's influence—its suitability and propriety as a gift to the thing that receives it—intimates a further, ethical dimension in the "becoming" of things in nature. We are told that virtues—which, like the ideas, can act as forms that apply and draw out virtue from matter—"do not err, but by accident." Why then do some things differ in quality from others formed by the same idea? One answer is that the forms are not omnipotent in working their persuasion because consenting matter can be variably disposed or insufficient. In fact, "all Celestial influences may be hindered by the indisposition and insufficiency [*confusionem & inabilitatem*] of the matter."[83] False or untempered mixtures can create monsters. And among truly formed things, the variability of an idea's influence is largely a matter of preparation in combination with the right application of virtue. The Platonists, Agrippa observes, stipulate that the highest, more powerful virtues are infused "according to the desert of the matter [*merita materiae*]."[84] The preparation of the disposition has to do with choice and habituation as well as the material limits of the thing disposed.

The ethical and devotional coloring in the formative workings of the virtues is clearest in Agrippa's discussion of the mind. He recalls Ptolemy's emphasis upon the mind's choosing its better nature: "he which chooseth that which is better, seems to differ nothing from him who hath this of nature." The magician should therefore make suitable to heaven's benefits all his "thoughts, affections, imaginations, election, deliberation, contemplations, and the like."[85] By quickening his faith in the suasory power he affects, his own effort resembles that of his object: "For our mind doth effect divers things by faith, which is a firm adhesion, a fixt intension, and vehement application of the worker, or receiver, to him that co-operates in any thing, and gives power to the work which we intend to do."[86] The mental image is a forming power that dresses the mind for the impression that perfects it from within and from above. "For our mind can through imaginations, or reason by a kind of imitation, be so conformed to any Star, as suddenly to be filled with new vertues of that Star, as if it were a proper receptacle of the influence thereof."[87]

Metaphors of ethical culture permeate Agrippa's discussion: "For so much the more perfect life things receive [from the stars], by how much their temper is more remote from contrariety."[88]

One might expect astrological influence to be wholly determining or at least impervious to sub-stellar beings' power to affect it. But even the lower beings influence astrological powers "so far forth as things render themselves conformable" to those powers.[89] They affect (or influence) what they affect (or imitate). The occult properties that stars then convey into things do not work without a kind of universal consent.

The preparation of the yearning *materia* is not all that is vital to natural influence. A decorum of time, place, form, number, proportion, pronunciation, stellar position, and even of the speaker's attention, vehemence, and the "violence" of his imagination, is necessary if a magician is to make use of the most effective instruments of natural magic, the hymns of Orpheus:

> They that desire further examples [of efficacious speech] . . . , let them search into the hymns of Orpheus, then which nothing is more efficacious in natural Magick, if they together with their circumstances, which wise men know, be used according to a due harmony, with all attention. . . . Such like verses being aptly and duly made according to the rule of the Stars, and being full of signification, & meaning, and opportunely pronounced with vehement affection as according to the number, proportion of their Articles, so according to the form resulting from the Articles, and by the violence of imagination [*per imaginationis impetum*: perhaps the inseeking or deeply impressed imagination, from *im* plus *petere*] do confer a very great power in the inchanter, and sometimes transfer it upon the thing inchanted, to bind, and direct it to the same purpose for which the affections, and speeches of the inchanter are intended.[90]

The complexity of the task is beyond the ken of calculation and yet necessary for appropriate persuasion. True consent is of the nature of things yet not always easy to effect. In fact, if wise men followed all of Agrippa's prescriptions, they would only "sometimes transfer" their influence by means of enchantment.

Given that all true names are written in heaven, and so signify by conveying and realizing the harmony of the stars,[91] Agrippa still insists upon the preparation of the namer and the named. The name should be uttered often, "in due place, and time, and seriously with an intention exorcised upon the matter rightly disposed, and that can naturally be acted upon by it." Thus the magician Appollonius, having swiftly and "accurately inquired into" the name of a maid who had died on her wedding day, "pronounced some occult thing, by which she revived."[92] His inquiry sought her precise signification, which he delivered in an occult fashion so as to lift or draw her toward the perfective conjunction for which she had been prepared: her wedded life. Such constraints upon the magician's naming power are limits that enrich its effects: "The *Platonists* therefore say, that in this very voice, or word, or name framed, with its Articles, that the power of the thing as it were some kind of life, lies [*latere:* lies latent, capable of excitation] under the form of the signification."[93]

Writing is itself a perfective ornament, being "the last expression of the mind" and hence "the number" or ultimate signification "of speech and voice" and their "collection, state, end, continuing, and iteration." Writing perfects speech in its use "to express [*enunciare*]" the interior of the mind and "to draw forth [*depromere*]" the secrets of thoughts, as well as "to declare [*pandere*] the will" of its maker. In its initially ornamental function it risks becoming a cosmetic pandering. Yet as array, in Agrippa's terms it forms the subject to which it is decorously applied. (The modern derogatory meaning of *pander* is at least partly the result of literary accident: the association in Chaucer and Shakespeare of the lovers' go-between, Pandarus, with bawdry.) Agrippa concludes that writing improves on speech because it makes "a habit, which is not perfected with the act of ones voice." More than the appearance or raiment of its object, writing is a habitual action that gives things their color as it completes them and brings them to light.[94]

7

The notion that all magicians are in fact demonic manipulators who blaspheme God's creation is the famous charge made by Augustine in *The City of God,* which attacks the misuse and ultimate impiety of Egyptian learning, including the myths of Isis and Osiris, as forms of idol worship that deny God's omnipotence. Such learning supposedly appeals to the demonic powers in the things of earth, air, and the heavens themselves.[95] Augustine is particularly outraged over the creation of gods modeled after men. In what seems to be the manufacture of statues which are then animated with spirits, the *magus* supposedly extracts and uses evil "demons," not the ennobling *daimon* he claims to be his guide.[96] To the author of the greatest Christian argument against the idolatry of the fallen pagan city, such image-making is the sink of Egyptian learning. The persuasion of a yearning matter by a decorous form can only be idolatry: "The demon attached to an image by an impious art has been made a god by man, but a god for this particular kind of man, not for all mankind. What sort of a god then is this who could only be made by a man who is in error, who lacks faith, who is estranged from the true God?"[97]

Agrippa's most explicit response to Augustine's charge occurs at the end of the second book of *De Occulta*, a moment he prepares for with scores of chapters outlining a comprehensive Timaeic cosmos. Frances Yates has referred to Agrippa's statement in that place as an unalloyed declaration of the power of the *magus;* in its context, however, his provocative questioning invokes limits on the magician's powers.[98] Agrippa's magician dares controversy, but in a manner that emphasizes the importance of his becoming suitable to the order of things, bending his thoughts toward their sources and ends so that he might move toward the archetype that forms his desire:

> But know this that such images work nothing, unless they be so vivified that either a naturall, or Celestiall, or Heroicall, or animisticall, or Demonicall, or angelicall vertue be in them, or assistant to them. But who can give a soul to an image, or make a stone to live, or mettal, or wood, or wax? and who can raise out of stones children unto Abraham? Certainly this Arcannum doth not enter into [*non penetrat*] an Artist of stiffe neck; neither can he give those things which hath them not. No body hath them but he who doth (the Elements being restrained, nature being overcome [*victa*], the Heavens being overpowered [*superatis*]) transcend the progress of Angels, and come to the very Archetype it self, of which being then made a cooperator [*cooperatur*] may do all things.[99]

The *magus* in his remarkable ascent is still "made" a cooperator in the passive sense of the verb. His power to overcome the world is supposed to strike wonder into Agrippa's reader; but that power is qualified by the Archetype's continuous forming of the *magus,* who is also a *materia,* however great his power to form, as he aspires to "all things" in operation *with* the Archetype.

Agrippa has already cited the authority of Aquinas's *De Fato* in arguing that celestial influence extends over artificial things. His point is to emphasize the celestial powers' superiority over what man makes.[100] If the magician gives life to anything, he does so in accordance with the constraints put upon him by his imitation of superior powers and his "respect" for the "beginning" of inferior things in entities higher than the *magus*. His soul's ability to cooperate, if it does transcend that of the Angels, is hence the result of its contemplation and imitation of things below and above, and the manner in which they animate what is to be influenced according to its degree on a scale of ascent: "Our soul therefore, if it will work any wonderfull thing in these inferiors, must have respect to their beginning, that it may be strengthened, and illustrated by that, and receive power of acting through each degree from the very first author." The magician's strength and light come from the very things he would influence, and from higher sources of influence that he must attract in order to act well in his calling. Hence to use the power of the sun, the *magus* must "return to the soul" of that higher source, imitating its "intelligible light." Only then might his own "intellectual sight" take it in. To work upon his object, he reaches for something beyond himself, then must imitate it rather than grasp at it, and draw its influence as a kind of gift.

Once drawn from these sources, the magician's power is capable of moving objects "unwillingly" beyond their "natural disposition," but not in violation of their nobler natures. Agrippa's example is the father who is moved unwillingly to labor for his son, "for to keep and maintain him, although he be wearied." Thus the parent's love for his offspring overcomes his baser nature as he imitates a nobler idea of his fatherhood. It is apparently this higher idea that the true magician is to discover and then apply to the unwilling being he seeks to move. Agrippa's second and final example broadens this principle, alluding to the manner in which nature's "indigency" or "poverty" moves men beyond their baser natural inclinations as they strive for riches.[101] Here the idea of plenitude, not mere deprivation, is at work. The magician who knows the power of the idea and of men's yearning can cooperate with the deprived man's higher and lower natures to move him out of his inertia.

Rather than defend or condemn a magical will to power, these tactful illustrations attribute extraordinary influence to the *magus* while alluding to a decorum in the way he and his objects imitate nature. Baser nature, even when willingly imitated, is not the only object of natural imitation. Conversely, the imitation of higher things need not spurn what is lower. The ideas of fatherly love and plenitude are supposed to draw their beholders away from their baser natures, but without severing fathers from fatherhood, or laborers from their understanding of poverty as deprivation—as a privation of something better.

8

For the modern reader, the plausibility and representativeness of these Timaeic formulations is severely tested when one applies them to ornamentation and persuasion in rhetoric and poetry. If writing is a perfective complement of speech, as Agrippa claims it is, it is also, according to Timaeic principles, an ornament that somehow forms and persuades the object to which it is applied or attached. Names are ornaments that call to and help form their objects. But if Timaeic ornament is a kind of clothing of speech, or a "coloring"—something applied to or juxtaposed with its object—how can it be more than an arbitrary device, one eminently suited to a speaker's false affectation? What do ornament's traditional Timaeic roles as a covering or an addition to its object have to do with the more firmly grounded Aristotelian conceptions of *potentia* and *energeia,* which inform Agrippa's speculations?

Commonplace Renaissance descriptions of the cosmos offer a preliminary guide to this quandary, for they often associate the created world with an ornament or a decoration. Some prominent instances define man's relation to the world as ornamental: as a microcosm of the whole, man supposedly affects that whole, since it is the creation of God. Man desires to be its ornament as the cosmos ornaments him. The *Asclepius* offers this idea in a paradox of visionary force:

> As [man] governs as though he were himself for the world—and the world for him—an ornament, so well it is that by reason of this divine composition of man that the Greeks rightly call the world *kosmos.* Man knows himself, he knows the world, this understanding having as a result that he recalls what is appropriate to his role, and recollects those things are useful, in his service and in what he must do, offering to God his praises and his most lively actions of grace, revering the image of God without forgetting that he is of God, he too, the second image [of God].[102]

Man and *mundus* ornament one another by perfecting their counterpart decorously, in worship of the Creator whom they image. Their decorum is praise. By definition, it is not congruent with its object. But ornament is also praise of that which man and argument are inchoately ready to become; it confirms what they seek to be. Or

rather, it confirms their *being*. Here the ornamental relation of man
to world, world to man, and both to God is, most decorously, a true
enameling of things, a surrounding and covering of their inspirited
light with glass so worked that it glows their life.

That God is himself a master of ornament is a remarkable commonplace of the period: the cosmos is said to be perfected by decorous
ornament, as though its creator adorned it in order to bring it into
being. Thomas Digges's free translation of Copernicus, *A Perfit Description of the Celestiall Orbes,* echoes the Vulgate's reference to the
stars as ornaments of the heavens: the orb of the fixed stars is "garnished with lightes innumerable."[103] According to Sir Walter Raleigh's
account of the creation in *The Historie of the World,* God first "distinguished and gaue to euery nature his proper forms," and in the last
three days "adorned, beautified, and replenished the world" with the
sun, moon, stars, and the generation of life on the earth. For Raleigh,
God's making and adorning partake of each other, for rather than
being formed in the first three days and merely decorated in the last
three, the parts of creation are "adorned with forme."[104] God demonstrates the double meaning of the Latin *figuro* by simultaneously
forming and embellishing the world, figuring forth the creation.

Raleigh's description would have had precedent beyond the *Asclepius.* Pliny emphasizes the affinity between ornamentation and the
act of creation in his definition of *kosmos:* "that which on account of
[its] ornament the Greeks called *kosmos,* we for the sake of [its] perfect
and absolute elegance name *mundus*" [*quem* kosmos *Graeci nomine
ornamenti appellarunt, eum nos a perfecta absolutaque elegantia mundum*].[105]

Augustine lends authority to the idea when he likens the history
of the world to the rhetorical figure of *antithesis,* the elegant ornament
made by the Providence of God:

> The opposition of such contraries [*antithesis*] gives an added beauty
> to speech; and in the same way there is beauty in the composition
> of the world's history arising from the antithesis of contraries—a
> kind of eloquence in events, instead of words. This point is made
> very clearly in the book Ecclesiasticus. "God confronts evil, life
> confronts death: so the sinner confronts the devout." And this way
> you should observe all the works of the Most High: two by two:
> one confronting the other.[106]

A failure to appreciate the philosophical elegance of these commonplaces is a special hindrance to our understanding of rhetorical

figures, and of ideas of persuasion surrounding Bacon as he approached maturity. The modern tendency to assume that copious additions and variations are redundant or beyond decorum—for example, that *accumulatio* is essentially the piling up of mass and that the inversion called *epanados* is variation that is valuable for its own sake—stems from a concept of matter and ornament alien to these views of nature and cosmos. The post-Baconian heritage encourages the notion that matter must either be actual or absolutely non-existent, and potency a stored force, though matter and energy are now tied problematically in equations of relativity. Concepts of material potential or perfective actualization seem irrelevant, at least to modern lay interpretation of such principles. But if we can look back through this perspective to the Timaeic and Aristotelian conceptions for coming-to-be, the Renaissance investment in the rhetorical figures begins to make sense in terms of a natural philosophy in which the augmentation of potency and the actualization of *dunamis* are mediated by deliberations concerning the means and ends of natural ornamentation.

9

This background for a re-examination of Renaissance rhetorical figures should allow us to glimpse something beyond modern commonplaces about color, including the popular view that "colors" in a non-scientific context are either aesthetic tools or false cosmetics. In the sixteenth century colors and figures of rhetoric tend to be associated in a generally scientific sense, though one need not go far to find a plethora of Renaissance warnings about false colors in cosmetics as well as language. The thematic and formal preoccupations of, for example, Sidney's sonnets seem to dwell upon a corruption inherent in false painting.

Color is certainly no simple talisman of virtue in an age that gives Bacon material and impetus for gathering an arsenal of tints for rhetoric, *The Colours of Good and Evil.* Nor can the virtue of color in rhetoric or in alchemy be entirely clear when in *Hamlet,* Polonius tells the innocent Ophelia to "color" her loneliness with reading so as to capture Hamlet's secret thoughts. Hamlet too assumes in his conversation with Rosencrantz and Guildenstern that color is false appearance.[107]

It would be a mistake, however, to conclude on the basis of ambivalent uses of colored appearances in Renaissance literature that tinting is merely a method or a deception. The influential traditions of sympathetic magic, astrology, alchemy, and their echoes in Aristotelian and Platonic commonplaces put the burden of proof on modern criticism. The proto-modern Hamlet is indeed skeptical of false coloring, but his distrust of tincture does not prevent him from aspiring to a revenge "of true color"—one that will draw blood instead of tears.[108]

Even though it often refers to daubed women as proverbially duplicitous, the love poetry of the age relies heavily upon ornament applied to its subjects, as though a special kind of poetical painting could set out or appropriately drape the lover's truth. Timaeic strands in English Renaissance theories of poetry and rhetoric lend support to the love poets' efforts, as will be discussed more fully in the last part of this chapter. In preparation for that investigation into poetical and rhetorical color, it would be useful first to examine the meaning of color in what was by definition an old science of coloring—alchemy—and to ask whether alchemical coloring illustrates more fully the Timaeic principles we have already set out.

For Aristotle, light and color are almost identical: "whatever is visible" is color.[109] When Henry Peacham defines description or *hypotiposis* as setting forth a thing "plainly," he invokes the Aristotelian view when he claims that the description will "paynt out each thing in its due collour."[110] Color in this sense is form's shadow; its shading gives the thing both hue and form. In Peacham the sight "decearneth" things precisely by means of "their fourmes, and colloures."[111]

Aristotle explains that light is "as it were the proper color of what is transparent," having "the power to set in movement" a substratum that "contains in itself the cause of visibility." Light exists "whenever the potentially transparent is excited to actuality" by the influence of fire or something resembling "the uppermost body" (the uppermost shell of the cosmos) of which light is the "activity."[112] In alchemy, color is supposed to do much the same thing. Stephen Toulmin has observed that "the theories of the alchemists . . . were largely concerned with surface-appearances: the crucial question for them being, how the visible properties of an object—of which colors are the most obvious—are related to its inner structure and constitution."[113]

Whatever might have been the true definition of the *materia prima* upon which the alchemist worked his skill, the alchemical tradition reflected and fostered the belief that certain procedures, especially tincture and heating, conferred qualities upon metals such as copper and silver that yearned for and were capable of an aureation that brought them to their most proper forms. Tincture was a byword for alchemical transformation. In the Pseudo-Raymond Lully's famous declaration, "*Mare tingerem, si mercurius esset,*" alchemical ambition is expressed as the desire to gild the sea.[114] The Egyptian Zosimus, some of whose ideas were known to the Renaissance, stresses that "the tinctural element" is "the useful thing" to bring gold from potentiality to actuality.[115] Jean de Meun equates alchemical coloring with all art, by urging art to imitate alchemy's power to stain metals.[116] In the context of these commonplaces, Shakespeare's artful praise of morning's "gilding pale streams with heavenly alcumy" is not without a certain philosophical earnestness.[117]

An alchemical metaphor in Stephen Hawes's *Pastime of Pleasure,* in which he compares alchemy with elocution, links rhetorical painting with a principle of natural philosophy. Elocution "doth ryght well claryfy" rhetoric's matter just as alchemists "gold from coper puryfy":

> . . . elocucyon with the power of Mercury
> The matter exorneth right well facundyousy.
>
> In few wordes swete and sentencyous
> Depaynted with golde harde in construccyon
> To the artyke [artist's] eres swete and dylycyous.[118]

Mercury as catalyst of alchemical transmutation and as the messenger-god of eloquence links rhetoric's painting with alchemy's perfective persuasion of matter. The ornamentation of plain matter is "facundyous," just as elocution's "few wordes," once painted gold, delight receptive ears with their sweetness.

In the Paracelsian *Lexicon,* the process called *elaboratio* develops and purifies metals in much the same manner as the subject matter of speech is ennobled. The essential substance of the thing is worked out by means of elaboration: "we separate the ignoble, or worthless, portions of any substance, and most powerfully draw out [*elicimus*] whatever belongs to its essential part."[119] Paracelsian *elaboratio* draws forth an essence or soul that possesses a kind of corporeality evident in its having color. According to the terminology of the *Lexicon* the soul is itself "the tincture withdrawn from the body,"[120] much as the mysterious "fifth essence" is the "color" that perfective art somehow draws from baser things. Tincture has "a certain essence, quality, and form."[121] All three are treated as various actualizations, not abandonments, of bodies' noblest beings: "[tincture] can impart, and so as it were, infuse its own appearance into a substance. If this Tincture be properly developed [*elaboratum*] . . . [I]t will impart an unchanging and persisting quality to a thing in proportion to its capacity for receiving it."[122]

A kinship between rhetorical and philosophical ideas of color, form, and actualization is evident in the definitions of several key words in sixteenth-century Latin dictionaries. According to Thomas Thomas's 1587 *Dictionarium*, what is *coloratus* is "set out and garnished with figures and ornaments," while *color* means actual appearance: "the external face or beauty of a thing."[123] As the outwardness of a thing, color is synonymous with "pretense," but "pretense" that is not what we commonly think of as deception. *Pretense, color,* and *pretext* are indeed allied in Thomas's list, as they are in John Rider's,[124] but Thomas defines *praetexere* as "to color, cloak, excuse, or pretend." To make pretext is "to border, or set out as a border along by," much as the similar term *praescriptio* means "a limiting, a forme, cloak, color." Thomas Elyot offers a way of understanding this phenomenon in his definition of *pretendere*.[125] To pretend is not only to conceal but to border a thing with a hedge. More positively, pretending is a carrying or bearing of something "afore." Color and pretext here set out something, or set before it its own nature, like an emblem in a procession, as though their clothing lighted and defined the character of what they cloaked.

Thomas's definition of addition lends support to the idea that rhetorical ornamentation which adds colors can have something to do with bringing forth. *Adjunctio* is thus among other things a "color of rhetoric," and *addere* can mean to "augment" or "prolong." In the Paracelsian lore, *addere* is *temperare*; addition becomes the method for drawing to the fore gold's true qualities, making it the most tempered of metals.[126]

IO

The alchemical literature of England, as it is collected by Elias Ashmole in the mid-seventeenth century, elaborates these principles according to Timaeic and biblical ideas of genesis and renewal. The English texts that Ashmole attributes to "our Famous English Philosophers, who have written the Hermetique Mysteries in their owne Ancient Language," suggest that the perfective testing of metals might have at least as much to do with composition and tempering as with firing and purgation.[127]

Thomas Norton's *Ordinall of Alchemy,* for example, concerns the use of natural magic that engenders what is proper to the perfective desires of nature's kinds. His alchemist would demonstrate what Frank Sherwood Taylor has called alchemy's "understanding of nature in terms of life."[128] He would second natural color and natural heat by awakening an "intellectual" potential in natural bodies:

> When the foure Elements wisely joyned be,
> And every-each of them set in his degree,
> Then of divers degrees and of divers digestion,
> Colours will arise towards perfection.
> For then worketh inward heate naturall,
> Which in our substance is but Intellectuall:
> To sight unknowne, hand maie it not feele,
> His working is knowne to few Men and seild;
> And when this heate naturall moved be shall
> By our outward heate artificiall,
> Then Nature excited to labour will not cease
> Many diversities of degrees to increase.[129]

The alchemist should seek "Tincture most specious"[130] in the archaic sense of the adjective: the true tincture is appropriate to the kind or species of what is colored, which is thereby moved as it would be by outer heat in a manner that brings it to itself.

When Norton condemns the "wondrous violence" of "Vicious men" who "mought lerne this *Science,*" he is anticipating Bacon's criticism of the destructive impatience of foolish alchemists.[131] But in so doing he gives greater attention to complex proprieties that allow nature "At her owne leasure to make Generation."[132] He desires to lead a "prudent Nature" between "extremities" by having it move through "all degrees / Of everie meane" until its potential were made actual.[133] His alchemist would moderate his aspirations so that they augmented his character's stature without doing violence to his *ethos,* the constitution of his character. The mean that man engenders in himself would be much like the mean of a prudent nature, both preserving their characteristic "substance" from violent destruction.[134] Decorum in these alchemical actions is physical and moral at once. The mind of the alchemist, his relation to his assistants, his use of his instruments, his choice of a place for his laboratory, even his expression of "love" for his work must accord with what perfects

each action and the work at hand.[135] To save the phenomenon, alchemy must therefore work in operations that are beyond calculation
or canvass.

It is true that the alchemist typically fires and grinds his metals,
and that his manner is sometimes called violent. Descriptions of radical reductions, calcinations, and purgations are scattered through
Ashmole's collection. The prevailing practice in these texts, however,
is more in keeping with the alchemical sections of Jean de Meun's *Le
Roman de la Rose,* which proposes poetically an integration of the
testing of metals with the perfecting of various mineral desires for
completion. When Norton says that true alchemical arts "serve Nature,"[136] he appears to make a similar projection: that such arts assist
a "virtue Minerall" that would attain to the fullest realization of its
species. The true species of the thing is assumed to reach toward the
heavenly sphere that engenders it.[137]

We can study this alchemical commonplace in George Ripley's list
of transforming operations in *The Compound of Alchymie,* where his
directions for feeding and giving drink to nascent gold are shadowed
in the rigors of alchemical reductions. Considered from a modern
perspective, no specious mineral desire would seem capable of surviving the corrosive, fiery purges of Ripley's "calcination," or the
putrifying rigors of the "fermentation" he supposes will destroy a
metal's primary qualities. His "exaltation" resembles a crucifixion,
and his "recapitulation" requires "vyolent hett."[138]

Yet when this Ashmolean alchemist tests his metal or discovers the
Philosopher's Stone, his fires and other purgations are typically means
of tempering and perfecting his object. For example, true calcination
will not proceed without preserving the "moyster" in the Philosopher's Stone, a feat that depends upon the alchemist's recognition of
inclination in analogous substances and his subsequent joining of
"kynde only wyth kynde; / For kynd to kynde hath appetyble incly-
nacyon."[139] Likewise, although the fires of alchemical conjunction
must "do thy bodyes wo," in a sense "against Nature"[140]—their action
imitates pregnancy,[141] or a purgatory from which "after paynys tran-
sytory" the metal is brought by devoted application into a golden
"paradyce where ys yoyfull lyfe."[142] The operation gradually conjoins
various natures into a harmony "wythoute stryfe," a union that can
then withstand more violent fires.[143] Here the analogy with Christian
salvation is strong, but the painful birth of the metal also persistently
recalls a climb toward perfection informed by a thing's nature: its

physical limits and the idea or form of its character beyond mere physicality. Its Christian counterpart would be something like that harrowing of souls described by the Shakespearean apparition who calls himself the dead King Hamlet. If the Ghost were telling the truth (his testimony about purgatory is controversial, as are the claims for a conjunctive purgatory put forward by the alchemists), his torment would be perfective as well as hellish. He visits the living Hamlet with this purgatorial ambiguity in his call to revenge.

Alchemical fermentation is another sort of reduction that Ripley calls a "natural" and "dew" application of proportioned influences for bringing gold to the fore. The examination of metals by means of purgative fermentation that removes some qualities and fixes others is in fact a way that the spirit "teacheth" the body to become more spiritual, while the body teaches the spirit what bodily suffering is. Just as all corporal bodies, Ripley argues, "May not show out ther qualytes effectualy" as gold "Untyll the tyme that they becom spyrituall," so the spirit needs instruction in privation: "For then the Body techyth the Spryt to suffer Fyer, / And the Spryt [teaches] the Body to endure to thy desyre."[144] It is as though fermentation of the mineral could be a natural and soul-making tension between body and spirit, an expectation of ascent that is both poised and pent in bubbles. In his conclusion Ripley reiterates the importance of "vyolent hett," but in the context of wishing for himself a "gentle" purgatorial fire after his death.[145]

The crucifying function of Ripley's "exaltation" submits to a similar analysis. What seems to be a general purging of body from spirit is more specifically a "naturall" rectifying of each element according to its "mene" or true form.[146] In the discussion of numerous accompanying operations, heat is supposed to be "nurryshyng . . . not vyolent,"[147] "temperate,"[148] and restorative of "naturall heate,"[149] until the metal can withstand the examination of greater fires.[150]

The Ashmolean *Hunting of the Greene Lyon* depends upon the true alchemist's moderation in a similar fashion: "the meane to hold is best."[151] Affinities between Christian history and nature's regenerative cycle give the author some opportunity to mix piety with a doctrine of generative moderation.[152] The savior-like child born to the sun and moon is sustained and purified by means of a furnace, but the sealed vessel for confining the testing heat is useful only insofar as the metal under scrutiny has been made progressively resistant to the ordeal.[153] John Gower seems to invoke this regard for a maturing mineral when he refers, in the Ashmolean selection from *De Confessione Amantis,* to the "desire" of "every mettal" to become true gold "With helpe and comforte of the fyre."[154]

Care for generation again tempers proof in the anonymous Ashmolean *Liber Patris Sapientiae,* which elaborates conceptions of a female Mercury. Mercury espouses and bears fruit to a suitable husband "in whome sche worketh all her myght."[155] She can kill and give life to any metal or alchemist she pleases, but her true power is in her moderate espousal of one "by nature of her selfe same sute." When she turns away from unkindly wooers who "would wedd her against her will,"[156] her catalytic potency bears fruit in the rigors of a conjugal love.

The stability of these syntheses of Christian and Timaeic paradigms is of course questionable. Theories of alchemical transmutation are extremely complex; in some instances they severely qualify or contradict the idea that alchemical operations perfect a *potentia* in baser metals as though they were animate beings. Taylor's history notes that in their frequent subjection of the nascent gold to fire, alchemists could have easily confused rebirth with redemption: "the bright metal became a black formless mass, a stinking corruption; then another process brought this dead mass back to the state of metal again . . . a more glorious and excellent metal."[157] Timaeic and biblical paradigms for this spectacle could be strangely combined, and made to change into odd parodies of themselves. Lynn Thorndike cites an example from the work of Arnald of Villanova, which sets out the preparation of the metal according to a peculiar mixture of husbanding and crucifixion. The alchemist beats the "son," puts him in bed for a kind of sexual enjoyment, delivers him over for crucifixion, then anticipates the moment when "the veil of the temple will be rent, and there will be a great earthquake." He turns up the fire in that apocalyptic moment, whereupon the son is supposed to "give up the ghost," presumably to show its true nature as gold, resistant to corruption and heat.[158] Carl Jung has gathered a host of texts giving similarly ambivalent and tortive accounts of alchemical purification and rebirth.[159]

Alchemical excess, of course, can lead to at least two kinds of catastrophe. The first comes to Ovid's Midas, who discovers too late the consequences of using any available means to make gold. The king is not only greedy; he converts food and drink into things that can no longer sustain earthly life. Second, the alchemist runs the danger of dissolving the lower and higher spheres into each other. If the *materia prima* is, as it is defined in the Paracelsian lexicon, the Philosopher's Stone, the gold that is "stronger than gold," the microcosmos, the chaos,[160] then the alchemical desire to find the perfection of matter threatens to end all earthly things, or to pull down the divine. Alchemy under these circumstances becomes a sublime parody of Midas, its mundane abuse merely pandering to greed.

Nevertheless, in deferring to nature's variety of kinds, with their various potentialities and perfections, the typical Ashmolean alchemist to a surprising degree recognizes and tends to mitigate these risks. Norton stresses the importance of God's grace and consent for success in the work of transformation,[161] while maintaining the alchemist's claim to "serve *Nature*."[162] The mere desire for profit ruins all,[163] whereas the willingness to undergo pain—foregoing haste, despair, and deceit[164]—permits the discovery of "pure Natures and simple."[165] "Unwise Doctours" are those who seek only superficial effects, who do not sufficiently reduce "Matters divisable" and fear to descend into the "fowlest" of "grosse Workes" necessary to reduce and purify the mineral foundations of aureation.[166]

This vocabulary resembles Bacon's as he applies religion to science in the *Meditationes Sacrae* and *The Advancement*. Indeed, Ashmole quotes from *The Advancement* to defend alchemical ambitions.[167] He goes so far as to preserve Chaucer's satirical *Canon's Yeoman's Tale* as proof that Chaucer, like Bacon, is in sympathy with alchemy because he "fully knew" its "mystery."[168] The tale told by the Yeoman, who is clearly not an adept, exposes the Canon's ruthless greed and the excesses of other alchemists; but it does not obviously demolish alchemy itself. Indeed, the disgusted Yeoman defers in his conclusion to Plato's supposed knowledge of the Philosopher's Stone, which he says the philosopher chose to keep hidden until Christ could reveal it "where it liketh to his deite; / Man to enspyre."[169] The Canon's fundamental error, if one can believe the repentant deceiver who exposes him, is to presume upon a grace not necessarily withheld from true alchemists.

The Ashmolean alchemist differs from Bacon in the manner in which he avoids such presumption. Bacon's new alchemical science, as we will see in a later chapter, is an encryption of ambition: it seems to put aside presumption entirely, while arming itself for an alchemical conquest of baser being. Ashmole's collection of alchemical opinion is closer to the spirit of the famous fifteenth-century declaration of alchemy's goal attributed to the Pseudo-Raymond Lully, who is remembered for a qualified boast: *if* there were sufficient catalytic mercury, alchemy could make golden the sea.[170]

The Ashmolean alchemical literature assumes that there are many kinds of gold. Such recognition of the variety of perfections does not lend itself immediately to speculation about the aureation of the world. Some gold is higher on the scale of perfection than other kinds, yet all are more or less golden in their "brightness, weight, color, lack of tarnish, and resistance to fire."[171] Perfection of individual species is supposed to harmonize with cosmic perfection. As Frank Sherwood Taylor puts it, the alchemist lends himself and his metals to "the whole purpose of things, which were impelled to seek perfection by their striving towards the perfect ideas of their kind in God."[172] The true color of gold is a tincturing pneuma that animates and realizes in various metals their highest and yet most appropriate, tempered virtues.[173] The purest gold moderates the alchemist's ambition because he seeks what is by definition the most tempered of metals.[174]

In an alchemical crux of *Le Roman de la Rose,* Jean de Meun frames his carefully ambiguous defense of alchemical art by accommodating the Aristotelian principle that kinds are preserved and perfected as species aspire to a higher being. In his highly conventional introductory argument, the poet claims that all art is delusion if it defies the idea that one species cannot be transmuted into another.[175] He goes on to describe the true alchemists as models for the artist, who open and temper their materials so as to bring them to perfection within their species and complexions. Even the most radical scourging of impurities, properly undertaken, returns metals to the sulphur and mercury from which they were born.[176]

Where Jean seems to describe fundamental changes in the metals that art leads toward nobler being, the alchemical reduction is ambiguous. Reduction shades into composition according to paradigms of natural birth and maturation. Alchemical operations disrobe—*desnuent*—the metals of their species,[177] bringing the metals to maturity as they molt and are molted into silver (*il[s] les muent / En fin argent*).[178] Rather than altering his object the wise alchemist can "open" them (*sagement en ouverrait*) and find marvels.[179] When he uses lesser metals to give others greater nobility, his additions adjust (*ajoustent*) or bring his object to temper. If he makes ashes and thence glass, he combines fiery reduction with a wise manner of making so that they "give birth to" (*font . . . naistre*) the glass.[180] A special cause "draws" (*tire*) the alchemist's matter toward a strange new individuality; the verb *tirer,* which here suggests opening as well as concealing, reaping as well as luring, is richly problematical—as is Jean's shadowy comparison of art and nature in the passage's conclusion.[181] The argument is finally an entertainment of the possibility that art has power over nature, but only in the wisdom of alchemists who know better than to proceed immoderately or without veils.

Bacon's opinions on alchemy are indices of the ways he uses Timaeic learning, as we will see in greater detail in Chapter 3. His most famous pronouncements are condemnations of alchemical idolatry; his less well known opinions draw a new science of gold-making out of Timaeic roots. At first glance, the newly scientific alchemy he proposes is a scourge of the old belief in natural tendency: the "dream" that nature somehow intended to bring about aureation. But Bacon's rejection of alchemical tradition also analyzes the old alchemy's inability to apply and pursue its means and ends systematically. The new science of metals is a resolution to complete the old techniques by gathering the means to enforce the old Lullean wish to turn the sea to gold.

Persuasion and Ornament

> In a picture, they which truly vnderstand
>   Require (besides the likenesse of the thing)
>   Light, Posture, Height'ning, Shadow, Culloring,
> All which are parts commend the cunning hand
> And all our Booke (when it is throughly scan'd)
>   Will well confesse; presenting, limiting
>   Each subt'lest Passion, with her source, and spring,
> So bold, as shewes your Art you can command
>   But now, your Worke is done, if they that view
>   The severall figures, languish in suspence,
>   To iudge which Passion's false, and which is true,
>   Betweene the doubtfull sway of reason, and sense;
>   Tis not your fault, if they shall sense preferre,
>   Being told there, Reason cannot, Sense may erre.[1]

I

Ben Jonson's dedication to Thomas Wright's study of the passions and their persuasion, *The Passions of the Mind in Generall,* takes for granted a relation between ornament, persuasion, and the nature of things. Ornament is required by those who "truly vnderstand," and the colors of Wright's art set forth and give limit or form to the passions they ornament. Discerning readers expect ornament to surpass simple imitation, and to do more than stir sluggish minds. Wright's art brings forth the perfection of his subject matter with its "source" and "spring." Rather than merely impressing or swaying his audience, the heightening and posturing effected by his rhetorical ornaments increases the likelihood that readers will become even more capable of distinguishing between and tempering the passions Wright has colored and shadowed.

Jonson makes another notable distinction, between a love of ornament's shadowing powers and a confusion in the face of rhetorical figures that leads to languor and suspense. A love of figures enhances the discerning audience's powers of distinction, but misunderstanding of their shadowing creates distress. Put in other terms, delight in ornament derives from delight in ornament's proper function. A failure to comprehend Wright is at least as much an error of the mind as it is a defect in the passions; one can presumably join the ranks of the discerning if one is informed by an expectation that Wright's rhetorical figures will transcend mere imitation and shadow the thing itself.

Of course, Jonson's confidence in the figural power of rhetoric contrasts with the doctrine of antipathy between truth and appearances that one frequently finds in the new learning. That doctrine requires experimenters to sever themselves from the world of colors in order to carry out their discipline of abnegation. Their antipathy toward appearances frustrates the development of sympathy between expert and layman, and between rhetorician and the mass of idolaters. Persuasion is by definition suspect: "generally let every student of nature take this as a rule, that whatever his mind seizes and dwells upon with peculiar satisfaction is to be held in suspicion" (*NO* IV.60).

One of Jonson's chief authorities, Cicero, puts the matter very differently. Crassus, his chief spokesman in *De Oratore,* predicates his description of rhetorical principles on the affinities of nature, language, and judgment:

> [E]verybody is able to discriminate between what is right and what is wrong in matters of art and proportion by a sort of subconscious instinct without having any theory of art or proportion of their

own; . . . they display this much more in judging the rhythms and pronunciations of words, because these are rooted deep in the general sensibility, and nature has decreed that nobody shall be entirely devoid of these faculties . . .[2]

Cicero carries this confidence in natural judgment over to some of his most basic assumptions about rhetorical persuasion. Rather than being deceived by words as though they were idols, an audience tends to judge the proportion and hence the meaning of words according to natural sanction. The power of persuasive language is its ability to draw the seed forth into a mature plant. Crassus' colleague Antonius explains that "the efficacy of the whole" of rhetoric is that it "fosters and stregthens" rather than "originates and engenders" the natural affections.[3] The rhetorician is a kind of intermediary or a warning voice supposed to stir and incite (*sedo, molior, incitare*), not to instill or remove. Rhetoric should excite (*excitare*) an audience with affections that are called forth (*ex* plus *citare*)[4] or help press them back into their proper form.

When Antonius seems to contradict these ideas, arguing that the goal of oratory is to have an audience "moved by something resembling a mental impulse [and] emotion (*animi et perturbatione*) rather than by judgment or deliberation (*magis quam indico aut consilio*),"[5] he is emphasizing the importance of the audience's animation, not necessarily its susceptibility to emotional coercion. By saying that impulse and emotion are moved *magis quam* the judgment or deliberation, he preserves the relation of emotion and intellect to the degree that the meaning of *magis quam* shades toward "more than," away from "rather than."

Oratory, says Crassus, puts all philosophy and specialized sciences "in their full light,"[6] not simply by making them known to audiences, but by bringing them into actuality: into an illustrious and praiseworthy being. Likewise, eloquence brings into view animate, breathing emotions that are "almost smothered" without the assistance of an art of oratorical imitation:

> [I]f reality unaided were sufficiently effective in presentation we should have no need at all for art. But because emotion, which mostly has to be displayed or else counterfeited by action, is often so confused as to be obscured and almost smothered out of sight, we have to dispel the things that obscure it and take up its prominent and striking points.[7]

The essential function of oratorical delivery is to clear away the confusion that obscures the adequate and nascent display of emotion, not to exploit feelings.

These premises are largely products of Cicero's adaptation of Aristotelian doctrines of matter and form, which he uses to explain the relation between subject matter and style in oratory. Bacon himself uses Ciceronian phrasing when he describes the illustrating or illuminating power of rhetoric; but Cicero's assertions carry more of a conviction that the form has the power to clothe unactualized matter in a way that brings it into being. In *De Oratore,* rhetorical illumination is presented as though it were a physical process known to the general culture of men: "one has to begin by accumulating a supply of matter . . . but the matter has to receive shape from the general texture and style of the speech, and to be embellished by the diction and given variety by reflection."[8]

Style ornaments a thing of beauty the way blood permeates and colors a living being.[9] As the colors or figures of style illuminate the whole,[10] they are assumed to bring it gradually into being: "nothing exists in the physical universe that emerges as a whole and develops completely all in a moment."[11] The style of speeches is designed to imitate and perfect nature by bringing forth the organism through various kinds of decoration. Decorously lighted, the matter becomes luminous and hence visible. Without this "lucidity of style" (*luce verborum*), no idea is lustrous or distinct to the view (*illustrem*).[12]

The *Orator* explains how decorum brings things to light: "there is no thought which bears fruit to an orator, unless it is fitting and perfectly expressed."[13] Crassus likens such embellishment to the pruning or grafting of trees so that they take shape and come into view as their true natures permit.[14] Cicero links decorum to the Greek term *to prepon,* what is conspicuous and shines forth.[15] Propriety in style is *quid deceat,* or what is simultaneously proper and seeming.[16] Thus in *De Oratore* the proper choice of words entails fullness (*plenum*) and sonority (*sonans*) that combine proper seeming with the fullest possible realization of the matter.[17] Consequently, only those metaphors are decorous that "either make the meaning clearer . . . [or] better convey the whole meaning of the matter (*res tota*)."[18]

Crassus acknowledges the possibility that ornament first appeared because it was a useful adjunct to the matter of the speech. But ornament's utility seems coincident with its beauty. Ornamental clothing that was "first invented to protect us against cold"[19] cannot now be discarded without committing a mutilation.[20] The notion that "the body has no part added to its structure that is superfluous" becomes for Crassus an argument for the perfective complementarity of matter and form: "in a ship, what is so indispensable as the sides, the hold, the bow, the stern, the yards, the sails and masts? Yet they all have such a graceful appearance that they appear to have been invented not only for the purpose of safety but also for the sake of giving pleasure."[21] He goes to the extreme of proposing that a temple would retain its pediments for channeling rainwater, even if it were constructed in rainless heaven, because all its parts contribute to its dignity. Without the ornament, it would be "entirely lacking" in virtue, as would any speech deprived of the least of its divisions, including the minute pauses of the speaker as he breathes his animating life.[22] The cosmos itself dissolves, should "even a slight modification" (*paula immutata*) occur.[23] The sailor drowns without his graceful rigging; the loss of a brick desecrates the temple; the tree that a gardener strips of its leaves ceases to be a tree.

Many of these ideas flourish in Quintilian's adaptation of the Ciceronian legacy for purposes of formal instruction. In the *Institutio Oratoria,* teaching is a preparation, an investiture and flexing of the soul that draws it toward its perfection. In Book II, when Quintilian asks, "[O]ught we not to nourish just as we clothe? (*non alemus et quasi vestiemus?*)" he is invoking the idea that nourishing and dressing are allied. Ornamental operations blend with the activities of the gardener:

> [I]f in some cases it is necessary to lower (*detrahere*) certain qualities, surely there are others where we may be permitted to add (*adicere*) what is lacking. Not that I would set myself against the will of nature. No innate good quality should be neglected, but what is idle or at rest (*quod cessat*) must be made to grow (*augendum*) and be inspired (*addendumque*).[24]

Ridding the student of inappropriate attributes stimulates the idle virtues as it presses back excesses into a more natural form. The process of growth and diminishing resembles (or is the same as—the grammar is ambiguous) giving the body a garment.

Quintilian's natural philosophy parallels his theory of ornament and his pedagogy. Nature suffers or permits (*patitur*) the embellishments of art to bring it to its most characteristic perfection.[25] Rather than being reduced by its suffering, nature comes to "attain its full strength" by means of a properly ornamental art.[26] *Emphasis* in rhetoric is therefore a figure in which "some hidden (*latens*) meaning is extracted from some phrase."[27] In a complementary fashioning, *flexus* or rhetorical detour gestures the animation of the thing it flexes: "the curve (*flexus*), I might almost call it motion, with which we are so familiar, gives impress of action and animation (*motus dat actum quendam adfectum*)."[28] Turning away turns up the true form, as in a picture of someone that conceals what is known to be an injury, or in a speech that adumbrates, in silence and understatement, Agamemnon's grief.

An awareness of these commonplaces, in classical sources highly accessible to the sixteenth century's understanding of classical rhetorical theory, should give us an idea of how a host of widely used terms could resonate with a philosophy of nature quite different from the biblical burthen of the new learning. The vocabulary of so ubiquitous a concept as dress partakes of Aristotelian ideas of quality and addition that linger in a host of words still common in the modern era. The notion that the attributes of things are a kind of clothing, which matter puts on to become its correspondent self, is Aristotelian. An *attribute* is literally a tribute given to something, yet there is little question of its somehow being *of* the thing itself when we use the word as a noun. Likewise, to *prepare* a thing is to dress it, while in fact preparation is in general thought to ready it, perhaps even to draw out what is almost there. A thing's *feature* is an attribute that we tend to suppose is a setting forth and heightening of what the thing is.

The syncretic poetic theory of the critic Girolamo Fracastoro, which George Saintsbury calls a *locus classicus* for Renaissance attempts to harmonize Plato and Aristotle,[29] concludes with similar commonplaces merging principles of eloquence with philosophical notions of natural matter and form. Like Cicero and Quintilian, he draws from Aristotelian and Platonic traditions, arguing that poetry is both true and beautiful because it manifests "the perfection and excellence of the subject." Fracastoro wants to defend the subject matter and style of poetry in terms of the perfecting complementarity of matter and form that he finds in nature:

[W]hat the painters and poets add to things for perfection is not extraneous, if we mean by "thing" not the bare object such as common artificers, or those who are controlled and restricted by some purpose, make, but the object perfected and given life. Such an interpretation the greatest artists make,—most of all the poet who wishes to arouse admiration in all. Then if what is added makes manifest the perfection and excellence of the subject, ought we not to concede for all its great usefulness and desirability?[30]

The passage does not argue that style merely covers and improves upon a naked subject. Fracastoro goes so far as to resist separating the addition from the thing. Appropriate style perfects and animates the matter by manifesting what style ornaments; it plays upon and draws forth the thing it seems to create.

Here the decorum for beautiful and useful style resembles Cicero's: everything the eloquent poet adds "is drawn from the nature of the subject, either by metaphor, or epithet, or the other means that are inherent in nature itself, causes and effects, and other devices of that sort."[31] The poet who adds for admirable effect "is he who is moved by the real."[32]

2

These commonplaces have not lately received the attention they deserve. In her study of imagery in Renaissance poetry, Rosemond Tuve made voluminous suggestions, more than a generation ago, that poetical ornament might have a more than merely instrumental connection with Renaissance poetry's enactment of ideas.[33] Yet the more recent analysis of Renaissance poetics by Thomas Greene treats Quintilian's idea of decorous, perfective imitation as though it were obviously a false compromise,[34] a failure to act upon the conflict between "the security of ritual" and "creative historicity" which "swerves" from such imitation.[35] The idea that ornament or any emulation can be a commendatory completion of what it praises now appears to have no standing in critical debate. "Affectionate malice" must be the more fundamental force in apparent imitation,[36] or all imitation must undermine itself in failing to attain perfection.[37] Richard Lanham dismisses the perfective forming powers of ornament because ornament "envaluates"—puts value into its object.[38] For Lanham, self-conscious ornament is more honest than plainness because it admits what it is: something the poet or rhetorician designs to be noticed. Lanham seems to support Timaeic principles of addition when he argues that "the way to naturalness is through artifice, not around it," but the artifice he has in mind is an unavoidable play of appearances that men must either claim is natural to what they make, or hypocritically disavow.[39] Naturalness is a self-conscious, self-willed, and inevitable play of ornamental addition. Addition is thought to be ornament precisely because it is reduced to play.

Even O. B. Hardison, who observes in *The Enduring Monument* the prevalence of a poetry of commendatory emulation during the English Renaissance, does not examine the affinities among traditional ideas of ornamental and natural perfection. Arguing that poetical ornament is no "sugar coating," he uses Fracastoro's authority to claim that it is effective in getting an idea across and—more importantly—serving as a suitable adjunct to what is beautiful, so as to render greater pleasure and more effective persuasion.[40] But his emphasis upon effect, and upon the transcendental movement of the poet's imitative praise, deflects attention prematurely from the interaction of form and substance presupposed by his own and by Fracastoro's arguments. Hardison is closest to Fracastoro when he maintains that the emulous poet supposedly ascends to the idea of the thing he imitates: "such an idea shifts the concern of the artist from moral and philosophical matters to essence." He "may choose external objects as a point of departure but these are not his basic concern. If they were, he would be like the artisan."[41]

Without taking issue with these assessments of *mimesis* in Renaissance poetics and rhetoric, one could argue that sophisticated modern theories of rhetoric have unnecessarily weakened themselves by neglecting the relatively immediate contexts of English Renaissance ideas of ornament and persuasion. What moderns are prone to call confusion, false compromise, ludic daring, or doctrinal conventionality the period often articulates in language freighted with commonplaces harmonious with Timaeic tradition.

3

John Sturmius's schoolmasterly advice in *A Ritch Storehouse* intones the age's ostensible faith, now often indulged or dismissed, in the consubstantiality of word and thing, such that "wordes are the images of thinges." He tells his students, "From this time forwarde you must ioyne together and combine the study of them both. And to that ende tendeth all my talke."[42] The imitation he teaches is "nothing else but a meanes and a way howe to expresse in your owne talke those maners and formes of speaking: which the Greekes call *ideas,* which be commendable and beautiful in the talke of another."[43]

Figures, praising and praiseworthy "forms of speaking," are in his work commensurate with ideas. Although Sturmius's text, like others of the age, distinguishes tropes from schemes, assuming that tropes alter the significance of words and sentences whereas schemes do not, his definitions do not obviously entail the assumption that figures such as metaphor and allegory are alien to the original significance of the words they displace. The same can be said of Richard Sherry, whose *A Treatise of Schemes and Tropes* reminds its readers that metaphor "sheweth the thynge before oure eyes more euidently,"[44] that tropes, along with schemes, arise either because language affords no other means to say what we intend, or because "to set out more plainly we be compelled to speake otherwyse then after common facion." If we will not be ignorant "in the sence or meaninge of the matter that excellente authors do wryght of, we muste nedes ruune to the helpe of schemes and figures."[45] The meaning of such statements is lost if the reader does not recognize that figures in this case are somehow thought to *effect,* not just affect, the understanding by their power to draw out, outline, and embroider what would otherwise not come to light—what would not become itself. When Sherry writes that metaphor "sheweth the thynge before oure eyes more euidently,"[46] he is saying that metaphor somehow brings the thing into actuality.

If he should lack an understanding of this true "name and propertye" of schemes and tropes, a reader will pass through the garden of good authors as though it were a mere thoroughfare that he beholds but does not see:

> For as lyke plesure is not to him whiche gooeth into a goodlye garden garnyshed wyth dyuers kindes of herbes and flowers, and that there doeth no more but beholde them, of whome it maye be sayde that he sente in for nothynge but that he wold come out, and to hym which besyde the corporall eie pleasure knoeth of euerie one the name & propertye: so verelye much difference is there in readynge good authors . . .[47]

In a similar vein, Peacham insists that tropes both alter and enforce "proper and naturall signification"; if they were not "proper," they are "nye and likely."[48] His catalogue of metaphorical tropes assumes that properly chosen metaphors manifest cosmologically genuine connections. Metaphors of sight and seeing set forth the powers of the mind "because the mind and sight ['the most principle and perfect sence'] so much resemble one another, we may wel borrow of the one and beare it to the other, for as the sighte decearneth thinges, by their fourmes and collours, and see what they be, so likewise the mind, by the power intelectiue, doth vnderstand truth from falshood. . . ."[49] Similarly, metaphors transforming men into beasts ("the envious man doth bite priuily") render men truthfully when their "manners be such as cannot be expressed with those words, which doe properly belong to men."[50] In cases where Peacham identifies what appears to be an essential discontinuity between figure and truth, there is an accessible relation between the "proper" signification and its alteration, as when a sentence using *ironia* "is understood by the contrary,"[51] or "cause" is figured by means of "effect": "So sayeth Christ, I am the resurrection of the dead. Yet he is not the resurrection, but the cause that make the dead to ryse agayne."[52] Dudley Fenner and Abraham Fraunce describe this proper turning of a word from its "natural signification" as though it were a process of courtship and matrimony, not of willful force or displacement: "This change of signification muste bee shamefest, and as it were maydenly, that it may seeme rather to be led by the hand to another signification, then to be driuen by force vnto the same."[53] For Fenner, even the garnishing of whole sentences, designed "for the forceable mouing of affectations," respects and enhances sense. It "doth after a sort beautifie the sence and very meaning of a sentence" because "it hath in it a certain manly maiestie."[54] One is hard put to distinguish here between ornament as technique and as the complementing maturity that praises (compliments) what it completes.

Like tropes, the schemes in Peacham's garden can be understood as alterations of the order of words and sentences that augment and orchestrate their meaning. Even in syntactical schemes such as *zeugma,* which allow for various omissions of key words, or *emphasis,* which Peacham, following Quintilian, defines as a figure that implies more than is stated,[55] the figure's force is its power to complete, which derives from the reader's recollection of what has been left out.[56] An extreme example of this ambivalent alteration is *metaplasmus,* "a transformation of letters, or sillables in single words contrary to the common fashion," that enables poets not simply to alter an isolated metrical foot, but to perfect the shape of the entire utterance.[57] And what might appear to be mere redundance, the figure of repetition, brings out something of import. Hoskins insists that "in speech there is no repetition without importance," just as "no man is sick in thought upon one thing but for some vehemency or distress."[58] *Re-*

petitio is assumed to manifest the passion that helps make the thought what it is.

Other rhetorical figures tend to be bound up with the sharp and vehement passions of the poet or speaker that are stimulated by their imitation of what the discourse would set out. Thus for Peacham *imprecatio* emerges "when we curse and detest some person or thing, for the euils that they bring with them, or for the wickednesses that is in them." The imprecation is a curse, a calling down of harm upon what is evil. Similarly, *ecphonesis* is not strictly a label for a verbal technique, since it is "an exclamation & outcry to expresse the passions of our minde."[59]

An interesting test of Peacham's theoretical convictions occurs in his discussion of *hyperbole*, which in his own definition is said to "surmounte and reach aboue the truth."[60] If in Peacham's general discussion of the term this form of exaggeration severed the rhetor's praise from the thing praised, we would have to dismiss the seriousness of his insistence that eloquence is truthful utterance. But Peacham justifies the figure by claiming that its overreaching power manifests the qualities being praised. Cicero's claim that Pompey fought more battles than others have studied, and conquered "more prouinces then any others haue desyred," draws out by imitation what is most significant about Pompey's virtue: "by making an incredible reporte, [Cicero] doth signify that Pompeius noble actes were so worthy, and hys victoryes so many, that they were almost incredible. . . . [W]e use an incredible sayng, to shew that the truth wee affirme, is almoste incredible."[61] Peacham contrasts *hyperbole* with *bomphiologia,* which also exaggerates but does not truthfully imitate: "for Poets by theyr trim Eloquence, oftentymes doe f[r]ame great commendations to the dead, and list them up ten tymes higher, then euer their vertues reached."[62] Genuine hyperbole has the power to evoke what is almost incredible if the exaggeration is true to its subject.

In a similar vein, Hoskins explains the workings of a closely related trope—metaphor—as a combination of varying (a special "going beyond"), seeing the whole, and hitting the mark. Like other passages of this sort, this one needs to be read with a measure of patience that calls forth assumptions embedded in its logic and premises.

[T]hough all metaphors go beyond the signification of things, yet are they requisite to match the compassing sweetness of men's minds, that are not content to fix themselves upon one thing but they must

> wander into the confines; like the eye, that cannot choose but view
> the whole knot when it beholds but one flower in a garden of
> purpose; or like an archer that, knowing his bow will overcast or
> carry too short, takes an aim on this side or beyond his mark.[63]

Metaphor allows men's minds to wander, but they err in a garden
planted with intention, in which they come to see each flower as part
of a whole, evoked by the metaphor's hyperbolical linking of part
and whole. Metaphor acts as though it were an archer's bow darkly
suited to the distance; when it is aimed properly "on this side or
beyond," its arrow hits the target. The archer's aim is indirect, not
false, and his indirection is responsible for finding the thing out.

It is of course fallacious to assert that Elizabethan rhetorical theorists
naively put their faith in the notion that all language is congruent
with reality. Although, as Peacham asserts, God "is well seene" in
"the paynefull rules of Grammer, in the subilityes of Logick, in the
flowers of Rhetoricke," the quadrivium, and theology,[64] it is not
obvious that everything looking like a trope or a scheme is thought
to be a genuine figure. Vices among schemes are what Peacham calls
"of the vngarnished order";[65] they are not only merely apparent, but
denatured figures unfit to be called garnishings. Warnings about the
abuse of the figures abound in Cicero and Erasmus. Cicero takes
pains to avoid seeming to argue for an unphilosophical eloquence,
and in the introduction of his *De Copia,* Erasmus immediately warns
students of the dangers of empty ornament.

Nevertheless, readers of all these authors should be struck by their
common tendency to treat rhetoric as something quite distinct from
a neutral tool to be used for good or ill according to the virtue or
genius of the rhetor, or in reference to a simple criterion of rhetorical
effectiveness. In *De Oratore* Antonius sometimes leans toward the
reductive position, but he does not abandon the assumption that
embellishment has an affinity for truth, if only because (he says) it is
easier to praise achievements and reputations that are real than to
fabricate them.[66] The ease of truthtelling does not obviously deter a
vicious rhetor from lying, but Antonius is alluding to a higher natural
ease that defines truthful rhetoric. This seems to be the remarkably
worked assumption of the medieval maker of *Cleanness,* who begins
his devoted praise of purity with the assurance that his invention of
"fair forms" will flourish as though powered by purity's virtue:

> Clannesse who-so kyndly cowthe comende,
> And rekken up alle the resouns that ho by right askes,

> Fayre formes myght he fynde in forthering his speche,
> And in the contrare kark and combraunce huge.[67]

This principle is acted out in the extraordinary manifestation of copiousness in Erasmus's book of exercises, a rhetorical display that imitates and augments what Erasmus seems to consider most real, most praiseworthy. It is better, Erasmus reminds his reader, to encourage an abundance of the appropriate figures, and then to trim the plant rather than to nurse a poverty-stricken style.[68] Those who misuse *copia* are as likely to say too little as too much,[69] not simply in violation of an isolated stylistic canon, but because they fail to realize that "everything must be exaggerated,"[70] that it is of the nature of copious expression to set forth voluminously what is. Thus the hundreds of variations in *De Copia* on a single sentence of praise for Sir Thomas More form an elaborate exercise of rhetorical facility that is also a *tour de force* of compliment for Erasmus's friend—an elaborate *demonstratio* revealing More's character.

In a similar spirit, Thomas Wilson's explanation of hyperbole as "mountyng above the truthe" argues that amplification truthfully "sets forth" what exceeds expectations, though it might seem to depart from truth:

> Mountyng above the truthe, is when we do set furthe thynges excedyngly and above all mennes expectacion, meanyng onely that thei are very great. And thus, God promised to Abraham, that he wold make his posteritie, equal with the sandes of the yearth. Now it was not so said, that there should be so many in deede, but that the nomber should bee infinite.[71]

Rather than simply conceding that God did not mean what he said, Wilson insists that the number of Abraham's descendants will indeed be "infinite." He rejects the interpretation that God merely equates the number of descendants with the sands; the hyperbole means that the number is truly beyond all expectations, beyond count.

Amplification for purposes of moral enjoining is also supposed to be veracious, even though its prime purpose is to persuade rather than to define virtue and vice. Thus Sherry observes that "when we praise chastitie in a yonge man, we go not aboute to perswade that he was chaste, but that vertue shulde appeare greater in floryshyng age."[72] The persuader calls the youth's attention to the form of virtue that he would take on as he matures, not in order to transform the young man's character or to coerce it, but to call it truly to its more perfect, "floryshyng" self later on.

It is sometimes difficult to appreciate how tenaciously the Elizabethan rhetoricians and the ancient authorities they cited seem to hold
to such suppositions. Taken in isolation, Cicero's emphasis on amplification as the defining characteristic of eloquence can reduce ornament, in modern eyes, to a tool that manipulates subject and
audience: "the highest distinction of eloquence consists in amplification by means of ornament, which can be used to make one's speech
not only increase the importance of a subject and raise it to a higher
level, but also to diminish and disparage it."[73] But raising or lowering
the importance of subject, when amplification properly takes on such
a task, is meant here to confirm what otherwise would not have been
realized. And the process appears to be not merely the result of applying attenuated rules of decorum, but of realizing the aspiration of
rhetor, audience, and subject matter. Richard Sherry provides a gloss:
"A greate parte of eloquence is set in increasing and diminyshing,
and serueth for this purpose, that the thyng shulde seme as great as
it is in dede, lesser or greater than it seemeth to manye."[74]

Although rhetoricians' warnings against the perversion of praise
are not uncommon, *praise* is commonly synonymous with virtue: "I
call it praise to suffer Tyrannie," says Sidney's Astrophil, who elsewhere insists that "Eloquence it selfe envies your praise."[75] Jonson
calls beauty "the Marke of praise," and Shakespeare fuses praise with
the perfection of virtue in Portia's *sententia,* "How many things by
season season'd are / To their right praise and true perfection."[76] For
Wilson, the amplifying figures are "precious stones set in a ryng, to
commende the golde,"[77] as though they were incorporated into the
whole that they praised. Eloquence "commendeth the matter" and
shows it "clad in purple" where before it walked "bare and naked."[78]
Honors in this sense are the realization of the character of what they
clothe. Not giving or taking on rich apparel is a defect in those who
should be capable of taking to themselves what is properly theirs or
their object's:

> What is a good thyng to a manne, if he neither knowe th[e] use of
> it, nor yet (though he knowe it) is able at all to use it? If we thinke
> it comelinesse, and honestie to set furthe the body with handsome
> apparell, and thynke them worthie to have money, that bothe can
> and will use it accordyngly: I cannot otherwise se, but that this part
> deserveth praise, whiche standeth wholy in settyng furthe matter
> by apte wordes and sentences together, and beautifieth the tongue
> with greate chaunge of colours, and varietie of figures.[79]

The confluence of notions of praise with amplication is a characteristic development in Elizabethan discussions of rhetorical ornament. In the sense that poetry and rhetoric are by nature
commendatory, they add praises to their subjects by amplifying, furnishing, adorning, and garnishing them. In George Puttenham's chapter on "ornament poeticall," he argues that poesy can "shew itself
best only in the gorgious clothes of ornament," which "must needes
yeld it [poesie] much more bewtie and commendation" than plainness.[80] Beauty is neither imposed by an entirely external addition of
ornament nor spontaneously expressed; it is effected by embellishment that the poet "setteth vpon his language . . . as the embro-
derer doth his stone and perle or passements of gold vpon the stuff
of a Princely garment."[81] Ornament is "a goodly outward shew" that
is "set vpon the matter";[82] its compliment is artfully attached to the
matter so as to complete it. Such embellishment resembles a jewel
placed in a setting, or a crown that tops—simultaneously overgoes
and finishes—that part of the body that already rules over the whole
and yet calls for a more ample and fitting sovereignty. From a related
perspective, it enacts the vegetable, Middle English meaning of the
verb *gemme:* it resembles a flower or fruit, an addition of bloom that
is the true flourishing of the tree.

Rhetorical amplitude, in contrast to "naked" logic, thus "useth gaie
painted sentences and setteth foorth those matters with fresh
colours"[83] because, in Wilson's words, "the Coloures of Rhetorique"
can be likened "to mannes eye sight." They make seemly what is
invisible or improperly realized, as does the appraising eye. As sight
is the master of sense, the colors are the masters among the parts of
rhetoric;[84] their characteristic function is to bring things before the
eyes.[85]

This pattern of associations is evident in prime Renaissance synonyms for *ornament,* such as *exornation* and *furnishing.* The prefix
of *exornation,* attached to the Latin verb *ornare,* to furnish, gives the
ornamental action an outward movement. Likewise, *furnish* draws
heavily from the meaning of *fornir,* retained in French: to complete.
Raiment is of course a shortening of *arrayment,* a setting forth or placing
in order. *Dressing* and *trimming* in their archaic senses have to do with
completion and perfection; each is a perfective addition as well as a
cutting away of dross.

Puttenham assumes that ornamental dress is not only customary
but "civil"—a characteristic of men and women who, according to

the commonplace, are human to the degree that they are civil. Nakedness, of course, is a *lack* of cover, and *nudus* the state of being
destitute of clothing rather than free of it. To lack cover is to need
what one should have, to be deprived of what is in some sense one's
own. Thus in her allegorical manifestation in John Lydgate and Stephen Hawes, Dame Rhetoric is pure and clear precisely because she
is glorious in garb and speech.[86] Her ornament affords a radiance even
in darker tropes that shine in obscurity, though Hawes cautions that
that light is not easily apprehended.

When Peacham calls eloquence "the instrument of our vnderstanding" and "the key of our conceptions,"[87] he is drawing from a similar
set of Latinate assumptions about the significance of eloquence as an
accoutrement. An *instrumentum* need not be a mere tool, but a furnishing or an instruction (drawing from *instrumentum*'s root *instruere*,
to instruct) whose address orders and manifests capacities not yet
formed in the understanding. In Peacham's description the instrument
of eloquence is therefore the "key of conceptions": the complementary configuration in little of the thing it unlocks in the understanding.

The apparent circularity of Richard Rainolde's definition of eloquence in *The Foundation of Rhetoric* is really a display of this affinity
among the rhetoricians' concepts of amplification, praise, and becoming:

> Nature hath indued euery man, with a certain eloquence . . . as
> Aristotle the Philosopher, in his Booke of *Rhetorike* dooeth shewe.
> These giftes of nature, singuler doe flowe and abounde in vs, ac-
> cordyng to the greate and ample indumente and plentuousnes of
> witte and wisedome, lodged in vs, therefore Nature it self beyng
> well framed, and afterward by arte and order of science, instructed
> and adorned, must be singularlie furthered, helped, and aided to all
> excellencie, to exquisite inuencion, and profounde knowledge, both
> in *Logike* and *Rhetorike*.[88]

In choosing the verb *indue* (*endue*), Rainolde makes use of the Latin
root *induco*. The entry for the word in Thomas Thomas's dictionary
lists an array of synonyms.[89] Following Thomas, nature's favorable
"indumente" of man could here be an inducing, persuading, bringing
forth, or succoring of eloquence in him by nature. The Latin root of
coerce is appropriately opposite, insofar as *coercere* means to shut up
and enclose, not simply to force. In Rainolde's language, nature en-
dues man with eloquence by which he freely adorns nature in turn.

Of course, not all "induing" of objects or audiences is favorable to their perfection and confirmation. Thomas's negative synonyms denote a tendency for false persuasion to seduce, deceive, abolish, and defeat. Indeed, the Reformation controversy over the nature of religious vestments puts a naive reading of this evidence in doubt. But we cannot read Rainolde and others properly if we miss the ample and cohesive evidence that clothing and praise tended to be master tropes for perfective persuasion in poetry and rhetoric.

4

Given alchemy's recognition of an affinity between color and essence, which Hawes touches on in his equation of alchemical tincture and rhetorical ornamentation, it is worth asking whether a major sixteenth-century English rhetorician such as Puttenham assumes that rhetorical figures produce an alchemical effect on what they ornament. Does his analysis of elision, repetition, and reversal assume that the figures perfect the "substances" they augment, emphasize, and transmute? Do the "auricular" figures work alchemically because they "satisfie & delight th'eare only by a goodly outward shew set vpon the matter with wordes"?[90] Finally, do the "sensible" figures, which "inwardly" stir the mind, somehow accomplish the sense they ornament?

Puttenham's choice of language to describe the figures tends to confirm that a general alchemical paradigm is at work throughout the chapter on ornament in *The Arte of English Poesie*. First, he assumes that auricular figures "of the smallest importaunce"[91]—the modifications of spelling in individual words—all make poetry "more tunable and melodious,"[92] more its lyrical self. The first major auricular figure, *eclipsis* or elision, is presented as though its "vertue" or power were to supply, rather than remove, "by defect": "And first of those [figures] that work by defect, if but one word or some little portion of speach be wanting, it may be supplied by ordinary vnderstanding and vertue of the figure *Eclipsis*, as to say, *so early a man,* for [*are ye*] so early a man . . ."[93] Along with the understanding, the figure's virtue fills or makes whole, insofar as "supply" revives the meaning of *suppleo*.

Similarly, although *zeugma* involves the omission of redundant elements in successive clauses, Puttenham presents the figure as though it "supplied" a word "to perfit the congruitie or sence of them

all . . . because by one word we serue many clauses of one congruitie." Its brother, *prozeugma,* "satisfieth both in sence & congruitie
all those other clauses that followe him."[94] With his first examples,
Puttenham shows that *enargia,* the "glorious lustre and light" that
characterizes the auricular figures,[95] really perfects the whole's proportion and sense. The most essentially auricular figure, rhyme, completes the line as though it were the archer's release of his arrow—a
gesture called the "loose" (Puttenham's name for rhyme) that is meant
"to finish the feate of his shot."[96] Rather than a merely accidental
decoration, rhyme is here a moment in which the poet, like the archer,
is most like himself in the turning "loose" of his line.

Similar principles influence Puttenham's discussion of the rest of
the auricular figures, as they do his classification of figures that are
"sensible" and "sententious." *Metaphora,* appealing to the inner
senses, is a departure from the ordinary use of words: it declares—
or excites a lightening or yearning in—the subject matter that ordinary language can not draw out. ("Here for want of an apter and
more naturall word to declare the drie temper of the earth, it is said
to thirst & rejoice."[97]) Some sensible figures such as *paradiastole* and
hyperbole ("the loud lyer"[98]) come close to flattering the subject matter
with false flowers. On the other hand, paradiastolic praise ("when
we make the best of a bad thing") is not, in Puttenham's scheme,
mere puffery; making the best of something is not the same as making
something bad into something good. Puttenham's language retains
the idea that however suspect such praise might become, when rightly
understood and applied it draws out what it praises. The relentlessly
hortatory mode of the English rhetorics, which critics today sometimes interpret to be a sign of gross naivete, is typically premised on
the axiom that the best and most effective use of the figures is only
in their decorous application, their abuse being by definition an ab-
rogation of rhetoric's commendatory nature.

The distinction that sixteenth-century rhetoricians make between
genuine and bogus suasion and ornamentation is of kind rather than
degree. False rhetoric denies genuine tendency; it is not simply untrue,
excessive, or indecorous. It is not genuine persuasion and does not
apply authentic ornament because it does not persuade or decorate in
what are assumed to be the true senses of those words. False persuasion in the strictest sense of the word does not exist. Sophisticated
modern observers of the rhetorical treachery of Shakespeare's villains
find this hard to accept. Yet the import of the rhetorician's position

is cosmological and ethical, as well as technical: there is something in the *nature* of coercive rhetoric that helps make it false; it is not false purely by reason of the villainy of its user, although in being false coercive rhetoric springs in part from that villainy. To say that Iago exposes the superficiality of the naive sixteenth-century rhetorician is to discount the debasement of his suasion—the meanness of its devices and the way they gnaw into the noble Othello's mind, which is painfully complicit in its own swerve toward murder.

For these reasons, hyperbole, as we have already mentioned, is a praising exaggeration that Puttenham can treat as though it were veracious. The figure should be outlandish enough that an audience does not believe it directly, moderate enough that one can give it credit and thereby advance or abase the reputation of the person being praised or condemned. Puttenham insists that the figure properly employed sets forth truth, that the hyperbolist can truthfully say, as Puttenham does, "I meane nothing lesse than that I speake."[99] Even the most extreme form of wrenching metaphor, *catachresis,* can be "commendably spoken," when in its proper fashioning it sets out the true form of its subject matter.[100]

The "sententious" figures, which combine appeals to the ear and the sense, also tend to be perfective catalysts and flowerings in the service of truth. Puttenham shows how the *anaphoric* repetition of a word at the head of successive lines sets the verse to its natural dancing: the head word "lead[s] the daunce to many verses in sute."[101] Another form of repetition called *anadiplosis* is an antithesis that in Puttenham's example glimpses, not simply identifies, the deeper moral significance of the repeated word:

> Comfort it is for man to haue a *wife,*
> *Wife* chast, and wise, and lowly all her life.

Or thus:

> Your beutie was the cause of my first *love,*
> *Looue* while I liue, that I may sore repent.[102]

An idea of the wife's true nature emerges in the clarifying figure, just as in the second example the nature of the speaker's first love does not come fully to light until the figure reveals a meaning hidden in the first line. Likewise, various plays upon words, such as nicknames and puns, "come all from one originall."[103] The lines Puttenham cites as an example of punning *prosonomasia* are meant to argue an affinity between the new word and the old, not only the poet's ability to make sport: "The lesse I *loue,* I *liue* the lesse."[104] A more extreme type of punning like *traductio,* in which a word generates numerous and distant variations in succeeding lines, is assumed to translate or "translace" the word into many shapes the way a "tailor" works upon a "garment." The new words not only "come all from one originall," but are various adjustments made upon a single piece of clothing.[105] Even a synonym (the figure *sinonimia*) is the "Interpreter" of the word it renames; when they are placed in a series, "one of them doth expound another."[106]

Finally, the ornamental transformations called "The Wonderer" or "The Doubtful" are interruptions that complete and ennoble ordinary language. By allowing the poet or speaker to express awe or doubt, the figures displace ordinary discourse with expressions that go beyond the affirmations and denials of ordinary speech; at the same time, Puttenham presents his examples as though he assumed the figures augmented rather than displaced the ordinary forms. Figures of praise and horror open up ordinary affirmation with awe; denial is augmented with a figure of doubt.[107]

Quintilian's explanation of that master-figure, *emphasis,* harmonizes with the bulk of Puttenham's discussion of ornament. For the Roman, emphasis occurs when "some hidden meaning is extracted [*eruitur*] from some phrase," as happens in the third line of the passage he selects from Dido's lament:

> Might I not have lived,
> From wedlock free, a life without a stain,
> Happy as beasts are happy?[108]

The rhetorician notes that "although Dido complains of marriage, yet her passionate outburst shows that she regards life without wedlock as no life for man, but for the beasts of the field."[109] His gloss assumes that emphasis unlocks the meaning of "From wedlock free," showing the deeper pathos in Dido's wishing for something—the life of beasts—that she knows she does not desire.

5

How far can we extend Quintilian's synecdochic summary of figural ornamentation to the more general forms and effects of persuasion? In the conclusion of his *Arte of Rhetorique,* Thomas Wilson cites Demosthenes' praise of delivery, including pronunciation, as the most important of the five parts of eloquence.[110] How does delivery conform to the Timaeic and Aristotelian paradigm of perfective action? What are we to make of Fraunce's assertion in the *Arcadian Rhetoric* that pronunciation is the key to the speaker's true disposition[111] and to tropic meaning itself: "Without . . . change of voice, neither anie *Ironia* nor liuely *Metaphore* can well be discerned."[112]

According to one of Cicero's spokesmen in *De Oratore,* delivery is supposed to embody, not mimic or exploit, the speaker's hidden passions.[113] The eye is best suited for making eloquent gestures because it is "the only part of the body capable of producing as many indications and variations as there are emotions."[114] The orator's eye in other words is thought to actualize the emotions. Rather than merely signifying, its tears combine what is seen with what is felt. (The *Timaeus* explains that a conjunction of incoming and outgoing rays in the eye causes a discharge of fire and water called a tear;[115] the result is a synthesis of internal and external motions.)

The style closest to the eloquence of the eye is the great or high style because it involves the fullest play of figurative language. In Dudley Fenner's words, the high style transforms "the more simple and plaine maner of speaking, vnto that which is more ful of excellencie & grace."[116] Like the gesture of the eye, it can be notoriously false when it is indecorous. But the travesty of either mode does not lead rhetoricians of speech and gesture automatically to conclude that the essential nature of high style and gesture is corrupt or neutral. Puttenham joins a chorus of rhetoricians condemning abuses of the high style, which make it "counterfait, and puffed vp, as it were a windball carrying more countenance then matter";[117] yet he insists that the essence of decorum is its natural "seemelynesse" and "comelynesse"—indeed its gesture of "pleasant approche."[118]

Delivery and high style are in this sense the fullest realizations of eloquence. They stand in the same relation to it as the Aristotelian greatness of soul to the other virtues. Greatness of soul is like delivery and the high style in being "as it were a crowning ornament (*kosmos*) of the virtues; it enhances their greatness." Without violating the lesser virtues ("it cannot exist without them") the great-souled character arrays them with a kind of excess by which they extend themselves to honor him.[119]

Of course, the danger in giving so much attention to the development and delivery of the high style is that no praising or praiseworthy virtue might be involved. As Aristotle mentions in the *Rhetoric,* style and gesture without ethos are ineffective and pretentious.[120] Castiglione's *The Courtier,* which devotes extraordinary effort to the art of noble display, sometimes warns against the twin excesses of false self-promotion and the overzealous pursuit of *sprezzatura;* there is a danger, in a world that attaches so much importance to courtly display, of trying too hard, either aspiring to grand gestures that cannot be one's own, or trying so assiduously to hide one's art that artlessness becomes affectation. Still, that dialogue's cautions against extremes are a way of endorsing true *sprezzatura's* decorous, high-minded performance of graceful artlessness. Style and delivery form the courtier's character, just as his character is assumed to form his self-presentation.[121]

The speaker must frequently act out the passions that he seeks to move in his audience, in order to show—as Thomas Wright says in his treatise on the passions—that the orator's reasons move himself.[122] He therefore feigns, but does not necessarily or typically deceive. *Feigning* is ambiguous in sixteenth-century usage: flatterers feign, but "the truest poetry is the most feigning."[123] We have a hint of the complexity of *feign's* meaning in sixteenth-century uses of *pretend.* Wright means to commend his audience when he says it "pretendeth to be ruled by reason."[124] Pretending in this sense is a legitimate aspiration for what one ought to take upon oneself, intend, or mean. Henry VI is not a good king, says one of his supporters in the play, because he does not pretend: "Why shall we fight if you pretend no title?"[125] Pretending is here a stretching forth or before oneself—in accordance with the word's Latin components *prae* and *tendere.* It is an affection, even an affectation (the words are interchangeable in the sixteenth century), that tends to be interpreted as a legitimate yearning for a higher good true to one's nature. When Shakespeare's Timon of Athens hears one of his followers praise a horse, he freely gives it to its praiser as a compliment to his virtue: "no man / can justly praise but what he does affect."[126] Timon's friend does eventually betray him, but the benefactor's main point of giving the horse away is to call out the friend's pretense to a higher nature. As Wright puts it, things naturally strive to "effect" their "affection."[127]

6

Renaissance methods of curing disease and training horses happen to contain elaborate discussions of matters crucial to sixteenth-century rhetorical theory and practice that are usually not explicit in the rhetorical treatises. Ideas of curing and training enact common Renaissance conceptions of persuasion and ornamentation. They reveal dimensions of Platonic and Aristotelian natural philosophy which are more complex than those we have referred to so far, and which have important implications for conceptions of rhetoric tied closely to ideas about nature and man's place in it.

Works such as Timothy Bright's *A Treatise of Melancholy* and Thomas Wright's *The Passions of the Mind* depend upon traditional natural philosophy, even though the ostensible purpose of their works is heavily didactic. In condemning the impiety of those who interpret humor psychology to mean that vice, virtues, and religion are simply products of the humors, Bright emphasizes the intricacy of passionate tendency, its complex interactions with the senses and the soul. And although Wright's book concludes with a long prayer in which he turns away from his practical examination of the passions, the magnitude of his study rivals the religiosity of his resignation.

The works of both men are concerned with the persuasion and ornamentation of natural tendency, as is the work of the rhetoricians. Sherry, in his treatise on rhetoric, writes that "there is nothynge desyred, but vnder the consideration of good or profite."[128] As Wright puts it, the passions "either prosecute some good, or flie some evil."[129] Of course, men frequently wander from the good, often at least partly influenced by their passions; but their error is typically an aberration or their own disease, however cursed the Fall may have made mankind. The passions participate in what Bright calls "a secret power of nature" that can overcome infirmities, and render to the body "a greater purity and firmness of health, than before the sickness it did enjoy."[130] Bright goes so far as to insist that a natural tendency toward ripeness and health can prevail when children are stricken with a fatal disease; they are known to experience a ripening of the passions and of the soul itself, defeating the baleful influence of the humors even as they proceed toward a death presumably brought on by accelerated aging.

> I have knowen children languishing of the splene, obstructed, and altered in temper, talk with grauite and wisedome, surpassing those tender yeares, and their iudgement carying a maruelous imitation of the wisedome of the ancient, hauing after a sorte, attained that by disease, which other haue by course of yeares: whereupon I take it, the prouerbe ariseth: that they be of short life, who are of wit so pregnant: because their bodies do receaue by nature so speedie

a ripenesse, as thereby age is hastened, through a certaine temper of their bodies.[131]

Philippe de Mornay's *The True Knowledge of a Manes Owne Selfe* ventures a similar argument for the affections' natural tendency toward health. Nature "being disrancked and made vnrulie" by Adam's Fall, the affections are not always "moderated by iudgement, deliberation, or honest councell"; yet when the influence of reason wanes, the affections' "mistress," the will, guides them: "the will, as mistresse of the affections, forbids the motive power, that shee transport not the members, to perpetuate vnreasonable or pernicious things. As a man hauing a Feuer, affects to drinke inordinately: but yet the will checks the hande, that it shall not approache to the cup or glasse."[132] The will has a tendency to check the passions, and to do so as their loving governor. In Wright's words, the affections for all their wanderings reside in "the very facultie and power of the soule"[133] which by definition is not controlled by the humors.

How then are the passions moved, and how do animate tendencies express themselves physiologically, as they commonly do? Bright explains the process by following Aristotle's dictum in *De Anima*[134] that animate movement is expressed and initiated in the heart and its affections, rather than by means of the chemical humors. Anger arises from intellectual and passionate movements of the heart regarding the idea of justice. The passion arises from the heart, and is accompanied by a boiling or heating of the humorous blood; but the contracting and dilating motions of the fluid are caused by the heart's "mislike of that [which] offendeth" and the consequent vehemency of its "reuenge."[135] The heart is "kindled with anger" because its preferences have been abrogated; it is not moved by coercive heat. Bright here agrees with Wright in arguing that the humors are not "organicall partes" or "instruments" of the healthy body.[136] In its fashion, the heart acts and elects as though it were a kind of soul.

A somewhat simpler account of the heart's action appears in Wright's chapter on the moving of the passions. Wright's title, *The Passions of the Mind,* complements Bright's argument that the passions partake of soul and mind, and therefore do not characteristically fall under the power of the humors. Wright does allow the humors a natural role in moving the passions, but only insofar as they are sympathetic with the soul's operations. Movement arises from "the purer spirits" flowing from the brain, the residence of the imagination. Those spirits act upon the sympathetic responses of the heart. Once sense and memory inform the imagination,

> the purer spirits, floeth from the brayne [where the imagination resides] by certaine secret channels to the heart, where they pitch at the dore, signifying what an obiect was presented, conuenient or disconuenient for it. The heart immediatly bendeth, either to prosecute it, or to eschew it and the better to effect that affection, draweth other humours to helpe him, and so in pleasure concurre great store of pure spirits; in paine and sadnesse, much melancholy blood; in ire, blood and choller; and not onely (as I said) the heart draweth, but also the same soule that informeth the heart residing in other parts, sendeth the humours vnto the heart, to performe their seruice in such a worthie place.[137]

What at first seems to be a series of clear cause-and-effect relations turns out to be an interplay of heart and soul. The purer spirits signify something to the heart; they do not alter it physiologically or even energetically persuade it. The heart responds to the purer spirits with an alacrity that shows a predisposition to "prosecute" or "eschew" what the purer spirits bring to it. When it calls the humors to support it, the soul simultaneously does the same, as though to leave no doubt that the movement is not merely physiological. Finally, the humors summoned by the soul do fealty to the "worthie" heart, as though they partook of animate tendency toward the good in the proper movement of the passions.

Of course, neither Wright nor Bright assumes that the influences exerted by tendency and the soul's hierarchy are absolute. The passions would never err if such were the case. Bright describes the government of the passions as essentially rhetorical: "a civill subjection ruled by counsell and no constraint."[138] Since the heart is not forced to make the affections conform to what is good, it is responsible for the excess and balance of the passions. On the other hand, its freedom is not total. Its natural tendency to be "disposed and framed to mediocrite of affection" opens it to the physician's persuasion,[139] which it accepts or rejects in light of its sense of the good. John Davies summarizes this idea in his description of the "voluntary appetite," which he calls "motions of the harte's Hart properlie."[140] They are bred from reason and will. The reason, revealing to the will "what is good or ill . . . rules hir not as though *will* could not choose, / But as one teaching Hir hir pow'r to vse."[141] Reason persuades a will that has a power to choose. (The will "makes Reason waite her will to kno.") On the other hand, the will's freedom to act on its own is not entirely independent of what is just, since the will naturally tends toward the just. The will "is free to doe that needes it must," not "the thing that is uniust." Davies adheres to the view that the choice of unjust action is a decision to become enslaved to sin, and thus to negate the will's freedom to affirm the organism's free tendency to do good.[142]

Like Davies, Bright and Wright attribute the proper moving of the passions to persuasion, not compulsion. In order to acknowledge and command the affinities of heart, mind, and soul, the physician must somehow appeal to their natures, no matter how disease might have obscured them. He cannot manufacture health or consent without abrogating the nature of what he intends to cure. Thomas Elyot's *Castel of Helth* seeks to remind the reader that no cure is successful if it is more than "a littell annoyance" to the patient's true complexion.[143] Following this dictum, Bright devotes most of his effort to refreshing the spirit, strengthening the brain, and comforting the heart,[144] in order to persuade the melancholic toward health. His treatise is a rhetorical appeal to a sick friend, an argument that endorses the Aristotelian principle, summarized in the *Ethics,* that the rational part of the soul "can in a manner persuade [*peitho*] the irrational [appetitive] part."[145]

Again, the "irrational" appetitive part is persuadable because it is in some sense rational. Davies reminds his reader that the seat of the appetites, the heart, is "the Mirrour of the minde."[146] Wright invokes the commonplace that certain appetites display intellectual tendencies toward the good: "the appetite of *honour . . . is due* vnto *vertue*" since it "encourageth often noble spirits to attempt most dangerous exploits for the benefit of their countries."[147] Fear "expelleth sinne," while "sadnesse bringeth repentance," and "delight pricketh forward to keepe Gods commandments."[148] Rather than being accidents or occasional occurrences, such appetitive aspirations are somehow within the nature of the appetites.

Certainly, the more disordered the soul, the greater the difficulty in persuading it. When the affections have erred into madness, or the body has fallen victim to powerful aberrations of nature like the plague, the physician's powers are most demonstrably limited. The temptation mounts for him to create a purely pharmacological cure.

Burton's great summary of remedies for melancholy demonstrates the medical literature's interest in persuasive cures even in extreme cases. His general plan for treating melancholy relies upon persuasion at almost every stage. He recommends that the sufferer first attempt to cure himself by tempering his passions in dialogue with his own reason. If that method fails, the sufferer must explain his condition to a friend, and seek comfort in his friend's speeches. If he must seek further assistance from a physician, the treatment must attempt to cure the mind as well as the body, first by reasonable explanation, then by persuasion: " 'Many,' saith Galen, 'have been cured by good counsel and persuasion alone'," for "the tongue of a wise man is health."[149] Although he advocates suppressing and excommunicating some sufferers of religious melancholy if all else fails, most of his attention is devoted to methods and kinds of exhortation intermixed with physic.

Burton takes the melancholic's opinions seriously. Since true persuasion affirms the soul's natural tendency toward health, the sufferer's opinions offer him a door to health as well as sickness. The sick man who refuses to eat might be cured if his condition resulted from his religious rejection of earthly foods, and if his physician, understanding the importance of that opinion, fed him while dressed in the garb of an angel.[150] The angel is "forged," but under certain circumstances, says Burton, "it is not amiss to deceive."[151] In fact a "feigned lie, strange news, witty device, [or] artificial invention" properly lends credence to the melancholic's opinion in a manner that encourages him to cure himself:

> Philodotus the physician cured a melancholy kind that thought his head was off, by putting a leaden cap thereon; the weight made him perceive it, and freed him of his fond imagination. A woman, in the said Alexander, swallowed a serpent as she thought; he gave her a vomit, and conveyed a serpent, such as she conceived, into the basin; upon the sight of it she was amended.[152]

Here the physician does more than teach an illusory power of positive thinking. He allows the sufferer to regain his senses by reasoning through his delusion, toward the sufferer's nobler idea for his actions. The king's helmet is not a deception, in that it enables the melancholic soul to realize that his head weighs upon him. A deluded woman is also able to regain her health by means of a cure that honors her notion that the snake is in her stomach, an evil not wholly out of reach, and hence susceptible to being expelled in a relatively simple operation. Similarly, the man who is afraid to make water, "lest all the town should be drowned," is cured when he is told that the town burns and that he might carry out his sense of political responsibility by making water to put out the fire.

Certainly, Burton gives accounts of pharmacological and surgical cures, including woundings and geldings that are designed to drive out one disease with another. But his discussion of these more purely physiological treatments, like his discussion of everything else, is qualified by his extensive use of second- and third-hand testimony and anecdotes, which he does not regularly recommend in his own voice. He places his most technical material about pharmacological treatments mainly in the later pages of his work, after he has established a philosophical groundwork that affirms the importance of having the passions draw toward health largely by themselves. And where provocative passages appear in the first parts of the work, the weight of his multitudinous references generally favors the attitude toward persuasion maintained by Bright and Wright. Wright summarizes that point of view when he explains that it is the sufferer's idea of the physician and of the "goodness of the cure" that ultimately stirs the passions, thus strengthening his constitution and curing him.[153]

7

The Renaissance notion that the passions are genuinely persuadable—not just forces to be repressed or released—is apparent in contemporary treatises on horse-training. Though we now relegate the taming, schooling, riding, and curing of horses to the hobbyist, in the sixteenth century these endeavors were an art of governance and persuasion resembling the more earnest discipline of eloquence and to some degree the political art. Sir Philip Sidney is not entirely facetious when he introduces his apology for poetry with the horse-trainer Pugliano's argument that the rider's art is superior to "skill of government." The voluble Italian means that it is, among other things, the art of government *par excellence:* "no earthly thing bred such wonder to a prince as to be a good horseman."[154] Pugliano is so convincing when he praises his art and his horse that, jokes Sidney, "I think he would have persuaded me to have wished myself a horse."[155] In fact, the Italian trainer is a master orator on the verge of transforming his audience into the praiseworthy horse he rides so well.

Sidney resists this rhetoric because, he says, he has had a bit of training in logic. But he cannot forget Pugliano's love of his art, nor the audacity with which he defends it. Pugliano's enthusiasm by Sidney's account is almost ridiculous, and yet it serves as the model for his own defense of poetry because poetry, like horsemanship, is in need of an advocate who will permit it to show its true virtues to the world. Pugliano carries his hyperbole too far, and so (Sidney warns with careful self-effacement) will he. But in so doing he will honor a more fundamental seriousness in Pugliano's defense of horsemanship, which is akin to Sidney's defense of the power of poetry to persuade. Before examining Sidney's tacit analogy between horsemanship and the rhetorical aspects of poetry, we must first look into the art of horse-training, especially its kinship with notions about how to govern the passions.

Roger Ascham compares horsemanship to education, not only because riding, like education, is "one of the few gentlemanly distinctions," but because the best schoolmasters are "wise ryders" who "by ientle allurements do breed up in [their students] the loue of riding." Men should take at least as much care in selecting children for studies and training them as they do in choosing and training a colt.[156] The comparison of education and wise horsemanship is no idle illustration, for it draws upon a principle of horse-training that the surviving sixteenth-century treatises on that subject emphasize. As John Astley in *The Art of Riding* puts it, "For whatsoeuer a horse doth by compulsion or force, he neither knoweth what he doth, nor how to doo it, neither will it become him."[157] In *The Book of the Governor*, Elyot invokes the pedagogical commonplace: "I would not haue [students] inforced by violence to lerne, but accordyng to the counsell of Quintillian to be swetely allured thereto, with prayses and such pretty gyftes as children delyte in."[158] A closer examination of the training manuals suggests that the educators' views were elaborated according to a widely shared philosophy of training and persuasion with roots in traditional forms of natural philosophy.

Any discussion of horses and rhetoric must take account of R. S. Crane's well-known article linking Jonathan Swift's supremely rational Houyhnhnms to the definition of *horse* in contemporary logic textbooks.[159] Crane argues that Swift reverses the commonplace definition of *horse* as an irrational animal—and the companion definition of *man* as a rational animal—so as to expose the irrationality of man. Shocked by the contrast between the rational horses and the

Yahoos, Gulliver finds he is more at home in the stable than in his own house.

Crane places great weight on the logicians' definitions of man and horse, derived from Quintilian and echoed in Sidney's claim to see through Pugliano by means of logic. In Swift's interpretation of the commonplace, Crane argues, man at least ought to be rational, whereas the horse as a contrary to man is an example of what he should not or can not be. But in fact, Quintilian in Book VII of the *Institutio Oratoria* is not so doctrinaire. His point is about definitions, not about the difference between man and horse: "It is a false definition if you say 'A horse is a rational animal,' for although the horse is an animal, it is irrational."[160] The sentence, like Sidney's joke in the introduction to his *Defence,* affirms a similarity between horse and man as well as a difference. The two are similar, insofar as their animal souls are distinct from vegetative souls; and the horse's animal soul possesses an appetitive faculty that might be partly rational. All animals are capable of achievements which, Quintilian says, "perhaps indicate the possession of a certain degree of reason," even though "they are called . . . unreasoning beasts."[161] Swift could very well be drawing from a cultural predisposition toward attributing a form of reason to the beast. This may be one reason why his utopian horses are not as ridiculous as the narrowly satirical structure attributed to Swift's book by Crane would seem to dictate.

A hint of the animate horse appears in Ficino's commentary on Plato's *Phaedrus,* which treats the horses pulling the chariot of the soul as appetites, one of which is rational.[162] In Plato's dialogue, the fairer horse responds to its master's words, though the second, which in Ficino's reading would be the irrational and concupiscible appetite, must be restrained forcibly. The question of whether the latter's training draws on a modicum of rational tendency even in the irrational horse is an important and complicated matter for the dialogue's discussion of the nature of rhetoric—an issue that will have to wait for a later chapter.

For now we can take John Astley's *The Art of Riding* as a reference point. Since he follows Xenophon—the classical authority in these matters—he seeks to make the horse "obedient by reasonable meanes." He concedes that rationality is only "proper vnto men," yet treats the horse the way Wright and Bright treat a passion—as a more or less rational being that "knoweth what he doth" as it is properly trained.[163] A successor to Astley, the logician Thomas Blundeville, writes a horse-training manual that begins with the idea that the horse is naturally capable of tempering.[164] It is an embodiment of the passions yet it is eminently "tameable, docible, and . . . obedient vnto man if trained without violence that would destroy its natural constitution."[165] Gervase Markham's manual argues the same point: violent correction takes "from the horse the *apprehension* of his evil."[166] Inexpert riders abuse their horses because "wanting patience" they do not "let the horse knowe his fault" before correcting him:[167] "all arte teacheth we are to fortifie our Horses vnderstanding"[168] so that it can "come to a perfit knowledge of your minde or intention."[169] Thus the proper training somehow enables the horse to correct his actions with a form of understanding, and "of his owne accord."[170] We could say that the trainers are waxing metaphorical in these passages, were it not for the degree to which the conception of the horse's rational tendency permeates the training literature.

The goal of the training draws out the horse's most characteristic passions, what Astley calls its "natural lustiness and courage and freshness of feeling which is proper to him by nature."[171] Markham seems to have this in mind when he stresses the importance of training the horse to take "an inward delight of his comeliness";[172] the horse's proper feeling is a reflective admiration of its coming forth. Burton echoes and expands upon this idea when he likens the persuasion of a melancholic patient to the proper training of a horse made skittish by loud noises: in both cases, the student should "be so manned by art, and animated, that he cannot only endure, but is much more generous at the hearing of such things, much more courageous than before, and much delighteth in it."[173] The training enables the man and the horse to be more reflectively and passionately themselves.

These are the goals, but what are the methods of the training? How are the powerful, sometimes willful animals tempered by their riders without violence? This is another way of asking if human beings can control their own passions and persuade others without coercing souls. Wright recalls St. Basil's analogy likening the uncontrolled passions to wild horses pulling a coach,[174] and recommends taming them by "ill usage" rather than pampering.[175] Ascham concedes that the "sharpe keepinge in and bridleinge of youth" is necessary, though it is to be carried out by fathers, not schoolmasters.[176] The question arises whether methods of training ultimately contradict the idea that persuasion unfolds, not violates, the self-moving soul, the rational appetite, and the passions' aptitude for tempering.

The horse-trainer's chief instruments of correction and guidance are the voice, the bridle, the spur, and the rod. Blundeville, explaining a principle that is implicit in the work of Markham and Astley, says that the voice is the most important: "For the voice correcteth without disorder: and it maketh the horse afraide without putting him in despaire."[177] That is, the voice can correct without breaking the horse's nature. It appeals to the horse's higher being, rather than making it faint-hearted.[178] Even dull horses, or those that are "vile of courage," often respond to the rider's art where vigorous spurring fails.[179]

Properly used, the nature of the rider's instruments is to correct and help the animal to become more finished, more perfectly its own horse: "the bridle correcteth both head, necke, and mouth, and maketh him to reane [rein] well, and doth helpe much to embolden, or to man him. . . , the Spurs do not onelie make him steddie and iust, but also subiect and quicke to vnderstand his Riders mind."[180] The rod would seem, unavoidably, to be a tool of abuse; but Markham tells how it is in fact an ornament, not a whip; its primary purpose is to represent the horseman's traditional weapons of war. When it is used on the horse, it scratches and "cherishes" more typically than it chastises.[181] Applying any of these instruments to chastise and guide the "mad and furious" nature of a rebellious mount, the horseman is "vpon euerie correction [to] instantlie cherish him, that he may vnderstand you correct him not for going, but for some other disorder in his going, and this shall not onely detaine him from stryving aginst the bridle, or running away, but also giue him so easie an apprehension of his fault, that he will in very short space amend it."[182] If the bridle can somehow temper and perfect the horse's nature, the spurs can stir its spirit. Blundeville says that the spurs, like the voice, are a means of "helping" the horse "to advance."[183] It seems that Markham can justify what he calls a "violent" means of urging such as spurring because it "stirreth" the horse's "spirit or alacrity." And although the rider can kick with his stirrups, he does so properly only once in every dozen paces.[184] Spurring is really a signifying gesture, "to show the horse it is being corrected."[185]

Applying the metaphor of the spur to civil life, particularly to rhetoric, Francis Bacon bows to the commonplace when he argues in *The Colours of Good and Evil* that because glory and honor are natural "spurs to virtue," rhetoricians would do well to study them in order legitimately to spur men:

> [S]ince the ordinary instrument of horsemanship is the spur, and that
> it is no manner of impediment or burden, the horse is not to be
> accounted the less of which will not do well without the spur, but
> rather the other is to be reckoned a delicacy than a virtue [the horse
> that needs no spur is more delicate than virtuous]: so glory and
> honor are as spurs to virtue: and although virtue would languish
> without them, yet since they be always at hand to attend virtue,
> virtue is not to be said the less chosen for itself because it needeth
> the spur of fame and reputation . . .   (*CGE* VII.80)

The horse or man who does not do well without a spur is in fact
more virtuous than the "delicate" specimen who is unable to benefit
from it. As an "ordinary instrument" of horsemanship, the spur does
not violate the virtue it consistently attends and stimulates.

There is an unspoken shrewdness and daring in Bacon's argument
that we will have to examine in a later chapter. Suffice it to say here
that what looks like a justification of appealing to the horse's rational
appetite—its reaching toward courage and the display of its native
beauty—might in fact subvert horse-trainers' (and traditional rhetoricians') concept of persuasion by implying that the spur is absolutely
necessary for the attainment of virtue. Bacon is being double, but his
doubleness does a certain homage to the trainers' principles of persuasion.

The notion that rhetorical spurring might incite, not coerce, genuine virtue appears in the notorious *The Philosopher of the Court,* even
though that work is an ironic attack on false persuasion's contorting
influence on genuine virtue. In an introductory poem, William Hitchcockes asks the reader to incite the translator to perform greater deeds
by giving him "The goade, the whip, the bat, and spur" in the form
of praise:

> Why then giue praise (which is the goad and spur,
> The whip and bat whereby each doth in vertue stur)
> To him, that did translate: thy selfe shalt thereby gaine
> To force him for thy sake to take muche greater paine.[186]

The poem is a sarcastic protest against flattery; on one level, there is
no distinction here between persuasion and violence. But Hitchcockes' verse works the horseman's commonplace that praise chas-
tens, not just comforts or deceives, its object. Praise would stir the
translator to "take much greater paine," perhaps to return flattery for
flattery for his patron's advantage, but also to make the poem a more

vigorous, perfective satire for its readers' true sakes. In the body of the text, a similar idea appears in advice to the courtier that he find something divine within himself that will "bridle hym with shame from doing euill, and prick him forward to do well."[187] The discipline is painful but not a torture. The courtier must ultimately find a higher being within and then take it upon himself, as one cherishes and spurs his greater being as a mounted man.

In *Musophilus,* horse-training provides important imagery for Samuel Daniel's praise of eloquence. Like a good rider, eloquence has the capacity to "stir" and yet "manage, guide, and master" the higher desires ("the eminence / Of men's affections") by means of "the strong reine of commanding words."[188] By such means, it can "let out" thoughts as yet locked in, and refine the world for speakers as yet "vnformed" and "vnknowing."[189] Cicero's Crassus uses a training metaphor to similar effect: the good teacher will use the spur and the bridle according to the characteristics of individual students' souls, much as the gardener grafts or cuts "to produce in each [plant] the configuration that the nature of each permitted."[190]

8

Sir Philip Sidney takes up many of these commonplaces in his *Defence of Poesie,* where he gives them a sometimes ironic force that tests their appropriateness as paradigms for the function and power of poetry. The introduction of the *Defence* in fact suggests that there is a noble analogy between the commendation of horsemanship and the praise of poets and poetry, between the managing of horses and the governing or persuading of men, between true horsemanship and making poetry. In the first lines of the treatise, the squire Pugliano's exaggerating praise of fine riders, their mounts, and the horseman's service as courtier to his prince is more than an amusing anecdote to catch the readers' attention.

In his joking resistance to Pugliano's hyperbole, Sidney admits or seems to confess that Pugliano's rhetoric begins to make him think himself a horse. The squire's argument is self-promoting and ludicrous, but because Pugliano loves his art, and because the horse, with its beauty, faithfulness, courage, and nobility reminds Sidney of the best courtier in his refusal to flatter, Sidney would be right to imitate the horse, and by extension the horseman courtier, in defending poetry as a nobly persuasive art.

Although in his introduction Sidney makes a point of wondering whether Pugliano is a flatterer, the deeper joke is that Pugliano's praise almost convinces Sidney to become the thing he desires to be: a clear-sighted and faithful member of the court. His wish to become a horse under the spell of Pugliano's rhetoric is admittedly absurd; but we see that the horse-trainer's eloquence draws Sidney after all into affinity with the noble horse. The ostensible purpose of the *Defence* as a whole seeks to do much the same thing with its audience, commending poetry with an exaggeration that would faithfully draw England toward nobility.

If this Timaeic dimension of Sidney's argument frames the *Defence*, how can it be reconciled with Sidney's famous assertion that poetry makes things "quite anew," not just "better than nature bringeth forth"? If Pugliano's enthusiasm can almost effect the metamorphosis of a man into a horse, it might just as well create a man-horse or a centaur, which Sidney points out is one of those beings poets make, "such as never were in Nature, as the Heroes, Demigods, Cyclopes, Chimeras, Furies, and such like."[191] Sidney's self-effacing, seemingly frivolous introduction therefore broaches the possibility that the true poet is one who ranges freely "only within the zodiac of his own wit." On the one hand, "there is no art delivered to mankind that hath not the works of Nature for his principal object, without which they could not consist."[192] On the other, "only the poet . . . lifted up with the vigour of his own invention, doth grow in effect another nature"[193] in imitation of the prerogative given to him by the "heavenly Maker," who sets only man "beyond and over all the works"[194] of uninspired nature. The latter poet, imitating God, would make a second genesis "when with a divine breath he bringeth things forth far surpassing her [nature's] doings."[195]

The actualizing, Timaeic conception of *materia prima* would seem to have no place in this scheme because the freely inventing poet must not be bound to a pre-ordained subject matter: "The poet only bringeth his own stuff, and doth not learn a conceit out of a matter, but maketh matter for a conceit."[196] Recent critical interest in this apparent contradiction has tended to explain it in terms of divided allegiances: Sidney's understanding of poetry as an Aristotelian mimesis of nature clashes with his idea of the poet's Platonic foreconceit, which transcends the limits of nature. But we have seen that the pervasive Timaeic tradition is not so precise. Its syncretism so routinely transposes and joins Platonic and Aristotelian principles that modern critical distinctions run the risk of ignoring the integrity of other distinctions more germane to that tradition. C. S. Lewis's warning about the premature analysis of the Platonic-Aristotelian nexus in Renaissance thought is a helpful guide to the *Defence:* "The men of that age were such inveterate syncretists, so much more anxious to reconcile authorities than to draw out their differences, that the Aristotelian and neo-Platonic views are not clearly opposed and compared, but are rather contaminated by each other and by many more influences as well."[197] Aristotle invited this confusion (Lewis believes "unwittingly," though his evidence points toward a purpose),

> when he allowed, in contexts which had nothing to do with poetry, that Nature often tends to or aims at . . . a greater perfection than the indeterminacy of matter allows her to achieve (*De Gen. Anim.* 778A; *Polit.* 1255B); words which Sidney remembered when he wrote in the *Arcadia* (1590, II. xi) of forms such as "Nature, often erring, yhet shewes she would faine make."[198]

Syncretic Timaeic principles are at work in subordinate sections of the *Defence.* In the conclusion of Sidney's argument that poetry is didactic, the Platonic foreconceit joins with Aristotelian mimesis. Poetry can "bestow a Cyrus upon the world, to make many Cyruses, if they will learn aright why and how" the poet made his energic image of Cyrus. The process is Timaeic in poetry's dependence upon men's learning rightly "why and how that maker made [them]" a Cyrus. That is, the poet's foreconceit is brought forward in the actualization of his audience's faculties as though they were intellectually analogous to the Timaeic *materia prima;* they become Cyruses in somehow taking cognizance of, and rising to, the end and manner of their being made so. In this sense the poet can make his ideas "manifest, by delivering them forth in such excellency as he hath imagined them." Indeed, poetry's faculty exceeds the workings of nature in the way it acts "substantially" upon character, to bring many potential Cyruses into being.[199]

Poetry draws out or holds up to scorn "what sould or should not be" rather than what merely "is."[200] The modal shift is toward the imperative, yet in Sidney's formulation it is also open to Timaeic illustration as the poet's perfection of possibility. The poet has the ability to coax into being what tends to be or "may be." He thus replaces the merely historical "is" with the lively, energic "is" of his golden conceit.[201] The spring of this poetry is the soul's judgment as well as its desire. Poetry's Horatian function, despite its seemingly superficial appeal to the passions and its emphasis on merely didactic ends, delights the affections in part because its models are admirable. It instructs the wit by showing to the understanding what it is capable of admiring.

In contrast, the moral philosopher, the historian, and the lawyer try to reform their audiences in a manner that condemns, contorts, or ignores tendency in those audiences' passionate judgments. The moral philosopher defines and analyzes "with a sullen gravity" that masks his own unnatural repression of all passion until he angrily bursts out in hypocritical condemnation of "the foul fault of anger."[202] The historian seeks primarily to impress and dominate with idle hearsay. His examples afford him no knowledge of "how his own wit runneth."[203] The lawyer tries to make men good, but only in the negative sense that they do no harm to one another.[204] Only the poet would have men love knowledge and virtue in a fashion that would actualize that love in "well-doing." His moving of audiences is superior to others' teaching because it is "well nigh the cause and effect of teaching." He persuades, "for who will be taught, if he be not moved with desire to be taught?"[205] As a lover, he witnesses and manifests his own desire so that he can draw forth the love of his mistress "by that same forcibleness or *energeia* (as the Greeks call it)."[206]

Tendency is at work in the poet, the audience, and the subject matter. Cicero is thus admirable for his often poetical power "to make us know the force love of our country hath in us."[207] His influence moves his audience toward a love that is in part already theirs, and which complements the orator by working its own persuasion from within. Elsewhere Sidney argues that the audience responds to the poet's "perfect picture" with the sight of its own soul, in which the poet's "lively knowledge" satisfies "inward conceits." Illuminated by the poet's pictures, audiences should "straightways grow, without need of any description, to a judicial comprehending of them."[208] No matter how recalcitrant, audiences wish to see the form of goodness,[209] and so can respond to its higher calling as well as the influence of the poet. The hard-hearted king cannot resist "the sweet violence of a tragedy" unless he does ungentle violence to his own longing "in despite of himself."[210]

These lines of argument partly emerge from, and shade back into, Sidney's reductive Horatian formula that poetry should teach and delight. To the extent that Sidney treats poets, audiences, and subject matters as though they called to one another's tendencies and were subjects of judgment, he resists the Horatian argument's turning away from desire—its treating delight simply as a tool, or its universalizing of delight to make it the same for everyone. In the final stages of the *Defence,* he strengthens his resistance by connecting delight with nobility. Insofar as comic delight is supposed to elicit a joy proportioned to nature and to an audience's judgment and character, the poet recognizes that to delight is to persuade aspiring souls, which are of as many kinds as there are judgments and characters. Laughter without delight is by contrast formless and ignoble, a "scornful tickling" concerned with the unfamiliar and the unnatural. Ignoring the distinctions of judgment and desire, it indulges what is alien to distinction and to character itself.[211]

These supporting arguments assist a reading of several of Sidney's more central, apparently anti-Timaeic contentions. The poet "never affirms," Sidney writes, and so never lies or "maketh circles about your imagination to conjure you to believe for true what he writes."[212] Might true poetry then abjure persuasion altogether as mere conjuring, along with any pretense to bringing true things into being? But Sidney here is talking about poetry's superiority to histories that merely tell "what is, or is not." What is true for the historian is merely what is, and poetry does not devote itself to affirming the truth of historical fact. Poetry's concern is with "what should be," and in that suasory mode it brings forth what is beyond historical fact. Xenophon's poetical Cyrus is truer than the historical one because the poet captures the very idea of Cyrian nobility, a reality one is presumed not to doubt. The centaur and the other mixed beings of poetical lore not found in nature are in this sense true to those foreconceits or ideas that make them most suggestive and compelling as residents of worlds beyond history. A certain kind of poetic conjuring might convert audiences into beasts or courtiers whose honesty made them more than human, as Pugliano's jest might have done if Sidney had not playfully confronted him. In the end of the treatise Sidney himself resorts to a conjuring ("I conjure you") that he makes seem as non-goetic as possible. The irony of the conclusion displays and tempers the persuasiveness of his public prose.

Sidney's second famous assertion, that nature's world "is brazen" while "the poets only deliver a golden"[213] is similarly ambiguous. What seems to be an obvious assertion of poetry's superiority to nature depends upon an alchemical metaphor. In one sense, the golden world is utterly beyond anything natural. In another, however, the metaphor suggests that poetical making might not sunder itself from less transcendent things: what is brazen is an alloy of copper, a metal that in alchemical lore has a propensity for becoming gold.

Analogously, Sidney's well-known comparison between the poet and the Maker of all retains a Timaeic coloring within an extended biblical analogy:

> Neither let it be deemed too saucy a comparison to balance the highest point of man's wit with the efficacy of Nature; but rather give right honour to the heavenly Maker of that maker, who having made man to His own likeness, set him beyond and over all the works of that second nature: which in nothing he showeth so much as in poetry, when with the force of a divine breath he bringeth things forth far surpassing her doings, with no small argument to the credulous of that first accursed fall of Adam, since our erected wit maketh us know what perfection is, and yet our infected will keepeth us from reaching unto it.[214]

The analogy suggests a genesis *ex nihilo* in the poetic maker's art; yet Sidney refers only to the making of Adam from dust, into which God breathes life. In that context, the imitating poet would bring forth, not generate from nothing, his own "second nature" as God engenders life in the latter days of creation from matter already created.

The elusiveness of Sidney's incorporation of Timaeic principles enables him to distance poetry from magic, much as his irony permits him to distinguish poetry from lying. In the way he argues that the poet affirms nothing, he raises a fantastical edifice of praise that overtakes Pugliano's playful praise of his horse. Yet the very mode of his distinguishing between poet and the conjurer is a persuasion that employs non-goetic, Timaeic power. His denial ("The poet never maketh any circles about your imagination"[215]) clarifies, rather than merely contradicts, the force of his concluding statement, "I conjure you."[216]

Sidney gives way to the authority of poetry's divine models without consistently aligning poetry with their anti-Timaeic implications. He goes so far as to condemn Plutarch's *Isis and Osiris*,[217] and to reject the moral philosopher's ancient adage, "follow Nature."[218] But he does so in the context of praising Plutarch's poetical superiority to pagan philosophers, and of showing that moral philosophers are no poets because they try to teach by denying desire. The Psalmist's desire, which Sidney praises above all, is anachronistically neo-Platonic as well as pious: David's poems show him "a passionate lover of that unspeakable and everlasting beauty to be seen by the eyes of the mind, only cleared by faith."[219]

Although Sidney quickly retreats from the argument that David's divine verse is paradigmatic of all poetry, he does not merely fall back to a defense of mimetic and didactic poetry. His turn away from prophetic poetry is "a more ordinary opening" of the subject that makes more "palpable" what has gone before.[220] It will not necessarily abandon higher things, for it draws them out more substantially and compellingly than non-poetical philosophers and historians can. It is at this point that the argument concentrates upon poetry that imitates "what may be, and should be," including that "well-doing" which goes beyond the mere avoidance of vice that is taught, badly, by the moral philosophers who harbor unjust contempt for "outward things," especially "glory."[221] Coming to the fore in this turn of the argument, Sidney's strident and tentative defense of poetical action covers and draws from models that are nearly coeval with the Psalms, more aspiring than Horatian imitations, and more telling than the teachings of didacts.

Nature and Concealment in Courtly Gesture

I

Sidney's dependence upon irony in the *Defence* is a reminder that although the persuasive forms of the sixteenth century's rhetorical figures are thought capable of revealing the true form of the poet's and orator's meaning and subject matter, they are also by their nature what Puttenham calls "abuses or rather trespasses in speach, because they passe the ordinary limits of common vtterance." According to that compendium of commonplaces, *The Arte of English Poesie,* those abuses "deceiue the eare and also the minde, drawing it from plainnesse and simplicite to a certaine doublenesse, whereby our talke is the more guileful & abusing." Thus metaphor, for all that may be said of its clarifying power, is "an inuersion of sense by transport," and allegory is "a duplicite of meaning or dissimulation vnder couert

and darke intendments."[1] Puttenham excuses the figures from the
censure of the Areopagites, who banned all figurative speeches, for
two reasons that call out for explanation: the poet engages in the
harmless pursuits of mirth and pleasure, not the grave business of the
courts where figurative expression might pervert the judge; more
important, the poet uses his figures in accordance with decorum,
which Puttenham defines as "a special regard to all circumstances of
the person, place, time, cause, and purpose he hath in hand." What
might be "heresies of language" in one context are decorous in others.[2]

The circuitous, shadowing course of Sidney's argument is decorous
in this second sense. The *Defence* leads to a conclusion that is self-
consciously incomplete, despite its glossy finish: "believe, with me,
that there are many mysteries contained in poetry, which of purpose
were written darkly, lest by profane wits it should be abused."[3] Right
poetry, as Sidney most prominently takes it up, is bright and lively,
as though it could shine forth the significance of everything to all
men; but the ingratiating eloquence of the *Defence* itself is a drape, as
Sidney hints in his recollection of Pugliano's power to delude.

Puttenham's defense of the figures does not disavow, despite his
defense of harmless pleasures in poetry, his original argument for the
dissimulative function of the figures. Decorum saves them from the
charge of linguistic heresy, but it does not efface the traces of their
affinities with dissimulation. He plays out this more complex argument in his discussion of allegory as the "Courtier," or the "figure
of faire semblant." At first, he embraces the notion that the end of
allegory, like that of the courtier, is "cunningly to be able to dissemble."[4] The properly educated courtier will "neuer speake as he thinkes,
or thinke as he speaks"; "in matter of any importance his words and
his meaning very seldome meete."[5] Although *The Arte* goes on to
condemn such courtly behavior as foreign and unbecoming to English
courtiers and poets, Puttenham's consequent defense of a proper poetic cunning actually perfects the courtier's concealing gestures in
terms that correspond with Castiglione's doctrine of *sprezzatura*:
"therefore leauing these manner of dissimulations to all base-minded
men, & of vile nature or misterie, we doe allow our Courtly Poet to
be a dissembler only in the subtilties of his arte, that is, when he is
most artificiall, so to disguise and cloake it as it may not appare, nor
seeme to proceede from him by any studie or trade of rules, but to
be his naturall."[6] Again the dissimulation is restricted to the "subtilties" in the poet's art; but these are his most "artificiall." The poet's

figurative grace proceeds most aptly from the maker who somehow hides his study of perfective ornament so that it may "be his naturall."

It is tempting to conclude from these matters that Puttenham is merely resorting to the hackneyed commonplace that art should hide art, so that he can escape the jaws of an argument in which he rejects artful concealment and yet tries to maintain the respectability of poetry. However, the idea that rhetorical or poetic figures can save and help form a subject by concealing it is not the same as the more general notion, explored in the previous chapter, that figures clarify their subjects and their users' meanings by working them toward perfection. Puttenham seems to be touching upon something more than standard definitions of suggestive figures such as those set out by Abraham Fraunce, in which for example the figure *praeteritio* or "pretended omitting" allows us to note what is missing "in the verie shewe of praetermission, as when we say; I let this passe."[7] Rather, it is something not altogether removed from Castiglione's principle of the mask, a means of concealment that protects what otherwise would not have been formed within its cloud. *The Arte* is relatively Horatian—certainly not Hermetic—in its emphasis upon appropriate effect; but the notion that concealment creates an impression of naturalness has broader implications in the context of sixteenth-century conceptions of revelatory disguise. Demetrius lends his ancient authority to the idea that allegory is a "hidden meaning" that establishes the importance of matters "likely to be considered commonplace" if presented as something "clear and obvious." On the other hand, the cryptic figure is not strictly a keeper of esoteric truths: it is "impressive, especially in threats," as though it had a superior power to embody the threat in cloaking it. Allegory in this sense covers what would otherwise be as unfigured as "men without their clothes."[8]

In *The Courtier*, Sir Fridericke argues without opposition for the necessity of the courtier's masking all his public exercises in dance and war. The disguise enables him to prove his virtue in ways that open dealing cannot. In Thomas Hoby's phrasing, "there is no way" to knowing the courtier's character "if a man will show himselfe in open sightes about such matters [e.g. his nimbleness], whether it be in armes, or out of armes":

> Because to be in a maske bringeth with it a certaine libertie and lycence, that a man may emong other thinges take uppon him the fourme of that he hath best skill in, and use bente studye and pre-

ciseness about the principall drift of the matter wherin he will shewe himselfe, and a certaine Reckelesness aboute that is not of importaunce, which augmenteth the grace of the thinge, as it were to disguise a yonge man in an olde mannes attire, but so that his garmentes be not a hindraunce to him to shew his nimblenes of person.[9]

The courtier in fact wears two forms: the one "he hath best skill in," the other—the guise of an old man—that allows him "a certain Reckelesness" that graces the whole of his action. The first is a covering that draws out and finishes his capacity for study and precision. The second, the old man's attire, is concealment by which the recklessness of youth is affined to the old man's privileged carelessness. Here the mask enables the courtier to display his skill. The audience might know the courtier beforehand, but in this case does not know him until he puts on the mask, which allows him to set forth his virtue with greater concentration and more liberal grace. Without masks, a prince can not long make real his authority because he "loseth the libertie to do all those thinges that are out of the dignity of a prince."[10]

As an ornament, the mask trims by taking away as well as augmenting: the visored prince is "stripping himself of the person of a prince" at the same time that he declares a prowess undisclosed by his merely "being a prince." Without disguise, "he might easily make men beleave that he keepeth the persone of a prince because he will not be beaten but spared of the rest: beside that, doing in sport the very same he should do in good earnest whan neede required, it woulde take away his authoritye in deede and would appeere in lyke case to be play also."[11] Gaming in his ornamental mask, the prince can be taken more seriously as he proves that his rule is a kind of regal play that enacts his virtue.

For Castiglione the courtier fashions his character by means of the concealing, discovering power of his ornamentation. He acts "by placing of the figures contrarie"[12] as a poetical painter uses line and light to "discover" depth and distance,[13] employing "shadow" to "make the lightes of high places to appeere, and so with light [to] make lowe the shadowes of plaines." He must "meddle divers coulours together, so that throughe the diversitie bothe the one and the other are more sightly to beholde." Shadows are here fadings of color that feign and shape. (*Faint* and *feign* derive from the Latin *fingere*: to shape, invent, feign.)

Sightliness is therefore not the same as clarity. "Lowlines is muche to be commended in a Gentilman that is of prowesse and well seene in armes,"[14] not simply because prowess shines brighter when it emerges from obscurity, but because prowess and lowliness can appropriately cloud one another. There is something necessarily cryptic in the courtier's self-fashioning; his success in the world of *The Courtier* largely depends upon how he withholds himself in the manner of his self-presentation. That paradoxical drawing of himself, as if he were an embroidered curtain opening and closing simultaneously, is his *sprezzatura*.

Sixteenth-century commonplaces about eloquent ornamentation and persuasion become more accessible to a modern understanding as one begins to appreciate the analogy between Castiglione's fashioning of character and the poet's decorous rendering of his subject. For example, the Count's complex pronouncements upon women's cosmetics and their relation to female virtue are complementary additions to the commonplaces we have just discussed. He refers to the dangers of false ornament, but also entertains the possibility that there is a manner of cosmetic veiling that might be commendable. Although such decoration is often merely "couriousness," whereby women "discover openlye unto everye man the over great desire that ye [women] have to be beawtiful," a woman might be graceful in showing "so litle" trimming that the beholder is "in doubt whether she be trimmed or no."[15] The doubt—the entertainment of the possibility of genuine trimming—can be more compelling than the certainty of purity.

The woman of enigmatical ornament is surprisingly similar to the woman of purity Bembo goes on to favor: the one who "is manifestlye seene" to have "nothinge uppon her face" even though she delights the eye with that play of apposite colors which comprises courtly grace. The shifting juxtaposition of paleness and blush upon her cheeks is taken in but "not regarded." And much as the woman who paints with a graceful restraint that leaves the beholder in doubt whether she paints at all, the woman of purer beauty shows herself "by happe out of order . . . without showing her self to bestow diligence or study." Bembo's praise of her apparent artlessness is in this sense applicable to the woman of cosmetics whose art is neither seen nor invisible. Art hides art in this sense: it "best pleaseth the eyes and mindes of men, that stande alwayes in awe to be deceived by art."[16]

In his preface, Hoby attempts to assure his moral reader that such art in the Italian book is virtuous; but he does so in terms that sustain Castiglione's emphasis upon grace as a genuinely cosmetic art. Cheek's letter, printed with Hoby's introduction, sounds a warning against England's borrowing "counterfeitness of other thinges to attire her self withall."[17] Hoby anticipates the objection in terms of a similar metaphor for covering, but one that affirms its ethical function. He dedicates the work "To Ladyes and Gentlewomen," as "a mirrour," by which they might "decke and trimme themselves with vertuous condicions, comely behaviours and honest entertainment toward al men."[18] In the later passage on cosmetics, attiring and covering for all their ambiguity come to be understood as the essential motions of self-definition; the "recklessness" of a character's disguise is a swerve away from an "over great desire" to impress.[19]

The courtier's ornamental gestures thus draw his character as though it were a curtain that closed as it opened, and opened as it closed. Insofar as the arras of his gesture is a tapestry of his ethos, it also outlines or forms the character in an action that must be woven and read over time and with adequate preparation. The special ceremony in the courtier's arraying unfolds his virtue, withholding and presenting it simultaneously. The ruling metaphor is of course organic, but of a particular kind. When Castiglione describes the courtier's figurative use of words in terms of the grafting of trees, his metaphor implies that the tree's temporal growth toward fruition drew out something that remained beyond the figure's reach:

> Sometime I would have him [the courtier] take certaine wordes in an other significacion then that is proper to them, and wrasting them to his purpose (as it were) graffe them lyke a graffe of a tree in a more luckye stocke, to make them more sightly and faire and (as it were) draw the matters to the sense of the verye eyes, and (as they saie) make them felte wyth hande, for the delyte of him that heareth, or readeth.[20]

The parentheses look two ways, toward qualification of the analogy as a mere figure, and toward the imaginative confirmation of a deeper truth about metaphorical language. "As it were" appropriately refers back to "wrasting," as though to deny the impression that metaphor is merely an arbitrary yoking of word and purpose. As the same time, the qualification casts doubt forward, to the adequacy of "graffe" as a metaphor for metaphor. The passage adumbrates the paradoxical function of ornamental figures as artful perfections of a tree's matter that are so palpable to the sense as to be "felte wyth hande," and yet so dependent upon the tree and its "matters," which they draw into view, that their existence as meaningful perfections is highly contingent. Such ripe fruit easily falls to the touch, separating itself with proverbial alacrity from its stock.

The almost accidental relation of courtly words and gestures to courtly character is for Castiglione an aspect of *sprezzatura*, which Hoby translates as "Reckelesness." In fact, as "the true fountain from the whych all grace spryngeth," it brings with it "another ornamente," by which the courtier's most accidental motions, like gracenotes, can greatly amplify his virtue:[20]

> [I]t imprinteth in the myndes of the lookers on an opinyon, that whoso can so sleyghtly do well, hath a great deale more knowledge then indeede he hath: and if he wyll apply hys study and dilygence to that he doeth, he myght do it much better . . . . in daunsinge, one measure, one mocion of a bodye that hath a good grace, not beyng forced, doeth by and by declare the knowledge of him that daunseth.[22]

Here the lack of knowledge "indeede" is no vacancy of knowledge, but a potency given signification in a nearly negligent grace. The deed will confirm what the courtier has already done so "sleyghtly" and "well" in his own covering disregard. Virtue is drawn forth by the courtly inadvertence of his gesture, as a line when "sleightly drawen" by a pencil "tendeth" toward "the peincters purpose" more truly than it does as the obvious result of study or of art.[23]

If the ultimate significance of the courtier's doings emerges from the turn or swerve in his manner, he must somehow transcend the mutability and corruption of manners, about which Castiglione cautions his reader and himself in his first pages:

> [S]ometime it proceadeth that maners, garmentes, customes, and facions whiche at sometyme have beene in price, becumme not regarded, and contrarywyse the not regarded, becumme of price. Therfore it is manifestlye to be descerned, that use hath greater force than reason, to bringe up newe inventions emonge us, and to abolishe the olde, of the whiche who so goeth about to judge the perfection, is often tymes deceyved.[24]

This is one reason for Castiglione to write a dialogue, a swerving from declarations of fashion-bound precepts, and why his dialogue develops as a mediated recollection rather than a direct and didactic projection. Whereas all teaching books set an order of rules, and thereby submit by default to the unreasoned flux of the very fashions they codify, Castiglione turns toward "renunge a gratefull memorye" of past conversation. The book will open itself by commending a memory, not by prescribing a model.

Castiglione's introduction forecasts other manifestations of graceful negligence. His remembrance will "repeat certain reasoninges," as though careless as to the meaning of their order; yet as he renews his "gratefull" memory, he will enter—without seeming to care for himself—the stream of the old, excellent reasonings. Since he has not heard the discussions first-hand he lets fall the news that he seeks to remember what his informant remembered. When he finally resolves not "to swarve from the pourpose" and to "arryve in good order at the ende," his actual purpose is to "*disclose* the cause of the reasoninges that hereafter followe"—not teach or analyze them as we might expect.[25]

Using these terms, Hoby praises Castiglione for resembling Cicero. *The Courtier*, like *De Oratore*, is admirable in not relying upon rules, and in its "call to rehearsall" of matters debated by eloquent men.[26] The rehearsal is most literally a repetition of the old debate, but as we have noted its enactment of the past is not direct, and not necessarily complete. *The Courtier* from the beginning is in this regard more indirect and playful than Cicero's self-consciously circuitous dialogue.

One of the Count's early pronouncements on the nature of his courtly conversation sets the work's tone of caution amidst levity, its shying away from trying overmuch to find the essence of courtly virtue in the power and ornament of a courtly style: "In everye thynge it is so harde a mater to knowe the true perfeccion, that it is almoste unpossible, and that by reason of the varieties of judgementes."[27] Here the operative term is "almoste." The subject is approachable, though only by indirection:

> Yet doe I thinke that eche thing hath his perfeccion, althoughe it be hid, and with reasonable dyscourses myght be judged of hym that hath knowlege in the matter. And for as much as the trueth (as I have sayd) is oftentymes hid, and I take not upon me to have this knowledge, I cannot praise but that kynde of Courtyers which I set most by, and allow that whiche semeth unto me most nigh the trueth, in my smal judgement . . . . also unto my self it may appere sometime one thing, sometime another.[28]

The verbs hold the thought. He will essentially *judge* that perfection, and so wait for it to emerge; he will not seek it out. He assumes that his judging, like that of the more knowledgeable man, is really praise ("I cannot praise but that kynde"). And in praising he *allows* (literally extols: the word draws from *adlaudare*) rather than prescribes. Finally, in his concession that the truth "may appere" variously to him, he maintains the relation—as well as the distinction—between the perfection he praises and its many possible manifestations to the imperfect eye. The entire subject is treated in terms adaptable to the melding of indirection and petition in a ceremony of reverence.

Castiglione's most doctrinal passage about how matter is perfected by form reveals some of the Timaeic complications underlying that ceremony. When his actors compare the virtues of men and women, the commonplaces do not settle the dispute. One speaker labors to prove that men are obviously superior to women, since men are forms that perfect material femininity;[29] his answerer discovers a complexity in the commonplace that justifies the argument that the "Species of *Homo*" perfects both men and women, whose difference according to their sexes is "an accidental matter and no essential."[30] Here the ethical meanings of gestures that distinguish female from male, by which courtly love attracts so much interest in the remainder of Book III, are as problematic as the courtly gestures of *sprezzatura*. Everyone supposes that the idea of the courtier informs the *materia* of its aspirants, and that "reckless" action is evidence of that perfection; but the essential relation between gesture and character, for all the dialogue's emphasis upon the courtier's ethos and his mastery of technique, darkens before the busy eye.

In keeping with the ephemeral nature of *sprezzatura* in *The Courtier*'s ready formulations of courtly virtue, the process of teaching that virtue is obscure. Hoby's phrasing emphasizes its ritualistic character, for example in the passage describing how the courtier might persuade his imperfect prince toward higher things. Castiglione's courtier would give the prince the bitter medicine of moral reformation, but do so as though the prince were a spirit to be well conjured and coaxed, his way covered with flowers, shade, and commendation. The courtier must lead his prince

throughe the roughe way of vertue (as it were) deckynge yt about with boowes to shadowe yt and strawinge it over wyth sightlye flouers, to ease the greefe of the peinfull journey in hym that is but of a weake force. And sometyme with musike, somtime with armes, and horses, sometyme with rymes and meeter, otherwhyle wyth communication of love, and wyth all those wayes that these Lordes have spoken of, continuallye [may] keepe that mynde of his occupyed in honest pleasure: imprintynge notwythstandynge therin alwayes beesyde . . . in companie with these flickeringe provocations some vertuous condicion, and beguilinge him with a holsome craft, as the warie phisitiens do, who manye times whan they minister to yonge and tender children in ther sicknesse, a medicin of a bitter taste, annoint the cupp about the brimm with some sweete licour. The Courtier therfore applyinge to such a pourpose this veile of pleasure, in everie time, in everie place, and in everye exercise he shall attaine to his end . . . .[31]

Read merely as advice on how to sway one's patron, the passage is a rule of manipulation: to win his prince's favor and guide him properly, the courtier must make his discourse a "veil of pleasure." But the device, like the mode by which it persuades, is a shadowy reflection of its end. The veil is like a "sweet licour" that covers the taste of a bitter medicine. In anointing the cup, the doctor honors the drink whose taste he hides: the sweetness of the veil is a remembrance of a higher thing, for on the previous page bitterness is said to characterize vice while sweetness marks that virtue which is "hid under that litle bitternesse."[32] The medicine of persuasion is thus here a reversed, cloudy image both of the thing it overcomes and the thing it affirms. The courtier does similar homage to the prince's way on the rough road to virtue, "deckyng" and "strawinge" it with "flickeringe" graces that suggest but do not presume to image the prospect of the prince's happiness. The courtier is himself an ornament of his prince—an allegory of high importance that the prince elicits for the sake of his own education in virtue. Carefully subordinate, almost accidental, the courtier is formed by the prince whom he forms. The ornamental, formative relation of microcosm and macrocosm in Asclepius comes to mind.

Insofar as Castiglione's courtier teaches his prince virtue, he does so with a kind of emblem, by inscription rather than prescription. His teachings, if they can be called such, are "vertuous condicion[s]" affixed to his ornamental activities by his "imprintynge" them in a manner "beesyde" and "in companie" with them. The connection between moral sign and delightful activity must be merely problematic as long as one supposes that the sign simply labels the ornament didactically. In fact, Hoby's diction intimates no sign or moral in the courtier's didactic turns. The courtier imprints a "vertuous condicion" upon the prince's entertainments: he somehow marks an attribute as though with an emblem, as though with a quality that seems to have been present to begin with, at least in some form, in the prince's regimen of "honest" pleasures. The hypothesis that Castiglione manipulates the prince, that he uses careful negligence to trick him up toward virtue, ignores these discursive facts.

2

If concealment is an essential function of figured speech, its status and meaning are richly problematic in rhetoric, as well as in poetry. In this regard Boccaccio's definition of poetry as veiling allegory is applicable, at least to a degree, to poetical rhetoric.[33] Some forms of discursive gestures, intended to set subjects forth and to persuade, envelop what they clothe. Indeed they cannot be discursive, cannot complement the gist of Castiglione or the traditional rhetoricians, unless they also withhold themselves. In terms of Timaeic rhetoric, inappropriate clarity can damage the character of the speaker, the audience, and his subject matter.

In the *Phaedrus*, of course, Socrates warns against hothouse rhetoric that forces audiences to grow into spindly plants incapable of inhabiting a world outside of false speech.[34] The delaying and unfolding of the dialogue has to do with the proper persuasion of various kinds of character without violating the soul. The dialogue's subject and meaning are elusive, and can be dangerously misunderstood or ignored if either participant's enthusiasm for speeches or his appetite for sleep were to prevail. The obscurity of Socrates' means of persuasion—the irony by which he draws Phaedrus toward a higher idea of rhetoric—needs the aid of an idea of definition and a powerful set of myths that can take Socratic garb and stir Phaedrus from his infatuation with the ready conclusions of manipulative oratory.

The spirit of Socrates' disguise is leagues away, but not entirely foreign to, the Horatian notion that art ought to hide art, which even for the oratory-minded Horace is an ethical as well as an artistic principle—and so not consistently reducible to calculation for effect. For Horace, the poet's proper veering from the "common matter" he imitates is meant in some degree to obscure his source in order to preserve his character as a maker rather than a copier.[35] To a degree, the maker's concealment of his model's matter and style expresses his respect for what he would not presume to copy directly. In Ben Jonson's phrase, it permits him to give evidence of his own wisdom in work "humour'd right"[36]—work that aspires to acknowledge its debt without foolishly declaring it.

To a critic such as Puttenham, the ethical undertone to the notion that art should be hidden co-exists with his praise for decorous display. Both principles inform the paradoxical conclusion to *The Arte*, where Puttenham finally makes the poet most admirable in seeming to act artlessly with "peculiar vertue and proper instinct" as nature does,[37] but then adds that the poet's feats of language "suggested and vttered" by nature are no better than those "polished" by art.[38] Puttenham yokes the two ideas in the next sentence: "Therefore shall our Poet receaue prayse for both, but more by knowing of his arte then by vnseasonable vsing it . . ." The knowing that characterizes natural eloquence, which does not show itself unseasonably, is akin to a fair dissembling that transcends those corruptions of character that come from false affectation and indiscretion. The true poet is "more commended for his naturall eloquence then for his artificiall, and more for his artificiall well disembled then for the same ouermuch affected and grossely or vndiscretly bewrayed, as many makers and Oratours do."[39]

This model of subtle unfolding is crucial to theories of style and ethical development in the sixteenth and early seventeenth centuries. Thomas Wright draws upon it when he defends the man who does not "blab out" his conceits. More than a moral cliché, his argument derives decorous speaking from the deliberate and appropriate preparation of the speaker's demeanor and the proper ripening of his subject matter.[40]

A locus for the commonplace is Eramus's *Ciceronianus*, where it develops into a rich defense of the imitation of Cicero. Erasmus rejects a false Ciceronian's attempt to transfer Cicero into the imitator's work as though the Orator were a package of figures. Proper Ciceronianism is really the cultivation of the imitator's character and subject matter, in accordance with Cicero's "facts and ideas" and the "power" of his "mind and judgment." The "surface" of Cicero's speech is not his essence:[41] "I favor imitation, but imitation that aids rather than hinders nature; that corrects rather than destroys nature's gifts."[42] Followers of the best ancient authors should find "what in each excells and accords with your own genius—not just adding to your speech all the beautiful things that you find, but digesting them and making them your own, so that they may seem to have been born from your mind and not borrowed from others. . . ."[43] Imitation that aids nature would thus conceal its parentage while enacting and perfecting it. It would be an "offspring" that reflected "the living image of the parent" in its own parenting. Himself citing venerable precedents in the advice of Cortesi and Politian, Erasmus wishes "to resemble Cicero not as an ape resembles a man but as a son resembles his parent."[44]

The common sense in Erasmus's tenor complements his complexity. Imitators must diverge from their models—and thereby partly obscure them—in much the way that children must learn to walk by following but not over-rigorously copying their superiors: "he cannot walk well who always puts his foot in the track of another." In more philosophical terms, the imitator follows his model in order to emulate, complete, and perhaps surpass it according to the predecessor's unrealized idea, perhaps not for the sake of making something similar or different: "an imitator does not desire to say the same things so much as he does to say similar things, nay sometimes not even similar but even equal; an emulator strives even to speak better if he can, and no one was ever so finished an artist that you could not find in his work something which could be done better."[45] Erasmus's advocate Bulephorus delights in the paradox of an "unlike" imitation's being "greater" than imitation in copying its model's desired form "more perfectly."[46]

But even this indirect imitation is not sufficiently circuitous if it does not cover itself with the aid of an Erasmian *sprezzatura*. One must spurn the pseudo-Ciceronian, straightforward directions for style in the popular *Rhetorica Ad Herenium*; they are written by "a stammerer in comparison with Cicero."[47] They are inadvertent parodies of directness because they are oblivious to the imperative to conceal: "I should not want this imitation to be sought too anxiously and too religiously; for this very thing hinders us from accomplishing our desire."[48] To follow Cicero properly, one must hide art with art as he advised.[49]

Erasmian concealment involves the imitator's honoring and perfecting his nature as he does his subject, improving "pliable nature" but not presuming, as the pseudo-Ciceronian Nosoponus would, to change every thing into something else by means of the "persistent labor" of a heedless alchemy. The aping Nosoponus had said, "there is nothing which persistent labor cannot overcome . . . . What hinders the genius of man also from being transformed by training and practice?"[50] Erasmus's advocate is more cautious, and more independent of Ciceronian excess. He is impressed by the deep-rooted differences among natural things ("earth is never turned into fire, nor fire into water"[51]) and the deceptive likenesses, as between the ape and man, that can hide those differences. He is also interested in how different things can be alike, in ways that man might imitate without presuming to identify himself with them or to master them: "no animal in all its members approaches nearer to the figure of man than the ape, and so like is it that if nature had added a voice it could seem a man; again nothing is more unlike man than a peacock or a swan—and yet, I think, you would prefer to be a swan or a peacock rather than an ape."[52] If one wishes to imitate Cicero properly, one must understand that he is ultimately complete not in his works but "in himself," and that therefore the imitator must somehow express his own nature in his imitation of Cicero. Without his proper transformation within, his speech will be a "false mirror" smeared with paints rather than decorated.[53]

The pseudo-Ciceronian encrusts his model with ornament the way a bad dressmaker makes the dress, and the image it clothes, conform to the ornaments.[54] Both are idolaters, not because they drape the image—Erasmus takes for granted the true dressmaker's archetypal role—but because they seek with vaunting directness to manipulate the dressing with ornamental figures that neglect at least three things: the image's true form, the animating power of decorous dress, and the aspiring nature of the dressmaker's being.

III

ADVANCEMENTS AND REFORMULATIONS

Baconian Nature

I

Books of the old magical learning, Bacon argues in the opening to Book II of *De Augmentis*, need not be burned to make room for the works of the new, since the new ones will be "of such a kind that like the serpent of Moses, they may devour the serpents of the enchanters" (*De Aug* IV.290). The reference to Moses' defeat of the Egyptian magicians, despite Bacon's accommodating tone, is an argument for the new learning's power to incorporate magic—and by extension the entire Timaeic tradition—by devouring it. Bacon uses Moses to bless the new learning's incorporation and transformation of the magician's lore and the complex of ideas that gives shape to the Timaeic tradition in the English Renaissance.

Bacon goes further in his Mosaic analogy. He is reported to have said (in a statement his secretary, William Rawley, set down in cipher) that "he thought Moses was the greatest sinner that was, for he never knew any break both tables [of the law] at once but he" (*RCB* VII.181). The reference is to Exodus 32.19, where Moses' righteous anger and revelatory mission justify his shattering of the tables when he sees the Israelites given over to idolatry. Although Rawley's anecdote is second-hand evidence, it alludes to a crux in Exodus that would have offered a ready comparison between Mosaic wisdom and a new learning that responds to men's worship of the idols of the cave, tribe, marketplace, and theater by breaking the old wisdom into aphoristic bits. In Exodus, the word of truth is re-introduced only after Moses subjects the Israelites to the ordeal of drinking the dust of their idol, which he has ground down and dissolved in water. The punishment is a test; according to Mosaic law, the drinking of dust tests a woman accused of adultery (Numbers 5). The new learning similarly takes in idolatries and bits of nature collected in the new natural histories, proving its abnegation of vain hopes so that the tablets of truth can be re-constituted.

Bacon strengthens the new learning's association with Moses in his description of the "rational knowledges" traditionally assigned to rhetoric: those having to do with invention, judgment, memory, and delivery. These austere "keys of all others arts" (yet to the masses the "least delightful" of studies) man has vainly spurned in favor of "knowledges that are drenched in flesh and blood" such as history, morality, and policy, which appeal to "men's affections, praises, fortunes." In sum, the mass of men have enacted the Israelites' rejection of the manna that Moses tells them the Lord has given them to eat.[1] In the same passage of De Augmentis, Bacon makes the identification explicit:

> [I]n that knowledge is *pabulum animi* [the food of the mind]; so in the nature of men's appetite to this food, most men are of the taste and stomach of the Israelites in the desert, that would fain have returned *ad allas carnium* [to the flesh-pots], and were weary of manna; which, though it were celestial, yet seemed less nutritive and comfortable. So generally men taste well knowledges that are drenched in flesh and blood . . . (*De Aug* IV.383)

Those men who eat "this same *lumen siccum* [this dry light]" partake of the manna that "doth parch and offend most men's watery and soft natures" (383). In partaking of the rational knowledges' "celestial" wisdom, they prosper before God in the wilderness of their mechanical abstinence from the passions.

The precise relation between wisdom and the transmission of revelatory knowledge in the new learning is explained in De Augmentis with reference to Moses' relation to Aaron, his brother and spokesman: "For what a distance there is between them [wisdom and eloquence] is shown in the words spoken by God to Moses, when he declined the office assigned him on the ground that he was no speaker." Following the passage in Exodus in which God says that Aaron will serve as the slow-tongued prophet's speaker, Bacon argues that eloquence is "doubtless inferior to wisdom" because Moses will stand in God's place as the oracle of what Aaron will speak (*De Aug* IV.454).[2] Solomon has said that eloquence is practically more effective than wisdom (*De Aug* IV.455); but the clear superiority of the law-giving Moses to his mouthpiece Aaron, as it is set out in this intro-duction to "the foundations and office of Rhetoric," is consistent with the deeper function of rhetoric throughout Bacon's works.

Commentators have observed, Bacon says, that there is sometimes "a natural" or "moral . . . sense or reduction of many of the cere-monies and ordinances" in the Mosaic law (*Adv* III.297). For instance, Moses' voice, which according to Bacon is what prevents him from freely imparting God's words to other men, is reduced, in the natural history of the *Sylva Sylvarum*, to an exceedingly mundane yet highly significant subject of physiology. The fact that Moses says he has difficulty speaking is evidence that he has a "defect of speech." The condition, Bacon says, is the result of a cold, dry mouth, which the new, fundamental inquiries into heat and moisture are presumably capable of curing (*SS* II.470). Whereas Moses' slowness of speech and lack of eloquence lead him to depend upon Aaron, the new sciences' promise to cure conditions such as his would give the new learning its own direct speech, which it could then exercise or disguise at will. Without his "defect"—his inability to speak to the multi-tude—Moses would not have to depend upon Aaron, the sometime idolater who is "less firm in character" (*HVM* V.244), in order to convey or carefully garb prophetic truths. There would be no need for a spokesman, no risk of falling into idolatry as Aaron does while Moses lingers on the mount.

One need not believe that these are Bacon's inferences in order to appreciate the relation between Moses' role in the new sciences and that of Orpheus. Moses and Orpheus are ostensibly opposites. Bacon makes the prophet's superiority to Egyptian learning emphatic by attributing the superiority of the righteous serpent to Moses rather than to Aaron, in contradiction of Exodus 7.12. In this context, we are reminded of the commandment against the idolatry of similitudes that Moses delivers from his isolation: "Thou shalt not make unto thee any graven image, or any likeness of any thing that is in heaven above, or that is in the earth beneath, or that is in the water under the earth."[3]

Orpheus is by contrast "the representation of universal Philosophy" because he is "master of all harmony." Bacon remembers that he "subdued and drew all things after him by sweet and gentle meas-ures." Orpheus seems wise, but not in any conceivable Mosaic sense. His chief accomplishment is the near-rescue of his wife from the infernal powers of death, which he effects by means of "the sweetness of his singing and playing" (*SV* VI.729). In that adventure, he is moved first of all "by affection," and moves others so. Although he does not finally succeed in bringing his wife back to life, he is renowned for his power to draw by his lyre "all kinds of wild beasts," as well as stones and trees, "in such manner that putting off their several natures . . . they all stood about him gently and sociably, as in a theater." The Helicon, the river sacred to the Muses, mourns his death (*SV* VI.721). Compared directly with Moses, the traditional Orpheus performs something very close to what The Wisdom of Solomon calls idolatry: the attempt to bring the dead child back to life. To console himself in his failure, he uses his powers "to insinuate into men's minds the love of virtue and equity and peace" and to build cities in which they seek a different kind of immortality "by merit and renown." The pursuit of fame and virtue, according to Bacon, is therefore the activity of a failed universal philosophy that seeks substitutes for a desire to overcome mutability.

There is, however, another Orpheus within or behind the myth of Orpheus, one who conforms to the Mosaic imperative to flee from idolatry. Precisely because the traditional Orpheus' attempt to rescue Eurydice is "moved by affection," he acts in an "impatience of love and anxiety" that proceeds "from no cause more" than from vain curiosity and meddlesomeness. The traditional Orpheus' passions are thus failures of scientific will. Because they are mere encumbrances, they are subject to the control of new Orphic methods of inquiry and transmission. If he had been properly prepared, Orpheus might have succeeded (*SV* VI.722). The possibility that the new methods can conquer the passions, especially the passionate imagination of fear, love, and anger, is foreshadowed in Orpheus' victory over the beasts. In bowing to the harmony of his lyre, the beasts forsake more than their natural passions; they discard their "several natures." The rebirth of Orpheus, which is promised in the bubbling up of new Helicons, entails a more fundamental putting off of yearning in order to control the world's affections with truly archaic harmonies.

Universal philosophy's "noblest work of all" is "nothing less than the restitution and renovation of things corruptible, and (what is indeed the same thing in a lower degree) the conservation of bodies in the state in which they are, and the retardation of dissolution and putrefactions." It is a goal that cannot be effected "otherwise than by due and exquisite attempering and adjustment of parts in nature, as

by the harmony and perfect modulation of the lyre" (*SV* VI.721).
"Perfect" modulation would transcend idolatry if the Orpheus who
brought it about could transcend his own yearning. He could then
turn his attention to the modulation of fame and virtue from the
standpoint of the "exquisite attempering" of science.

2

We can test Bacon's reconfiguration of the myth of Orpheus and its
assimiliation with Bacon's view of Mosaic law by examining the place
of poetry among the new sciences. This is best done by referring to
the theories of genesis in Bacon's natural philosophy, which are a
pattern for his theory of poetry and, by extension, his theory of
rhetoric.

When Bacon speaks of poetry directly, he intones a variety of
commonplaces that passages in other works can most properly gloss.
He declares that poetry can be understood in two senses: as mere
style, having to do only with words, not with matter; and as a conveyance of matter that makes it "one of the principal branches of
learning" (*De Aug* II.315). In its latter role, poetry is supposed to
combine biblical and Orphic functions, though Bacon carefully limits
his assertion with a double qualification: poetry "may" be thought
to partake "somewhat" of a divine nature, "because it raises the mind
and carries it aloft, accommodating the shows of things to the desires
of the mind, not (like reason and history) buckling and bowing down
the mind to the nature of things" (*De Aug* III.316). Poetry shows that
"there is agreeable to the spirit of man a more ample greatness,
a more perfect order, and more beautiful variety than it can any-
where (before the Fall) find in nature" (315–316). Still, what is "agreeable" is, according to the primary doctrines and methods of the new
learning, fundamentally misleading as a source of higher truths.
The similitudes of poetry are effective conveyors of obscure truths
to the senses (317), but the relation between poetical similitude
and truth is here at least as ambivalent as Aaron's translation of
Moses.

Poetry's power is really esoteric. It conceals, enfolds, and sets forth
the higher mysteries of "religion, policy, and philosophy" in fables
and parables that are as significant as they seem to be absurd. There
is a Moses behind Aaron whom the masses do not hear, or do not

know that they hear, or do not realize is different from his spokesman. The truths of poetry are evident in ancient myth if one can detect their signals in absurdity; the true interpreter must leap routinely to something that no man could have conceived: "when a story is told which could never have entered any man's head either to conceive or relate on his own account, we must presume that it had some further reach" (*SV* VI.697).

The myths lack connection with the poets who are thought to make them. Primordial poetry is more likely to be true because it flows from "ancient tradition," "as sacred relics and light airs breathing out of better times," rather than from a poet's vision or the collaboration of poets' memories. The transfer of truths in the ancient myths has been entirely unconscious because no one poet has known what they mean. What poets have added to the source is only "embellishment" that the enlightened interpreter must strip away to get at the unrecognized stratum underneath (*SV* VI.697). The more he removes the passions and imaginations of a single man and of the ancestral affiliations of the poets, the more truthful the residue of his analysis will be.

The interpreter's imagination must therefore become a servant of esoteric truths that do not "excite the faculties of the mind" as the doctrines of Plato have done to mankind's detriment (*FL* III.504). Imagination can then be at home with matters of faith and religion, where similitudes and parables are beyond the reach of scientific analysis or judgment. When imagination prevails over reason in matters of true faith, Bacon declares, its rule is unquestionably pious. In the lower regions, its rule over reason is a guise, no matter how useful it may be in the hands of the enlightened or the inspired: "in all persuasions that are wrought by eloquence and other impressions of nature, which do paint and disguise the true appearance of things, the chief recommendation unto Reason is from the Imagination" (*Adv* III.382).

The permissible functions of the imagination are set out in Bacon's doctrine of the soul, which "must be bounded by religion, or else subject to deceit and delusion" (*Adv* III.379). The new Orpheus is therefore best known for his religious devotion. The last lines of Bacon's demonstration of the wisdom of the ancients in mythical poetry are given to his praise of the power of Orpheus' song to subdue all pleasure in the Sirens' singing: "by singing and sounding forth the praises of the gods," Orpheus is superior to Ulysses and Solomon because he has "confounded the voices of the Sirens and put them aside" (*SV* V.764).

3

Much of Bacon's most esoteric theorizing in universal philosophy is found in two works on the origin of things: *Cogitationes de Natura Rerum (Thoughts on the Nature of Things)* and *De Principiis atque Originibus (On Principles and Origins)*. Here we see his attempt to join Orpheus with Moses and other biblical authorities by modifying the atomism of Democritus. The new Baconian conception of natural "bodies" and their motions, which largely derives from Democritus, is the new Mosaic serpent that Bacon uses to consume the old magicians and to save Orpheus from heresy.

A clue to the maze of Bacon's discussion of matter and its origins is his myth of Coelum, whom he labels "the Origin of Things." In his commentary on the birth of this "most ancient of all the gods," he adumbrates the new learning's transformation of prominent non-biblical commonplaces about the birth of the world. The myth is supposed to confirm the speculations of the atomist Democritus, who claimed that matter was eternal while the world was not. The history of Coelum's offspring denotes the history of matter as successive struggles between father and son ending in the emasculation of the father-gods, and the removal of "all power of generation" from matter's parents. The atomistic axiom of the eternal fixedness of matter is thereby guaranteed. Conversely, the extreme mutability of matter's configurations is evident in what happens next: matter fumbles about, creating "ill-compacted structures of things" and then an unstable "fabric." It threatens to "relapse into its ancient confusion" as long as the emasculated father, Saturn, remains alive. Venus and the Sun can bring only a measure of concord to the continuing "convulsions of the lower regions" (floods, tempests, earthquakes, and so on) until things have "settled at last into a more durable state of consent and harmonious operation" (*SV* VI.723).

Here Bacon uses the Coelum myth to efface Timaeic notions about matter being clothed by form. Order comes to "ill-compacted" matter only by way of vaguely defined beneficent influences such as Venus and the Sun, acting in a manner both obscure and ambiguous. We see that matter moves from extreme disorder to compact structures as soon as Jupiter cuts off the source of new matter that has caused the perturbation. Bacon adds that this ordering occurs when Venus (and so concord) becomes predominant; but his sequence of events emphasizes Jupiter's limitation of the *quantity* of matter, not his divine influence, as the means for making the world coalesce. Jupiter need only free himself, and (according to the logic of Bacon's speculation) thereby threaten to regain the power to generate offspring, for the world to be endangered by that increase of matter that Bacon argues is responsible for the old disorder.

Bacon's commentary outside of the conventional bounds of the biblical Genesis is couched cautiously as a mere "fable" of philosophy: "For we know (through faith) that all such speculations are but the oracles of sense which have long since ceased and failed; the world, both matter and fabric, being in truth the work of the Creator" (*SV* VI.725). But Bacon's theory of interpreting the wisdom of the ancients assumes that the myths are buried oracles that the new learning's hermeneutics can bring back to light. The myth suggests, to those sons of science who know what Bacon is doing with interpretation and the doctrines of Democritus, a theory of matter that accommodates biblical doctrine with the influential though attenuated powers of Venus and the Sun. The new Orpheus, who would know the atomistic mechanism and power of matter, could take advantage of the fixity of true bodies and their apparently unlimited potential for combination.

Just how seriously Bacon takes the Coelum speculation is evident in another prominent rendering of a genesis story in the myth of Pan, or nature, which he embeds in his Latin translation of *The Advancement*. There he surprisingly approves of what he considers to be the anti-atomistic theories of Plato and Aristotle for having "approached much nearer" than the atomists to "the figure of the parable" that tells the story of Pan's birth. His purpose is to use these prominent authorities as perverse approximations of Democritus' belief that nature originates from immutable yet extremely adaptive atoms.

Plato and Aristotle, Bacon explains, "have made Matter as a common harlot, and Forms as Suitors." Indeed, they and their followers "have represented Matter as being entirely despoiled, shapeless, and indifferent to forms." Such a formulation would thereby support the opinion that Pan is the child of Ulysses' wife Penelope, born after her alleged "promiscuous intercourse . . . with all the suitors" (*De Aug* IV.320). The Platonic Ideas, as well as Aristotle's duality of potentiality and actuality, are here reduced to a theory of the perverse exploitation of passive matter by strangers.

In *De Sapientia Veterum*, Bacon distances himself from this interpretation by making it one possibility among three for explaining Pan's origin, and by employing the respected though sometimes contrary authority of Plato and Aristotle. He also disavows such ideas in the *Cogitationes de Natura Rerum*. In that text he calls the association of matter with harlotry "a weak and popular opinion, arising out of superficial appearances and superstition" (*CNR* V.347). Invoking a traditional, Timaeic opinion that the heavens have tendency and the regions below them have characters that are not entirely mutable, he discounts the idea that the heavens and the earth are entirely dissimilar in regard to permanence and change. At the same time, however, his argument intimates that the celestial sphere is far more mutable, and the terrestrial more invulnerable, than is commonly believed. He adapts, for the sake of a new atomism, the story of a defiled yet chaste sublunary Penelope:

> What is further held,—that celestial bodies do not suffer changes, while sub-lunary or, as they call, elementary bodies do; that the matter of the latter is like a harlot, always seeking after new forms, while that of the former is like a matron, delighting in a wedlock constant and undefiled,—seems a weak and popular opinion. . . . For neither is heaven indued with that eternity which they suppose nor the earth with that mutability. . . . For it is only heathen arrogance that endowed the heaven with this prerogative of being incorruptible; whereas the Holy Scriptures assign eternity and corruption to heaven and earth alike, though not to each an equal glory and veneration.   (*CNR* V.437, 439)

What starts out as a comparison of the two regions' passions becomes an identification of their common ambivalence as eternal yet corruptible things.

The theory of invulnerable and mutable substance that replaces these misconceptions is set out more completely in the treatise *On Principles and Origins*. There Bacon praises the pre-Socratic, atomistic consensus that matter by definitioin has form and "the principle of motion" enclosed in itself (*PO* V.467). Matter always has form; their relation is a given in the myth of Cupid, where we see the first atom is already "a person" at its birth (468). The more complex speculations of Plato and Aristotle are mere thoughts and words; "nor can any one think otherwise, unless he plainly deserts experience," not having "submitted" his mind "to the nature of things" (*PO* V.467). The idea that matter is formed in being ornamented over time according to the complex decorum of emulative desire will not stand up to the fact that Cupid is "naked," independent of adornment, and utterly obscure in the ends and sources of his sympathies. What ornamentation and furnishing of matter there is must "be the consequence and emanation" of matter's three undividable components: substance, form, and motion. "[T]hese three are by no means to be separated, only distinguished; and matter (whatever it is) must be held to be so adorned, furnished, and formed, that all virtue, essence, action, and natural motion, may be the consequence and emanation thereof" (*PO* V.468).

It is important to see how Bacon dovetails this adaptation of Timaeic categories with the strictures of Holy Writ, and with the goals he assigns to Orpheus as the personification of the new philosophy. Since Democritus, as Bacon uses him, comes closest to the unwritten "primitive wisdom" of the ancients, Bacon argues that atomism properly interpreted conforms to a principle of faith: the world passes away while God-created matter, which forms all appearances, does not:

> [T]he eternity of the world (such as we now see it) is denied; and this was the conclusion both of the primitive wisdom, and of him who comes nearest to it, Democritus. The same thing is testified by Sacred Writ; the principal difference being, that the latter represents matter also as proceeding from God; the former as self-existing. (*PO* V.491)

Although from the biblical perspective "the existing configuration of the world" could not have grown by matter's own collisions and attempts to combine, Democritus' vision confirms God's power to dispose the world's appearances as he wills them. What we see as eternal is not, and what we see as ephemeral is fixed and infinitely combinable.

Bacon wonders "whether it would have been possible for this created matter, in a long course of ages, by the force which was given it, to have gathered and shaped itself into that perfect configuration (as it did at once without any rounding about at the word of command)." Atomism suggests to him that God might not have had to dispose or order what was made because the nature of matter might have compelled it to take on the appearance of things by itself. But to pursue this matter might entail a heretical inquiry, "a question perhaps not to be asked" (*PO* V.491). Bacon immediately refers his reader to the myth of Coelum, "where I will discuss more fully what now I glance at" (*PO* V.492); but his rendering of that allegory in *De Sapientia Veterum*, as we have seen, avoids the issue again.

In *On Principles and Origins* Bacon does provide a more complete argument. There he describes the atom in terms that are consistent with his theory of "bodies" that are more basic than the atom, have a kind of desire and form, and yet are invulnerable to change:

> [A] necessity plainly inevitable drives men's thoughts (if they would be consistent) to the atom; which is a true being, having matter, form, dimension, place, resistance, appetite, motion, and emanations; which likewise, amid the destruction of all natural bodies, remains unshaken and eternal.   (*PO* V.492)

Such bodies are more truly atomic than the atoms of Democritus. They are irreducible, generative of motion, and available to the maker of a panoply of configurations (*CNR* V.422).[4]

The consequences of this adaptation of Democritus are immense. In positing as fact that "all things are changed, and that nothing really perishes," and that the sum of matter like the fundamental bodies of nature "remains exactly the same," Bacon can set down three "precepts" of experimental procedure that resonate throughout his discussions of the natural and rational knowledges (*CNR* V.426–27). The first is "that men should frequently call upon nature to render her account" whenever a body evident to the senses disappears. That is, the experimenter can and should act as an inquisitorial judge in such cases, examining the accused about what it must have hidden. The severity of the questioning is perfectly justified by the principle that true bodies are not annihilated. The judge must not accept or interpret the account of nature "before it has been shown . . . where the [disappeared] body has gone to" (427). There can be no question that the body has been hidden or transformed, since "nothing [that is, no body] really perishes." The most basic tangible and intangible bodies can only cease to exist by the will of God. Consequently, the experimenter "should omit no way of vexing and working" nature to verify nature's account of itself, and thus to "bring out its ultimate operations and powers of resistance." Here again is the paradigm of Menelaus' torment of Proteus, to which Bacon refers on an adjacent page in his justification of using all possible means to bring nature to a true confession: "we should try to enchain Nature, like Proteus, for the right discovery and distinction of the kinds of motions are the true bounds of Proteus. For according as motions . . . can be spurred on or tied up, so follows conversion and transformation of matter itself" (*CNR* V.425).

A third rule completes the judicial interrogation of matter: men should reject the conventional idea that all change occurs when spirit separates from the tangible substance within which it is confined. It is precisely the confinement or imprisonment of substances and their spirits that provides the best conditions for discovering the nature of bodies. "[T]he greatest obstacle which a man meets with" in his experiments is his inability to vex matter unrestrainedly without permitting some part of it to escape (*CNR* V.428). The conventional error that would render the new plan for experiment useless is "a common opinion that the spirits of things, when they are raised by heat to a more intense degree . . . , escape" (*CNR* V.428). Bacon does not doubt that bodies contain spirits, which can sometimes elude scrutiny. He even grants them appetites and motions when he uses the terminology of Timaeic natural philosophy. But his point is that only experimenters who properly seal the subject of their inquisition from any prospect of escape will succeed. Only under comprehensive duress will matter and matter's spirit be drawn to confess.

Successful inquisition is what Bacon has in mind when he treats the study of bodies under extreme pressure, focusing on projectiles. Hammering or firing hard bodies from a cannon is the best means of discovering their natures because under extremes of pressure the bodies will act in a Protean fashion: "to an accurate observer it is manifest that hard bodies are most impatient of pressure, and have, as it were, a very acute perception thereof; so that when forced ever so little out of their natural position, they strive with great velocity to free themselves and return to their former state" (*CNR* V.434). Hard bodies suggest what all bodies do in less arduous circumstances. When escape is impossible the projectiles try to "extricate and free themselves in any way they can" (435). In so doing, they give the experimenter the information he needs to use them more effectively, confirming his knowledge of their nature. The explanation of bodies' natures in terms of their response to such "violent and mechanical motion" is the very "fountain of practical operation" (*CNR* V.435). Similar ideas, rendered with almost identical phrasing, are found in the *Novum Organum* (especially *NO* IV.234–35).

The upshot of these findings, which have great importance for the new knowledge of rhetoric and poetry, is that the new universal philosophy makes no distinction in principle between natural and violent motion. In the companion treatise, *De Principiis atque Originibus*, Bacon rejects "the common philosophy of the school" that distinguishes between these terms: "For these words, *nature, art,* and *violence,* are but compendious phrases and trifles." Violent motions such as those used in the new learning's experiments are in fact more natural than motions that do not show the nature of bodies: "Nay, those very motions which they call violent may be said to be more according to nature than that which they call natural; if that be more according to nature which is stronger, or even which is more according to the system of the universe" (*PO* V.499).

The fundamental, tangible or intangible bodies of which all things are comprised may have appetites, but as is the case for the atom Cupid, their sources, ends, and purposes are ultimately beyond speculation. The sons of science can indeed say that certain bodies "desire" to rise into the sky, and try to congregate with similar bodies, but only because the principle governing their movement is a law of density. Motion's true governors are necessity and chance: "all violent motion is in fact natural: the external efficient simply setting nature working otherwise than it was before" (*NO* IV.68). Natural motion is really a dislocation of, a collision with, or a reaction to another body. It is no seeking of a home between heaven and earth: "For place has no forces, nor is body acted on except by body; and all swift motion of a body, which seems as if it were seeking a place for itself, is really in pursuit not of location or position simply, but with reference to some other body" (*PO* V.500).

In the *Novum Organum* Bacon notes that although explicitly violent means may not be responsible for the "more remarkable transformations" in natural bodies, the new learning ought to embark upon experiments that would attempt "by violence" to induce bodies— those most likely to strive to free themselves from control and fixity— to take on configurations contrary to the motions of their appetites and wills so that their new "constant" forms can "become a kind of nature" (*NO.* IV.236). The creation of this nature would obviate the idea of nature, while it would bring out what Bacon paradoxically contends is a characteristic human ability to master violence more aptly than other types of motion (*NO* IV.236–37).

We have detected inklings of these reasonings in Bacon's account of the new learning's tests and transformations of human beings. In the essay "Of Adversity" the various afflictions visited upon man by his fall discover his faith and virtue, "like precious odours, most fragrant when they are incensed or crushed" (*E* VI.386). The pear Bacon squeezes is forced into its ripeness, as the crushing of a flower reveals its truer, more homogenous color (*NO* IV.235–36).

4

Spirit, according to Bacon's descriptions, is the most Protean of bodies. Its motions being the most powerful, it is the most invulnerable; yet it is highly volatile, and easily opened to the configuring powers of external forces that set it in relation to other bodies. As Bacon argues in *De Augmentis*, intangible bodies are "above all other things both strenuous to act and soft and tender to be acted on" (*De Aug* IV.400). Spirit has the unique power of generating growth, though confined in the "prison-house" of the tangible body. When held in a body, it makes its own "trials and experiments" on the tangible matter that encloses it (*NO* IV.196), as though it too were a son of science—a being that was tested and testing all at once.

In *De Sapientia Veterum* Bacon describes the spirit of bodies in terms of the myth of the virgin Proserpine, whom Dis carried off by force into the earth, the realm of tangible, material nature. Dis keeps her there by dissimulation as well as force; his captive loses her chance to escape by eating three seemingly harmless grains of a pomegranate that sentence her to the underworld (*SV* VI.758). The deep lesson Bacon draws from Proserpine's captivity is a direction for manipulating the motion of spirit in tangible bodies, the goal he sets for experimentation in the *Novum Organum*. Proserpine's adversity demonstrates that

> there are two ways of confining and restraining spirit in old and earthy matter; one by constipation and obstruction, which is simple imprisonment and violence; the other by administering some suitable aliment [the pomegranate seeds], which is spontaneous and free. For when the imprisoned spirit begins to feed and nourish itself, it is no longer in a hurry to escape. (*SV* VI.760)

All natural bodies, both animate and inanimate, have spirit (*HVM* V.219), but they cannot be preserved from death nor brought back to their prelapsarian existence until men learn how to keep the intangible Proserpine imprisoned in tangible bodies. In order for the new philosophy of nature to achieve "its noblest work of all"—the "renovation" and "preservation" of natural bodies from dissolution (*SV* VI.721)—Orpheus must master the deflective and enthralling techniques of Dis.

Bacon's history of life and death, *Historia Vitae et Mortis*, explains precisely how spirit can be kept or put into tangible bodies so that they do not dissolve. Since spirit is essentially a stranger to what is tangible, various forms of violence or deception are necessary to effect the preservation. The spirit must be "tempered" so that its "unruly and turbulent" nature does not cause it to escape or to "prey upon" its cell. Either excess is fatal to the natural body, which must be a composite of the intangible, spiritual body and its tangible prison.

Experimenters have four options. First, they can violently put the spirit "to flight" within its confinement so as to condense it, making it more dense and less excitable, and so less likely to escape (*HVM* V.269–70). As we will see with Bacon's experiments with highly spirited wine, the confinement also allows the son of science to observe and measure the spirit as it undergoes the ordeal. If its closed chamber is strong enough, it will be unable to vaporize fully and so will not escape, even though it might be subjected to tremendous heat and pressure. The closed vessel becomes the perfect manacle for surprising and holding Protean matter.

The other three methods seem more friendly. Indeed, Bacon makes a point of saying that one of them, the method of "cooling," is "without any malignity, or unfriendly quality" (*HVM* V.269). The others are called "soothing" and "quieting down." However, the original guiding principle is in force. In his introduction to the treatise, Bacon stipulates that experimenters can maintain life only when they detain spirit by "confinement" or "voluntary detention." The friendly methods for the latter are also forms of imprisonment, though less obviously violent. "Soothing," for example, are those methods that succeed in making spirits "contented with themselves" (*HVM* V.275), though in fact they must reside in alien, tangible beings. Although spirit in some sense controls its habitation, being the "masterwheel" of the body (*HVM* V.330), its imprisonment diminishes its spiritedness for the sake of the tangible body's survival: "all spirit (which like flame is fanned by motion) by being shut up becomes languid, and therefore less active and less able to propagate itself; hotter no doubt, as flame is, but slow in motion" (*HVM* V.287). Ultimately, Proserpine must be kidnapped, then tricked into eating the pomegranate, much as Proteus is forced and deceived so that his powers can be known and used.

In the *Novum Organum*, one can see these ideas in practice as Bacon recounts an experiment on wine: the "rarest" and hence one of the most volatile and difficult to control of natural bodies. He starts from the premise that "everything tangible that we are acquainted with contains an invisible and intangible spirit, which it wraps and clothes as a garment" (*NO* IV.195). To discover the proportions of its tangible and intangible bodies in the composite, and so to learn more about what wine is and how to make it, Bacon tells how the liquid can be subjected to heat, "the great instrument of operations" both in nature and in art (*NO* IV.237). He puts the wine in a vessel on hot coals, and arranges a bladder so that the wine's rising spirit will be confined within it. At this point, he shows surprising caution—given the new learning's appropriation of atomism's license to violence— in taking care that the heat is not so great that it breaks the glass vial, nor the the bladder so impervious that no steam escapes. He goes so far as to prick a hole in the bladder in the belief that a tiny opening will prevent the captive steam from condensing. The apparatus would seem to compromise the new philosophy's principles of force and confinement, but for the manner in which Bacon describes its use. He wants most of all to discover what happens to wine's spirit when it is heated, and makes these adjustments toward that end. Since the wine's spirit is really "neither wholly detained nor wholly discharged" (*NO* IV.197), the experimenter can take it into his charge in the same way as a hidden inquisitor might overhear a suspect.

Bacon appeals to what sound like Timaeic ideas in order to criticize those experimenters who, "without attempting to imitate or emulate nature," destroy "by the use of violent heats and over-strong powers all that more subtle configuration in which the occult virtues and sympathies of things chiefly reside" (*NO* IV.199). Nevertheless, his experiment in this case reduces the heat in order to calculate its effects and to keep the spirit conscious and testifying. He puts the hole in the bladder so that the opening will lure the spirit or steam away from its tendency to return to liquid (*NO* IV.198). The result is a kind of window on the spirit's cell; the confinement is complete, though it eludes the captured spirit's power to perceive it.

5

Perhaps the most revealing illustration of Bacon's transformation of Timaeic notions of matter and form is his treatment of alchemy, which Paolo Rossi argues is evidence of Bacon's debt to conflicting traditions.[5] It is more precisely an adaptation of traditional alchemical ideas for the sake of a newly atomistic science of gold-making. From the fragment, *Inquisitions Touching the Compounding of Metals*, one first gets the impression that all alchemy is false science. The hope of the alchemists "seemeth a thing scarcely possible; because gold is the heaviest of metals, and to add matter is impossible." Pretending to add matter to the world runs counter to atomistic doctrine as well as divine prerogative (*ITCM* III.803, *CNR* V.427). The alchemical faith in the natural tendency of metals to affect gold in the caves of the earth or the crucible of the laboratory would seem to be heretical.

Skepticism toward alchemy is consistent with the doctrine of color that Bacon sets down in the *Novum Organum*. There his theory is atomistic: color is an accident, the result of the positioning of a thing's most minute bodies rather than any becoming quality. This idea is adumbrated in *The Advancement*:"And this is one cause why colours have little inwardness and necessitude with the nature and properties of things, those things resembling in colour which otherwise differ most" (*Adv* III.238). More specifically, "we easily gather that colour has little to do with the intrinsic nature of a body, but simply depends on the coarser and as it were mechanical arrangement of the parts" (*NO* IV.156).

Not only is alchemy bereft of true tincture; it is deprived in Bacon's analysis of the assumption that gold draws into being more gold. The Timaeic idea of persuasion in alchemy seems to be irrelevant. To make gold, one would have to effect a "condensation" that would "drive" the metal "into a narrower room" than its "natural extent beareth."

But this heating and confinement of matter is standard practice for the new experimental sciences, as we have seen. Hence Bacon's qualification: the process "seemeth" impossible, is "hardly to be expected," but is not beyond men's capacity *if* they use the new science. Bacon's hedge about the idea of making gold conceals a new alchemical doctrine which he reveals with disarming frankness in his book of scientific recipes, the *Sylva Sylvarum*.

It is the means, says Bacon, not the end that is defective in the alchemists' pursuit. Although "the world hath been much abused by the opinion of making gold," gold-making is itself "possible." If one can free oneself from the "dream" that nature intends metals to become gold, or the superstition that man can free nature from impediments so that she can do her work, then a new prospect for discovering gold in "the true ways and passages of nature" comes to hand (SS II.449–50).

The old alchemists failed because they did not see a deeper truth in their own principles. They vainly anticipated success, and overfired the nascent gold in violation of their belief in an alchemical midwifery of nature. The new science would by contrast master a temperate heat without anticipation. By denying their worldly hopes and by focusing on a nature without its own purpose or *telos*, the new alchemist might use heat to quicken metals' spirits in accordance with the true nature of things.

The real difference between the old alchemy and the new is that traditional alchemists are failed dreamers who assume that nature has intention, and so cannot know nature with the sort of certainty that would become routine were they to stop wondering about the relation between natural, cosmological, and human ends. The new alchemist would not have to consider whether he travestied nature if he discovered and used it with unwavering obedience to the basic laws of its invulnerability and flux. The new alchemist could aspire to make gold precisely because nature's limit on the creation of new matter is inviolable, and hence provides an opportunity for the free play of his actions upon existent matter, in obedience to the few true laws of matter's composition. Bacon's doctrine of Protean matter, summarized in another treatise, clarifies the new alchemical principle: "when men consider the inexorable necessity there is in the nature of matter to sustain itself, and not to turn or dissolve into nothing, they should omit no way of vexing and working it, if they detect and bring out its ultimate operations and powers of resistance" (CNR V.427). All transformations of matter depend upon nature's being "spurred on or tied up." No mutation of bodies can be effected unless one tries "to enchain nature, like Proteus" (CNR V.425). To abjure violence or to use it hypocritically, as the old alchemists do, is to remain ignorant of the license available to enlightened alchemists who follow those laws.

The fundamental inferiority of the old alchemists' practices lies in their lack of wise nerve. They do not confine the metal long enough

in its molten state "detained" yet "opened," thus vulnerable to manipulation without being dissolved (*SS* II.449). Properly confined and
persuaded as rigorously as becomes necessary, the metal can be made
to take in certain less noble substances, which it makes appear more
golden. The process protects the metal from dissolution, but only by
imprisonment that ensures that "no part of the spirit" escapes. Likewise, the temperateness of the new alchemy's crucible is really an
instrument for preventing the nascent gold from becoming churlish
like a prematurely awakened Proteus (450). Six months of fiery confinement "vexes" the metal to yield itself to the uses of the experimenter, as though nothing of consequence to the noble metal could
be lost. The gold that comes from these exertions has, in the final
analysis, no need to be gold. This is the conclusion of Bacon's recipe
in the *Sylva Sylvarum*: "let men dispute whether it is true gold or no"
(*SS* II.450).

The practical application of this argument appears in Bacon's treatise on metals, where he emphasizes that gold-making can be "a thing
of great profit" to regimes that promote the new methods. Success
depends only upon whether the combination of baser with higher
metals is detectable: "For if a quantity of silver can be so buried in
gold, as it will never be reduced again . . . and also that it will serve
all uses as well as pure gold, it is in effect all one as if so much silver
were turned to gold" (*ITCM* III.802).

What happens to alchemy in the new learning illustrates the new
sciences' efforts to restore magic "to its ancient and honourable meaning," as Bacon describes that meaning in *De Augmentis*. The "sublime
wisdom" of the enlightened sciences looks behind what the Persians
called the "knowledge of the universal consents of things," and finds
"the science which applies the knowledge of hidden forms to the
production of wonderful operations" (*De Aug* IV.366–67). Care for
consent and tempering is finally a new effort to master mutability by
detecting and manipulating the fundamental bodies.

What follows is an analysis of the implications of Bacon's philosophy of nature for his ideas of rhetoric and method, and for his vision
of the culmination of scientific endeavor in *The New Atlantis*.[6]

Bacon and Rhetoric

But yet notwithstanding it [rhetoric] is a thing not hastily to be
condemned, to clothe and adorn the obscurity even of philosophy

itself with sensible and plausible elocution. For hereof we have great examples in Xenophon, Cicero, Seneca, Plutarch, and of Plato also in some degree; and hereof likewise there is great use; for surely to the severe inquisition of truth, and the deep progress into philosophy, it is some hinderance; because it is too early satisfactory to the mind of man, and quencheth the desire of further search, before we come to a just period; but then if a man be to have any use of such knowledge in civil occasions, of conference, counsel, persuasion, discourse, or the like; then shall he find it prepared to his hands in those authors which write in that manner.

But excess of this is so justly contemptible . . . there is none of Hercules' followers in learning, that is, the more severe and laborious sort of inquirers into truth, but will despise these delicacies and affectations, as indeed capable of no divineness.   (*Adv* III.284–85)

I

What precisely is the role of rhetoric within Bacon's universal philosophy? In this crucial passage from *The Advancement*, he invokes the traditional analogy between clothing and rhetorical adornment. Ornament makes sensible and plausible what was obscure; it seems to be necessary, at least for conducting civil business. The passage as a whole, however, assigns to ornament and rhetoric a function no higher than that of a necessary tool. Rhetoric is in fact a harm to inquiry. Since its users recall learning from a ready store rather than searching it out, rhetoric deceives in the subsequent ease of its operation; it closes inquiries prematurely. Bacon has designed the passage so that his praise of rhetoric's usefulness in civil discourse is peculiarly limiting. The true followers of Hercules employ rhetoric, but despise its "delicacies and affectations" when they do Herculean things. If rhetoric can convey no "divineness," it can have nothing to do with the truths toward which they labor.

These charges are also partly traditional. Bacon draws from old rhetorical doctrine when he makes his famous diagnosis of a threefold malaise in traditional learning. He re-enacts expressions of concern over false rhetoric that one finds in Erasmus, Cicero, Aristotle, and Plato. Similar symptoms of rhetorical corruption have been derided in every age, certainly by Plato's criticism of the Sophists, Aristotle's disapproval of the vices of ambitious lawyers, Cicero's warnings against mechanical, small-minded rhetoric, the humanists' attack on scholasticism, and the skeptics' rejoinder to Ciceronianism. Up to a point, *The Advancement* is an extension of currents in the humanistic tradition favoring a more accessible, methodical dialectic and a pedagogical rhetoric to replace false Ciceronianism, obscure scholastic logic, and contentious theological disputation.

The famous definition of rhetoric in *The Advancement* echoes the ancient concern that eloquence be understood in relation to reason, not only in regard to what acts upon the affections. Properly understood, rhetoric applies and recommends "the dictates of reason to imagination, in order to excite the appetite and will" (*De Aug* IV.455). Insofar as rhetoric is "ornament," it can be a true complement of learning if students have first mastered "stuff" and "variety" for rhetoric to ornament (*Adv* III.326). Bacon's characteristic distrust of opinions (the idols of the tribe, the cave, the marketplace, and the theater) does not prevent him from endorsing the traditional rhetorical idea that common notions—the opinions and commonplaces so useful to rhetoricians—have something to do with a higher realm of ideas and universal observations. Their light, "though it be a faint and superficial light, is yet in a manner universal, and has reference to many things" (*NO* IV.65). Bacon also makes a bow to the Aristotelian assumption that speeches favoring the cause of truth are more influential, constructed more easily than those favoring falsehood (*De Aug* IV.455–56), and he goes on to defend the delights of rhetorical speech by noting Plato's argument that beauty can make manifest the instructive similitudes of virtue (*De Aug* IV.456).

Extending his concessions to the rhetorical theory of the Platonic and Aristotelian tradition, Bacon occasionally asserts that rhetoric must not coerce if it is truly to persuade. There are times when he insists that he does not wish "to force or to ensnare men's judgments, but to lead them by the hand with their good will" (*NO* IV.91). Scientific authors should give counsel, not dictate (*Adv* III.289). As a herald of science addressing King James I, Bacon claims to foreswear persuasion itself. At least in the case of the king, he makes use of a traditional Timaeic principle of rhetoric when he presumes only to "excite" his auditor's soul so that it moves itself: "though I cannot positively or affirmatively advise your Majesty, or propound unto you framed particulars, yet I may excite your princely cogitations to visit the excellent treasure of your own mind, and thence to extract particulars for the purpose agreeable to your magnanimity and wisdom" (*Adv* III.264). By the same token, learning establishes a kingship over men's understanding in which knowledge commands "men's willing natures" (*Adv* III.316) and makes a "just and lawful sovereignty" (315).

One is struck by the earnest tone in Bacon's warnings about the coercive practices of false rhetoric (*Adv* III.279–80). His prohibition of manipulation and interference often seems to extend to those who study nature's works. Since "the subtilty of nature and operations will not be enchained in the bonds [of words]" (*Adv* III.388), nature must be wooed "with due observance and attention," not forced by those who wish only to conceal their errors in studying her (*SV* VI.736). In the midst of his discussion of "effecting works" from knowledge of nature, he asserts that the student of science, whatever his transforming powers might be, ultimately joins and divides only what already exists; nature does all the rest by working within (*NO* IV.47).

An affinity between Bacon's project and Timaeic persuasion is also evident in the titles of two of his most important treatises, *The Advancement and Proficience of Learning* and its elaborate translation, the *De Dignitate et Augmentis Scientiarum*. Each title identifies the purpose of the two parts of each work: to praise and to extend human learning. In the first title, the meaning of "advancement" is problematic. If the word is parallel to *dignitate* and therefore refers to the praise of learning in the first part of the work, "advancement" is essentially a kind of extolling promotion of what already exists, a setting forward rather than an innovation. The second part of each work of course emphasizes advancement in the sense of desirable innovation. But here as well the meaning of *augmentis* is twofold. Bacon argues for the superiority of augmentation over improvement, calling the latter an activity of compilers and commentators who seldom bring about a "natural generation" of learning (*Adv* III.294–95). Yet the organic metaphor latent in *augmentio* preserves to a degree the notion that generation occurs out of something that already has a character of its own. In fact, augmentation is assumed both "to preserve and augment whatever is solid and fruitful" (295). It makes knowledge resemble "a spouse, for generation, fruit, and comfort" rather than a courtesan, who is used for pleasure, or a servant who merely carries out a master's practical ambitions (295). Augmentation is a kind of discovery distinct from the recollective invention of eloquent speakers, but it is also the "addition or amplification" of knowledge, as though it were knowledge's eloquent manifestation (389–90). Similar ambiguities attend Bacon's description of his work as an *instauratio* or restoration of learning.

The ambivalence in the titles emerges again in Bacon's explicit response to the quarrel between the ancients and the moderns. His paradoxical assertion that modern man is really an ancient, an aging survivor of a young classical world, blurs the issue of whether the modern world essentially completes or departs from the past. "Ancient" modern man, in the scheme of the new learning, is both a herald of the new learning and a mature perfection of his heritage.

In fact, Cicero's insistence that philosophy and rhetoric not be separated becomes a pillar in Bacon's grander scheme to uphold "continuity" in the sciences (*De Aug* IV.373). Though he sometimes seems to dismiss rhetoric as "indeed capable of no divineness," he condemns other men's efforts to break rhetoric away from philosophy; they would deny that rhetoric studied properly is one of the rational knowledges.

To a degree, these ideas harmonize with the new learning's apprehension of nature and Bacon's occasional use of traditional alchemical terminology. As we have seen, the language of his natural philosophy is often informed by a traditional Timaeic physics, including the assumption that nature is animate, and hence that matter possesses a kind of yearning for form. Despite his claim that men idolatrously project their images onto all of natural and civil life, he repeatedly makes use of the Aristotelian language of appetite. The virtues or qualities of matter, such as density, solidity, and heat, he calls passion or desires (*NO* IV.29). His explanation of motion in anthropomorphic terms is difficult to overlook, especially when he applies principles of physics to moral and civil philosophy. Like the natural object, which "tendeth to the conservation of a more general form," men take up their civil duties for the good of all (*Adv* III.420). And somewhat as men are, matter is capable of "abhorence of motion," restraint, and excitation (*De Aug* IV.356). In *The New Atlantis*, the narrator tells of the breeding of precious metals in deep caves as though another widespread Timaeic belief—that metals behave almost like living things—could have standing in Solomon's island of science.

In *De Sapientia Veterum*, Bacon calls the atom Cupid—love being "the apptite or instinct of primal nature" (*SV* VI.729). The *De Augmentis* records and upholds, if erratically, the traditional view that "all natural bodies have a manifest power of perception, and also a kind of choice in receiving what is agreeable, and avoiding what is hostile or foreign" (*De Aug* IV.402). In response to this and other passages, Alfred North Whitehead has found in Bacon an organicism that has helped keep alive the Aristotelian concept of an animate tendency that is responsive to a formal cause.[1]

2

Despite these nuances, the charges Bacon makes in *The Advancement* against false eloquence help to subvert Timaeic rhetoric. If traditional rhetoric and logic have barred men from comprehending nature, they must be reconceived. Rather than revealing a nature free from man's fallible tendencies, the old eloquence and logic have projected men's beliefs and aspirations upon nature. Traditional rhetorical and logical discourse cannot approach the truths of nature because nature does not conform to man's effort to find his own order in it. Neither does nature cooperate with rhetoric's characteristic hyperbole. Suspicion and doubt must be the new guiding principles of reformed inquiry and the adaptation of rhetorical techniques. The health of mind that Cicero considers natural to man's experience of art contrasts with the congenital error that Bacon spies in men's minds: "the human understanding is like a false mirror, which, receiving rays irregularly, distorts and discolours the nature of things by mingling its own nature with it" (*NO* IV.54).

Only partly softening the old arguments used by Cornelius Agrippa to condemn learned vanities, Bacon mixes inquisitive ambition with a disdain for scholars' false aspirations. The fall into idolatry has thrown everyone down from an edenic kingdom in which man had the power and wisdom to name all living things. Enlightenment is as near as the smashing of the idols, and yet it would seem that only a few students of nature, if any, can heed Bacon's call to transcend a self-deception that characterizes fallen man.

Into question comes the principle, so important in the traditional rhetorical theory of Plato and Aristotle, that public discourse can have some degree of philosophical import when it addresses ordinary audiences. In Roger Ascham's words, it is "that good councell of Aristotle, *loquendum ut multi, sapiendum ut pauci,* [:] use speech as the meanest should well understand, and the wisest best allow."[2] Bacon cites a less elevated, more schematic version: "*Loquendum ut vulgus, sentiendum ut sapientes* [a man should speak like the vulgar, and think like the wise]" (*Adv* III.396). In Bacon's phrasing, the multitude is clearly base, and the speaker's thought and experience are set apart from his speech. Elsewhere Bacon rejects even this version of Aristotle's notion by arguing that since words originate from the vulgar commerce among men, their fallen and irremediable separation from what they name condemns their unsophisticated users to misapprehension. Only the arduous mechanic of inquiry Bacon adumbrates in the *Novum Organum* and elsewhere seems to offer a prospect of saving a few students of nature from the "fallacies and false appearances" of words (*Adv* III.397).

The deeper cause of this divorce of *res* from *verba* is, Bacon contends, a pandering to the masses, for which prominent ancient philosophers and modern religious and academic reformers are responsible. Their attempts to persuade and inform the mass of men have damaged inquiry into nature. The learned who speak to others like themselves have fallen into the same error. Their addresses to the multitude of their peers have injured science with feats of "magnificence and memory" that block "progression and proficience" (*Adv* III.322). Amplification and memory, which in Timaeic, Aristotelian, and Ciceronian rhetoric tend to draw substance and form from shared conceptions of value and heritage, are incapable of augmenting scientific inquiry because they have been corrupted by public associations and private perception. The only means of escaping this condition, according to Bacon's fundamental critique of the idols, is to submit to a mechanical guide that is immune to vainglory or accident.

> There remains but one course for the recovery of a sound and healthy condition,—namely, that the entire work of the understanding be commenced afresh, and the mind itself be from the very outset not left to take its own course, but guided at every step; and the business be done as if by machinery.   (*NO* IV.41)

The machinery is an armor to protect the intellect from false tendency and chance. Bacon claims to have "surrounded the intellect with faithful helps and guards, and got together with most careful selection a regular army of divine works" for "a safe and convenient approach" to nature (*NO* IV.31). True learning becomes battle and deception directed against the seditions and invasions of desire and accident.

In this regard, the true renovation of learning resembles a medical cure carried out by a dictatorial physician on a compliant patient who, strangely, is at once uncontrollable and docile. The patient cannot be

reclaimed by eloquence, and yet he must submit with "precise obedience" to the prescriptions of a "more exact knowledge":

> It were a strange speech which spoken, or spoken oft, should reclaim
> a man from a vice to which he were by nature subject. It is order,
> pursuit, sequence, and interchange of application, which is mighty
> in nature; which although it require more exact knowledge in pre-
> scribing and more precise obedience in observing, yet is recom-
> pensed with the magnitude of effects . . . the *truth of the direction*
> must precede *severity of observance.*   (*Adv* III.377)

The old idea that the rhetorician and physician are akin in eliciting
rather than prescribing health gives way to "mighty" methods for
conforming the inquirer to the deepest foundations of nature.

Many of the attributes of Bacon's "inductive" machine are well
known, though the degree to which they are designed to thwart
tendency has not been adequately appreciated. Chapter I has reviewed
the function of scientific aphorisms. In the *Novum Organum* Bacon
sets out the virtues of making comprehensive lists of them and of
constructing more general maxims by rigorously sifting the aphoristic
evidence. Such devices restrict their own subject matter to the analysis
of experience, and so control man's innate love of perverse generalization. Their form demands that nature be taken to pieces. As dis-
crete, often contradictory units of discourse, they frustrate idolatry.
Finally, their interpretation would seem to call for an almost auto-
matic "due process of exclusion and rejection" carried out on the
simplest possible basis: by noting similarities and dissimilarites among
instances, and by gathering those instances from experiments designed with mechanical thoroughness so that the enumeration of cases
is complete. The system is supposed to hold the unaided senses away
from the "thing": "I contrive that the office of the sense shall be only
to judge of the experiment, and that the experiment itself shall judge
of the thing" (*NO* IV.26). But how is it possible for an experimenter
to devise a machine that is not influenced by his own nature? If he
somehow succeeds, how will he then bring himself and others to
learn and benefit from something designed to prevent mankind from
being itself?

Methods for interpreting nature, as they are set out in the *Novum
Organum*, are responses to such questions. The new procedure, which
seems to be mechanically straightforward, is predicated on the notion
that the strangeness of an effect is primary evidence of its truthfulness.

Bacon explains that interpretation is an acquaintance with the "Forms" that proves its validity by embracing a unity in "substances the most unlike" (*NO* IV.120). Bringing to light what no one could have anticipated is the essential function of aphoristic inquiry. The new interpretation leads to "truth in speculation and freedom in operation" precisely because it reveals a knowledge of things "never yet done, and such as neither the vicissitudes of nature, nor industry in experimenting, nor accident itself, would ever have brought into act, and which would never have occurred to the thought of man" (*NO* IV.120).

Bacon implies that these sudden revelations appear after a prolonged period in which the seeker must be ignorant of his essential goal. Scientific inquiry resembles a game in which children search for things hidden by a greater being; they must know they are looking for something, but for the game to be a proper decoding they must have no idea what their object is until they find it. They are supposed to make hypothetical collections of data to arrive at tentative formal laws before their surveys are complete, but their inferences from preliminary hypotheses are best when they contradict, not just disrupt, expectations.

"Writers on natural magic (very frivolous persons, hardly to be named in connexion with such serious matters as we are now about)" are "everywhere parading . . . similitudes and sympathies of things that have no reality" (*NO* IV.167). Bacon too proposes to detect order in "Instances of Conformity," but his goal is to discover conformity in the most disparate, least likely instances, by means of "a certain sagacity" (167–68). Although he takes pains to explain dozens of less revolutionary ways to identify similarities between instances, he emphasizes the insight that discovers the most unusual conformities in cases that at first seem utterly different. His chief example reaches out to the ends of the earth in order to reconcile the antipodes. The old and new worlds, he observes, are conformable in two ways: Africa and "the region of Peru" have coast lines of complementary shapes, and the old and new worlds are both "broad and extended towards the north, narrow and pointed towards the south" (*NO* IV.167). The machine and the goals of the new method of inference draw him toward the hidden symmetry of opposite continents.

Like truths gathered from the study of petty "juggling and conjuring tricks," a surprising similitude offers information about nature that the study of less unusual instances can not. Tricks and surprising comparisons are a necessary "preparative for setting right and purging the understanding," since "whatever draws the understanding from the things to which it is accustomed, smooths and levels its surface for the reception of the dry and pure light of true ideas" (*NO* IV.172–73).

3

The method that deceives anticipation, like the new rhetoric, is Janus-faced. It offers the results of experimental inquiry and indoctrination as though they were the plain and open testimony of the senses, while withholding its deeper truths—as it must do, given the deep-rootedness of men's idolatrous tendencies and their imaginations' need for comfort. The famous goal of the new learning's enterprise, set out in *De Interpretatione Naturae*, is "to disclose and bring into sight all that is hidden and secret in the world" (*IN* III.518), given that "the formula itself of interpretation, and the discoveries made by the same, will thrive better if committed to the charge of some fit and selected minds and kept private" (520). Vulgar wits will eventually see evidence of the new learning, but only through its utility and effects (*NO* IV.42).

Bacon's modified atomism is important in relation to the new methods of inquiry because it supplies paradigmatic support for the ambivalence of the new learning's account of itself. On one level, the fundamental bodies are perfectly self-evident; they strike constantly upon everyone's senses. Experience is in this sense everyone's encounter with them. But Baconian experience, as we have seen, is far more problematic. As immediate and universal as all sense experience, it is yet so remote from ordinary life that the testimony of the senses, controlled by the idolatrous mind, must be ruthlessly denied. Once the proper mechanisms of inquiry and communication are established and followed, the senses are again supposed to be able to give evidence of the minute bodies. But then another paradox arises: the only real bodies that strike us are tiny beings "of a perfectly dark and hidden nature" (*PO* V.464). Their physiognomy and appetites must remain cryptic; like Cupid the atom, their essential natures are "positive and inexplicable" (*SV* VI.729). They are the most perfect embodiment of matter as code. Vulgar wits, who sense them without proper preparation, experience only what Democritus calls "figments" (*NO* IV.58).

The modified atomistic paradigm is consistent with Bacon's approach to mathematics, which has been considered one of his failings as a precursor of modern science. Bacon is not intensely interested in numbers as means of calculation, partly because instrumental numbers would be relatively accessible to laymen. He adapts the examples of Democritus and Pythagorus to maintain that figures and numbers are the principles and natures of things, not countable attributes. Numbers properly understood are formal clues to "the woods and enclosures of particulars." Moreover, there is no likelihood of discovering even similitudes of such principles in the opinions of the inexpert, as Plato seems to assume. In the new learning figures are clues to the labyrinths of nature, and thus cryptic aids available to the few (*De Aug* IV.370). Those who put great stock in mere calculation are like the old logicians: they are idolaters who impose their vain "generalities" (attributes of quantity) upon things without effect.

4

Given this bifurcation of knowledge into idolatry and wisdom, what finally is rhetoric's role? Man's worship of the idols of the cave seems to be inevitable, so long as he does not dare to step out of the world of tendency. When he has separated himself from the delusions of society, the cave-dweller is still unable to understand experience because he embraces his enslavement to vain hopes and to chance. The wayward ambition of his imagination and intellect creates arbitrary images he worships as real, unless the charade before him can somehow be made to yield itself up as something he can despise.

The idols of the marketplace, the words men share in their daily commerce, are similarly counterfeit in their origins and their use. Men do not see their currency for what it is: a thing to be mastered like the coinage of gold. Bacon's market metaphor grows from the notion that people coin and thereby corrupt the medium of exchange, their use of words creating a demeaning trade in which the value of exchanged things fluctuates according to fortune and whim. Similarly, the idols of the theater, those confused systems of the world's philosophies, impose themselves upon the fancies of the learned so long as men do not embark upon the road of true experiment.

How can idolaters be urged to escape these conditions? *De Sapientia Veterum* teaches that they must meet and subdue "science," which Bacon makes synonymous with the Sphinx. But that prospect is terrifying. The deeper myth makes success seem all but impossible.

In the Baconian account, we discover very little about science's origins, or how idolaters can make science their own. The Sphinx simply haunts "every turn" on the roads men walk (*SV* VI.756). They must confront it, not aspire to it or approach it by means of deliberation. By a kind of default, the Sphinx impinges upon men's lives as a destiny or fate. Almost everyone has become its victim because men cannot solve its riddles. The riddles come from Muses that cannot be called upon; yet the Sphinx's challenge must be answered immediately to avoid the cruel "destruction and laceration of the mind" that is the Sphinx's mangling of its victims. Science is a prodigy that threatens the mass of men with torment, but gives a kingdom to the one who can answer its queries.

The Sphinx's action in human affairs has little to do with teaching or bending, or an articulated hierarchy of understanding. The ignorant it dislimbs; it rewards the ambition of one who is capable of taking in "the greatness of the prize" (*SV* VI.755) and yet has to make his way on hobbled and deformed feet, "for men generally proceed too fast and in too great a hurry to the solution of the Sphinx's riddles; whence it follows that the Sphinx has the better of them" (*SV* VI.757–58). Oedipus prevails, but Bacon's interpretation of the myth implies that other riddles of science will continue to haunt the roads, perplexing and driving men mad if they do not do what Oedipus did. Without a riddle-solver, the axioms and arguments of science will penetrate and hold fast the mind "as though they were the monster's claws," or "as goads, and as nails driven in" (*SV* VI.756).

In order to gird his audience to undertake or tolerate such a quest, Bacon's rhetoric moves in two directions at once: steering away from his audience's anticipations of the course and end of the Baconian program, and turning toward his audience's need for reassurance. The *Novum Organum* stipulates that "Our purpose is not to stir up men's hopes, but to guide their travels" (*Adv* III.235), yet it includes Bacon's pledge that he will

> not unfrequently subjoin observations of my own, being as the first offers, inclination, and as it were glances of history towards philosophy: both by way of an assurance to men that they will not be kept for ever tossing on the waves of experience, and also that when the time comes for the intellect to begin its work, it may find everything the more ready.   (*NO* IV.30)

So that men are not "sad," so that they do not harbor "a worse and meaner opinion of things" than is warranted, he will "make hope in this matter reasonable"—just as Columbus before his voyage set out the reasons that gave him hope of success (*NO* IV.91). Bacon will condescend to encourage the tendency to hope, even though hope must be alien to his scientific method.

The implementation of such a plan is a complicated matter. Bacon repeatedly returns to the idea that "vain apprehension" and "the new birth of science" are absolutely distinct (*NO* IV.84). The "promise of the thing" is not "the thing itself," just as preparing men's minds is supposed to have nothing truly in common with discovering truth (*NO* IV.91). Near the end of the first book of the *Novum Organum*, Bacon discloses that the opinion he rouses in men to turn back delusion and despair cannot be a "legitimate interpretation" (*NO* IV.105). Utterly contingent, his suggestions "are to serve only for the time, and by way of interest (so to speak) till the thing itself which is the principle be fully known" (103). Yet the very reference to the provisional nature of his coaxings encourages as well as blocks anticipation.

Behind this emphasis upon the possibility of discovery despite the imperfections of men's capacities, there is the hopeful doctrine that idolatry might pass in an instant if ignorance could once give way. The remoteness of a transformation of the old learning is somehow proof, in the new learning's alembic, of the revolutionary possibilities of the new sciences. The unlikelihood of science's being born again is reason to expect that science can be renewed, perhaps all at once (*NO* IV.91). One step beyond the prison of delusion and chance could change everything. Alexander's unprecedented conquest of the known world began with a pedestrian departure from the past: he "had done no more than take courage to despise vain apprehensions" (*NO* IV.94). The idols of the tribe are universal patterns of misapprehension because men are enthralled by vain hope, particularly the belief that "it is consonant for the affirmative or active to affect more than the negative or privative" (*Adv* III.395). Their enslavement verges on the conqueror's freedom if they can seize upon the principle of negation.

One means of breaking the hold of appearances and of tendency is to use a form of rhetoric that prepares for the proper sort of Baconian inquiry, and so deliberately stimulates the scientific activity of its audience: "initiative" rhetoric. Whereas the old "magistral" rhetoric calls only for credulity, and indeed cultivates its audience's anticipation of what is to be said (*De Aug* IV.449), the new "initiative" rhetoric would be like "a thread to be spun on," something unfinished that leads the true student of nature to examine and augment it. The old rhetoric "lays the understanding asleep by singing of specific properties and hidden virtues, sent as from heaven and only to be learned as the whispers of tradition" (*De Aug* IV.367). The new aphoristic method deprives its students of illustration, generalization, oratorical circumstance, and any pre-established pattern of inference, "so there is nothing left to make the aphorisms of but some good quantity of observation" (451). The very deprivation of initiative would enforce the independence of its users. The result would be a strangely ceremonious initiation into the mysteries of the sciences in which the aphorisms are to be read as shards that are blanks to credulity. Bacon has in fact borrowed the term *initiative* from "the sacred ceremonies," which the word here parodies and emulates (449).

5

This natural rhetoric of reversal, surprise, and contradiction helps to explain Bacon's interest in hieroglyphs. In the codes of nature and of discourse, tendency and appearance reduce to "surds" or empty characters. And yet one kind of character, the hieroglyph, is "real," and thus capable of revealing the true nature of things in itself (*De Aug* IV.439). Hieroglyphs are "real," not "nominal" because they represent "things and motions" in gestures that are somehow congruent with the thing signified. In *The Advancement*, Bacon cites approvingly the authority of Cicero to establish the connection between natural motions, human gestures, and the mind: "the private and subtile motions and labours of the countenance and gesture" are "as Q. Cicero elegantly saith, . . . *animi janua*, the gate of the mind" (*Adv* III.457).

However, the conjunction of the hieroglyph with facial expression and Janus—the gate and the god—points up a deep Baconian irony. One learns in his writings on civil discourse that countenance and gesture are the faithful testimony of the mind *if* the observer reads wisely the code of a person's expressions. A person who knows the power of the hieroglyphic gesture uses it as a veil, as a probe, or for effect (*E* VI.387–89); its fidelity to the user's mind is often therefore cryptic and nominal.

In *De Augmentis*, Bacon likens the sacred Egyptian writing to parabolical poetry. Hieroglyphs come before letters as parables come before arguments. Like hieroglyphs, parabolical poetry is unique in its power to illustrate and "infold" the relationship between man and divinity. It is "sacred and venerable," the highest kind of poetry (*De Aug* IV.316–17). But just as parabolical poetry that is not religious and revelatory is misleading, the non-religious or cryptic hieroglyph must be misleading as well. Its truth can be read only by those with knowledge of the Protean lengths to which nature and man will go to escape the faithful dictation of their true characters.

In Bacon's project this natural, cryptic play of appearances, which the sciences imitate, has repercussions for civil life and civil rhetoric, although Bacon carefully mutes the analogy. He does not deny that the exploitation of appearances for the sake of a hidden intention is a Machiavellian act, at least when it is carried out for the sake of private ambition. He condemns such behavior (*De Aug* IV.471). Men who sever their acts from their intentions, he argues, are ruthless and dangerously ambitious. Taking pains to avoid the charge that he is a Machiavel, Bacon is careful to present his survey of the gestures, the more or less visible actions of moral and civil life, in light of religious principles. All of moral philosophy is in fact the "handmaid" of religion. Though it is capable of making its own decisions in service to its mistress, it is essentially her servant (*Adv* III.441).

The proper study of all human gestures, including the actions of rhetoric, supposedly discloses the intent and nature of the gesturer, since the mind signals disposition as much as disposition signals mind (*De Aug* V.34). Properly understood, gesture is therefore a "thing real" (*Adv* III.360), not a mere tool. And the disclosure of intention is preferable to absolute secrecy, since it is necessary to communicate at least some aspect of one's purposes to others in order to succeed (*Adv* III.466–68).

The Advancement and *De Augmentis* defend the commonsensical view voiced by Livy that the cultivation of countenance and gesture should adhere to a mean, "Lest [one] should appear . . . either arrogant or servile" (*De Aug* V.33). Bacon is willing to argue that one cannot give up all ostentation without doing harm to one's dignity. But the deeper premise of the discussions of moral and civil knowledge in *The Advancement* and *De Augmentis* seems to be that civil knowledge, or policy, "requires only an external goodness" (*De Aug* V.32). In private, men value a good that has no substantial relation to the good of society (*Adv* III.425).

The passage in *De Augmentis* seems at first to move in the opposite direction. It initially praises traditional philosophical studies of a good that embraces private and public spheres, and it allows for a weighing and balancing, rather than a strict separation, of virtues associated with active and passive lives. But giving his account of past writings, Bacon resolves "to reinforce the doctrine of the exemplar" with a very different approach. He will be the first moral and civil philosopher to consult systematically and clearly "the nature of things, as well as moral axioms," to "cleanse the fountains of morality" (*De Aug* V.6). Nature tells him that "in everything there is an appetite toward two natures of good," one that is "total . . . in itself," the "self-good" of private ambition, and a second that is a "Good of Communion" (7). These are supposed to be shadowed in the motives of the fundamental bodies of matter, which seek their own as well as higher likenesses. The obvious superiority of the second motion is a reflection of Christian charity's now decisive demonstration that the active, self-sacrificing life is superior to a passive one (7–10).

The natural evidence of universal charity rests on an almost opaque analogy. The idea that natural bodies are attracted to their likenesses could be richly Timaeic; but here it becomes an axiom engraved in the bodies themselves. The bifurcation of the Good separates private from communal appetite, as if the aspirations of the bodies toward their terrestrial likenesses were fundamentally opposed to higher yearnings as well as the duties of Christian charity. Were it not for the obvious superiority and power of a communal good "engraven upon man" (*De Aug* V.7), public gestures would be hollow or manipulative performances.

The idea that political life and morality sometimes diverge is not new; but Nature teaches Bacon the lesson, which he says is muddled or ignored by traditional moralists and political philosophers, that private good and communal good are incommensurable, whereas communal good imposes its prerogative upon all men who are not "degenerate" (*De Aug* V.7). Rhetoric in such circumstances has a merely accidental and scientific relation to the higher good. It cannot appeal to aspirations except in deception that is the exercise of a scientific principle. Persuasion cannot act upon the communal desire except to enforce it among the degenerate, or to second it redundantly where it is already active. Its ambivalent action suppresses and obviates distinctions between power and violence.

Once one begins to appreciate the comprehensive force of Bacon's scientific cleansing of moral and civil philosophy, his discussion of civil ostentation becomes more problematic, especially as it relates to his philosophy of rhetoric. His attempt to justify men's temperate efforts to promote themselves in others' eyes runs counter to his axiomatical distinction between public and private aspiration. Tensions between the two positions repeatedly spur him to speculate about how to exploit radical differences between private and communal motives: "For as it is said of calumny, 'calumnate boldly, for some of it will stick,' so it may be said of ostentation (except it be in a ridiculous degree of deformity), 'boldly sound your own praises, and some of them will stick' " (*De Aug* V.67).

On one level, the advice urges men to "spread all sail in pursuit of their honor," to present themselves "to the first degree of vanity" because their sails are indeed their own. Men should promote themselves so that they do not lose their dignity. Yet the passage takes advantage of the power of the Machiavellian proverb: just as slander will discover shortcomings in anyone if it is unscrupulous enough, boasting will be believed if it is sufficiently incredible. This is the moral equivalent of the scientific principle that the least similar things should be discovered to have the most compelling likenesses. Although Bacon disavows the comparison with Machiavelli by distinguishing calumny from decent self-promotion, the argument derives strength from the example's shocking power. It draws attention to the possibility of creating any reputation one wishes, limited only by one's scruples, not at all by the nature of public ostentation.

Bacon's attempt to justify "good mediocrity in the declaring or not declaring a man's self" is susceptible to the same contradictory cross-currents of morality and ambition (*Adv* III.466). As he explains how ostentation might be acceptable for reasons that are not strictly moral and religious, he tends to emphasize the power one can gain by employing temperate display. Rather than praise temperate display as a virtue in itself, he argues that it is more "prosperous and admirable" than deep dissimulation. In the end, moderation is more successful because deep dissembling is not as effective: extreme secrecy creates traps that ensnare the dissembler himself (*Adv* III.467). Thus Lucius Sylla, Julius Caesar, and Augustus Caesar carefully disclosed part of their ambition in order to further their plans to rule Rome, whereas Pompey, who hid all his plans even from friends whose help he needed, utterly failed to realize his ambition (468). Pompey's deep dissimulation was in fact not cunning enough: "not greatly politic" (468). If he had been cunning, he would have been more moderate.

6

Bacon dampens the Machiavellian tenor of these arguments by referring, very early in his discussion of moral and civil action, to the limits that nature and fortune place upon ambition. In *The Advancement* and *De Augmentis* he labels his discussion of these matters a "Georgics of the Mind," an endeavor to teach the new husbandman that like the tiller of the field he "cannot command neither the nature of the earth nor the seasons of the weather" (*Adv* III.433). But the bounds of nature and fortune are not nearly as definite for Bacon's husbandman as for Virgil's. The former can "proceed by application" to overcome natural barriers through suffering that is "wise and industrious" (*Adv* III.433–34). In fact, the new husbandman's inquiry into what he cannot do is "the groundwork of the doctrine of remedies" (*De Aug* V.20). The limits are to be studied so as to be transformed or removed. In succeeding passages, Bacon urges the study of all human dispositions, natures, and characters so that the student of human nature might effect their remedial transformations.

Unfortunately, the master of remedial inventions is Daedalus, who—as Bacon recalls him in *De Sapientia Veterum*—is a murderer (*SV* VI.734). He is also a master of nature who creates devices for the sake of pleasures that are "wicked" and monstrous. He gives Pasiphae the means "to satisfy her passion for the bull; so that the unhappy and infamous birth of the monster Minotaurus, which devoured the ingenuous youth, was owing to the wicked industry and pernicious genius of this man." The labyrinth he makes for Minos to hide the monster is "wicked in its end and destination" (734). Yet Daedalean invention, as Bacon describes it, does not in itself violate nature or religious principles. The artificer makes "the furniture of religion and ornament of state" as well as the machinery of perversity, his devices being indifferent to their uses. Indeed, his works "dissolve their own spell" by offering a thread to their labyrinthine construction (735). The evil done by the artificer falls into obscurity as Icarus did, if the wise and charitable act upon his clues to his devices.

The challenge that Daedalean ingenuity poses for sagacity and charity is especially great when the sons of science act upon the "immateriate virtues" of the minds and spirits of men (*SS* II.652). In the *Sylva Sylvarum* the experiments that Bacon outlines in his natural history are studies of the deepest springs of influence and persuasion, where the "immateriate virtues" are those qualities of minds and spirits that persuade and undergo persuasion. The goal of one important set of experiments is to learn ways that one imagination can secretly "bind" another, using those "effluxions from spirit to spirit" that take place "when men are in presence one with another" (652). Bacon says he is here not interested in the question of whether strong beliefs might fortify the imagination. He wants to search for a key to a more fundamental influence, one that would allow one imagination to control or fix another to itself.

In the aphoristic shorthand that attenuates yet enriches this late collection of suggestions, Bacon works in stages. He hypothesizes on the basis of the practice of magicians that the most successful way of influencing a person is by impressing the imagination of his ignorant, naive servant or follower. To impress the servant's imagination, "authority" rather than experience or reason is most effective (656). The more the persuader detects his own imaginings binding this vulnerable subject, the more powerful he becomes (654–5).

Proposing a medical experiment, Bacon sets forth a routine yet stunning illustration of the new sciences' dependence on charitable resolve. To prove the susceptibility to medicine of the patient's spirit in its sleep, Bacon recommends using the faithful servant to administer the potion undetected:

> The body passive and to be wrought upon . . . is better wrought upon (as hath been partly touched) at some times than at others: as if you should prescribe a servant about a sick person (whom you have possessed that his master shall recover) when his master is fast asleep, to use such a root, or such a root. For imagination is like to work better upon sleeping men than men awake.   (*SS* II.659)

The effluxes of the servant's imagination are bound into service thanks to the physician's persuasive and presumably charitable prediction that the master will recover. To these influences Bacon adds the potion itself, and the patient's somnolent state. All are circumstances amenable to a benevolent cure, if the physician is benevolent. Conversely, they are extraordinary opportunities for abuse. No mention is made of the patient's previous knowledge of the treatment or of his consent. There is no discussion of whether the physician's prediction has a basis in fact. The proposed cure follows, with striking fidelity, the binding of Proteus. The cure is scientifically appropriate in the sense that it is true to the new learning's conception of how the imagination can be bound; yet its legitimacy depends on extraordinary resources of charity in the practitioner, the servant, and the reader.

7

The scientific rhetoric that arises from these principles is, as we have noted, one of laborious, self-depriving induction and sudden insight into the springs of power. Plato, Aristotle, Cicero, and Quintilian share the idea that a combination of restraint and display is characteristic of rhetorical expression. What is remarkable about Bacon's departure from their consensus is that beneath his careful attention to moderate gesture, prudent expression, illustration, and orderly presentation, his scientific rhetoric aspires to contradictory extremes. It sets out to frustrate expectation while it approaches the full disclosure of universal laws; it imposes screens as it anticipates revelation; it disavows an interest in Aristotelian formal and final causes as it seeks to detect, in the simplest uses of all natural things and civil gestures, the very secrets of their natures, of nature itself, and the power—if not the image—of its divine maker. The implications of this outlook for all Baconian rhetoric come to light most intriguingly in *The New Atlantis*, which figures a polity ruled by the legacy of a Solomonic king.

The voyage to Atlantis is sometimes called a pleasant fiction that Bacon did not bother to finish. From its opening page, however, the narrative is a highly coherent play of light and shadow that intimates the paradoxical power of the new universal science and its wisdom of persuasion. As the narrator begins to describe his heretofore unknown destination, he says he can "plainly discern" it; but what he sees is "full of boscage, which made it show the more dark" (*NA* III. 129–130). Entering the harbor, he discovers a fair city, only to be motioned away from the shore by its inhabitants. Their unmistakable warning is "without . . . fierceness," just as their first messenger prohibits a landing in terms so hospitable that the narrator confesses "we were much perplexed" (130). The natives show their charity and reveal their history to the strangers in a manner that combines extremes of generosity and reserve. They tell the sailors that they can stay on the island and freely enjoy all its comforts. But to all this they append the absolute provision that the sailors leave in six weeks, and not venture from their rooms for three days, thereafter not traveling more than a mile and a half from their lodgings (135).

Curiously, the limits on the time the strangers can stay are quickly enlarged so that the sailors are free to live on the island for the rest of their lives. But this sudden liberalization also reveals a restriction more serious than previous ones: the sailors discover that the island is unknown to the rest of the world. That is, the New Atlantis discloses its inner life to visitors who have left the world behind. Their knowledge of their isolation and their indulgence in the comforts of the isle enforce the regime's secrecy by removing the occasion and the desire to communicate with the outer world. The narrator, like thirteen other visitors in the course of history, has presumably been able to make his way back so that he can tell his story, but like the others who have returned he knows he risks not being believed. The New Atlantis's citizens venture abroad without that concern, but only because their sole purpose is to spy.

The island tells its history with a similar play of light against darkness. A spokesman reveals the miraculous details of the place's ancient conversion to Christianity, without saying anything about the hundreds of years that followed the founder Salomon's interdict on traffic with strangers (137–39). Likewise, the scientific revelations freely offered by one of the fathers of Salomon's House are given to the narrator alone, and the list of utopia's accomplishments, though it stimulates speculation that man might master nature following the island model, yields only meager hints of how such mastery works or of what nature is (156–66). The lone auditor receives almost no opportunity to observe or test the achievements about which he is told. What he hears and sees comes from that side of the world opposite his own, from an archaic city living in a future beyond the bounds of idolatry.

The mixture of extremes of disclosure and secrecy is a conscious policy of the House of Salomon, which creates experiments in order to effect all things possible (156), but reveals only a portion of its findings. The editorial deliberations of the house's publishing board are wholly internal, and the authority who mentions them reveals no principle upon which a decision to publish might be made (165).

The disarming factuality of the narrator's account of New Bensalem's achievements therefore borders on myopic obscurity. The story the utopians have helped him create is a kind of oracle, encouraging speculation about an ideal fusion of charity and scientific enlightenment and yet reminding the audience that the island is a closed society impossible to seek out, jealously protective of its security, curiously frightening in its affording of comfort to strangers who are swept into its harbor.

The islanders' religion is in itself a mixture of extraordinary charity and distance, of ceremonial display and disguise. The barriers it erects against the infidel are speedily lifted once the stranger gives a sign of common faith, and yet the narrator immediately senses that the sailors welcomed as brothers are under close surveillance (134) and might be banished to the sea-storms again if they misbehave. His warning to his fellow sailors conveys hope fighting against fear, of praise for God's mercy and the island's charity amidst dread at the prospect of being lost again at sea, thrown out either by God or the islanders' willingness to act swiftly and secretly to protect themselves:

> It is a kind of miracle hath brought us hither; and it must be little less that shall bring us hence. Therefore in regard of deliverance past, and our danger present and to come, let us look up to God, and every man reform his own ways. Besides we are come here amongst a Christian people, full of piety and humanity: let us not bring that confusion of face upon ourselves, as to show our vices or unworthiness before them. Yet there is more. For they have by commandment (though in form of courtesy) cloistered us within these walls for three days: who knoweth whether it be not to take some taste of our manners and conditions? and if they find them bad, to banish us straightways; if good, to give us further time.   (NA III.134)

The sailors, though greatly impressed by the comforts New Bensalem provides them, are at first careful only to ask about the circumstances of the city's conversion to Christianity. The narrator does not ask the scientific questions that one would imagine Bacon would be most interested in posing. Instead, the sailors mimic the piety of Solomon. Upon assuming power, the wise king prays to God for wisdom and grace, rather than luxuries; the rescued strangers inquire about their hosts' faith, not about how the utopian society manages to command nature so impressively. The Solomonic reticence of the narrator would be ludicrous were it not for the extreme uncertainty of his own and his company's circumstances, which so effectively stimulate extremes of hope and fear. For several days the sailors do not know whether they will receive "sentence of life or death" (135).

The strangers are given information about New Bensalem's scientific innovations only after a period of isolation in closed quarters, in which they demonstrate—much as Bacon's spirit of wine in the heated vessel—their most essential attributes: gratitude and humility, and their fear of being denied the salvation that Providence seems to have offered them. The first hints of the utopians' power over nature the sailors hopefully interpret as evidence of the islanders' piety. The island's medicine is supposed to exhibit New Bensalem's charity. The islanders' indifference to gifts shows their honesty. Their lack of concern for the distinction between gold and silver testifies to their generosity. Only toward the end of the tale does the narrator hear about utopian powers to lengthen significantly the body's lifespan, not just cure its diseases (158), and about the acceleration of the growth of precious metals in artificial caves. He must check his discoveries with the knowledge that the island's experimenters are admitted masters of deception; their "house of deceits of the senses" represents "all manner" of fallacies in a growing repertoire of devices and principles that they keep secret (164).

The manner in which Bacon admits the initiate into the presence of these mysteries plays upon the narrator's and the audience's hopes and fears. Bacon's conscious effort to rewrite the precursors of his tale, the *Timaeus* and its sequel the *Critias*, is nowhere more striking than in his exploitation of these two passions, which Plato's dialogues, particularly the *Timaeus*, routinely temper in favor of different ends.

The *Timaeus*, of course, describes a utopia in speech. The participants in the dialogue attempt to recall a story they have heard, from others who have heard it from others, about a virtuous, primordial Athens that was destroyed in a natural catastrophe. Their discussion is a gradual recovery of an admittedly uncertain history about a lost city. It depends upon testimony almost comically contingent upon the limits of memory; yet that testimony is capable of evoking their interest in the possibility that they might gradually recover knowledge of a flourishing city like the one described in the *Republic*. The speakers' desire to recover the memory, coupled with the fact that Athens has again come into existence, suggests that the old lost city is not inaccessibly remote from living recollection. Still, a knowledge of the finality of the ancient catastrophe tempers anticipation that the old polity, if it ever existed, will be flesh again. Timaeus' discussion of the birth of the world is similarly muted by the remoteness of the recollection, by the fancifulness of the conversants' departure from their primary task of remembering the virtuous ways of the lost city, and by the observation in the conclusion that knowledge of the beginnings of nature, if one could gain it, is not sufficient for training men how to temper their characters and their cities.

Bacon introduces the utopian city in an entirely different context. New Bensalem and its island society are supposed to have existed throughout history. They have survived natural upheavals, a sign of providential favor and their own resources for mastering the sometimes disastrous swellings of uncontrolled natural forces. Even today, vessels can sail to New Atlantis; the island is eminently more accessible, in a narrowly physical sense, than Plato's "nowhere." On the other hand, the sailors who find it are also utterly lost, with no idea of what they have found until they land. Plato's speakers seek the old Athens from the start of a leisurely and challenging discussion, in which they gradually approach something they desire to understand better. Bacon's sailors are at first intent upon finding trade, not utopia. The strange winds that take them to New Bensalem force them entirely from their course, and though the sailors hope they are being carried by Providence, they are not confident—even after they land—that the experience will not wrench them from their lives. After he is saved, the narrator likens the sailors' experience to Jonah's (134). The uncontrollable winds that propel them take the sailors into a new kind of darkness, then cast them up on a land from which the narrator must try to carry news of utopia's religion and science to an ignorant world.

The passions that teach the castaway are extremes of fear and hope: terror of death in the open sea followed by an extraordinary elation at having set foot upon—not just having heard about—a kind of heaven on earth. Yet it is an elation qualified by a fear that unless he is rigorously pious, God and the utopians will expel him.

The winds that move him over the sea are of two kinds. The first, the trade winds, stymie his progress and so resemble, in Bacon's scheme of things, the fickle influence of chance and the vagaries of traditional learning, selfish ambition, and the commerce and language of the marketplace. The second wind is the rush of air that takes him straight to the island. It blows north "with a point east" (129), or true north. It is a wind contrary to the ordinary currents of nature. Its direction, violence, and mathematical regularity sever it from the tendencies of natural gales. To have made the observation of its heading, the mariner would have had to consult a magnetic needle—one of the new clues to the labyrinth of nature that no inventor could have known to wish for in its true form (*IM* IV.18). Without proper initiation or knowledge, the narrator sees the clue but does not draw meaning from it. The journey exaggerates the Baconian method, for contrary to all the sailors' expectations it forces them with tortuous, mechanical regularity, in hope and despair, toward a utopia they do not know they approach or desire.

The result of their exquisite torture is a spiritual readiness that is difficult to distinguish from passivity. When the narrator is eventually admitted into the house of mysteries he is remarkably silent. One of the experimenters simply begins to inform him of the institute's activities, without submitting to or being prompted by questions. The initiation appears to have obviated the mariner's ability to question the pious science that has tested and formed him.

The New Atlantis embodies and portrays the scientific rhetoric Bacon explains and exercises in other parts of the *Works*. It is to be read as code: on the surface an engaging, pious account of moral, civil, and physical reality; in a deeper sense, an initiating journey. For the narrator talking to his men, their deliverance is a "miracle" (134); for the informed reader, its self-abnegating movement is designed to be at least an intimation of apocalypse, a revelation of the possibility and the means of mastering nature and civil affairs. Insofar as the reader comes to believe he knows what is happening in the House of Salomon, he is given a vision of nature's power, and the power of nature's maker. The tale also trains its sympathetic listeners to imitate the enlightened utopians' secrecy, not just in order to hide their achievements from envy or theft, but to protect their piety from their own unreliable dispositions. The rigorous ceremony of New Bensalem is in part a device to persuade the narrator that the more he knows about the manipulation of natural motions, the more he must devote himself to charitable duties that do not unleash or betray new powers to do all things possible.

The pious caution of the vision almost empties it. The initiate is told about scientific and social activities, but hears almost nothing about how they have come about. Moreover, the holy man's bland enumeration of astounding scientific achievements seems instantly to render the miracles of science routine. One is reminded again of Oedipus and the Sphinx. The instant the hero answers the riddle, the monster dies. Oedipus throws its body on an ass for all to see, a revelation resembling the speedy circulation of the new scientific knowledge, whose emblem in *The Wisdom of the Ancients* is the Sphinx's wings (*SV* VI.756). In Atlantis, the initiated narrator is within the miracle, yet nowhere. He lives in a utopia that preserves his life, comforts him, and holds out the possibility of mastering nature; but he is barred from real mastery as long as he does not know the code. Insofar as he does know it, the exotic secrets of Atlantean science, once revealed, threaten to become as banal, as silent to the imagination as the dead Sphinx.

~⌒ IV ⌒~

CONTRASTING AND ANTECEDENT TRADITIONS

The *Phaedrus* and the *Rhetoric*

I

The consequences of the new learning's transformation of rhetoric are strikingly evident in Bacon's rendition of Plato's myth of the cave, which *De Augmentis* uses to illustrate men's idolatry. He would have the champions of the new learning imitate the man whose escape from the cave Plato describes in the *Republic*. They should somehow live "in the contemplation of nature, as in the open air," rather than being taken in by the cave's idolatrous puppet-show (*De Aug* IV.433). If they do not succeed in detaching themselves from the cave for good, their spirit "must needs be filled with infinite errors and false appearances." They will remain bound within their delusions even "if they come forth but seldom and for brief periods from their cave, and do not continually live in the contemplation of nature."[1]

Although Bacon puts aside "the exquisite subtlety of the allegory," his gloss hints at a new role for rhetoric once the sons of science see the light. Those who are freed, or who free themselves, must perpetually remain above ground. If they return, their spirits will be filled with "infinite errors." Bacon omits the fact that in Plato's myth the philosopher returns, albeit upon peril of his life and not strictly by choice, to give some version of what he has seen to those who have not escaped.

In much of his writing, Bacon seems to be addressing the shackled spirits himself; but the doctrine attacking the idols of the tribe, the cave, the marketplace, and the theater does not allow him to speak as a philosopher underground the way Socrates can. How then will the new learning's arts of transmission work, especially those that seem to appeal to non-specialists? If the philosopher of the new learning must enter into the rigorous exile of perpetual contemplation and yet participate in the world below, it would seem that his only course is to adopt the manner of Plato's puppeteers. He must return to the underworld as Orpheus does—or rather, in the manner that a charitable Orpheus should have entered it: by withholding himself from passion and yet playing upon the passions of infernal powers to deprive them of Eurydice.

Thus in *The Advancement*, once Bacon finishes with his critique of irresponsible rhetoric, he dwells upon its "strength" and "subtilty" rather than its relation to reason. He is blunt about the general similarity of rhetoric and sophistry: "There is a seducement [in rhetoric] that worketh by the strength of the impression and not by the subtilty of the illaqueation; not so much perplexing the reason as overruling it by power of the imagination" (*Adv* III.295). The paradox in these views is that although the cave is a place of rhetorical deceit, the new sciences can discover and master the forms of seduction.

In this way the new rhetoric demonstrates its incorporation into the new universal philosophy. Rhetoric, like natural philosophy, is a branch growing from "the root and stock of universal knowledge" (*VT* III.228). Cicero was correct in arguing that Socrates wrongly "divorced them and withdrew philosophy and left rhetoric to itself, which by that destitution became but a barren and unnoble science." But Cicero did not go far enough. If eloquence is "a treasury and receipt of all knowledges," it is more than a knowledge of how to use other sciences "for ornament or help in practice" (229). Like all true sciences, which use the others to frame the "very truth and notion" of their axioms so as to perfect a universal knowledge of mutually corrective sciences (229), rhetoric uses other sciences "for the framing or correcting" of "axioms." This is Bacon's version of Cicero's argument that philosophy and eloquence are one. The development of sciences of the human faculties and of the means of working them will ensure that reason finally has its way. The new rhetoric will expose the falsehood of Plato's likening of rhetoric to a cookery that ruins or falsely garnishes the food it works upon (*De Aug* IV.456).

The gist of Bacon's defense of rhetoric is a variation upon Aristotle's well-known rejoinder, in the *Rhetoric*, to the notion that his subject can be dangerously mishandled:

> *Bacon*: For abuses of arts only come in indirectly, as things to guard against, not as things to practise.   (*De Aug* IV.456)

> *Aristotle*: If it is argued that one who makes an unfair use of such faculty of speech may do a great deal of harm, this objection applies equally to all good things except virtue, and above all to those things which are most useful, such as strength, health, wealth, generalship.[2]

Aristotle's reasoning differs from Bacon's in that he compares the faculty or power of rhetoric with good things, which include the useful and expedient. Rhetoric and the other goods are means of a sort, but also steps on a scale of goods, not strictly tools or elements of knowledge in a higher science or for the use of entirely separate, charitable intentions. Genuine expedience, as the *Rhetoric* treats it and as the *Ethics* discusses it at length, is conducive to happiness because real expedience has to do with the good.[3] On this count Bacon criticizes Aristotle for focusing on probative concerns that draw attention away from practical applications of rhetoric, the study of which would enable rhetoric to become a full science capable of doing what the rhetorician wants (*De Aug* IV.458).

Aristotle's original definition of the "art" of rhetoric preserves a connection between technique and philosophy without driving them into a single category. Rhetoric, like dialectical discussion, develops no special science of its own; it harbors no specialized subject matter. Yet an art of rhetoric is also capable of examining "any subject whatever" for the sake of "discovering the possible means of persuasion."[4] Rather than an application of persuasion, it is essentially an art or *technē* that discovers the grounds of persuasion, much as a science discovers what is most pertinent in its own field.[5] This rhetoric is an "offshoot" of dialectic and "the science of Ethics." J. H. Freese's translation tries to clarify the idea by adding the word *merely* where Aristotle says rhetoric is a faculty;[6] but the metaphor of the offshoot does not so strictly suppress rhetoric's affinity with the sciences.

Bacon uses Cicero's praise of philosophical eloquence to justify rhetoric as a rational art whose stature as a part of universal knowledge would rival other sciences. Aristotle on the other hand warns against defining rhetoric by "crossing over into the domain of sciences, whose subjects are certain definite things, not merely [*monon*: only] words."[7] The *Rhetoric* does not systematically separate words from things or downgrade the rhetorician's dependence on words. But neither does it identify rhetoric with the specialized subjects and demonstrations of the sciences. This seems to be the sense of Aristotle's statement that rhetorical proofs have a bearing on "matters that are in a manner within the cognizance of all men and not confined to any special science."[8] Proofs are persuasive instruments with a range and pertinence that can lift them beyond what is unphilosophical and unscientific. Rhetoricians err when they "claim to possess" a science, as do false rhetoricians who assume that they are experts in politics.[9]

Turning at this point to a closer analysis of Platonic and Aristotelian ideas of rhetorical persuasion, we can pursue the meaning of Bacon's appropriation of the Timaeic heritage.[10]

2

To the old question whether the *Phaedrus* is more fundamentally about love than rhetoric, Ficino's Renaissance commentary offers the preliminary answer that the dialogue, in having to do with the beauty of souls and of gods, "talks about love for beauty's sake." It is not therefore irrelevant "that Plato inserts Lysias' speech and argument over oratory; for beauty pertains to the intelligence, to sight, and to hearing. Consequently, in dealing with the beauty of souls and of divinities and likewise with the body's beauty, Plato is correct to discuss the beauty of speech."[11] For Ficino, the *Phaedrus* is concerned with the beauty of speech for the same reason that it is concerned with the beauty of the soul, the gods, and the body: all appeal to intelligence, sight, and hearing. True rhetoric is itself beautiful to the intellect as well as to sense.

Socrates almost immediately asks Phaedrus to read a speech by Lysias, a daringly seductive oration enthusiastically reported by Lysias' young admirer. A kind of beauty in Lysias' words has already cast a spell over Phaedrus. The youth, enamored of rhetoric and, one suspects, of the power over a beautiful audience such a speech can give him, has studied his master's eloquence all night.

Socrates himself seems caught up in the enthusiasm for hearing Lysias' speech, though he is also intent on questioning Phaedrus about it in their conversation. ("I'm so anxious to hear you out that even if you walk as far as Megara . . . I'll not be left behind."[12]) Both speakers are in a sense carried away by the occasion that Lysias' oratory has created, though Socrates has from the start opened the discussion to the distinctions between true and false suasion. Socrates and Phaedrus take themselves or find themselves taken "outside the walls" of the city, out along the Ilissus, the river flowing nearby, and then into the river itself as they walk shoeless to their destination. They finally sit in the lush grass under a tall plane tree, amidst fragrant flowers and pleasant shade, where Socrates expresses his pleasure with the surroundings (though he soon observes that outside the city walls he feels like a stranger).

The two men are, it turns out, near the place where Boreas is reputed to have carried away the maiden Oreithyia. As they recline on the slope in a breeze akin to that windy god, their feet dangle in the moving waters. Their strange new situation is "a spot sacred to Achelous and the Nymphs."[13] Achelous, in Hesiod's *Theogony*, is a river god born to Tethys and Oceanus. He is "the silvery swirler"[14] who works in concert, as do the other river gods, with the nymphs, who act as "nurses" and helpers to men.[15] The nymph who happens to head Hesiod's list of Achelous' company is Peitho, a spirit of persuasion, whose name embodies the Greek assertion "I persuade." Socrates and Phaedrus are thus carried along—almost carried away— by a river of persuasion.

If, as Jacqueline de Romilly has argued, Plato sets Socrates against the conjurers, especially rhetorical conjurers such as Lysias and Gorgias, the encounter with Phaedrus would be a likely occasion for him to do battle with them.[16] Here, however, Socrates confronts Lysias as though he were a conjurer himself. He imitates and parodies sophistic rhetoric in order to converse with Lysias' student, and he works upon Lysias by persuading Phaedrus. The dialogue's proximity to the river helps form it as a work of persuasion, though much more must be said about its use of rhetoric against rhetoric.[17]

The opening of the *Phaedrus* enacts a kind of rapture, though in their very movement beyond the city's walls the two men enter a discussion about distinguishing false persuasion from true. The dialogue moves toward a clarification of the difference between seduction and elevating transport, and the relation between transport and philosophical dialectic. Socrates leans toward that end when he immediately agrees with Phaedrus that Boreas carried away Oreithyia near the spot where they now recline, but then adds that the exact location is further along the riverbank, not where they sit. In other words, the two men are in the general but not precise location of the mythical transport. They have been surrounded by the powerful influences of the river, but in their power to observe a distinction of place, they see that they are not exactly in the situation of Boreas and Oreithyia.

The conversants move toward a definition of philosophical persuasion by undergoing various forms of persuasion that the dialogue gradually and only partially transcends. Socrates and Phaedrus speak from within a cave not unlike the one in the *Republic*. The young man's love of Lysian oratory enables him to see only the puppets' shadows. He slowly recognizes a distant similarity between shadows and puppets, then an affinity between the puppets and things in nature. He beings to acknowledge something superior to, yet drawn from, his own opinions. Conversely, Socrates slowly doffs his parodic disguises as the dialogue begins to respond to his thirst for inquiry into the nature of opinions about rhetoric.

The opening oration composed by Lysias is a remarkable anticipation of the new learning's posture of antagonism toward tendency, affection, and all affectation. Lysias uses the passions, despite his disavowal of passion in himself, to bring Phaedrus under his influence. Socrates observes a certain beauty in the speech's diction and arrangement, a beauty that has obviously stirred the young man it addresses. Lovers, says Lysias, "cannot control themselves" and hence are "incapable of good judgment."[18] Lysias then offers to break the spell that lovers try to cast over their beloved. As a non-lover, he says he can be objective, immune to the damaging excesses of the lovers' madness. He instructs his handsome audience of one in the sober principles of self-interest: surrender to me, he argues, for your own good. Let us take our pleasure rationally, without endangering one another with lovers' false ambitions, and without the danger of desiring new beauty once the old one fades. Let us enjoy love without being lovers.

By pointing to the damage that tyrannical, fickle eros can do, Lysias gives the impression of being a rational companion. He plays on the possibility that the young man will be abandoned or hated by a lover. He then immediately reminds him of the danger of lovers' jealous embraces. Moving rapidly between illustrations of both excesses, the speech creates the impression that the young man will never escape the torments of eros unless he acts in his rational self-interest.

The paradoxical fruition of this strategy is Lysias' request that the young man favor him, even though self-interest would seem to dictate that neither should favor anyone. Here the speaker cannot completely hide his own passion, which he expresses as a dislike of impartiality not his own. His argument is at bottom a warning against revealing passion, and a secret indulgence in the thing it denies. Lysias issues that warning by appealing to the young man's sense of self-interest, saying that indiscriminate impartiality in choosing companions will multiply the chances that private affections will be made public and bring shame upon him. The young man will suffer disgrace, Lysias predicts, if he does not minimize detection by favoring only the speaker. The argument as whole constructs a love that is bound to self-indulgence and the sort of rationality that devotes itself to self-preservation.

The power of the speech, arising from Lysias' complex disclaimer of passion, has overwhelmed Phaedrus and continues to intrigue him, since he has thought of nothing but Lysias' words since daybreak. It soon becomes apparent that he has spent his time memorizing the work, presumably to use it as a secret script to appeal to an unsuspecting audience. Nevertheless, his attempt to hide the written text upon meeting Socrates expresses his shame at his utter dependence on the words that have so powerfully taken him in fear of love's evils. He is eager to try the speech out on Socrates in the guise of his own delivery, but his shame exhibits an awareness of a better manner of persuasion.

It is important to notice that Socrates, who is far from unaware of what is going on, seems to welcome Phaedrus' advances by asking to hear Lysias' speech verbatim once the conversation discovers Phaedrus' ruse. Socrates then offers an almost enthusiastic revision. He has requested Phaedrus to read the speech so as to shame him; but Socrates is also eager to take up something of Lysias' erotic spirit in his own oratorical revision. He draws Phaedrus back to the notion that love is questionable, at the same time that he waxes more eloquent than Lysias when he amplifies the original speech about eros. He speaks his parody with his head covered, in shame of imitating a speech that condemns and exploits Eros, the god, while his elaboration of love's dangers compels him to admit afterward that he had "begun to utter epic verse."[19] He manages to break off without praising exploitative pleasure, and he declares that he will recross the stream to escape being carried away again by the Muses, or perhaps by Phaedrus' company.[20] But he resists the compulsion to flee. A desire to continue in Phaedrus' company, in a pursuit of a definition of rhetoric which is not without risk to the desire to look beyond mere pleasure, prevails. His decision to remain under the tree with Phaedrus, the river, the hypnotic songs of the insects, the heat, and the rhetoric of Lysias is thus partly a decision to dedicate the dialogue to Eros, though of a progressively higher kind. Under the circumstances, only a discussion with Phaedrus has the prospect of clarifying what Eros and rhetoric are. Apparently spurred on, as Phaedrus is, by shame, Socrates also listens to his inner voice, which he says moves him to atone for not praising the god of love. In this way his shame and his demonstration of longing for an understanding of persuasion combine. He says he will invent an encomium to Eros that will correct his error in seeming to follow the blaspheming Lysias.

Socrates neither commands the exile of love nor freely indulges it. In some respects, then, he resembles Lysias. He depends upon rhetorical appeals to the passions though he eschews passionate coercion. And like Lysias, he is highly erotic. The all-important differences between the two master orators emerge in the manner and substance of the dialogue's gradual development of a higher or more accurate understanding of the idea of eros and persuasion. The route from false rhetoric to philosophical truth is presented throughout the dialogue as a graduated, complex movement toward higher or more perfect forms of rhetoric.

Significant differences between Lysias and Socrates begin to appear in the manner of their speaking, when Socrates chooses to express his pious resolve to praise the god. Whereas Lysias both righteously condemns the god without naming him, and uses love for rational pleasures, Socrates praises Eros with a hint of irony. He likens himself to Stesichorus, the poet blinded for speaking ill of Helen, and quotes the notorious lines that won Stesichorus mercy from the gods:

> It is not true, that tale!
> You never embarked in the well-decked ships,
> Nor came to the towers of Troy.[21]

Stesichorus apologizes for questioning the virtue of Helen of Troy, but he does so by declaring that the real Helen was not *of* Troy. The virtuous Helen could not possibly have been there; the Helen of Troy described by the poets was not the real Helen, and the real Helen was somewhere else. In its mixture of piety and ironic reservation, Stesichorus' recantation is a fitting model for Socrates' praise of Eros. Socrates' speech will be a powerful encomium to the god, and will indeed almost overpower Phaedrus, but it will also qualify its zeal with parody and with the discursive rigors of dialectic. Likewise, the myth of the charioteer will be, according to what Socrates says following the speech, both a revelation and a suspect enchantment.

The myth of the charioteer, the famous centerpiece of the dialogue, carries these contrary attitudes to a height from which eros and rhetoric can be redefined at the same time that they are experienced with greater awe. The vision in one sense inspires Phaedrus to seek a nobler love, one that aspires to truth, in a climb toward the heavens. In another sense, however, the myth touches on the problematic nature of erotic persuasion. The very essence of the soul, Socrates tells Phaedrus, is its ceaseless *self*-movement, which makes it immortal; when its self-movement ends, it no longer exists.[22] Likewise, "every body that is moved from without is soulless"; only the body that "derives its motion from within itself has a soul."[23]

The myth embodies the problem of understanding persuasion. Can a self-moving soul be persuaded without being coerced? Socrates grants that the soul "moves something at one time, [and] may yet have its motion transmitted to it by another at another time,"[24] as long as its self-movement somehow continues unimpeded. The myth overwhelms and yet presses the question of how such a combination of influence and self-motion can be possible.

Socrates impresses Phaedrus' imagination with a tale of souls that are chariots drawn by pairs of horses, all following in the train of Zeus's chariot. The vision is one of harmony between the soul's self-motion and external persuasive forces. The soul combines motion and rest: the straining horses pull the standing charioteer, who guides them in his aspiration to reach the orbit of the gods as the influence of the highest god draws them all forth.

Zeus's influence on the other souls compares to the charioteer's over his team. Although the god governs souls as he sets in order and cares for all things, his rule consists most literally in setting his retinue in array (*diakosmon panta*),[25] not merely in "imposing order," as one modern translation has it. The squadrons of angels fan out in his trail, set forth (*kekosmēmenē*)[26] in harmony with the order of the cosmos, as though subordinate to him yet seeking what he seeks: a sight of reality beyond the turning heavens. Though the human souls in Zeus's train are not so harmoniously disposed to accompany him to the summit, they resemble in varying degrees the aspiring, self-moving chariots of the gods that revere and harmonize with what leads them upward.

In presenting that harmony, Socrates faces the difficulty of explaining the persuasion of the imperfect soul that once saw the higher realities but now is so troubled by the appetites of the dark horse that the only resort to move the chariot properly seems to be the whip.[27] The fallen soul, which easily forgets what it saw at the peak of its journey, would seem to be no soul at all if a vision of the summit must now be imposed upon it so that it can ascend again. The dark horse, as one of the three parts of the soul, cannot simply be whipped into submission if the soul is to be defined as self-moving.

The narrative presents two kinds of persuasion: of the charioteer and of his team of horses. The soul as a whole seems to be moved with a kind of violence when in the presence of worldly beauty; part of it is "stricken with amazement and . . . no longer able to control" itself.[28] The reaction, however, is not merely coerced. The charioteer has recalled in the sight of worldly beauty his true nature and his end beyond the earth. The human soul has by definition seen the highest things.[29] It forgets but then suffers perturbation because it does not abandon the memory that most defines it even in its fallen state.

Sometimes the charioteer appears to be coerced by the dark horse; for a time, it drags him and the good horse toward an object of beauty in order to satisfy its carnal appetite. But Socrates specifies that the rider and the good horse are finally dragged "yielding and agreeing [*eixante kai omologēsante*]"[30] as though in their resistance they could not refuse to approach the image suggesting their original vision. The chariot's struggling, consenting movement toward the beauty of the beloved reveals its object's "radiant face," which carries the charioteer's memory "back to the form of real beauty."[31]

Socrates describes the effect of the recollection in a manner that partially resolves the difficulty of the self-moving soul's being threatened with violence from within. As the charioteer approaches the beloved, he remembers the beauty he once saw at the rim of the cosmos, and so "falls backwards in awe and reverence, necessarily pulling the reins so violently that both horses are brought down to their haunches."[32] The beast increases its suffering to the degree that it violently resists the reins erratically controlled by recollection. The struggle pits the force of divine vision against irrational appetite. At the same time, the horse's appetitive lurches have the effect of doubling the force of the reins. The repeated motions finally subdue it, and the horse shows forth its animal soul in a fear that is a shadow of the self-moving soul's proper awe before its beloved.[33]

Once the lover subdues the dark horse, new difficulties await him in the manner he persuades his beloved. He approaches with a desire not only to serve and to honor, but to form by "sportive persuadings [*paidika peithontes*] and discipline [*ruthmizontes*: bringings to measure]."[34] How then do the lover's actions distinguish themselves from the false lover's efforts to make his beloved a mirror-image of his own corruption, a soul without access to philosophy? If the lovers are "bringing the beloved to be as much as possible like themselves,"[35] how can they avoid violently transforming him as Lysias would?

The myth suggests that a soul-confirming persuasion is possible if the lover leads the beloved to imitate the god the lover honors, rather than the lover alone. That divinity is supposedly shadowed forth in the beloved himself, to the degree that he wins the lover's attention because he resembles the god most appropriate to the perfection of his character. The effort to bring the beloved to a kind of temper or measure is in this circumstance an aspiration to confirm the beloved's highest self, rather than to create him anew. Instead of appealing to the beloved's self-interest, the lover's attempt to persuade is in this regard an act of reverence, its end being the beloved's more perfect imitation of the god. Struggling and prevailing as a charioteer and his team, the lover finally persuades the beloved only insofar as the beloved freely welcomes his attentions, much as the god would choose to show kindness to a suppliant.

These solutions to the problem of persuading self-moving souls are severely tempered with the rule that fallen souls cannot regain their wings for ten thousand years, unless they pursue wisdom with such dedication that they grow wings in three thousand.[36] Phaedrus complicates the discussion by not taking the cycle of years as a caution. He falls in love with Socrates' long speech, pronouncing it the last word on the subject, far better than anything Lysias has said or will say in speeches about love. The dialogue must resume in order to overcome Phaedrus' false enchantment, despite the success of the myth's rhetoric.

Each of the dialogue's three orations has blunted as well as agitated Phaedrus' desire to pursue these matters. In the work as a whole he moves only gradually toward greater dialectical acuity, first seeming to threaten Socrates with violence if he does not match or exceed Lysias' speech. Socrates continues, despite the danger, as though he were ashamed for Lysias and dependent upon Phaedrus for the pursuit of these matters, which takes place most appropriately in dialogue. After Socrates delivers his parody of Lysias, Phaedrus again appears to be on the verge of passionate excess in his praise of the new speech, until Socrates tells of his own shame in delivering it, and of the inner voice that warns him to make amends by speaking again.

Finally, after Socrates presents the myth of the charioteer, both conversants seem to be in danger of falling asleep. Phaedrus had suggested, just before Socrates' final performance, that since the disabling heat of noonday was almost upon them Socrates should stay and rest. Socrates himself had said he wished to recross the river to elude the danger of falling completely under the spell of the nymphs, of succumbing to the persuasion of persuasion (Peitho). While he unfolds the myth of the chariot as an act of purification, mid-day arrives and the cicadas are singing at top pitch. When he finishes he acts as though his speech in obedient praise of Eros had generated in himself an enthusiasm most difficult to control.

The cicadas intensify the temptation to sleep that follows the great speech, but their influence does not contradict the power of the speech to call the passions to higher things. The cicadas reward those who hear them and are wakeful. Modifying the tale of the Sirens in the *Odyssey*, Socrates has the cicadas praise those who in being transported by the Muses honor them in their arts, which include persuasion and dialectic, while staying clear of sleepy harbors.[37] If Phaedrus can join Socrates in sailing their discourse past the insects' Siren call, both men might find philosophical happiness.

The encounter's high point in the myth of the charioteer, occurring in the midst of the exchange, is not yet an adequate close. Phaedrus passionately misunderstands it, concluding that Lysias will never write a speech again, that Socrates' last oration has rendered all further speeches inferior. Having witnessed Socrates' power to extemporize a magnificent praise of Eros, Phaedrus projects onto Lysias his own novel and exaggerated disgust with premeditated, written oratory.[38] Socrates must go on to remind him that premeditation and writing are not in themselves the cause of sophistry: the dialogue must go within or beyond the myth of the charioteer to examine the differences between good and bad rhetoric, and to address Lysias himself.

No formal orations follow, but not because Socrates has entirely abandoned erotic rhetoric. He now turns toward the art of influencing souls in private gatherings, which he suggests is another manifestation of the art of speeches.[39] The discussion that follows enacts and suggests the nature of true rhetoric, in which it offers instruction. As Richard Weaver has argued, the suasory array of the dialogue's dialectic offers a rhetorically complex analysis and synthesis of what Socrates says should be pursued.[40]

The dialogue at mid-point turns more explicitly to souls, speeches, and the manner in which they are related, but Socrates does not exile himself from the arena of oratory. He invokes and recognizes numerous audiences other than Phaedrus: Lysias, Isocrates, and the gods. His irony enables him to characterize the dialogue's continuing inquiry as an epideictic display of daring, self-deprecating commendation rather than hostile censure, though there is an edge to his praise.[41] He praises an ass (Lysias and false love) as though it were a horse, drawing friendly ridicule that discovers Lysian love's inadequacies while introducing a higher praise of eros.

The numerous rules for carrying out philosophical oratory according to dialectical principles seem extraordinarily demanding, so much so that they raise questions about why the rest of the dialogue is necessary to introduce them, and whether they can be practiced. But these are questions which the dialogue addresses indirectly throughout. As we have seen, rules about analyzing and relating souls and speeches are at work at every stage in Socrates' encounters with the ruthless Sophist Lysias, his precocious student Phaedrus, the tepid Isocrates, the fickle Aphrodite, and the mantic Apollo. The reader of the dialogue must also sense Plato's attention to the diverse audience of his writings. The structure of the dialogue is to some degree a record of its organization of speeches according to the shifting of occasion, Phaedrus' predisposition, and the demands of dialectical procedure and principle in light of their application to multiple audiences. Observing these matters in practice—in the dialogue itself—is the way the student of rhetoric learns what philosophical rhetoric is, "through the sharp use of his senses." "If he does not do this, no part of the theoretical knowledge he acquired as a student is as yet of any help to him."[42]

Throughout the dialogue the disclosure of the unreliability of written or merely premeditated speeches paradoxically enables the reader to begin this inquiry. He is invited to proceed by way of the speeches that come under analysis because he is encouraged to encounter them as objects and instruments of ridicule and commendation in regard to something that might be true. Rather than being freed from the text of the dialogue or bound to its terminal doctrine for good rhetoric, the reader is supposed to enter into a play of speeches, coming to know his insufficiency and his readiness to defend what his words adumbrate.[43] The dialogue itself within Plato's written version of it (if it is possible to speak of such a thing) stands in similar need of a questioning and exposition that takes it beyond mundane fixity, into the nobler being of its self-movement and its aspiration. What is true of the speeches and the dialogue is meant to be applicable to the participants. One could say that the dialogue exists because it takes shape and moves within the form of its speakers' "amusement" with speeches, the activity that Socrates says characterizes the entire exchange.[44] When the dialogue finishes, the amusement must end; but the manifold activity of the amusement predicts its continuation in ready souls.

We see that what Lysias might and ought to have said about eros is turned over again and again. Socrates cannot let the matter rest with himself and Phaedrus alone. Earlier he had challenged Lysias "to write as quickly as may be" a purifying clarification of his first speech.[45] His dialogue with Lysias' beloved Phaedrus is in part an attempt to converse with Lysias *in absentia*, to urge him to defend his writings in response to questions of the kind that have already inspired another writer of speeches, Isocrates, to pursue philosophy. The dialogue will end with a challenge to Lysias to "come to the aid of what he has written . . . to demonstrate from his own mouth the poverty of his writings,"[46] and thus through dialectic to display either his greater wisdom or his vacuity.

In the dialogue's contest of ridicule and praise is a demonstration of how a philosopher might re-enter the cave of the idolaters and move his audience in stages to higher things, without remote control or the rigorously coded speech so necessary to the new learning. In the Platonic setting, the philosopher routinely undergoes a ludic yet dangerous encounter with opinion, and then by means of ridiculous and challenging praise attempts to coax opinion toward something higher.

It remains true that the dialogue's amusement is to some degree frivolous, to be discarded at the end. The possibility that Lysias will reform himself with the spur of Socratic dialogue is not great. We know that the more philosophical orator Isocrates is now an old man preoccupied with stylistic niceties; Socrates' prediction of his rise in future years to philosophical rhetoric is a barb as well as an invitation.[47] Phaedrus himself has difficulty grasping and remembering what has just transpired. He must ask Socrates to summarize,[48] and Socrates has cast doubt on the veracity of his own recollection of enthusiastic speeches. To the end, nevertheless, the dialogue's outward manner is one of praise rather than hostility and censure. Its irony continues to take up received opinion in a commendatory manner, to see "whether there is anything in it."[49] Its commendatory mode is to the end a form of ridicule, but one that tempers the ambitious rhetor with emulative, cautionary praise of his unacknowledged aspirations. Plato's hostility toward rhetorical sophistry is undeniable; what is remarkable about his discourse in the *Phaedrus* is its acknowledgment that the cave and the difficult, aspiring ascent from the cave are the context for all true rhetoric.

3

The *Rhetoric*, which Bacon recognizes most explicitly as his precedent in the making of a new system of rhetoric, differs in many ways from the *Phaedrus*, but without necessarily abrogating its precursor's work on matters of concern to us here. W. Rhys Roberts has documented the commonplace that Aristotle devised his *Rhetoric* to respond to the challenge Socrates lays down in the *Phaedrus*: to develop an art that is cognizant of the nature of truth, of the soul and its affections, of what the soul acts upon and what draws it out.[50] For Aristotle, the true master of rhetoric "can reason . . . can analyze the several types of character and the virtues, and thirdly, the emotions—the nature and quality of each emotion, the sources and modes of its production."[51]

The *Rhetoric* has sometimes been read as a handbook of techniques. In devoting most of its pages to a taxonomy of speeches, subject matters, affections, dispositions, arguments, and stylistic devices, the work to some degree encourages the purely utilitarian view propagated by Edward Copes's commentary and by Thomas Hobbes's highly reductive translation, which for two hundred years was the popularly definitive English version of the *Rhetoric*.[52] Book I's focus on proofs and facts, to many modern readers, seems to give ground in Books II and III to narrowly pragmatic studies of emotions, dispositions, arrangements of speeches, and forms of style, as when Aristotle's initial criticism of the manipulative arts of coercing judges leads in Book II to an inquiry into the methods of influencing judges' dispositions.

Writing in the sixteenth century, Peter Ramus (Pierre de la Ramée) sees Aristotle's rhetorical enterprise as a subversion of the true di-

alectic, which can have no counterpart in its proof-making and an-
alytical activities. Bacon writes that Aristotle does not go far enough
to make the *Rhetoric* a complete catalogue of sophisms. Friedrich
Solmson's modern analysis concludes that the work is an accretion
of texts without a controlling purpose.[53] But as Carnes Lord has
recently argued, the *Rhetoric* has a coherence—often underestimated
by readers intolerant of doubleness that is not purely rational and
practical—as a defense of high-minded rhetoric that persistently qualifies the status of the rhetorical faculty. For Lord, Aristotle answers
and engages the Sophists with a defense of philosophical rhetoric in
which he distances himself as much as possible "from those aspects
of rhetoric which he considered low and potentially dangerous, yet
necessary for effective persuasion."[54] The *Rhetoric* thereby enforces
the irony and inquisitive interest that mark the treatment of rhetoric
in the *Phaedrus*.

The matter and method of Aristotle's argument go further than
Plato does in delineating an affinity between rhetoric and academic
discussion, and in highlighting a similarity between rhetorical enthymemes and higher science or philosophy. But the *Rhetoric* is also more
guarded than the *Phaedrus* in its definition of rhetoric as a counterpart
of a dialectic of probable reasoning. For all its arguments in favor of
rhetorical endeavors, the *Rhetoric* does not attempt to define a philosophical rhetoric in a precise relation to the Socratic dialectic, as Socrates' irony seems to do at the end of the *Phaedrus*.

Aristotle begins with a definition of rhetoric that depends upon the
complex meaning of "dialectic" and on a problematic term for the
relation between dialectic and rhetoric: "Rhetoric is a counterpart
[antistrophos] of Dialectic."[55] Dialectic, we are immediately told,
resembles rhetoric at least in being concerned with "matters that are
in a manner within the cognizance of all men and not confined to
any special science." The comparison, whatever the precise meaning
of "counterpart," hints at rhetoric's limitations as well as its scope.
In its concern with probable reasoning, rhetoric, like dialectic, is a
comprehensive faculty restricted to no specialized subject matter. Yet
like dialectic it is also more or less confined to probable opinions
accessible to relatively general audiences. Neither endeavor begins,
as Aristotle's sciences do, from principles the specialists would accept
as primary and true in their own disciplines.[56] In the *Topics* Aristotle
observes that dialecticians, unlike philosophers, must take for granted
the presence of an audience. Their art "always involves a relation
with another party" whereas the scientific philosophers' need not.[57]

Aristotle's complex notion of opinion ennobles rhetoric in the way he limits rhetoric's character. In Aristotelian dialectic, opinion is called *endoxa*: seeming truth that need not merely seem. Those who uphold the truth of such opinions are, according to the *Topics*, "all" men or all of "the wise," or "the majority" of the wise, or the most "famous and distinguished" of them.[58] The list of authorities is all-inclusive and yet hierarchical. Dialectical opinions are literally *in* the *doxa* (common opinion) without being necessarily identical to it. In the *Rhetoric*, although Aristotle refers to opinion as seeming truth and *doxa*, he uses *endoxa* in a crucial passage referring to the probable reasoning that characterizes rhetoric.[59] And throughout the treatise, he presents various kinds of *doxa* from which the rhetorician is to draw proofs, the respectable ends of rhetoric.

If rhetoric is the "counterpart" or *antistrophos* of dialectic, how then does one explain the rhetorician's favoring of the uneducated speaker, and his taking for granted an audience's inability to follow scientific instruction? If rhetoric is not the same as the dialectic of academic discussion that Aristotle describes in the *Topics*, is it essentially a maker of false similitudes? The meaning of "counterpart" clarifies and complicates the issue. In its most literal sense, an *antistrophos* is the countermovement of a dramatic chorus as it responds to the first part of the choral ode. The chorus moves slowly across the stage to deliver the *strophē*, then turns to give the antistrophic response, a repetition or elaboration of the *strophē*. In paraphrasing the sentence, Cicero extends Aristotle's dramatic metaphor by making the movements equal actors: rhetoric is "an art as it were to answer to dialectic from another direction or location [*artem quasi ex altera parte respondere dialecticae*]".[60] But the meaning of the term in the *Rhetoric* is more complex than Cicero's gloss, which expresses an ambition to make rhetoric the equal, if not the superior, of dialectic and philosophy. Aristotle rephrases his comparison in more general, less binding terms: dialectic and rhetoric are like a plant and its "offshoot" (*paraphues*), a genus and its division or sub-set (*morion*), and a thing and its likeness (*omoiōma*).[61] Rhetoric therefore might be an adjunct, a subordinate, or a likeness of dialectic. As an offshoot it resembles something organic to the main plant. The species might be best understood as *of* the genus of dialectic, having to do with ethics and politics, and as a likeness that might be capable of evoking what it reflects. The more precise nature of these relations emerges only gradually in the course of Aristotle's discussion.

Correspondences such as these fire Ramus's sixteenth-century criticism of Aristotle as a master of misleading redundancies. For Ramus, of course, precisely because dialectic and rhetoric are comparable they should be resolved into two entirely distinct arts, with invention and arrangement going to dialectic, style and delivery to rhetoric. Yet the Ramistic attempt to remove rhetoric entirely from dialectic has a paradoxical effect, exhaustively documented by Walter Ong.[62] In taking over rhetorical invention and arrangement, Ramistic dialectic absorbs rhetorical elements in a way that weakens dialectic's logical status while strengthening its power to capture the pedagogical fervor of sixteenth-century schools. Ramus's three methodological laws, designed to ensure that dialectic proceeds by means of unassailable and unambiguous propositions about what is "most clear," recognize no difference between what is plain to the commonality and what is evident to the wisest of dialecticians.

For Aristotle, the power of rhetoric is assumed to reside in its proofs, be they devoted to demonstrating the argument itself, the speaker's *ethos*, or the grounds that enable a yearning audience to be moved: "We entertain the strongest persuasion of a thing when we conceive that it has been demonstrated."[63] The example and the maxim, which might seem to be mere assertions or tools for effect, are residual proofs. The most manifest proof is the rhetorical enthymeme, the most persuasive of such proofs in its resemblance to the scientific syllogism:

> It is manifest that the artistic Rhetoric is concerned with proofs. The rhetorical proof is a sort of demonstration, for we entertain the strongest persuasion of a thing when we conceive that it has been demonstrated. A rhetorical demonstration is an enthymeme,—this being, generally speaking, the most authoritative of proofs. The enthymeme again is a sort of syllogism, and every kind of syllogism alike comes under the observation of Dialectic, either generally or in one of its departments. Hence it is clear that he who is best able to investigate the elements and the genesis of the syllogism will also be the most expert with the enthymeme, when he has further mastered its subject matter and its difference from the logical syllogism.[64]

Here the overlap is neither identity nor illusion. The enthymeme differs from the syllogism, and the master of the enthymeme is the expert of the syllogism who knows that difference. He is the positive version of the sophistical rhetorician described in the *Phaedrus*, who must know true things in order to use likenesses effectively.[65] Al-

though the Aristotelian scrutiny of likenesses and differences introduces the idea that rhetorical proofs are probable, it does not abandon
interest in philosophical verity. The rhetorical enthymeme differs
from other kinds of syllogism in not drawing its conclusions "from
too far back"—too many steps removed from the immediate proof—
and in not including all stages of the argument.[66] Its form could be
said to compromise truth by taking into account the defects of its
hearers; but Aristotle emphasizes the power of the enthymeme to
avoid what is obvious and so already known, as well as what is
obscure. Although the general audience may not be able to follow
educated speakers who use necessary premises and generalities, it is
impatient with redundance, and it is persuadable by means of opinions
that are at least true "as a rule" (*epi to polu*).[67]

By contrast, Bacon's crucial definition of rhetoric does not mention
proofs. The means of illustration and transmission, as they are taken
up by various branches of the new learning in the *De Augmentis* and
the *Novum Organum*, are presented either as highly specific positions,
as general methods of presentation, or as signs—not as units of discourse claiming attention as arguments. In Bacon's hands, Aristotle's
commonplaces (*koina*) are all sophisms to be catalogued and employed
for purposes of rational and charitable manipulation. They cannot be
endoxic similitudes, despite their powers of influence, because they
are cryptic.

The lack in Bacon's major treatises of a sustained consideration of
endoxic similitudes and proofs, other than in his careful praise of the
old learning in Book I of *The Advancement*, is an indication of the
new learning's effort to free rhetoric from opinion in order to use the
influence of opinion for rational ends. Bacon frequently takes pains
to show his support for the customary moral and religious doctrines
of the day, but his plan to examine all sophistical opinions, those not
included in "doctrine," is designed to master opinion.

The difference between Aristotelian and Baconian approaches becomes clearer when one looks at Aristotle's delineation of the three
kinds of oratory and their most characteristic proofs. For example,
he insists that forensic speeches rely on the facts of the case,[68] even
though he devotes much of his discussion to pathetic and ethical
proofs, and to style. The lawyer restricted to the facts must in the
final analysis "prove that the fact in question is or is not so" and
"whether it is important or unimportant, just or unjust."[69] Rhetoric
has to do with proofs, and proofs are about something. Discourse

has a subject matter having to do with significant ideas. In forensic discourse proofs are concerned in some fashion with the meaning of justice, since to discover his arguments the rhetorician must study the motives and predilections of the victim and the accused, who in their desire for vengeance and testimony of innocence appeal to an idea of justice. In the deliberative discourse of the assembly the rhetorician will examine notions of expedience or practicality that take him to a consideration of the nature of happiness; in epideictic speeches of praise or blame, toward the idea of virtue.

A speaker appeals most powerfully to the disposition of his audience on the basis of his "ethical proof," which turns upon his presentation of proofs showing "good sense, virtue, and good-will."[70] Character emerges most persuasively through these "artificial" proofs, not from what Aristotle considers to be "inartificial" displays of credentials.[71] In the *Rhetoric* the verb for showing or constructing oneself as a persuasive character has to do with making proofs: *Kataskeuazein.*[72] To "develop a certain character in himself," the speaker resists the sophistic tendency to concentrate on rhetorical effect.[73]

The so-called "pathetic proofs" likewise rely upon the speaker's understanding of emotions, dispositions, and occasions whose meaning turns upon intellectual ends. The dovetailing of proof and persuasion is strengthened by a host of assumptions and arguments about the tendencies of animate things to aspire toward their appropriate ends and toward the good. Aristotle's collection of opinions concerning anger and pity is largely in proof of the existence of aspirations toward an idea of justice, whatever the errors and excesses of individual plaintiffs and defendants. Beneath the discussion of the objectivity of judges there is the assumption of a passionate tendency that enables judicial conviction. The lawyer legitimately appeals to the judge's disposition not to arouse inappropriate emotions of anger or jealousy but to elicit a conviction that leads to the judicial act.[74] It is in *not* engaging their passions in response to their own and others' persuasions that judges are particularly susceptible to corrupt rhetoric.[75] They succumb to falsehoods when their passions are "warped,"[76] not because they simply allow themselves to act with any kind of passion. Conversely, members of a deliberative assembly who are regularly involved in debating their own affairs are relatively immune to false rhetoric. Their common attachments to their own interests and the practical good of the city tend to focus their passionate attention upon the facts.[77]

The assembly's seemingly narrow deliberation over what is expedient in terms of the legislator's original intent is itself supposed to be a consideration of an end—happiness—and other means that are greater goods leading toward a higher end.[78] Here the discussion of expedience draws from the treatment of the efficient cause in the *Physics.* Although one might assume that the efficient cause is the most neutral of devices for achieving an end, in the *Physics* it too has teleological tendency.[79]

The list of topics appropriate to all three kinds of speeches hints at a tendency present in the instruments themselves. Indeed, Aristotle's own exposition discloses organizational preferences. When he explains the topic of the possible and the impossible, he lists only the arguments that establish the possible. He presents his list of merely "apparent" (hence false) enthymemes only at the end, in a much shorter series. Even there he argues that sophistries, rather than being simply false, are incomplete or misdirected: "in the case of sophistical disputations, the argument becomes fallacious when the circumstances, reference, and manner are not added."[80] Hence the most notorious of sophistical devices, the *Corax,* typically is not a fundamental mistake or a will to prevail, but an inadequate, inappropriate development of a reasonable principle. Corax claims to prove, as all Sophists are accused of pretending, that equally plausible arguments could be constructed on opposite sides of any issue. Corax's emphasis upon the unlikely possibility is probable, but "only," Aristotle adds, "in the conditions mentioned." It is in being misapplied that the argument "becomes" fallacious.[81]

Other sections of the *Rhetoric* that seem essentially sophistic and which are treated as sophistry in Freese's translation are best read in light of the design in these passages. The discussion of praise and blame, for instance, which in Freese's version seems to be an endorsement of mere flattery, draws upon a deeper notion of praise as *auxesis:* an augmentation that perfects. Praise in this sense amplifies, confirms, or predicts the actualization of potential virtues. Narrowly construed, Aristotle's advice seems to advocate what he condemns as shameful flattery that "overpraises" the good and "palliates" the bad:[82] "thus the cautious man may be called cold and designing; the foolish man may be called good-natured, or the unfeeling man mild . . . . [A] fallacious argument may be drawn from the motive [of the man being praised]."[83]

Nevertheless, what Freese calls a fallacy is more literally a reckoning beyond calculation, a hyperbolic excess *(paralogistikon)* conducive to stirring its object to act within its truer, higher nature.[84] The argument impinges upon the *Ethics'* treatment of excesses as unsuccessful attempts to hit the mean. In this sense praise augments character by drawing out or arraying the harmonics of what it is capable of playing, bringing before the object of praise what it has reached for and might by nature become. Such flattery resembles proper medical treatment, which makes its applications in order to elicit, not impose, the soul's movement toward health: "it is not the function of medicine to restore a patient to health, but only to promote this end as far as possible; for even those whose recovery is impossible may be properly treated."[85] The effect is in accordance with the *Rhetoric's* definition of pleasure as "a certain movement of the soul" that is a "settling down into [the soul's] natural state" or source of being.[86] The soul's cure is its proper self-movement, which is more important than any imposed health. False flattery can entail this curative principle.

In the same vein, the rhetorical proofs, like scientific syllogisms, can be distinguished as real or apparent,[87] in part because "that which is true and better is naturally always easier to prove and more likely to persuade."[88] Where we see Bacon stressing the inadmissibility of all but charitable and scientific motives in the use of rhetorical tools, Aristotle upholds veridical tendencies in the persuasive rhetorician's instruments as well as his subject matters.

Across this commendatory current, Aristotle endeavors to maintain a prudent distance from the excesses of opposite shores: an uncritical embrace of rhetorical conjury, and a deceptive antagonism toward everything rhetorical. Reminders of his caution occur throughout: rhetoric, he says, indeed proves opposites, as sophistry does in its most characteristic activity;[89] it addresses inexpert audiences unable to follow scientific reasoning;[90] the attractions of rhetorical style and delivery, especially in contemporary practice, are commonly vulgar.[91] Like rhetorical style, rhetoric itself is a "real or apparent" process of bringing to light.[92] The opposite of a dialectician is a Sophist, but we have no word to distinguish the false from the genuine orator: both are rhetoricians.[93] The panoply of translators' phrases for rhetoric's action draws out something of its ambiguity: rhetoric "assumes,"[94] "slips into the garb of,"[95] or "masquerades"[96] as ethics and politics. We see this caution in the *Rhetoric's* treatment of style and delivery as *prosthēkai:* though they are "of the greatest importance,"[97] they remain accessories to proofs, which "form the only artistic elements" of rhetoric, "all else being appendage."[98] Jebb and Freese translate the concluding phrase as "mere" accessory and "mere" appendage, emphasizing the derivative nature of all that is not proof in rhetoric.

Still, the *prosthēkai* have to do with the more literal meaning of the Greek term as something placed near something else, something more than accidental, as *prosthēkai* derives its meaning from the root verb *prostithēmi:* to set out, set forth, display, or show. The prosthesis is secondary to the organic whole; yet like the thing that occurs second it can be understood in appropriate circumstances as a completion and perfection, as something more final and primary than the thing it completes. Likewise the end toward which something moves as it is perfected by its accessory can be more primary, depending upon its relation to circumstances, than its source or beginning.

The *Rhetoric*'s Book III turns upon these ambiguities in the meaning of style as accessory to proof. What would seem to be an ideal occasion for Aristotle to expound upon style's power to perfect is not developed as one might expect. The book is curt, tempered by its reference to the ready corruption of contemporary interest in display and delivery. It moves with increasing speed and brevity, its ambivalence deflating sophistic ambitions to make style the center of the rhetorical art.

In Book III Aristotle therefore downplays, though does not deny, the possibility of an essential connection between style and proof. The outstanding feature of rhetorical style, the metaphor, he calls the most decorous when it is most perspicuous.[99] While style in Athens is a preoccupation that damages political life, *lexis* (style or diction) "contributes much toward determining [*pros to phanēnai:* toward making appear] the character [*poion:* nature or quality] of the speech," since "it is not enough to know what we are to say;—we must say it in the right way."[100] Aristotle takes up the matter most explicitly in a passage of extraordinary ambiguity:

> As . . . the whole discipline of rhetoric aims at appearance, we must give our attention to this subject [style], considered as necessary, not as desirable in itself; for, strictly speaking, our sole aim in our language should be to give neither pain nor pleasure; our facts ought to be our sole weapons, making everything superfluous which is outside the proof. Owing to the infirmities of the hearer, however, style, as we have said, can do much. (At the same time, style has necessarily a certain small value in every kind of exposition; the mode of expression chosen makes some difference to the clearness—

not such a very great difference, however; it is all imagination
and . . . [concerns] the hearer; thus, no teacher commends geometry by graces of style.)[101]

The passage goes further than any other in the *Rhetoric* to frustrate
sophistic enthusiasms. Its judgment upon style and delivery elevates
rhetorical proof above its additions, though it acknowledges style's
contribution to intelligibility. At one point the passage defends the
superiority of proofs on such narrow and rigorous forensic grounds
that style seems necessary only for attending to the least expert of
audiences. What style achieves does not seem to make a great difference. Style is *phantasia,* or outward show that "concerns the audience"
and so seems irrelevant to the teaching of a philosophical subject such
as geometry.

Aristotle makes his case, however, without reducing style to an
appendage. His defense of proofs, which compares rhetorical style
unfavorably to a science of numbers, is so restrictive that it retracts
some of the argument's derogatory bite. Moreover, the principle of
perspicuity (*saphē*),[102] which combines the truthful with the manifest,
sets the Aristotelian canons of style apart from those of the Sophist
who sees nothing philosophical at stake in choosing from synonyms
that generally refer to the same thing. For Aristotle, an individual
word "may be more appropriate [*kuriōteron:* having more authority]
than another because it is more in the image of our thought [*ōmoiōm-
enon:* more of a likeness], and thus better suited [*oikeioteron:* more
becoming, suitable] to set it [the matter] before our eyes." Metaphors
and other figures and schemes "must be taken from things beautiful,"
as though they stood more within the image of truth by coming from
the beautiful.[103]

Book III roughens all of these arguments with a brusqueness of
manner that serves as a proof of Aristotle's reservations. Much as
Socrates belittles the rhetorical handbooks by summing up their teachings in a few lines in the *Phaedrus,* the *Rhetoric* gives style and delivery
short shrift. Book III sticks to the facts. Since style offers no art of
proof susceptible to the modes of Aristotle's analysis in Books I and
II, the discussion can end quickly, plausibly, and logically with a terse
peroration in parody of the ideal forensic speech Aristotle described
in Book I: "I have spoken; you have heard; you know the facts; now
give your decision."[104]

Aristotle's argument is finally a commendation of rhetoric's teleological power when that power is drawn from its proofs. Style is a kind of proof too, in some ways the most important proof in the rhetoric that fills Aristotle's world. But the *Rhetoric* finally treats style much as Socrates handles rhetoric, by turning his audience's attention to the pressing and difficult problems of speaking and writing about philosophy, even as one recognizes the affinities between philosophy, persuasion, ornamentation, and the contest of dialectical disputation.

Agricola and Ramus

When it adapts the old arts of words to the new sciences of things, the new learning redefines what it uses. In making rhetoric and dialectic more available for certain kinds of inquiry and for the transmission of learning, it changes how rhetoric and dialectic are understood. The new learning is supposed to take in such things as the Aristotelian topics, their categories, and Platonic dialectic by systematizing and comprehensively indexing the resources of invention, removing Aristotle's vainglorious omissions and Plato's misapprehensions. But while this adaptation preserves much of the Timaeic tradition, it threatens the tradition's reason for being.

I

Far more systematically than does Aristotle, Bacon explicitly segregates the old arts of words from the arts of inquiry. Traditional rhetorical topics or sources of invention discover only arguments, not true arts (*De Aug* IV.407), and their invention is "not properly an invention" because it only recovers what is already known (421). The old rhetorician and dialectician have behaved like the self-satisfied baron who hunts game in his own enclosed park. The new arts of discovery would search out or dare to stumble upon nature's secrets in the forest beyond the park (422).

On a deeper level, the new learning assimilates the topics, as it does the strictures of Plato's dialectical method, by embarking upon a project to map their complete workings and to make them available for the new inquiry into nature. Comprehensively catalogued and ready for use, the new topics would perfect the old ones by extracting knowledge from nature, not just drawing it from the memory: "The same places therefore which will help us to shake out the folds of the intellect within us, and to draw forth the knowledge stored therein, will also help us to gain knowledge from without" (*De Aug* IV.423).

The "particular" or specialized topics, the most useful to the sciences, are in Bacon's argument surprisingly legitimate forms of "anticipation" (423) and allowable "precepts of invention." Even though the new learning predicates its reforms on the suppression of expectation, the best topical sources will be useful until the most perfect forms of inquiry are discovered and applied. Although the new topics are provisional, they allow investigators to get "a nearer view of that which is to come" (424).

This conversion of the topics into scientific instruments has a venerable precedent in the work of Cicero, who sought to improve upon Aristotle by developing a highly systematic, philosophically veracious system of topics in his *Topica*.[1] However, the new learning's "particular" topics would go far beyond Cicero in their power to flush game from the park of the world, or to prove its absence. Bacon demonstrates how one follows the heads of the topics to determine the nature of the attributes "heavy and light." For example, the experimenter asks "what bodies are susceptible to the motion of gravity," and inquires into the "effect the quantity of a body has in the motions of gravity"(424). Each topic begins with the command to inquire. The roster and its parts express the intent to experiment: "Inquire touching the motions of air; whether it rise upwards, or is, as it were indifferent. And this is hard to discover, except by some subtle experiments" (427). The topical questions, which for Aristotle in the *Topics* are a means of clarifying and pursuing the meaning of categories as they function in the arguments of others, here ease into roles as tools that work upon what is instrumental or manipulable in nature. They create a dialogue insofar as nature is made to answer. The partners in the exchange are locked within the bounds of an inquiry that makes what is alterable and what is factual identical as encoded equivalents. The new topics drag the field, and their honed categories, naming all conceivable attributes, impale their answers on the code-breaker's probes.

The goal of the hunt of Pan is to prove the presence or absence of something that precisely matches the terms or categories of the topical questions. The Aristotelian idea that the topics address an animate audience or that the attibutes are categories or predications—that in their most literal sense they call out, predict, or accuse something within—is replaced by the Baconian calling of the roll, and by the capture of attributes. Concern for the manner in which the calling or drawing out takes place—especially its relation to the predilections, intentions, and various circumstances of the object—has no true place in the new routine of hit or miss, unless those facts can be captured the same way.

2

In his discussion of the topics, Bacon probably had in mind certain humanists for whom the Ciceronian topical tradition was a spur to develop dialectic into a pre-modern science.[2] Although the new learning thrusts toward a new natural philosophy rather than a renewal of the humanist reformers' "dialectic," it shares the concerns of some humanist manifestoes intent upon breaking the spell of false logic and rhetoric. The pseudo-dialecticians and false Ciceronians were of couse objects of disdain for a large group of reformers that included Erasmus, Melanchthon, Vives, and Rainolde as well as Agricola and Ramus.

Despite Bacon's praise of aspects of the old learning in Book I of *The Advancement,* he does not express high regard for the humanists as a group. Lisa Jardine has documented his rich debt to his humanist education,[3] but the precise degree of his debt to humanist ideas about the topics is unclear. Bacon notes that the specialized topics have received "some slight mention in some writers, but . . . have not been fully handled, according to the dignity of the subject" (423). He occasionally criticizes Ramus's theories, and in one place, the posthumously published *Masculine Birth of Time,* excoriates him.[4] But Bacon also expresses approval of a portion of Ramus's work, and he recommends, to Sir Henry Savill, a course of study that includes the reading of Ramus and Agricola, for whom the topics of invention and the ways of detecting and conveying the truths of subject matters are famous preoccupations. Written at about the mid-point of his career, when he probably also wrote the damning *Masculine Birth of Time,* Bacon's brief study list puts Agricola and Ramus under the heading "Arts, Logic, Rhetoric" along with Agrippa and the authors of a few reference works (*LD* VII.102).

Of course, both Agricola and Ramus devote themselves to the development of a logocentric curriculum, not the new learning. But as Walter Ong has argued, revealing analogies can be drawn between their highly systematic emphasis upon visual or "objective" dimensions of dialectic and Bacon's rigorous transformation of the old top-

ical theory into a probe of empirical reality.[5] Agricola in fact attempts
to convert the Greek and Roman categories and topics into *loci* of
"things," as though the old topics that served rhetoric and disputation
could serve as heuristic treasuries for the world of objects as well as
the realm of language. Similarly, the schematic dichotomies of Ramus's "cartography of the mind," as Ong calls it, are conducive to a
conflation of rhetoric, dialectic, and a kind of observational inquiry
that Ramus equates with the Aristotelian meaning of *apodeixis* or
scientific demonstration.

More important for our purposes, the analogy between these humanists' programs and that of the new learning suggests another way
of understanding what happens to rhetoric and dialectic when the old
arts are simultaneously spurned and idealized by an aggressive, highly
schematic pedagogy that outlines a scientific dialectic. Strangely,
when that new dialectic has been entirely separated from rhetoric, its
credibility as science makes it more rhetorical. Conversely, its companion rhetoric, now more subject to schematization, gives the
impression of being more scientific, both in theory and in enlightened
practice.

Ong points out that although explanation by its nature tends to
rely upon visual analogies, and although the Greeks' privilege sight
as the intellectual sense,[6] something new happens when Agricola and
Ramus set out to teach a seemingly scientific, pictorial scheme of
dialectic that demotes words in favor of visual schema. An understanding and appreciation of the power of utterances to express the
inner being of their speakers and subjects is in danger of being lost.
The precise scale of the reformers' emphasis on visual judgment is a
matter of debate;[7] but a brief analysis of the Agricolan and Ramistic
programs, in light of their ambivalence toward older forms of rhetoric
and dialectic, will at least suggest what happens when an influential
branch of the humanist movement—the one that won Bacon's particular attention—sought to give unambiguously scientific substance
to the classical logic and eloquence it emulated, especially the Platonic
and Aristotelian traditions transmitted by Cicero and Quintilian.

Lisa Jardine has argued that the humanists intended most of all to
create a better pedagogy of learning, to project what they had re-
covered from the ancients, not to create a better learning in the sense
of discovering something new. The recovery of Plato and Aristotle,
along with Cicero and Quintilian, would have also entailed an encounter with their various claims for the philosophical respectability
of dialectic and rhetoric.

We have already noted the teleological power of humanist schol-arship in Erasmus's *De Copia*. In the work of Abraham Fraunce, one detects the assumption that teaching is a function of learning, not just a technique of logic, illustration, and self-instruction: "The nature of this art [of logic] . . . is seene not onely in teaching others, but also in learning thy selfe." The teacher must come to understand what he is doing by "meditating" and by examining others.[8] Melanchthon for his part draws from the sorts of metaphors and analogies of illumi-nation we have seen in Ciceronian rhetorical theory: the true (hu-manist) philosopher takes a doctrine "out of obscurity and makes it practically useful,"[9] "to serve all mankind well, by digging out and revealing truth."[10] Eloquence is "divinely bestowed" so that instruc-tors may teach "correctly and clearly concerning great and necessary things."[11] Learners must, according to Melanchthon's Plato, have "some god" as their guide, although the reference is quickly reduced to mean that inspiration from the god is an aptness of nature and a convenient, clear instruction.[12] Although such declarations of interest in the search for truth tend to be logocentric, the humanists have an interest somewhat similar to Bacon's in reforming learning by re-newing its sources of inquiry and rededicating its means of trans-mission to truth and faith.

The way Agricola and Ramus interpret that legacy illuminates some of the goals of *The Advancement of Learning*. In their own ways, they force an old issue: the meaning of the relation between pedagogy, rhetoric, and truth. In spurning or transforming the old inventive powers of rhetoric and in elevating dialectic to the realm of what Aristotle calls demonstrable or "scientific" truths, Agricola and Ramus put dialectic and rhetoric into a highly volatile combination, mixing their drive for dialectical certainty with their appeals to the most common opinions and susceptibilities of large audiences.

Agricola for his part preserves some of the old assumptions of Timaeic rhetoric. He would allow the existence of a rhetoric that brings things out of obscurity by ornamenting and disposing them. He also attributes to dialectic the power to arrange the subject's "po-tential" so that it is apt for teaching,[13] as though unfolding rather than conversion were his paradigm. However, the thrust of Agricola's *De Inventione* is not in this direction. In his assumption that the tools of the new art, his dialectical *loci* or "places," are "the shared charac-teristics of things," he reduces all subject matters to topics which "contain within themselves all that can be said about each thing."[14] As a result, "substance" is a place because it is in all things; the physics of natural matter and subject matter combine to dictate the truth of the locus. Conversely, if something that appears substantial produces belief, it manifests its own physics: "whatever is used to produce belief in a subject must in some manner be connected with it."[15] There is something of Aristotle's *Rhetoric* here; but Agricola pushes such declarations in two directions: as requirements that dialectical appeals to the mind use things of absolute certainty, or as references to an absolute certainty inherent in whatever is convincing. As belief and fact converge, teaching and learning oscillate between rhetoric and science.

Following and consulting the *loci* of substance, cause, effect, and so on, the dialectician can "survey the entire nature, parts, compatibilities, and incompatibilities of a thing" to discover suitable and convincing arguments. The identification of places and things is scientific in the sense that it instructs him in what is certain[16] by telling him what all things share. The ephemeral is not nearly as significant as shared certainties, and most of the liberal arts are passing things.[17] The topics are not only a "treasury" that contains the instruments for finding "all that can be said about each thing"; they "contain within themselves . . . every possible argument."[18]

When Agricola criticizes Aristotle and Quintilian for neglecting the philosophical dimensions of the dialectical topics,[19] he has in mind the topics' persuasive and revelatory power as much as their logical force: "dark places need the presence of light from some source if they are to admit of sight and vision."[20] The power to "paint" and "carve" the nature of things is what draws Cerberic truths out of hidden depths. Although such instruction is for "the more homely and inexperienced" rather than the learned,[21] its rhetorical force results from learned inference according to the *loci*.

The manner of the places' operation is of far less interest to Agricola than the convertibility of places, things, persuasion, and scientific demonstration. The best style is one that has "captured" the mind, and "as it were snatched away" the soul by the repetition of "the same thing"[22] or by making present the necessary "things." Thus Cicero is a good dialectician in arousing pity because he skillfully includes the two "things" necessary to teach what is tragic as well as to prove a case: the victim's misfortune and his appearance of innocence.[23]

In his care to downgrade persuasion that merely gives pleasure, and to favor argument that teaches and moves, Agricola declares that delight "cannot be the goal of any discourse," just as gluttony is not the goal of hunger (412); and yet, as the most striking instance of delightful language, poetry is one with dialectic because it is "of all things the most capable of [giving] this pleasure." Although its language "does not follow the thing" in adapting it for pleasure,[24] it instructs best in pleasing best.[25] "These things are so inter-related that the language which is especially pleasing also instructs best, though sometimes pleasure takes the place of belief."[26]

A typical passage in Agricola's paradoxical argument is his interpretation of Plutarch's saying that "a poem is a speaking picture." Giving himself the choice between the pleasing picture and the factual thing, he appears to decide in favor of the thing, for "one is brought to tears pre-eminently by things."[27] But then his example of a speech in which "tragedies and achievements" are more important than the language in which they are rendered equates subject matter both with the "tears" of the speaker's delivery and the "tearful inflections" of his style. Thing and delightful style become indistinguishable:

> [O]ne is brought to tears pre-eminently by things: no one would believe that the tears of the Roman people were as ready as appears in certain phrases of Cicero's perorations, even though these words were, to be sure, brilliantly and very aptly designed to arouse pity, were not the tragedies and achievements of noble clients laid before the eyes and commended by tearful inflections as well as by Cicero's own abundant tears. And it is too obvious to need pointing out that we are likewise delighted both by things and words.[28]

In his desire to stress the certainty and the power of dialectical inquiry and presentation, Agricola collapses into one another the *loci* of things, speeches, pictures, delight, knowledge, persuasion, pedagogy, belief, and truth.

3

Ramus's program is built out of a similar, though more sweeping conviction that the true dialectic is a kind of ontological instrument that reveals in its systematic pedagogy the nature of all subject matters. The new dialectical revelation is put to work everywhere, demolishing with veracious power distinctions between inquiry, instruction, and persuasion as it dichotomizes all subject matters according to its basic laws. Ramus acknowledges Agricola's *De Inventione* as the starting point for his own work.[29]

The new Ramistic dialectic is, like Agricola's, readily convertible to a radically rhetorical art. Its analyses of subject matters create striking schema, emphasizing clarity and discounting the problem of reconciling what audiences apprehend or opine with what they ought to see or believe. One of the means by which Ramus's theory of dialectic expands upon Agricola's is through his doctrine of the "generals"—the terms and propositions that he supposes should head all dialectical discourse because they are at once absolutely true and most accessible to men's minds. Where Agricola identifies the topics, the things they name, and the mind that sees their congruence, Ramus blends dialectical analysis, absolute truth, and what is best known or "common"—as though Aristotle's scientific truth, *endoxa,* and *doxa* were everywhere the same.

Ramus claims to have drawn inspiration and license from Plato and Aristotle. He cites the authority of the *Phaedrus'* definition of philosophical rhetoric,[30] and Aristotle's discussion of definition in the *Analytics*. He goes so far as to chide Aristotle for not holding to his own insistence in the *Rhetoric* that the study of moral philosophy should not be confined by the study of rhetoric.[31] But Ramus's famous demotion of rhetoric to an art of ornament and pronunciation also partly restores and improves upon the two ancient models he respects most. He presumes to perfect Plato and Aristotle by means of their own principles. Writing in 1588, his English follower Abraham Fraunce tries to summarize Ramus's position: "where Aristotle deserueth prayse, who more commendeth him then Ramus? Where he hath too much, Ramus cutteth off, where too little, addeth, where any thing is inuerted, hee bringeth it to his owne proper place, and that according to the direction of Aristotle his rules."[32] In Gabriel Harvey's words, Ramus is most to be praised for recovering the ancients from themselves as well as from time. Much as the Baconian interpreter of ancient myths, Ramus is responsible for "clarifying with amazing brilliancy the philosophic thoughts, and . . . unearthing from the records of history the venerable patterns of old and the knowledge of facts buried from our memory by antiquity."[33] Ramus's Aristotle is the faithful though sometimes wayward student of a not wholly reliable Plato, both misunderstood and misused by the commentators.

Ramistic dialectic concerns "mind and reason." All else has to do with "mere speech."[34] Ramus's reading of Plato and Aristotle leads him to the preliminary conclusion that opinion is irrevocably false (*saepe fallunt*).[35] In defining and analyzing the arts by means of the new dialectic, "one should follow not the wavering error of the mob but the fixed law of truth."[36] Rhetoric is an art of mere ornamentation because arousal and delight are not the proper ends of any reasonable art. "Arousal and delight do not have any proper arts,"[37] though once properly diminished the art of ornamentation is, like dialectic, "an art almost as fixed as arithmetic or geometry." Dialectic's powerful rigor makes it a universal art that clarifies "most easily and plainly all questions, all parts of speech, and finally all subjects."[38] Rhetoric's narrow principles and applications reduce it to an art so accidental it "can be perfected and completed without philosophy."[39] Gabriel Harvey's praise of Ramus for focusing "not only on the word (*logos*) but much more on comprehension (*sunesis*) and knowledge (*gnosis*)"[40] should be read in light of Ramus's declaration that anything to do with subject matter is "completely out of place and absurd in the art of rhetoric."[41] Ramus makes absolute the old adage that comprehension of subject matter (here the dialectical mastery of it) is "the proverbial 'marrow of persuasion' "[42]; yet rhetoric has no core.

As with Agricola, Ramus's severe restriction of rhetorical theory and practice in the name of the ancients tends to transfer many aspects of traditional rhetoric to dialectic, even though dialectic is supposed to be purged of them. Finding a cue in his reading of Plato and Aristotle, Ramus's theory of "generals" and their disposition makes over all the disciplines according to a theory of dialectic that is strikingly rhetorical. The common rhetorical topics of Aristotle are now "generals," or universal terms and propositions that are more true and hence "better known" than "specials," or specific instances, and so precede them in order and importance in true explanations of things.

The passage Ramus uses in the *Phaedrus* describes "two ideas" or procedures for true dialectical discussion: definition that collects scattered notions and observations, and division that "in the other direction" distributes the thing into appropriate categories or parts, typically pairs. In the *Phaedrus* itself, Socrates does not specify whether one "direction" is more veracious or prior, for his definition of philosophical rhetoric requires that the audience's souls, as well as the speaker's subject matter, be taken into account in the ordering of the speech or discussion. His definition appears late in a dialogue full of oratorical gesture heavily qualified by the suasory flux of the exchange with Phaedrus. Ramus, however, interprets the passage in isolation as Plato's doctrine of the one true method, without reference to souls or to their variation among audiences:

> [T]his text of Plato establishes a single method, a single kind of carefully arranged procedure, going from what is first and most general, through subalterns, to individuals. This he teaches should be carried out first by defining the supreme genus, then by dividing what has been defined. . . . [H]is examples [in the *Phaedrus'* discussion of eros] should have removed all doubt.[43]

The general in coming first "exerts a greater causal influence than the specific," and because it is more fundamentally true, it is "better known."[44]

The real dialectic for Ramus is equivalent to what Aristotle calls scientific demonstration (*apodeixis*), which the Stagirite but not Ramus often distinguishes from the probable reasoning of dialectic.[45] Ramus simply transfers Aristotle's definition of *apodeixis* to an absolute dialectic, and so abandons the old distinction between scientific and probable reasoning. Ramus's words have a bearing upon Aristotle's, but Aristotle is not saying the same thing: "demonstrative knowledge must proceed from premises which are true, primary, immediate, better known than [*gnōrimōterōn*], prior to, and causative of the conclusion."[46] Aristotle immediately qualifies the meaning of "prior to" and "better known"; Ramus does not. For Aristotle, something "absolutely most clear" does *not* tend to be clear to everyone or almost everyone at all times. Universal concepts are furthest from the perceptions, and the meaning of "better known" is complex:

> There are two senses in which things are prior and more knowable. That which is prior in nature is not the same as that which is prior in relation to us, and that which is [naturally] more knowable is not the same as that which is more knowable by us. By "prior" or "more knowable" in relation to us I mean that which is nearer to our perception, and by "prior" or "more knowable" in the absolute sense I mean that which is further from it. The most universal concepts are furthest from our perception, and particulars are nearest to it; and these are opposite to one another.[47]

Ramus's works are full of his disputations with Aristotle's commentators about the meaning of such passages. Is Aristotle allowing for two kinds of truth, one absolute and one probable, or is he merely saying that novice learners rely upon their senses until they understand what is prior by nature?

Ramus is willing to concede the existence of two levels of understanding, but he assumes that the first is simply the child's preparation for real learning, or the activity that establishes the principles of the dialectical art, not their application in genuinely dialectical teaching and learning. He is impatient with Aristotle's elaboration of the understanding's movement from one level to the other. In his commentary on the *Physics,* he is particularly offended by Aristotle's assumption that the movement is gradual and difficult, and that generals and particulars are "very, very commingled" in the process. Ramus declares that "the whole thing is opposite to the thing having been argued"; Aristotle's lack of complete clarity on this point contradicts his own "law of wisdom"—that we must move from clear universals to more obscure particulars. "Therefore," Ramus concludes, "it is proper to proceed from the universals to the particulars." The commentator who tries to explain the contradiction "searches in the clouds and shadows for an excuse for [Aristotle's] apparent refutation."[48]

Ramus's famous clarification of the Aristotelian doctrine, which he here claims has been betrayed by Aristotle, is set out in a sixteenth-century translation of the *Dialectica:* "The forme and methode which is kept in this arte [of dialectic] comaundethe that the thing which is absolutely most clear, be first placed: and secondly that which is next clear, and so forthe with the rest. And therefore it continually procedethe from the generall to the speciall and singuler."[49] This "law of wisdom" is "the sole law conccrning form, namely that thc things perfectly most familiar, known, and clear should go before."[50]

The result is an extreme displacement of the conception of dialectical arrangement Aristotle presents in the first lines of the *Topics,* to the effect that "he who reasons well demonstrates his propositions from more generally accepted and more familiar premises."[51] Again, the crux of Ramus's new law is its suppression, and consequent preoccupation with, the concept of "generally accepted opinion": the *doxa* and *endoxa* so vital to the Aristotelian tradition. By merging "the general," as Aristotle defines the universal in the *Posterior Analytics,* with the "most clear," Ramus allows "general" and "clear" to define one another. "General" may be what is immediately clear, and what is clear may be what is most general. "General" itself may have predominantly logical or rhetorical meanings. It may simply stand for what is immediately most clear "in general," that is, to everyone— and thus have nothing necessarily to do with generalization—or it may be the primary proposition of a syllogism. In the logical sense, what is general is clear, since the major premise of a syllogism needs no proof for the syllogism to operate on a purely logical plane and because the highest generals are axioms which Aristotle says by definition require no proof. But in Ramus's rhetorical sense, "clear" and "general" are the same.

Ramus displays his oratorical skills when he elucidates these ideas in his discussion of "the one method of establishing a science," part of his commentary on Aristotle's *Organon*. He likens the generals (here "genera") to a bright torch that is obviously "better known to us" than the tiny candle (the special or "species") that lights it. Inexperienced learners do indeed proceed from specifics to universals, but "it does not follow that, if the species is better known to us in point of time, it is better known to us than the genus." By "better known" Ramus here means "better known" *to the senses,* and thus to everyone:

> If from a tiny candle I light a great torch, it does not follow that genera are less well known and less clear than species, although the genera arise from the species. The truth is quite to the contrary: the more common the knowledge, the better it is known to us, just as, the larger and thicker the lights, the brighter and clearer they are. So also, in our perceptions of individual things, those general notions come first *even into the senses* [my italics]. What moves in the distance we judge to be an animal first, then a man.[52]

The appeal to the senses abolishes all Aristotelian distinctions between a logic of science and a logic of opinion. As the Ramist Fraunce puts it, "the Arte of Knowing and Reasoning . . . is only one and the same, as the sight of the eye in perceyuing all colours, bee they chaungeable [opinions] or not chaungeable [scientific truths]."[53]

One of the most striking effects of Ramus's compression of sense and intellect is the disappearance of distinctions between the intention of the arranger and the minds of the arranger's audience. According to Ramus, the ancients confuse the issue by allowing for a difference. A passage in Quintilian, for example, teaches a principle of *dispositio* the opposite of Ramus's: "we follow [in speeches] an order quite different from that which we employ in actual speaking. For that which as a rule occurs to us first is just that which ought to come last in our speech."[54]

Quintilian does recognize a rule similar to Ramus's—that "we should descend from the common to the particular" (*a communibus ad propria*)[55]—but he assumes that it governs only interior speech as the rhetor silently anticipates arguments that might oppose him. He argues that a separate, "natural" order is appropriate for the public presentation of ideas, and although it too may begin with common principles and specific applications of such principles, it must use different forms of arrangement when the common principles are weak.[56]

To Ramus's disgust, Quintilian assumes that disposition is an art that escapes strict codification. Like his predecessors, Quintilian cultivates the notion that *dispositio* is often double without being duplicitous. Its private and public arrangements work playfully yet seriously, to some degree in tandem, to some degree apart. Ramus does allow for a prudential or cryptic method of organization that is useful when one confronts "accomplished adversaries";[57] however, his precepts for that method, which involve the inversion of normal ordering principles so that an opponent in a debate is caught off-guard, receive almost no elaboration. He lists them in his commentary on Book VIII of Aristotle's *Topics,* in a form so truncated it is not surprising that he stops referring to prudential method in his later works. His list of organizational techniques in the *Scholae* is extremely brief, and significantly alters and omits items in the Aristotelian list it copies.

In the *Topics,* Aristotle is careful to recommend a kind of guile in the dialectician's aspiring, agonistic encounter with his audience: "The necessary premises, then, by means of which reasoning proceeds, ought not to be advanced immediately in their original form . . . .[Y]ou must keep as far away from them as you can."[58] Ramus boils this down to the innocuous, self-evident rule, "Bring together reasoning beforehand, through which the syllogism is made."[59] Aristotle has in mind the contest of interrogation and counter-interrogation that takes place in classical dialectic and which prepares for public discourse, whereas Ramus represses even the prospect of indirection for rhetorical or dialectical purposes.

Similarly, where Aristotle next insists upon a degree of doubleness for the sake of a sufficiently strenuous dialectical instruction, Ramus would simply create suspense:

Aristotle: "[Y]ou should not state the conclusions, but establish them by reasoning all at the same time at a later stage; for then you would keep the answerer as far as possible from the original proposition."[60]

Ramus: "Do not state the conclusion, so that because of this, when at last it is stated, it will be searched for."[61]

Ramus's third principle is a radically compressed version of an argument in Aristotle's *Topics* that runs counter to Ramus's key assumption in the *Dialectica*. His commentary barely preserves Aristotle in its unexplained advice, "Do not mention claims in succession." To say more would overturn the *Dialectica*'s main point: that there must in fact be a succession of claims from the more general to the more specific. The original passage in Aristotle explicitly entertains the possibility of subverting syllogistic order: "It is useful practice not to establish the admitted propositions, on which the reasonings are based, in the order of syllogisms."[62] For Aristotle, the disposition of discourse is not in principle so stringent that it jeopardizes the very idea of dialectical contest or rhetorical depth.

In the *Rhetoric,* true oratory calls for discovering the possible means of persuasion, and so has built into itself a doubleness of possibility and verbal act. Likewise, in the *Topics,* the truth-seeking nature of the dialectical enterprise coexists with a game of inquiry which distances the participants to some degree from their pursuit. Book VIII sets out methods of delaying and accelerating academic play for the expressed purpose of detecting or warding off sophistry. The best players know they are in danger at every stage of giving false refutations or merely pretending to knowledge. The game and the inquiry thrive on assertion and refutation that distinguish, in stages of discussion, between caution and timidity, between the reasonable thrust and parry and the imprudent lunge. The Aristotelian rhetorician is engaged in a somewhat similar agon with himself and his anticipation of his audience's thinking as he prepares for speaking to a general audience. Thus, although wise participation in dialectic and rhetoric is almost inescapably double, it obligates one to act as wisely as possible to reduce the gap between what audiences, speakers, and inquirers know, and what they might be capable of knowing.

It is the supreme paradox of Ramus's position that he attacks the ancients' duplicity while demolishing the traditional claims of probable reasoning and persuasion that might help close the gap between audience and speaker. The theory and practice of Ramistic dialectic declare the matter closed. Once the ancients' duplicitous logics are identified and done away with, the one true art of dialectic can invoke the Ramist laws of certitude and right order to save men from confusion and error. It is no accident that Ramus spends at least as much of his time refuting the errors of the ancients and their commentators as he does in more direct instruction; his system of dialectic is based on the assumption that misapprehension, far more than the inveterate difficulty of apprehending true axioms and ordering principles, bars the revelatory triumph of the new dialectic.

4

Bacon of course concludes that Ramistic dialectic, for all its force, is a highly contrived method of exposition, not a mode of inquiry. Taken too seriously, it is a Procrustean bed that contorts the laws of nature (*De Aug* IV.453). Bacon is careful not to claim that his methods of inquiry and exposition are monolithic, nor does he make Ramus's aggressive argument that his new approach analyzes and judges doctrine and nature indifferently. Bacon's discussions of expository method suggest numerous approaches; his explanation of scientific inquiry involves many stages of collection and analysis. Most important, Bacon is careful to stress his conformity with prevailing moral and political doctrine, and to eschew the impression that he engages in the more radical doctrinal disputes of the Reformation, with which Ramus, the inveterate controversialist who died in the St. Bartholomew's Day massacre of Protestants, was closely identified. Bacon does not often indulge in diatribes against ancient authorities by name, preferring to be seen as one who praises and perfects Plato, Aristotle, and Cicero for the sake of his charitable program. He tries to limit the connections between his work and the reform of established religion. His project tests but does not confront the view of his countryman Ascham, who links radical reforms of the arts of discourse to heresy and sedition:

> For he, that can neither like *Aristotle* in Logicke and Philosophie, nor *Tullie* in Rhetoricke and Eloquence, will, from these steppes, likelie enough presume, by like pride, to mount hier, to the misliking of greater matters: that is either in Religion, to have a dissentious head, or in the common wealth, to haue a factious hart.[63]

Nevertheless, Bacon follows much of the pattern of thought in the reforming work of Agricola and Ramus, and develops what they engender but denounce: an art of discourse that is as rhetorical as it is scientific.

Somewhat like Ramus's generals, the laws of the forms are accessible to all, once they are pointed out. They therefore resemble the testimony of the senses. If men could listen to their senses as they are opened to them by the new methods of the sciences, nature would give itself up to everyone with the alacrity of the Sphinx when Oedipus answers its riddle. But much as Ramus's selection of the generals and his arrangement of his great charts of learning hide other purposes in the silence of his visual schema, the new learning hides its secrets. Agricola and Ramus dismiss the contradictory persistence of the cryptic in their doctrines by repeatedly denouncing all concealment. Bacon hints that meticulous prudence is necessary in releasing knowledge of inventions to the public so as to protect the sciences from persecution and misuse; but he criticizes other kinds of secrecy as attempts to conceal false knowledge or to pretend to hide from God.

The new learning's arts of discourse reflect in their structure and in the mode of their decipherment the new learning's natural philosophy and its idea of man. The radical ambivalence of those arts—their conduciveness to cryptic conceit while they convey or seem to convey their fitness for faithful inquiry, moral instruction, and the transmission of knowledge—can now be examined in the essays, Bacon's most compressed efforts to exercise and reconcile these paradoxes in the new learning's enterprise. The following chapter, a reading of successive editions of the *Essays,* will be a gathering effort to judge the significance of these complexities for the new practical rhetoric that Bacon there sets forward.

V

THE *ESSAYS*

Bacon's *Essays* anticipate and image his other work not only in their outline of the studies he advocates or carries out elsewhere, but in their compact rendering of the philosophy of "business" and civil discourse that so strongly informs—and is influenced by—Baconian science. The opening essay of the original 1597 edition, "Of Studies," is a fitting introduction to all the essays, and in some sense to all of Bacon's works. It projects many of the formal and thematic concerns of the later writings, giving precedence to inquiry and experience over book-bound studies; to corrective exercise over display; to aphorism over disquisition; to ordeal over satisfaction; to rhetorical effectiveness over rhetorical delight and ornamentation.

I

"Of Studies" is a key to the whole, though its problematic nature testifies to the hidden complexities of Baconian keys. Like the code-maker's closely guarded chart of equivalences, it offers the possibility of defining the relation between studies and wisdom. Yet it is designed for publication in a world where idol-worshippers are more plentiful than sons of science. Bacon claims only to have delivered a series of *essais* or attempts, not a table for decoding the nature of things. The true import and shape of his arguments must be gathered from the art and gloss of the essays' enameling.

"Of Studies" begins in seemingly conventional praise of learning's usefulness for pastimes, argument, and ability, and its commendation of the superiority of the learned man over the expert in his fitness for making judgments, hence for disposing or forming things rather than merely following directions. From the first, however, another pattern of argument borders the conventional one. The essay defends studies according to their utility. The first predicate Bacon chooses for studies is "serve," and his first clarification defines them in terms of "their chiefe vse." There is not only a limit to the time one can profitably spend in delightful contemplation before it turns to sin ("To spend too much Time in *Studies, is sloth*"); there is also a strict limit to what studies can do without a deeper study: they might be said to "perfect Nature," but they are themselves "perfected by Experience." They depend upon wisdom, which is "without them, and aboue them, won by Observation" (*E* VI.525). Thus they "teach not their owne Vse." True observation and experience subject the inquirer to trials from which the deepest truths must be "won." Reading histories may make men "wise," as Bacon says in his conclusion, but the argument merely contradicts itself unless one sees that reading must be a deliberate suffering too if it is to be sagacious. *The Advancement* argues that it is "the true office of history to present the events themselves, together with the counsels; and to leave the observations and conclusions thereupon to the liberty and faculty of every man's judgment" (*Adv* III.339). The liberty of observation is, in the deeper sense, a freedom to undergo the wisdom-making ordeal. A similar meaning can by hypothesized in the essay's claim that "Naturall Phylosophie" makes man "deepe." There are really two kinds of studies: conventional ones instruct; wise ones test.

To read wisely is "to waigh and consider," not "to contradict, nor to belieue." The advice conforms to the proverbial notion that contentiousness and credulity are no substitute for active thought. But "to waigh and consider" in the context of the essay is to experience the text much as Bacon says the text must endure its reading: those few books to be studied carefully must be broken down, "chewed," before they are digested.

The 1625 edition's version of the essay marks and elaborates Bacon's differentiation of this wisdom from ordinary studies. In the revision, Bacon sharpens the original hint by indicating that true studies prune ("Proyn") the student's natural abilities so as to perfect them. In the more superficial sense the cutting is a sculpting of the student's nature; in its deeper import the pruning is a cutting back— a severing of wisdom from easy worldliness. In parallel clauses, studies are described as though they were themselves "bounded in by experience" so that they do not "give forth direction too much at large" (*E* VI.497).

The later version of the essay adds a passage recommending study of the schoolmen, whose exercises supposedly cure defects in the wit:

> Nay there is no stond or impediment in the wit, but may be wrought out by fit studies: like as diseases of the body, many have appropriate exercises. Bowling is good for the stone and reins; shooting for the lungs and breast; gentle walking for the stomacke; riding for the head; and the like. So if a mans wit be wandering, let him study the mathematicks; for in demonstrations, if his wit be called away never so little, he must begin again. If his wit be not apt to distinguish or find differences, let him study the school-men; for they are *cymini sectores,* [splitters of hairs].   (*E* VI.498)

In the comparison between physical conditioning and mental discipline, the exercises of the body are conducive to health in the Timaeic sense. They remove impediments by allowing the body to become more itself. The diseased body can enact its own perfective catharsis by throwing, shooting, gently moving, and—most appropriate for the head—riding and managing the great corporeality of a horse. At first glance, the scholastic discipline seems to do the same, but Bacon's examples ultimately run against the grain. They call for a discipline that scourges yearning from wit. Exercises in mathematical demonstration are valuable because they do not tolerate the slightest shift of attention. The schoolmen are valuable teachers because their fixation on distinctions is greater than their care for truth. They are notorious, according to the myth of the Sphinx, for splitting what ought not to be divided. The illustrative purging of the body, which through exercise imitates healthy action, clashes with Bacon's actual subject: the purgation of the wit, which strips away tendency and so prepares the wit for the renunciative wisdom of the new learning.

The first of the twelve *Meditationes Sacrae,* which follow the ten essays of the 1597 edition, echoes these arguments in the context of religious devotion. The pairing of essays with meditations in the first edition sets up a powerful juxtaposition. In the first meditation, Bacon reminds his reader, in terms that recall the separation of wisdom from studies, that there must be a strict division between the works of God and those of man: "if thou labour in God's works . . . thou shalt take rest in the leisure of delightful contemplation. But if thou follow after the mighty things of men . . . thou shalt look back upon thy work with disgust and reproach" (*MS* VII.243). By characterizing the faithful man's labor as taking place "in God's works," Bacon invokes the language he uses to describe natural philosophy: arduous direction of learning according to the work of God's encoding power. To "follow" the mighty things of men—in studies, for example—errs in this deeper sense, unless one sagaciously labors there too, inquiring into the way God's physics plays out in men's works.

The 1597 edition enforces the separation of studies and wisdom again in the first entry of its third section, *The Colours of Good and Evil*. The preface to this work declares that the studious ideas of the old Stoics, Epicureans, and Peripatetics cannot be judged or applied without "a very universal knowledge of the nature of things" (*CGE* VII.77), which is distinct from that gained from the study of their arguments. The colors of argument are themselves only "popularities and circumstances," not "true and solide reasons." The latter "perform" the persuader's labor whereas the colors only "represent" it. Although the colors represent good and evil, as do "true and solide reasons," they have a power "to alter the nature of the subject in appearance," which leads into error unless sagacious minds dispose them to advantage. After themselves, the old schools prefer the most studious of the schools, that of Aristotelian Peripetics, and so reveal their "enervation and weakness" (*CGE* VII.78). Their interest in ordinary studies unsuits them for the strenuous sagacity that would discover their own nonsense and give them mastery over the colors.

The new, scientific catalogue of the colors would surpass Aristotle's seemingly fragmentary, pretentious catalogs in the *Rhetoric* by making itself available to "full understanding and use." That understanding is for the discerning reader who sees into Bacon's "new manner of handling this argument to make it pleasant and lightsome," not pretending like Aristotle "to have overcome the nature of the subject." Within the humility of this statement is the persistent principle that true wisdom is wise digestion of "the full understanding and use" of the colors, which remain "somewhat dark, and best pleasing the tastes of such wits as are patient to start the digesting and soluting unto themselves of that which is sharp and subtile" (*CGE* VII.70–71).

The tensions between conventional studies and sagacious analysis are detectable in all ten of the essays of the original 1597 edition, which Bacon disposes according to an interchange of explicit moral advice and hints of sagacious principles. Digested into aphorisms framed by brief disquisitions, the quasi-Solomonic arguments of the essays offer themselves for ready didactic purposes, as they must do in order to encourage the charitable morality upon which the new learning depends the more it severs itself from conventional wisdom. The same aphoristic style of discourse that is conducive to a display of unaffected sincerity and free counsel is "sharp and subtile" for minds that know the rigor of the new learning's uses for pedestrian studies.

The subjects of the 1597 essays are humdrum when compared to those of the dozens of essays Bacon adds in later editions. But their ordinariness suggests a way of thinking about civil and natural philosophy and the rational arts of discourse that discovers intimations of civil and natural science in what is obvious, overlooked, and unattractive. The essays offer counsel about civil discourse: its general applications in language and public ceremony (2 and 3); its relation to friends and participants in legal suits (4 and 5); its usefulness in the management of one's personal estate (6, 7, 8), and its pertinence to the interaction between factions, neutrals, and adversaries (9 and 10).

2

After sounding a keynote in "Of Studies," Bacon devotes a pair of essays to the workings of wisdom and technique in civil discourse and comportment. "Of Discourse" begins by warning the reader that simply "being able to hold all arguments" is inferior to "judgment in discerning what is true" (*E* VI.526). The study of discourse, without such discernment, can lead to a "tedious" poverty of wit. "The honourablest part of talk" is "to guide the occasion and againe to moderate and passe to somewhat else." "Discretion of speech . . . is more than eloquence"; and it is "more than to speak in good words in good order" (526).

Bacon has hinted at the meaning of this discretion by the time he delivers the essay's first commendatory sentence, about "the honourablest part of talke." In saying that the end of discourse is "to guide the occasion, and againe to moderate and passe to somewhat else," he ostensibly commends a polite mastery of conversation that defers to others and to other subject matters. But this is an idea of deference that holds within it a deeper principle of civil control. By influencing the conversation's initial premises, by tempering its manner, and by shifting its subject matter, true discretion shapes the discourse. To rephrase Bacon's lines for interpretation is to reveal his care in describing the operations as though he were giving advice on the niceties of dialogical style: "It is good to varie and mixe speech of the present occasion with argument, tales with reasons, asking of questions, with telling of opinions, and iest with earnest" (*E* VI. 526). The strategy for guiding the occasion by asking questions pleases the interlocutors' vanities while strengthening the questioner's hand: the inquiry "shal give them occasion to please themselves in speaking" while its author may "continually gather knowledge." The next sentence, set off as a self-contained aphorism, in fact glosses the previous one without committing Bacon to an explanation: "If you dissemble sometimes your knowledge of that you are thought to knowe, you shall bee thought another time to know that you know not." At first glance, this is advice to refrain from imposture: Do not pretend to know, for otherwise you will later be thought to know, and perhaps be called upon to explain something of which you are ignorant. But the aphorism supports the preceding one: the wise affectation of knowledge, either in speech or silence, magnifies the pretender's authority in areas about which he knows little, and frees him for further observation of his fellows. The exception to wise secrecy proves the sagacious rule: "Speech of a mans self is not good often, and there is but one case, wherein a man may commend himselfe with good grace, and that is in commending vertue in another, especially if it be such a vertue, as whereunto himselfe pretendeth" (526).

The essayist's shifts between moral suasion, utilitarian advice, and wise signaling are at work again in "Of Ceremonies and Respectes," which complements the first essay in its discussion of the general tone and shape of civil conversation. Rather than immediately condemning affectation as he does in "Of Discourse," Bacon opens with a defense of minor "good formes," which are useful in winning commendation and respect. He soon qualifies his injunction with the commonplace that art must hide art: one must not "care to express" the forms, lest one "leese their grace, which is to be naturall and unaffected."

Here Bacon's *sprezzatura* recalls Castiglione's; but the stark pointedness of his advice seems to encourage what he would condemn:

> To applie ones selfe to others is good, so it be with demonstration that a man doth it upon regard, and not vpon facilitie. It is a good precept generally in seconding another: yet to adde somewhat of ones owne; as if you will graunt his opinion, let it be with condition; if you allow his counsell, let it be with alleadging further reason. (527)

This very proof of regard—of one's respect for one's opposite in civil discourse—is also, in this aphoristic setting, a clue to mastering the other person's contribution, of exercising *virtu* rather than virtue.

As the 1597 edition proceeds, these trends of argument are more pronounced. "Of Followers and Friends" turns more rapidly between narrowly practical pointers, moral axioms, and hints of a higher wisdom. Beginning by warning against costly followers and false friends, Bacon acknowledges that retaining certain kinds of followers is good, as long as one honors their service and virtue without encouraging "too much pompe and popularities." He also advises monarchs and states to prefer those who merely seem virtuous—"the more passable"—over those followers whose virtue might come too close to the prince's own (528). False honors become in essence the means of rule.

The second half of the essay indulges the idea that followers can be treated justly in a manner that benefits their superior. But Bacon then immediately presents opposite advice about what that just treatment might be, casting doubt upon the virtue of friends since they turn insolent and ungrateful without the most careful government:

> In gouernment it is good to vse men of one rancke equally, for, to countenance some extraordinarily, is to make them insolent, and the rest discontent, because they may claime a due. But in favours to vse men with much difference and election is good, for it maketh the persons preferred more thankefull, and the rest more officious, because all is of fauour. (528)

The effective dispensing of favors "because all is [or seems?] of fauour" converts from a recognition of virtue to a tool of wise manipulation.

Finally, the essay compresses the value of friendship into the friends' power to give helpful advice, making it appear that detached intelligence, not devotion or virtue, is what matters most: *"For lookers on many times see moe then gamesters, and the vale best discouereth the hill"* (528). The traditional esteem for friendship is qualified by the particular value Bacon attaches to the friend's power to "comprehend" or survey a counterpart's doings. The essay's conclusion that "there is little friendship in the world" abstains again from linking devotion and virtue to affiliation. The equation, in the essay's last lines, of friends and "lookers on" confirms the ambivalence of the essay's compound title. Mere intelligences are more like followers than friends, and indeed, as observant spies, their narrowly practical value is greater. Wisely understood, friendship is the perfection of following and looking on.

The 1612 edition counters this movement again, but toward the same end. It inserts a new, almost sentimental essay on friendship, and moves the old discussion to thirty-second place in a series of thirty-eight. The new essay revises the gist of its precursor by insisting that society is a desert unless there is friendship. "It is friendship," moreover, "when a man can say to himselfe, I loue this man without respect of utility" (559). Friendship adds something to society that society distinguishes from mere "meeting." It is a union of two "naturall" motions, in which each is strengthened (558). But Bacon's analogy, in comparing the two parties to all natural bodies, hints at another reversal: the natural motion need not be a specifically human affiliation. The illustration from natural philosophy readily converts, if one notes its implications for all terrestrial movement, to an axiom for the affiliation of all natural bodies, in which like simply attracts like: "And as it is certaine, that in bodies inanimate, union strengtheneth any naturall motion, and weakeneth any violent motion; So amongst men, friendship multiplieth ioies, and diuideth griefes" (558). Nature supposedly illustrates friendship, but in such a way that the distinction between natural and violent motion, between friendly and utilitarian relation, depends upon physical proximity rather than admiration or consent.

The drift of the comparison becomes more apparent as Bacon likens life without friendship to painful servitude as fortune's "hierling." Yet again, friendship's value shrinks: it lightens the burden of fortune, but more in the manner of a redoubt than of brotherhood. The argument comes to rest upon the danger of friendlessness, and the necessity of making life easier by using friends as sounding boards, for emotional catharsis, and to prepare "business."

Bacon seems to turn away from business when in his conclusion he distinguishes between "true use" of friendship and a dependence "vpon facility." A man might not open every corner of his mind to his friend, for example, in order to show his friendship does not amount to facile confidentiality. But the meaning of such advice threatens to become more facile than what it would replace. "True use," if it is not an oxymoron, is a phrase obscured by the clipped aphorisms of the conclusion: "Perfection of friendship, is but a speculation. It is friendship, when a man can say to himselfe, I love this man without respect of vtility. I am open hearted to him, I single him from the generality of those with whom I liue; I make him a portion of my owne wishes" (559). The pessimistic conclusion of

1597 is now superseded by the optimistic notion that friendship is possible, even necessary; but the essay's definitions are almost all negative, and the lead sentence of the conclusion puts the idea of friendship into question. Friendship can not be perfect; it can not be based on facility; it can not be common; it must involve sharing "a portion" of one's wishes. The open heart must reserve something to itself in order to prove that it does not share everything for advantage.

3

If friendship is one of the foundations of civil society, the outcome of Bacon's deliberations tells us a good deal about his idea of civil association and virtue. Following Aristotle's *Rhetoric*, the *Essays* are glimpses of Bacon's own politics and ethics, which his teachings about persuasion draw from and implement. His implicit definitions of movers, means, objects, ends, and manners of persuasive action define his own rhetoric of influence among men, which we can compare to his rhetoric of nature itself.

The fact that Bacon moves from the cursory "Of Followers and Friends" to a separate discussion of friendship in 1612, and then generates a new essay on the subject, one of his longest, for the edition of 1625, lends weight to the supposition that he approached the subject with unusual seriouness. "Of Friendship" is the only completely re-written essay in the canon.

From the outset of the final version Bacon carefully hedges against the suspicion he attempted to scotch in the 1612 version: that the true end of friendship is utility. In doing so, he complements his two most prominent predecessors writing on friendship: Aristotle and Montaigne. Aristotle of course outlines three kinds of friendship as they are determined by their ends: for use, for pleasure, and for the sake of goodness. He argues that the third is superior to the others. Montaigne's essay "Of Friendship," which was probably available to Bacon for a number of years prior to his writing his final version, clearly distinguishes between the highest friendship—such as Montaigne's own with Stephen de la Boetia—and the "common" utilitarian type, characterized by a concern for "offices and benefits."[1]

In the first paragraph of the revised 1625 "Of Friendship," Bacon intones the sentiment of 1612, that society without friendship is a desert. He goes further, to the notion that friendship is "love," not simply an alternative to superficial association: "For a crowd is not

a company . . . where there is no love" (*E* VI.437). But the 1625
version's allusion to the traditional Aristotelian view is faint. Bacon's
predication in the key sentence is embedded and implicit; the sentence
is not a declaration of what friendship is. Its reference to love is set
in the much larger, negative definition of friendship as the opposite
of "miserable solitude." The positive characteristics of friendship,
when they are identified in later paragraphs, are its effects or "fruits,"
which benefit the person who spurns solitude. Friendship is finally
defined in terms of its advantages to those who have given up solitude:
in friendship, one gains civil piety and purification of one's health:

> A principal fruit of friendship is the ease and discharge of the fulness
> and swellings of the heart. . . . We know diseases of stoppings and
> suffocations are the most dangerous in the body; and it is not much
> otherwise in the mind; you may take sarza to open the liver, steel
> to open the spleen, flower of sulphur for the lungs . . . but no
> receipt openeth the heart, but a true friend; to whom you may
> impart griefs, joys, fears, hopes, suspicions, counsels, and what-
> soever lieth upon the heart to oppress it, in a kind of civil shrift or
> confession.   (*E* VI.438)

The languages of physiological and mental therapy play hide-and-
seek with one another. The paragraph enforces an analogy between
the effects on body and mind, then emphasizes the quality of their
difference, then closes the comparison with a higher yet more questionable analogy between shrift and discharge. Both comparisons, the
bodily and spiritual, veer away from the idea of affiliation.

The high value Bacon places upon friendship presents itself with a
similar electrical charge, one that switches to its opposite the moment
one sees that the powers of friendship can be turned to advantages
heretofore unknown or unappreciated. For example, Bacon's third
paragraph ostensibly argues that friendship is far more than mere
utility because kings, who have everything else, buy it at a price that
can jeopardize their fortunes. The example paradoxically intimates
that friendship is a supremely unencumbered instrument, and thus
that kings who need friends set friendship at a high "rate," and indeed
"purchase" it. The notion that friends might be bound to one another
by means other than loyalty and purchase does not come into play.

Bacon charges this pole of the argument with the disturbing observation that kings without friendship eat their own hearts (*E*
VI.440). Unable to communicate his secrets to anyone, the friendless

king will "impair and a little perish his understanding" (439). The appeal to fear and ambition gives way to a discussion of the "most admirable" power of friendship to redouble joys and lessen griefs as they are shared with a friend. But this argument entails reliance upon "contrary effects" rather than sympathy, and draws a comparison between friendship and alchemy, a ready tool for the enlightened maker of fool's gold: "it is in truth of operation upon a man's mind, of like virtue as the alchymists use to attribute to their stone for man's body; that it worketh all contrary effects, but still to the good and benefit of nature" (440). Bacon returns to a principle of natural philosophy like the one he used in the 1612 edition, where he argued that the union of all bodies enhances their natural motion and diminishes violence. In the 1625 text alchemical friendship seems indifferent to finer distinctions between affiliation and antagonism.

The remaining third of the essay confirms Bacon's effort to charge his terminology by means of this reduction, so that a sagacious reader might experience the sparks that suddenly change the essay's polarities. He introduces the "second fruit of friendship" in highly positive terms readily convertible to opposite and subversive ones. Having a friend, he begins, is a boon to one's thoughts because they become clearer in friendly discourse. Opened to friends, thoughts *"appear in figure"* rather than *"in packs"* (*E* VI.440). The speaker "tosseth his thoughts more easily," makes them more orderly, and "seeth how they look." At last, "he waxeth wiser than himself" more quickly than he would by meditation. In all these phrases the gain in facility competes with the confirmation of non-utilitarian friendship. The struggling reader must quickly adjust to the idea that any acquaintance—indeed any thing—will serve man as long as he can unpack his thoughts in its presence: "In a word, a man were better to relate to a statua or picture than to suffer his thoughts to pass in smother" (440–41).

To this Bacon adds the perfection of the second fruit of friendship, which promises something more. He first praises a friend's ability to cut through self-flattery with freely given and accurate appraisals of his friend's manners and business. There is a distinction between "good" and piecemeal counsel (gathered from various specialties) that seems to put the good of friendship over its utility. But here the essay's refinements of these views prepare the ground for another turn in the meaning of "good" advice toward what is useful in business. Piecemeal advice is bad not because it is generally wrong, but because it proves unsafe, or damages a man's many other kinds of business—pursuits that a true friend would know enough about and could therefore protect. The superiority of the friend's advice to merely "scattered counsels" might ultimately be the result of his knowing all the facts of the case; it suggests the true friend's capacity to go beyond scattered counsels, after his comprehensive observation, toward something like the laws of the forms. The practicality of friendship would in that case project the activities and goals of the new scientific endeavor, which is governed by charity and wisdom, not friendship.

The essay's concluding paragraph takes this line of argument further. It first stresses the utility of friendship as an aid to doing those good things one takes most to heart, such as "the bestowing of a child, the finishing of a work" (442). In this sense, the friend is "far more" than oneself. But the next sentences argue that the friend who is the perfect deputy also does everything a man is too modest or ashamed to do in person. "How many things are there which a man cannot, with any face or comeliness, say or do himself? A man can scarce allege his own merits with modesty, much less extol them" (442). The line between a high-minded praise of fraternal devotion and a scouring enthusiasm for the basest techniques for having one's will done by another begins to blur again. The hint of calculating friendship for self-promotion is quickly obscured by the example of the faithful father who needs a friend to advise his son, since the father "cannot speak to his son but as a father" (443). The final sentence of the paragraph is a wood of cross-purposes, a retreat into conventional morality that adumbrates the suggestion that the friend is really the self's necessary disguise in the play of power: "I have given the rule, where a man cannot fitly play his own part; if he have not a friend, he may quit the stage" (443).

4

The essays in the original collection are variations upon these formal and thematic principles. "Of Sutes" and "Of Faction," like "Of Expence," move from endorsement of traditional commonplaces (in their cases the traditional rejection of the misuses of suits and factions), toward analyses of success and intimations of the laws of power. For example, within the crosscurrents of "Of Expence," the initial declaration that riches are for spending is immediately refined by a concern for the limits put on magnificence by "the worth of the ocasion." The principle is then whittled down—in the case of "ordinarie expence"—to the limits of "mans estate" (530). Bacon devotes the remainder of the brief discussion to the techniques of maintaining solvency.

Within that catalog of highly practical advice, Bacon then weaves assumptions that link mean estates with great ones. There is a universal and grander utility in all wise expense: *"woundes cannot bee cured without searching"*; "he that hath a state to repaire may not despise small things." Much as the new learning will dare with the blessing of the sun to inquire into all things mundane—especially the smallest and the most corrupt—to cure man's estate the wise man of ordinary means should not hesitate to look into his financial condition, the hearts of his servants, and the intricacies of markets. The great estate is not so obviously in need of repair; but if it is to use riches properly, it must search itself too, studying its own "undoing" for God or country, as Bacon stipulates in his second sentence. Where the ordinary man tries to cure himself by inquiring into what is corrupt and trivial, the magnificent man who is not a saint must calculate how to dispense with himself without falling into ruin. Thrift is virtuous, but wise thrift follows the drift of the new sciences.

In "Of Sutes," Bacon's seemingly begrudging toleration of the study of techniques for making petitions combines with his aphorisms advising how to carry off unsavory actions virtuously. Again, the interchange prepares for the conclusion that suits can be used wisely by those who know how and when to take action. Whereas mere contrivers bumble and delay, wise users are masters of tactics; they know that "the tyming of the Sutes is the principall." The best timing comes, as does all wisdom, from observation—in this case garnered about the person petitioned and those who might disrupt the request (529).

"Of Faction" condemns the argument that a prince ought to rule by manipulating factions. Yet it briefly subjects the reader to the discipline of considering how factions work and how they might be used according to a better wisdom. Following Bacon's initial disavowal of interest is a seemingly disjunct collection of observations that in fact overlap. The essay amounts to the argument that although the great man ought to be neutral, the factions can be worked to advantage by assuming they will always exist in one form or another, and by using their changeable natures. If his timing is good, a true student of factions can be a prosperous shifter from one faction to another: "The traitor in factions lightly goeth away with it, for where matters have stucke long in ballancing, the winning of some one man casteth them, and hee getteth al the thankes" (553). In this sense the wise "mean" man whose loyalties jump at the right time between well-chosen parties is as independent of faction as the great man who stands neutral for the sake of moral, kingly principle. Their wisdoms converge.

Somewhat similar generalizations arise from "Of Honour and Reputation." Its opening sentence strikes a balance between winning honor and the "revealing of a mans vertue and worth without disadvantage" (531). The exposition, however, is a highly compact, vexatious mixture of ethical and technical advice: men should purchase honor by preferring the unprecedented over the more difficult or virtuous course; they should "temper" their action, but only to win greater applause by appealing to "euerie faction"; they should attribute their successes to Providence rather than to themselves, in order to frustrate envy. The final half of the essay, a list of honorable offices, is a monument to established hierarchies, as well as a ladder to success. A brief catalog, it is strikingly distant from the disjointed introduction; yet it offers itself to the wise reader as a glimpse of the structure of political power.

Another essay, "Of Regiment of Health," claims that "there is a wisdome" in the ordering and discipline of health that is "beyond the rules of Phisicke," rules which exclude "a mans owne obseruation what he finds good of" (530). But the end of that wisdom comes to resemble the effect of medicine rather than a good. Health appears not to be a good in itself so much as an absence of disease. To ensure that absence, one must anticipate and turn back all threats to well-being. Observation and vigilance protect from corruption. The essay discovers the dangers of excess, given the weakening of nature with age, and it commends cheerful disposition at meals, not to affirm something to be cheerful about so much as to insure "long lasting" life (531).

Observation detects the flatteries of doctors who try to please the humors of the patient, and the overly mechanical approach of physicians whose art ignores the humors. Bacon advises observant patients to search out a physician "of a middle temper," as though a positively good physician might exist. But the essay continues at greater length to describe the procedure for making one doctor out of two bad ones, to provide for the eventuality that no physician possesses a knowledge of humors as well as arts: "Compound two of both sorts, and forget not to cal as wel the best aquainted with your body, as the best reputed of for his facultie" (531). Throughout, the meaning of the wisdom "beyond" physic descends to the level of detecting the most minute hints of disease: "despise no new accident in the body, but aske opinion of it." The true regiment of health, if it is read as a lowering of oneself into wisdom, becomes the wise patient's mastery of the means of averting disease, including the manufacture of his own physician.

The culminating essay of the 1597 edition, "Of Negociating," is the most obviously utilitarian of the first series, though its fixation on effect is at least as ambiguous. One could say that here Bacon finally excludes any explicit consideration of moral or ethical reasoning because he reveals an unalloyed Machiavellianism; but that exclusion rigidly maintained is really another way for Bacon to argue that the wisest morality is a purer calculation.

"Of Negociating" introduces the new learning's problematic equation of knowledge and mastery: "All practise is to discouer or to worke" (553). As Bacon's Latin version makes clear, practice is negotiation.[2] Negotiation so defined is a heuristic. The description of how men can be made to expose their natures and how that knowledge is to be used is a call to something darkly synonymous with winning advantage; the wise man discovers other men's natures presenting themselves for his use as they are betrayed by excess and adversity:

> [M]en discouer themselues in trust, in passion, at vnawares and of necessitie, when they would hauve somewhat donne, and cannot find an apt precept. If you would worke any man, you must either know his nature and fashions and so leade him, or his ends, and so winne him, or his weaknesses or disaduantages, and so awe him, or those that haue interest in him and so gouerne him.   (*E* VI.534)

In retrospect, the methods are familiar to readers of Bacon's discussion of inquiry into nature. Men are best dealt with by means of instruments: in the case of negotiation, instruments are other men. The best agents of the negotiator do not have to be friends; indeed the best ones are plain and lacking in all cunning. In general, the best observations are done by deputy, from a distance, by surprise, and at times that one's object is most likely to betray himself because he is overtaken by his appetites. When the negotiator's opposite is cunning, the wise inquirer, like the inquirer into nature, must read him like a code, and proceed cryptically himself: "In dealing with cunning persons, we must euer consider their endes to interpret their speeches, and it is good to say little to them, and that which they least look for" (534). The advice is moderate, unless one sees in it the violation of Bacon's resolve not to "work" another man secretly. The violation is in fact wisely moderate because it honors the victim's true nature, discovering it by means of manipulation.

5

The preoccupations of the original series of essays are remarkably consonant with those of the *Meditationes Sacrae,* which devote themselves to the charitable use of religion purged of ostentation, vain anticipation, and imposture. In Chapter I, we noted the coincidence of the new learning's doctrines of experiment with the meditations' religious arguments to "try all things" in fearless examination and trial of "infection" and "pollution."[3] Meditation five, "Of Moderation of Cares," distinguishes between attempts to "bind divine providence" and wise actions that take advantage of turns of fortune (246). The next meditation, on "earthly hope," interprets wordly aspirations as misleading anticipations, the central subject of Book II of *The Advancement:* "For it is the nature of the human mind, even in the gravest wits, the moment it receives an impression of anything, to sally forth and spring forward and expect to find everything else in harmony with it" (*MS* VII.247).

The solution to the problem of indulging earthly hopes is to show a contempt for the world, a repression that paradoxically offers a greater earthly, as well as heavenly, reward: "If the good be beyond the hope, then no doubt there is a sense of gain: true: yet had it not been better to gain the whole by hoping not at all, than the difference by hoping too little?" (*MS* VII.247). The principle is apt for the new sciences as well as religion: "Therefore all hope is to be employed upon the life to come in heaven: but here on earth, by how much purer is the sense [*sensus:* VII.237] of things present, without infection or tincture of imagination, by so much wiser and better is the soul" (*MS* VII.248). Scourging of the imagination purifies the senses, thereby increasing wisdom. Reasoned hope is "the work of the understanding and judgment," accompanied by a rational, "just inclination of the feeling" (248). Even reasoned hope is unavoidably subject to "anticipation of good," which "makes the mind light, frothy, unequal, and wandering" (248) as long as the scourging of the imagination is not complete.

The next five meditations examine false religion in terms of the new learning's task of detecting, controlling, and eradicating secular idolatries. The lesser sinners—the hypocrite and the impostor—lie by means of pompous rhetoric in the church, a rhetoric of praise for God which masks their unwillingness to benefit men by means of charitable deeds. Their "ostentation" is typical of the false rhetoric that Bacon ascribes to the idol-worshippers. It is either the false art of the scholastics, who order everything in their minds without engaging the inner self, or it is the vanity of poets who presume that their fictions will give instruction to true religion. It might also be the "high speech" of obscurantists who allegorize and so encourage deception. Like idol-worship, hypocrisy is defined by its satisfaction of the hypocrite's desires (*MS* VII.240). Although Bacon is careful not to condemn monastic prayers of praise (*"a great office in the Church"*) he points out that their "near neighbour" is "self-exalting" hypocrisy (244). The way to arrest false praise is to break the hypocrite from his habit of "sacrifice"—that is, of giving bounteous public praise for the Maker—and "to send him . . . to the works of mercy." This is the way to "convict" the hypocrite, to detect and judge him at once through a method of crossing his desires. One can then have him do the "duties of charity" rather than those of commendation, or face him with the prospect of revealing his "pretended holiness."

The most serious duplicity, that of the true heretic, is far more difficult to discover because he performs deeds that appear to be charitable. His false piety is not nearly as vulnerable as the paradings of the hypocrites and the imposters. To find Bacon's response to the problem of unmasking the heretic, we need to recall his recommendation in meditation three for men "of perverse and corrupt judgment," whose naivete resembles the heretic's sophistication in assuming that the appearance of honesty and goodness is all that matters. Bacon's strategy for exposing foolishness is appropriate for reducing the heretic's charity. The inquisitor must know as much as the heretic knows about his vagrant heart. Only when the "deepest reaches" of the cunning heart's "rottenness" can be "thoroughly sounded and known" (*MS* VII.245) will it be subject to faithful persuasion.

Bacon's emphasis upon the radical duplicity of the corrupt soul, as well as the means for unmasking it, threatens to put the inquisitor in a position analogous to God, who see into every thing. From the perspective of the meditations, however, the inquisitor is humbly doing God's bidding in bringing the unfaithful to account, and more importantly, in shining like God's sunlight into the sink of corruption, scourging and affirming the purity of his soul through a daring inquiry into sin (*MS* VII.245).

The Baconian adept takes a special risk in his rhetoric, for in adapting his outward speech and behavior so as to conform with any audience, he seems to do what the heretic does. The truly pious man's "carriage and conversation towards God is full of excess, of zeal, of exstasy . . . His bearing and conversation with men on the contrary is full of mildness and sobriety and appliable demeanor: whence the saying, *I am all things to all men* [*omnia omnibus factus sum*], and the like" (*MS* VII.250). This is the line from 1 Corinthians 9.22 in which Paul justifies a preaching that is at once "free from all men" and "servant unto all."[4] His claim is that his public speech and gesture can accommodate itself to all audiences and be "free from all men," as long as he eschews worldly glory and lives the gospel he preaches. In this sense Paul speaks against his will,[5] in fear of not preaching the gospel with which he crosses himself: "woe is unto me if I preach not the gospel!"[6] The new learning's devotions and practices must imitate Paul's sincerity or risk that woe.

Charity is for this reason an especially important term in the *Meditations*. Charity severs the misleading appearances of a connection between good deeds and good intentions. All degrees of charity short of "pure charity" share "something in them of ostentation. . . . For where a man feels that virtue is proceeding from him, it may be that he feels pride in it, and is taking delight more in the fruit of his own virtue than in the welfare and good of his neighbor" (*MS* VII.246). True charity will not permit even the most secret of vanities. It requires the mortification of personal anticipations because they are all self-aggrandizing, all illusions. Charity knows itself by selfless sacrifice, not by material achievement.

The rigor of true charity is thus highly conducive to a separation of means and ends in the new learning. The more advanced the new arts and sciences become, the greater the gap between anticipation and discovery, between the appearances of their operations and the course of true investigation, exposition, and rhetoric. It is this very self-abnegation that leads, or is somehow meant to lead, to the conformity of the new learning's accomplishments with the works of God. Unencumbered by vanity, the charitable arts and sciences would exhibit to their practitioners the workings of God's power in laws of manipulation and in what is then useful and beneficial to mankind. To opine a connection between God's works and purposes, as Bacon frequently reminds his reader, is vainly to presume to know the ways of Providence.

An appreciation of the significance of these competing imperatives in Bacon's works helps us to read the essays published after the 1597 edition. What follows are readings of several key texts appearing for the first time in editions between 1597 and 1625, and then again in the final supervised edition of 1625.

6

Twenty-four new essays in the 1607 edition, augmented by six more in 1612, expand upon many of these ideas, often in new modes of argument. As testimony to the significance of charity in the new learning, the second and third entries in the 1607 edition are entirely new discussions of what Bacon calls the secular partner of charity—goodness—and its contrary: the false wisdom of self-love. It is highly significant that for all three major revisions of the 1597 edition (1607, 1612, and 1625) Bacon drops the *Meditationes Sacrae* while creating new leading essays, sometimes clusters of them, concerned with the relation between charitable religion, goodness, and wisdom. In 1607, the new "Of Friendship" takes first place as an almost sentimental corrective to the shrewd "Of Followers and Friends," which falls from fourth to fourteenth place in 1607. Following "Of Friendship," in the third and fourth place, are new essays on the viciousness of self-love and the virtue of charitable goodness. In 1612, another new essay takes the fore: "Of [Unity in] Religion," which discusses the relation of policy to charity in making religious unity possible. Finally, the 1625 edition commences with the new "Of Truth," perhaps the most famous of Bacon's efforts, which is in essence a declaration of the new learning's fidelity to religious principle.

"Of Wisdom for a Man's Self" formulates an imperative that is common to all of these works but malleable in its implications and development: "Divide with reason between selfe love, and society: and bee so true to thy selfe, as thou be not false to others" (*E* VI.561).[7] Embedded in the appeal to reason is a remarkable equivocation: be *so* true to thy self *as* thou be not false to others. Shakespeare's Polonius, on the boards and in the stalls several years before Bacon's words were published, is more clearly if unthinkingly high-minded: "This above all: to thine own self be true, / And it must follow, as the night the day, / Thou canst not then be false to any man."[8] Bacon's command is to "divide" rather than devote oneself, and to do so on the basis of "reason," which establishes the division between society and self-love. Being true to oneself is a tolerated and carefully controlled evil rather than a formal principle. When Bacon says the prince should prefer those who "haue not this marke," he means that all men have it but that a few allow it to be made "the accessary" to the public weal (*E* VI.562). Only the prince, who by his nature fuses private with public, would seem to be able to follow Polonius's advice wisely.

This argument is augmented in the 1625 edition so as to suggest that lesser men might be able to imitate the prince's wise government. Ordinarily, self-aggrandizing men would seem to jeopardize their own fortunes by presuming to control events with their limited and idolatrous "self-wisdom" (433). But if such men could refrain from trying to control fortune with their misguided wisdom, they might escape becoming "sacrifices" to fortune's "inconstancy." If they chose rather to act at opportune moments, they could gain control of time. The wisdom that would enable them to see when it is right to act, here barely glimpsed, resembles the wise prince's ability to act as though public good and his own wise private good were the same.

If a basis for that wisdom could be found in man's nature, the problem of reconciling private and public goods would be more tractable. The original, 1607 version of "Of Goodness and Goodness of Nature," prominently placed fourth in the series, addresses this possibility in a manner that inducts the reader into a more elaborate struggle to prove and justify the existence of goodness in mankind. Bacon takes up the defense as no casual matter, since goodness is the sympathetic counterpart of charity. It "of all vertues is the greatest, being the character of the *Deitie,* and without it Man is a busie, mischevous wretched thing." Goodness like charity saves business— and by extension the new learning itself—from becoming idolatrous.

Bacon recognizes the chief objection to this view as coming from thinkers such as Machiavelli, who wonders how goodness can be useful, especially how the assiduously good and charitable man can defend himself from "those that are tyrannical and uniust."[9] Bacon takes the challenge seriously enough to characterize his essay as an effort to save Christianity and charitable learning from "the Scandall" of the faith's alleged sacrifice of its adherents to their enemies.

Rather than attempting to argue that goodness is part of human nature, the 1607 edition surprisingly begins by advocating the investigation of the errors of good men. If we review the schema of the argument before considering its modal complexities, we see Bacon reduce the cause of the difficulty to two abuses conducive to correction under the tutelage of the new learning: the good man's naive dependence on others' "faces, or fancies,"[10] and his indiscriminate giving to all men whatever their needs and virtues. The model for overcoming those errors is God, who cuts through the dilemma by means of an all-seeing and absolute prerogative. God controls the weather. He rains, and his sun shines, on every man; but he gives wealth and honors to some men and not to others. Good men should likewise find the power to benefit all, and to distinguish some with special gifts.

Most important, the guide to determine the giving of gifts is divinity's Golden Rule, which in Bacon's interpretation is much like the prince's god-like principle, set out in "Of Wisdom for a Man's Self," of acting in regal self-interest. In "Of Goodness," divinity "maketh the love of ourselves the *patterne;* the love of our Neighbours but the *portraiture.*"[11] Loving others as oneself is a divinely ordained means of self-protection. Kindness toward others is the image of the true pattern that is wise self-love: the capacity to give benefits advantageously.

Bacon joins this remarkable gloss of the Golden Rule with another biblical precedent, this one to show that self-interest and charitable deeds are coincident when a man retains his estate in order to do good. Acknowledging that charity and goodness would seem to dictate that a man give all away, Bacon's argument implies that to do so without a "vocation"—without a true calling—is presumptuous, hence uncharitable as well as financially ruinous: "For otherwise in feeding the streames, thou dryest the fountaine."[12]

All these points, made on the basis of right reason defined in terms of advantage, of piety linked with prerogative, finally do not address the possibility that there is a natural basis for charity, or a less ambiguous relation between the idea of good and the embodiment of a goodness in nature. Bacon's array of arguments invites the conclusion that the true ground of charity is a decidedly uncharitable calculation. Although he does not abandon the possibility of natural goodness, he notes it only in a single clause isolated from the thrust of his argument: "there is in some Men, euen in Nature a disposicion towards it [goodness]."[13] But then, following a pattern in many of the essays, "Of Goodness" turns its attention to natural malignancy. It marks the fitness of evil men for roles as "great Pollitiques," good "timber" for ships on the high seas of controversy (*E* VI.405). Only in a final phrase, which observes that politicians do not make good builders of houses, is the earlier seed of goodness acknowledged. A lone illustration of the natural basis of charity, which Bacon adds to the introduction of the 1625 version, is almost grotesquely tortive: even the "cruel" Turk is charitable by nature, for in stoning to death a Christian boy who has strangled a bird, he shows a love for animals that is in fact his own repressed love for his fellow man (403).

Some of the true indications of a man's charitable nature are set out in another 1625 addition as "the parts and signs of goodness" (405). From an initial perspective, Bacon's concise eloquence in the aphorisms listing charitable attributes is an enforcement of charity's faithful simplicity. However, in the context of the entire essay and its place in the series, the list of aphorisms is perfunctory, and their perfunctoriness an illustration of the difficulty of showing or proving true goodness except as a sign—a glimpse of something out of nature because it can only be sovereign and divinely given. The good and charitable man must "above all," as Bacon says in the final sentence, "wish to be an *anathema* from Christ," like Paul a persecuted sacrifice, if he is to show "a divine nature" that makes him conformable to the true charity of his faith.

Appearing with "Of Goodness" for the first time in the 1607 edition, "Of Marriage and Single Life" picks up the problem of defining true charity without recourse to the idea of natural affiliation. When Bacon observes that a natural family drains the churchman's charity, he poses the question of whether charity is bound to be purer in those who are unencumbered by the natural ties of marriage.[14] Single men do seem capable of greater charity toward mankind; nevertheless, he notes, they are in general "more cruell" than married men, and "hard hearted"—good "to make seuere Inquisitors."[15] In a 1625 addition, Bacon heightens and interprets the paradox: "*single Men,* though they be many times more Charitable, because of their Meanes are lesse exhaust; yet, on the other side, they are more cruell, and hard hearted, (good to make seuere Inquisitors) because their Tendernesse is not so oft called vpon" (*E* VI.392). Without having their affections drawn forth in familial routines, single men whose charity is liberated from nature are also cruel in their neglect of nature.

The highly uncertain status of charity in human nature makes charitable persuasion difficult. Hence the problem of maintaining the unity of charitable religion, a matter which comes to the fore in the new leading essay of the next edition, published in 1612. "Of Religion," later entitled "Of the Unity of Religion," paints charitable religion's environment as a place where dangerous conspiracy and disunity are rampant, but where religion can abide by charitable principles to protect itself. But if charity is a sign of *anathema,* a severing of oneself from the compromising affiliations of nature, then exactly how does it appeal to its friends, and turn back or convert its enemies in order to maintain "the bonds" of religious unity (*E* VI.543)? The answer, which Bacon broaches in the text of 1612 and later strengthens in the much larger 1625 version, is to "deface" men's schismatic reason: in moments of division, "it is better that Religion should deface mens vnderstanding, then their piety and charitie" (*E* VI.543). The argument is meant to quiet both sides of religious controversies: heretics whose misunderstandings lead them to change the course of established beliefs, and faithful practitioners whose vain reasonings invoke God's wrath to perform aggrandizing purges.

The principle of following charity over reason is the double doctrine of the essay's gnomic center: "For it is better that Religion should deface mens vnderstanding, then their piety and charitie; retaining reason onely but as an *Engine,* and *Charriot driuer* of cruelty, and malice" (543). Here the Phaedrean chariot takes a new form: reason powers charity as an engine, and directs the dark horse's cruel excesses into the service of charitable ends. The third figure, the good horse, is absent. Conflict between religion and reason discounts the possibility of harmonizing a being's anger and love with its incipient reason.

Charity can thus exercise extreme force to preserve its purity in the affairs of mortal believers and heretics. In arguing that disunity in religion threatens civil peace as well as the purity of the church, the essay calls upon princes, churches, and all kinds of "learning" to "ioyne in the damning to Hell for euer" of the violent subversives, by means of princely "power" and ecclesiastical "decrees," as well as Mercury's rod of eloquence (544).

Bacon tempers this declaration, as he often does elsewhere, with an almost parenthetical qualification that seems closer to his deeper intent: strife might be avoided if "Counsels concerning Religion" took not the Lord's name in vain. Here though, the afterthought is an extension of the earlier argument: when churchmen consult among themselves—that is, when they are already in more or less unified bodies—they ought not to act with violence. Heretics are to be kept at a distance, or sent by whatever means are available to an infernal punishment.

In the 1625 version of this essay, Bacon takes the rare step of erasing his reference to religion's defacing and retaining of the understanding. In its place, he inserts a paragraph that elaborately qualifies the meaning of the missing sentence by warning against zealous delusion:

> Concerning the Means of procuring Unity: men must beware, that in the procuring or muniting of religious unity they do not dissolve and deface the laws of charity and of human society. There be two swords amongst Christians, the spiritual and temporal; and both have their due office and place in the maintenance of religion. But we may not take up the third sword, which is Mohamet's sword, or like unto it; that is, to propagate religion by wars or by sanguinary persecutions to force consciences; except it be in cases of overt scandal, blasphemy, or intermixture of practice against the state; much less to nourish seditions; to authorise conspiracies and rebellions; to put the sword into the people's hands; and the like; tending to the subversion of all government, which is the ordinance of God. For this is but to dash the first table against the second; and so to consider men as Christians, as we forget that they are men. (*E* VI. 383-84)

Extremists jeopardize "all government" by making righteous armies of the people to force conversions. Bacon equates their crusades with the destruction of the first Mosaic "table" (the first commandments regarding the proper worship of God) by smashing it against the second (the commandments that have a more direct bearing on civil life).

Here William Rawley's recollection of Bacon's private remark, to the effect that Moses became the greatest outlaw when he broke both tables after descending from the mountain and finding his people rapt in idolatry (*RCB* VII. 181), is given its apposition in the *Essays'* public doctrine. Whether or not Rawley heard the remark, it is ironic praise of Moses that is pertinent to Bacon's appropriation of Mosaic principles to reduce idolatry and to fragment the world itself, for the sake of its reformulation by the new sciences. In the *Essays,* by contrast, a repetition of Moses' act by the righteous masses is a terrifying prospect. Bacon reminds us that men who are Christians remain men. Thus the essay broaches once again the problem of accommodating charitable persuasion to challenges posed by righteous defenders of charity.

The rest of the essay turns and inverts itself at least two more times on analogous issues. First Bacon allows that the "temporal sword" can be drawn, but only "with great circumspection," which he contrasts with the manner of its use in the hands of "the common people." The charitable forcing of consciences is commonly an expression of an idolatrous interest in one's own ends (*E* VI.384). Circumspection is the clue to the right use of charitable force; but the meaning of circumspection, like the meaning of wisdom, is evident here only in terms of its opposite. As an instrument to be used against seditious heresy, which is punishable by all manner of damnation, circumspect force again knows no limit. Only wisdom can save charity from self-deception, but wisdom is not at all available to the masses in the way it is accessible to the sons of science. Lawful behavior, temperance, and conventional religion must somehow hold the masses within bounds even though the wise circumspection which enforces those limits is utterly remote from conventional civility and belief, and so does not need to know such limits for itself.

Bacon's focus on the relative poverty of nature, its inability to assist charity's climb beyond idolatry, is evident in works such as "Of Nature in Man" and "Of Ambition," where nature is a tendency or condition to be repressed or done away with, or to be used by its wise repressor for ends wholly distinct from the origin of affections. The new learning's idea of charitable persuasion is more informatively presented in the deceptively conventional essays on love, beauty, and praise, which bend traditional topics of philosophical rhetoric toward the principles and purposes of the new learning.

In "Of Love" conventional Christian arguments against corrupt earthly desire support *The Advancement*'s attack on idolatry. Lovers' infatuations, the essay argues, epitomize the faults of the old learning. As in a theater, they "kneel before a little idol," flatter themselves, and indulge in a dangerous carelessness rather than gain wisdom and well-being (398). They depend upon the false ornament and exaggerated proofs of inflated rhetoric, which has no place but in the vain eloquence of earthly, idolatrous desire. Their language "braves the nature and value of things"; they use the "perpetual hyperbole" that "is comely in nothing but in love" (397).

Love is not only a fatal passion; it is proverbially inimical to the "wise" management of appearance and advantage: *"it is impossible to love and to be wise"* (398). Love is a "weakness" that "doth . . . appear to others" and so shames the lover by uncovering his vulnerability to others' strengths. Like an experiment that tests nature for its weaknesses, love gathers strength when the sufferer fails to endure "great adversity" or prosperity. Unchecked, love gains the lover no worthy "reward," but rather turns him, as it did Paris, from the goals of the new arts and sciences.

Love not only interferes with business; it wrecks even heroically fortified hearts "if watch be not well kept." Heroic figures such as Marcus Antonius and Appias Claudius are chief examples: Antony in losing an empire to wantonness despite his unparalleled soldiery, and Claudius in losing a government to love despite his austerity. Love is so dangerous that men must learn how to pen it up or sever it from their business. It cannot be tempered because a single lapse ruins all: "They do best, who if they cannot but admit love, yet make it keep quarter; and sever it wholly from their serious affairs and actions of life; for if it check once with business, it troubleth men's fortunes and maketh men that they can no ways be true to their own ends" (*E* VI. 398).

In the end, the essay acknowledges the existence of another kind of love, a positive "inclination" in man "towards love of others," but this love is "secret." It might be the root of charity, for it "doth naturally spread itself toward others"; still, it is only "seen sometime in friars." The illustration severely curtails the possibility that such love might exist in man's nature. Friars are single men who, we have learned elsewhere, are apt to transgress nature. Love might be inclination that "maketh mankind" in married love, and "perfecteth" mankind by means of friendship; but these last concessions are covered by the rapid cross-hatching of the essay's aphoristic weaving. Quickly, the last part of the sentence returns to the theme that "wanton love" corrupts what noble loves engender and perfect.

The churning of Bacon's aphoristic argument is particularly well-suited to a demolition of positive conceptions of love, not only to make a conventional didactic point but to hint at the true order of things. In "Of Love," the relentless juxtaposition of ideas forecloses upon hyperbolic praise of love. The essay captures its findings and sets them against one another so as to drive out erotic tendency.

In the closely related "Of Beauty," an aphoristic structure seems to work differently. For once the essay ascends to a relatively sustained mode of commendation, though it is ultimately assisted by much the same sort of purgative counter-movement as the one which purges vain anticipations in "Of Love." Bacon uses negative findings to burnish positive ones: "Virtue is like a rich stone, best plain set; and surely virtue is best in a body that is comely, though not of delicate features; and that hath rather dignity of presence, than beauty of aspect" (478–79). After these lines, the commendation vaporizes into the austere admiration of the most transitory of beauty's attributes. The idea of comeliness immediately prevails over beautiful "features"; "presence" overcomes "aspect." The essay's structure, like its subject, veers from its epideictic mode by systematically rejecting the first sight of beauty for a rapid survey of examples from which true beauty has fled. Thus one reads that beauty and virtue almost never combine in persons. There are exceptions, but in listing them, the essay makes them extraordinary proof of the ordinary rule. Beauty is most essentially motion, an elusive grace: "In beauty, that of favours is more than that of colour; and that of decent and gracious motion more than that of favour. That is the best part of beauty, which a picture cannot express; no nor the first sight of life" (479). Beauty is achieved in the painter's art by "felicity, . . . not by rule." It possesses "some strangeness in the proportion" that artists can not capture. Hence an older, autumnal face is for Bacon more beautiful than a younger one, as though a harvest of beauty on the verge of decay were the only "decent motion" of beautiful maturity.

The incidence of this admirable virtue is finally fortuitous, utterly beyond the painter's art, if one were to judge by the new list of corruptions supplied in the essay's last sentence. Admirable beauty is pointedly beyond the grasp of the mind itself, though it would seem to be detectable to the wise eye that knew that grace and motion, not features, are essential to beauty: "if it [beauty] light well it maketh virtue shine, and vices blush" (480). This little peroration, eloquent in its confinement, hints at the notion that true beauty, like charitable love, is absent from the ordinary sights and passions of the world, and is shadowed only in the systematic inquiry and care for acting at the right moment, in the light that only wisdom can effect.

Such beauty is like the true praise defined in "Of Praise," which must not be any "flower" or ornament, but an "ointment" that "filleth all round about." The metaphor of spiritual penetration displaces the organic metaphor drawn from traditional notions of decoration. Here beauty, like all true praise, might be an anointment that blesses—

an application that some magicians use to hold spirit in (*HVM* V.285)—not an addition that draws it out. Beauty is thus neither a perfective form nor a gracing of form.

Lacking the ointment of true praise, other virtues, such as those discussed in "Of Vainglory," are the factious puffery of ambitious imagination. They are the "scorn of wise men" (505). They commend themselves only to the creation of false appearances, as though they could reverse an irreversible physical law and make something "of nothing" (504). There is a "natural magnanimity" apart from vainglory, but it is an "art of ostentacion" best defined as praising others for perfections in one's self (504).

Whatever the wise man might do to manipulate the appearances of virtue, his effort to win honor, according to "Of Honour and Reputation," must not swerve to "woo" or "affect" it. Wooing and persuasion can have little to do with a character that declares itself wisely, by choosing the advantageous moment to make itself known. Virtue properly reveals itself when it wisely determines the most opportune circumstances for its action; it protects itself from envy by claiming that Providence, not policy, brings it success (505). The terminology of blessing and revelation casts down the metaphors of courtship and aspiration.

The greatest exception to this pattern is an example that confirms its more fundamental significance. The greatest of commendations— the triumphant parade—traditionally celebrates a military victory in a manner (as Bacon describes it in "Of the True Greatness of Kingdoms and Estates") that transcends "gaudery" in its power to kindle "all men's courages" (452). It is the form of praise Bacon finds "one of the wisest and noblest institutions that ever was." And yet, he argues, in a time of monarchy it is one of the most frivolous and dangerous. In "Of the True Greatness" he explains that the triumph is "not fit for monarchies," since a king cannot permit another greater than himself to be at the head of the triumph as victor. The king cannot afford to make use of even wise triumphs because they inflame the nobles who might surpass as well as save him in his battles. Bacon's technical guide to putting on such events, "Of Masques and Triumphs," devotes only a clipped, terminal paragraph to the ceremony after calling it a toy (467–68).

The noble persons the triumph commends are potentially dangerous. A noble class, Bacon says, can support the king largely by deflecting the masses' envy. But only in the sense that the king makes his nobles serviceable, bending them toward his business ("Of Nobility," 405), can they be said to complement him. Like a mere ornament, a nobleman "addeth majesty to monarch, but diminisheth power," unless the king finds "able" noblemen to do the real work of his will (405). Virtue, insofar as it is embodied or manifested in noble character under these circumstances, finds a place in monarchy as a tool rather than a perfective complement. As a complement, the noble class tends to be accidental or dangerous.

In his relation to the nobility, the king paradoxically endures the danger of seeming a mere user of tools that might be more virtuous than he is if he cannot control them. For Bacon, one of the crises of the Elizabethan age would have supplied evidence of that danger and its severe control: the Earl of Essex's attempt to enter London as a scourge of the court, in a kind of triumph he hoped Queen Elizabeth would approve. The aborted march on London was proof, from Bacon's perspective as a witness against his friend, that Essex despite his ambition should not have tried to be anything more than the queen's instrument. Essex's error ran counter to Bacon's life-long effort to prove the instrumentality of himself and the new learning to the monarch.

With the notable exception of *The New Atlantis,* the wise sovereign's manipulation of nature and of men is Bacon's model for the establishment of the new charitable sciences. The king or queen by nature acts wisely in isolation, making use of nobility without needing any commendatory perfection or completion by noble retainers, because it is fundamentally unnecessary and dangerous to the regal person. *The Advancement* counsels King James to rule as a god of Providence in cryptic but effective obscurity; it applauds Moses' use of Aaron as the deputy of his speech; it holds up for emulation Solomon's power to enjoy the riches of his kingdom without indulging his wise soul. Such kings, Bacon argues in various places, do not reveal their designs to others except to make use of others' services. And like Solomon they ensure their charity by means of their piety, which gathers power in presuming no independence from God's providential design. The cryptic, austerely resplendent, pious yet all-powerful rulers of the New Atlantis are monarchs in this mold.

In "Of Truth," the new opening essay of the 1625 edition, we read that truth teaches the "sovereign good of nature." A kind of kingly wisdom seems to be available to those who are the instruments of kings, if they are wise enough to hear it. But what is that wisdom if the teachings of truth, according to the essay's first lines, scourge men of their "affecting free-will" so that unlike Pilate they can "fix a belief"?

The new opening essay begins with Pilate's refusal to listen to Jesus: Bacon recalls his question "What is Truth?" and the impatience which "would not stay for an answer" (*E* VI. 377). The question is embedded in the Gospel's account of the interrogation of Jesus: Pilate has just asked whether he is king of the Jews. Jesus' twofold answer defines Christian doctrine: he has said that he was born into the world so that he "should bear witness unto the truth," and that "every one that is of the truth heareth" his voice. Pilate's exasperated response dismisses Jesus' preaching by giving up the possibility of finding that truth.

Pilate's doubt expresses, in Bacon's interpretation of this moment, "a natural though corrupt love of the lie itself." He embraces "vain opinion, flattering hopes, false valuation." Truth, on the other hand, is "a naked and open day-light." True inquiry, the first step toward "sovereign good," is a "love-making and wooing" of truth that Bacon parallels not with aspiration in nature but with God's creation of the senses; the "presence" of knowledge he aligns not with virtue but with God's gift of reason to man; man's "enjoying" of truth is linked not with aspiration but with God's election of "his chosen" (378).

In adjacent sentences, the close associations of religious and secular terminology confirm and elevate the Baconian argument that the knowing mind can undergo or traffic with lies without falling prey to them. God created "the light of the sense" as well as "the light of reason" so that the mind might wisely partake of falsehoods: "But it is not the lie that passeth through the mind, but the lie, that sinketh in and settleth in it, that doth the hurt" (378).

In "Of Truth," the true pleasure of knowledge is the wise possession of an all-seeing and charitable perspective on the "errors" and turmoil below. Bacon quotes from Lucretius to describe that perspective in Olympian terms, though he adds the parenthetical imperative that the wise never seek to command the hill of truth, and always have pity on those whose wanderings below they see so clearly. Those who know Olympian truths must be as pious as they are regal, as Solomonic in their charity for other men's conditions as they are in their comprehensive experience of what is conducive to pride.

The last section of the essay extends this reasoning to "the truth of civil business." Here we get an inkling of the argument's practical edge, which indicates how the wise man might hide his wise purposes from his civil appearances. Bacon loads the argument with conventional sentiments about the superiority of plain and upright dealing over "winding and crooked" lies (378). In the interstices and echoes of his phrasing he notes the sovereign mind acting far above, though in pity for, the erring minds below:

> [I]t will be acknowledged even by those that practise it not, that clear and round dealing is the honour of man's nature; and that mixture of falsehood is like allay in coin of gold and silver, which may make the metal work the better, but it embaseth it. For these winding and crooked courses are the goings of the serpent; which goeth basely upon the belly, and not upon the feet. There is no vice that doth so cover a man with shame as that to be found false and perfidious. (378–79)

The homage vice pays to honesty is some measure of honesty's validity as an honorable attribute. But Bacon's claim that everyone would liken perfidious dealing to the debasement of coinage is an ambiguous proof of a universal truth. The exchange of money is by its nature an idolatrous commerce of what is called, earlier in the essay, "false valuations." Honesty would be subject to the same false valuation, unless the alloy could be detected. The higher alchemy, as we have seen elsewhere, would be able to blend gold with baser metals that could not be discovered. So the principle that all men share—that alloys debase golden virtue—is a convention that the new alchemy would be able to maintain or manipulate according to its charitable will.

The essay's middle argument has already suggested that the wise might engage in a form of doubleness. When Bacon writes that lies "passeth through" the minds of the wise without hurting them, the ostensible argument is that the mind is a more or less passive conveyance that can wisely deliver itself of the idolatries of others without allowing them to sink in. But the mind's action need not here be construed as passive or silent. Bacon's phrasing is so general in this crucial phrase that it leaves open the possibility that the Solomonic mind might convey lies without suffering taint.

The Last Judgment enforces an equation of civil virtue and religious faith: "Surely the wickedness of falsehood and breach of faith cannot possibly be so highly expressed, as in that it shall be the last peal to call the judgments of God upon the generations of men; it being foretold, that when Christ cometh, *he shall not find faith upon the earth*" (379). Quoting Montaigne, Bacon argues that a liar blasphemes when with his untruths he "faces God" yet "shrinks from man" (379). In contrast, the charitable man would permit manipulation of his public visage of honesty while his actions in civil life were Solomonic in God's sight.

These principles prepare the ground for Bacon's most elaborate discussion of secrecy and disguise in civil affairs: "Of Simulation and Dissimulation," which inquires into when and how to tell truth (387). It is here that Bacon most clearly sets out, in an argument capped by an emphatic aphorism, an argument for the morality of secrecy: "set it down, that *an habit of secrecy is both politic and moral.*"

Secrecy is wise. It is superior to the much fainter wisdoms of dissembling and simulation, though it depends upon them. Yet the knowledge of "when to tell truth, and to do it," as Bacon describes it in his first lines, would seem to be the furthest thing from secrecy. "Certainly," he says in the first paragraph, "the ablest man that ever were have had all an openness and frankness of dealing; and a name of certainty and veracity." But openness, one soon discovers, is really the ability to "discern" what to disclose and when, and so conversely what to keep secret under the right circumstances. It is prudent to make openness reserved, and closeness the hidden agenda of frankness. Using an analogy from the more explicitly scientific writings, Bacon likens the open man to a well-trained and well-guided horse that knows "when to stop or turn." The simile is brief, but rich with implications for the essay's conception of the honest gesture. The apogee of the "open" horse's achievement is not its well-managed stature, gait, or expression of spirit or restraint so much as its ability to halt its self-disclosure or veer away. Discernment is the ability to stop, to reverse one's field, or to go straight ahead. All are relatively mechanical motions with little of the modality of living gesture. The perfectly open man, when he uses his reputation for frankness to cover his sudden turns and stops, becomes "almost invisible," a kind of pneuma. His discerning judgment distinguishes him from the base dissembler who merely develops an unthinking habit of closeness. The secret man's closeness is a more comprehensive "habit," as Bacon calls it in his final sentence (389). He knows how to cover up and yet set himself forth in all circumstances.

The secret man—the frank, secret man—is described in the next paragraph as though he were a new Proteus, a being more Protean than his predecessor. Bacon's saying that the secret man is "invisible" when he wants to be is another way of saying that he "leaveth himself . . . without hold to be taken" (387–88). Whereas ancient Proteus is within reach of inquirers who capture him in his sleep, the new man in his invisibility eludes everyone, while his simulation and dissimulation enable him to capture his opponents as though they were beings he could "surprise" in their sleep (389).

The secret man can use a reputation for closeness to surprise those who merely dissemble and who, attracted to a seemingly confidential listener, give over their burdens to him. There is a resemblance between the secret man and a wise confessor, to whom people think they are speaking without risk of disclosure (388). The wise confidant's reputation for secrecy enables him to open men's hearts to his will.

The secret man knows how to use invisibility to make inquiry by severing his tongue from his countenance as he observes how erring men's faces betray their inner life. One of the chief tasks of the new sciences—to inquire into the gestures of the face and body as signs of the body's relation to the mind—is thus a most suitable project, which Bacon in *The Advancement* accuses Aristotle of neglecting. The true inquirer would see into the relation between gesture and mind in vainly dissembling men, while he acted upon his knowledge with a covering mobility of gesture. Whatever connection there might appear to be between his own motions and purposes would be instrumental to his cryptic, though presumably charitable, intent.

Insofar as he discloses his "inclination" in speech, the secret man does so to protect himself from the charge that in silence he takes sides. Such disclosure is really dissimulation: "no man can be secret, except he give himself a little scope of dissimulation" (388–89). Openness is presented in terms of its usefulness in employing others for one's ends, or for "fame and opinion" (389). Inquiry is itself a form of lying, but a kind of lying that may be the only way to truth (389). If it creates adversity or turnings against appearances, it leads nature and men to make themselves "adverse," and so to confess or betray their true selves.

As charitable ciphering, secrecy does good to mankind without needing the mass of men's least sympathy or knowledge. Indeed, as it benefits the mortal body of men and of all natural things serving them, its secretly powerful foresight need not answer to men's minds at all except to protect its secrecy, to appeal to the wise, and to discover incipient sons of science who can undergo the Solomonic ordeal.

The sovereign man's rhetoric is in this sense identical to his intent. The utility of his gestures figures the nature of power in charitable hands. Yet because the true rhetoric of nature and of civil society—the idea and practice of rendering nature and men for the charitable benefit of mankind—remains as inscrutable to the unanointed as it is straightforward to the wise, the *Essays* must somehow fill the gap with generally acceptable counsels about civil virtue and piety.

7

Modern disagreements over the ends and means of the new learning, not to mention Bacon's character as its architect, seem to have ignored the interdependence of religion, science, and moral teaching everywhere in his works, and particularly in his *Essays*. If Bacon's conception of the new learning were obviously Machiavellian, the intensity of his interest in its relation to religion and civil virtue would border on the ludicrous. He does not combine sinister and high-minded designs with ease; neither does Machiavelli. For Bacon, the problems of justifying the new learning's innovations pose significant challenges to the idea of persuasion, to religious belief, and to the civil and moral orders—challenges which he addresses in the context of a lifetime of inquiry and debate. Defenders of Bacon as a benign rationalist underestimate him in another way: they do not address sufficiently his near obsession with covert practices, and his repeated descents into subject matters and methods of inquiry and presentation that are morally suspect. An easily sinister or benignly rational Bacon would not have been interested in a study of codes that linked natural philosophy with wise virtue, and that required him to justify his endeavor with didactic essays as well as scientific treatises, in both of which he ventured and disguised daring interpretations of established religion.

POSTSCRIPT: THE NEW SCIENCES AND BACON'S TRIAL

Any study of Bacon's works, especially of his theory and practice of rhetoric, must eventually take up his arraignment for bribery in 1621, an action by Parliament that led to his removal from his seat as the king's Lord Chancellor. The event is significant as a test of Bacon's character in light of his idea of morality in civil business. What is perhaps more important, the crisis called upon him to exercise his powers of eloquence to the utmost in his defense, powers that, most remarkably, he appears not to have used. This brief postscript is an opportunity to touch upon the fragmentary evidence of this painfully crowning moment in Bacon's public life, and to examine its illustration of the conclusions drawn in previous chapters.

The letter to Parliament that advances Bacon's explicit public defense is most surprising in its immediate "submission" to the Lords. In the center of the brief message is a sentence confessing Bacon's guilt as charged, and a seeming abdication of any right of defense: "I find matter sufficient and full, both to move men to desert the defence, and to move your Lordships to condemn and censure me" (*LL* XIV.243). Whether Bacon acted to deflect enemies of his king, served as an unwitting sacrifice, or was a repentant miscreant, the letter as a whole is a striking retraction and doubling of its seeming confession. Its eloquence startlingly embraces and defies the judgment, in a manner that offers glimpses of Bacon's application of the new learning to what he claimed was the most excruciating ordeal in civil affairs that a holder of his office could experience.

Rather than arguing Bacon's case, the brief letter begins with a request for "a benign interpretation" of its contents. The writer's spirit and mind are in such poor condition that they need the protection of "a noble construction"—a fortress of high-minded understanding supplied by the reader to the writer. There follows "a very strange entrance" to the rest: the daring, ironic argument that despite his extreme afflictions he is glad to have helped inaugurate "a golden world," in which all judges of the highest station will be brought to justice if they are guilty (242). The writer then seems content to pile on the charges; what has been said thus far passes "from the motions of my heart, whereof God is only judge" (243).

Much the same thing occurs in the next phase of the text, in which Bacon takes for his model Job's declaration that *"I have not hid my sin"* (243). Here the letter's confession shows a willingness to go beyond whatever Parliament might have wished Bacon to admit, just as Job surpasses the fallen Adam by fearlessly telling all. The rush to tell all, however, obscures what is being confessed. There are few details. Bacon turns to the list of Parliament's specific charges, but eludes them by saying he will not presume to bother his judges with a discussion of their inaccuracies (243). He is not only guiltier than Parliament can know; he is guiltier than they can say—but ultimately not in the way they have specified.

Some members of Parliament specifically protested the ambiguous result: was Bacon confessing errors or defending his case (248, 250)? The very way Bacon emphasizes his guilt has the effect of dismissing the specific charges against him and elevating his case to the higher court of the king. (This was indeed his intent as it was expressed to the king in private correspondence [241].) The punishment he proposes for himself would circumvent Parliament: giving his seal of office to the king "may serve I hope in itself for an expiation of my faults" (244).

The letter undermines the Parliament's judgment in another sense, by recommending a verdict that mixes radically opposite sentences. Parliament must act, it seems, with implacable severity as well as grace (245). The Lords should follow their "chief pattern, the king our Sovereign, a king of incomparable clemency" and "inscrutable for wisdom," who, like Henry VII before him, performs "acts mixed of mercy and justice." Bacon's Parliamentary judges should carry out the most severe punishment Bacon says a Lord Chancellor can undergo—the loss of his seal of office—and yet "not break the bruised reed" (244). The request is to have Parliament do the wise king's office, but Parliament cannot do so without parodying "incomparable" mercy and "inscrutable" wisdom. In welcoming their judgment on him, Bacon almost taunts his accusers with the prospect of his escape.

Bacon can play sovereign himself in writing to the Lords rather than standing before them. Reportedly ill, he is beyond the reach of demeaning cross-examination, and he can use his distance from the proceedings to augment the letter's achievement of rhetorical distance from the immediate facts of the case. His remoteness draws him closer to the king as God's lieutenant—for whom Bacon is himself the executive—who is the judge beyond Parliament, and indeed, in Bacon's definition of kingship, beyond any ordinary persuasion.

The letter's confession transcends secular judgment in another way, by invoking the relatively esoteric paradigm of Solomonic suffering and by aligning itself with the doctrine of wise Solomonic indulgence in the luxuries of power. In the letter and Bacon's later elucidation of the twenty-eight points of his guilt (a statement which the Lords, disgruntled with his enigmatic apology, required of him) the confessions draw a cryptic strength from Solomon's ability to endure, and to maintain his purity amidst corruption. Thus Bacon can freely admit his guilt in accepting gifts from petitioners whose cases he judged, while ignoring the charge that the presents tainted his verdicts (*LL* XIV.252–61). Likewise, he can welcome inquisitorial searches, following a late Roman precedent that requires judicial confession and torture, by approving of the "terror" of his own interrogation by Parliament. Arguing that such interrogation has much greater power than any merely physical or monetary penalty, he can follow the Solomonic path without sacrificing his entire estate (244).

"Of Envy," which first appeared four years after these proceedings, offers suggestive commentary on Bacon's rhetorical rationale in 1621. It is difficult to appreciate the intensity of the essay's attack on envy without recognizing envy's old meaning as opprobrium or public disapproval. Bacon's interrogation by Parliament was in this sense a confrontation with the embodiment of envy, and his response to that persecution a representative display of the rhetoric his essay later recommends as an answer.

For Bacon, envy infects all persons who have no virtue, who are superficially busy, who seem noble but are not wise (*E* VI.393). In short, envious people are as common as idolaters. All but the wise are envious. Envy ranks only with love in its ability to "fascinate or bewitch" mankind (392). As the counterpart of idolatrous love, it is the creator of evil influences by means of an "irradiation of the eye" (393). Bacon fell, or so it seemed, immediately after he had been charged. To turn back envy's magical action, he writes, there is ultimately "no other cure . . . but cure of witchcraft." Tactics developed to turn spells away must be used to deflect the envious eye.

Bacon advises confronting the witchcraft of envy with the radical displacement of the spell to another "lot" or target: "the wiser sort of great persons bring in ever upon the stage somebody upon whom to derive [Spedding's note: 'turn from its course'] the envy that would come upon themselves" (395–96). To turn the eye's attention, the deflecting machine uses one magic over another.

The rhetorician seeking to overcome envy is in a curious position. He cannot seem to persuade his envious detractors in any conventional manner, for "plausible actions" on his part will be—or will be interpreted to be—signs of weakness (396). In a world full of idolaters, commonplace proofs and shows of good faith are typically the tools of *naïfs*. If the persecuted rhetorician wishes to persuade others of his virtue, he can do so only ineffectively, by remaining silent. His only resort is a calculated persuasion that gives envy what it wants—a target for its mischief, which gives the persuader the freedom to move undetected.

There is something of the master-magician in the man who can escape the binding of envy. In his history of life and death, published after his abortive trial, Bacon refers to an ancient magus, Apollonius of Tyana, who performed such a feat: he was a man "truly wonderful; regarded as a god by the heathens, as a sorcerer by the Christians," who despite his "immense renown . . . towards the close of his life . . . had to undergo accusation and disgrace" (*HVM* V.253).[1] The circumstances of his ordeal go undescribed; Bacon only comments that Apollonius successfully "contrived to escape to safety." The full story was available in a biography by Philostratus. Apollonius was a famous universal philosopher (or magician, the account is ambiguous) who criticized the old Orphic rites[2] and distinguished himself from conventional magicians,[3] but who also had the power to escape all attempts to confine him.[4] His most notable feat was the one Bacon alludes to without specifying its circumstances. Brought into a courtroom on charges of practicing magic, Apollonius suddenly disappeared, leaving behind his written defense. By citing Apollonius for his long life, Bacon thus provides a note upon the success of this ancient's power to elude the envious imagination, providing it with a distraction—a defensive text—that perpetuates his power.

But how would one take upon oneself the mantle of such a magus? If envious idolaters are everywhere, how can one turn invisible in their gaze and escape the charge that one is oneself a magician? In the thousandth and last observation in the *Sylva Sylvarum,* published posthumously, Bacon offers one more clue to the new rhetoric. He hypothesizes that power and powerlessness, fame and subjugation, can be suffered and controlled through mere thoughts and words because the spirits of men are created from "one divine limbus." The "delight" that men have in winning fame and subjugating others substantiates the existence of that limbus, and implicitly justifies and excuses the success of the master persuader who knows how it works (*SS* II.672).

As the quintessential medium for action at a distance, the limbus is more than a medium of influence or the spells of the old magic. It draws everyone into its sphere because all are born there. All take it with them in their being. Hence it is the ideal medium for envy's ravaging of its victims; men in disrepute fall ill from envy's power to transmit disapproval through the limbus. It is also divine, a kind of limbo, a region from which one might rise up, or plunge into perdition, depending upon one's wisdom. Wise persuaders who knew the mutability as well as the universality of envy's influence would know something about how to use the limbic power with envy, or an ambition for fame. Wise men who knew their liminal natures would have a key to influencing and resisting the spirits of others, and to projecting or withholding themselves. Before the ignorant, they could become invisible. They might then act charitably, perhaps calling out to the spirit's divinity; or more dangerously, they might stir and deflect the limbic being without inhibition or in full confidence that what was divine in it would endure.

In the context of Bacon's entire project, the limbus makes uniform, immediate, and all but inescapable the old Timaeic universe's influence over its various parts and levels of being. Indeed, persuasion in the limbic world seems to be an absolute necessity, with few fundamental variations in its effects. All things persuade and are persuaded in every motion. Some fall into disfavor while others rise to fame or something higher. At the same time, one's power to influence, along with one's vulnerability to the influence of others, seems so much greater than it is in the Timaeic cosmos that persuasion bifurcates into two radically different activities: the instantaneous identification of the mover and the moved as one being, and their absolute opposition as coercer and coerced.

This hypertrophy of Timaeic tradition, which we have followed in many of Bacon's works, transforms the old white magic into a science of influence. As he drives out the old ideas of universal, per-suadable tendency, Bacon is reifying a universal tendency that is ap-propriate to a higher science rigorously governed by the force of necessity and the power of the rational will. In this new context, the persuader's purpose disappears yet asserts itself everywhere, much as Bacon describes God's encoding of his purposes in nature. The result of this paradoxical doctrine is a sort of higher magic, one that makes Timaeic nature strangely different by drawing it out of itself. To the degree that the real medium of influence is limbic in Bacon's sense of that word, the new learning also analogizes persuasion with the operation of divine influence or judgment upon all things. Bacon's well known disavowal of an interest in joining divinity with natural philosophy ends up creating a secular science vibrating with his idea of the Maker's encoding power.

NOTES

INDEX

NOTES

INTRODUCTION

1. Apollodorus, *Library* I.9.25.
2. Apollonius Rhodius, *Argonautica* IV.900–911.
3. For an account of the medieval commentary on Orpheus, see John Block Friedman, *Orpheus in the Middle Ages* (Cambridge, Mass.: Harvard University Press, 1970).
4. Francis Bacon, *The Works of Francis Bacon,* eds. James Spedding, Robert L. Ellis, Douglas D. Heath, 14 vols. (1868–74. New York: Garrett Press, 1968). All volume and page numbers refer to this edition. Unless otherwise noted, English translations are Spedding's. See the list of abbreviations at the head of this book.
5. Elizabeth Sewell, *The Orphic Voice: Poetry and Natural History* (New Haven: Yale University Press, 1960).
6. Barbara Shapiro, *Probability and Certainty in Seventeenth-Century England* (Princeton: Princeton University Press, 1983).
7. Cited by Shapiro, ibid., 67.
8. Stanley Fish, *Self-Consuming Artifacts* (Berkeley: University of California Press, 1972), 78–155.
9. Plato, *Phaedrus* 270a.
10. Lisa Jardine, *Francis Bacon: Discovery and the Art of Discourse* (Cambridge: Cambridge University Press, 1974).
11. Graham Rees, "Francis Bacon's Biological Ideas: A New Manuscript Source," in *Occult and Scientific Mentalities in the Renaissance,* ed. Brian Vickers (Cambridge: Cambridge University Press, 1984), 308.
12. Jerry Weinberger, *Science, Faith, and Politics: Francis Bacon and the Utopian Roots of the Modern Age* (Ithaca: Cornell University Press, 1985), 177 and passim, points out the importance of this passage in *The Advancement of Learning.*
13. Fish, *Self-Consuming Artifacts,* 145–146.
14. Ibid., 150–151.
15. See Brian Vickers, *Francis Bacon and Renaissance Prose* (Cambridge: Cambridge University Press, 1968), including a voluminous bibliography; Ann

Richter, "Francis Bacon," in *The English Mind,* ed. H. S. Davies and G. Watson (Cambridge: Cambridge University Press, 1964); J. L. Harrison, "Bacon's View of Rhetoric, Poetry and the Imagination," *Huntington Library Quarterly,* 20 (1957), 107–125; Benjamin Farrington, *The Philosophy of Francis Bacon* (Liverpool: Liverpool University Press, 1964); Karl Wallace, *Francis Bacon and the Nature of Man* (Carbondale: University of Illinois Press, 1967), and *Francis Bacon on Communication and Rhetoric* (Chapel Hill: University of North Carolina Press, 1943); James Stephens, *Francis Bacon and the Style of Science* (Chicago: University of Chicago Press, 1975); and Paolo Rossi, *Francis Bacon: From Magic to Science,* trans. Sacha Rabinovitch (London: Routledge and Kegan Paul, 1968).

16. Jardine, *Francis Bacon: Discovery and the Art of Discourse,* 219.
17. Ibid., 241.
18. Ibid., 244.
19. Stephens, *Francis Bacon and the Style of Science,* 180.
20. Ibid., 149.
21. Ibid., vii.
22. Ibid., 180.
23. Ibid., 67.
24. Charles Whitney, *Francis Bacon and Modernity* (New Haven: Yale University Press, 1986).
25. R. S. Crane, "The Relation of Bacon's *Essays* to his Programme for the Advancement of Learning," in Brian Vickers, ed., *Essential Articles for the Study of Francis Bacon* (Hamden, Conn.: Archon, 1968).
26. C. S. Lewis, *English Literature in the Sixteenth Century, Excluding Drama* (Oxford: Oxford University Press, 1954), 61. See 1–65 passim.
27. For background on the relation between theology and science in the Renaissance, I am indebted to Amos Funkenstein, *Theology and the Scientific Imagination from the Middle Ages to the Seventeenth Century* (Princeton: Princeton University Press, 1986).

I. NATURE ACCORDING TO SCRIPTURE

1. R. B[ostocke?], *The difference betwene the ancient phisicke and the Latter phisicke* (London, 1585), li$_v$.
2. William Tyndale's 1549 Bible 84:1 (my italics).
3. Proverbs 1:20–33 (Revised Standard Edition).
4. Ibid., 1:5–6.
5. The Wisdom of Solomon (Revised Standard Edition) 7:17.
6. 1 Kings 4:33.
7. Ibid., 16:17–18.
8. Ibid., 3:6.
9. Ibid., 2:19–20.
10. Ibid., 11:17–12.2.
11. Ibid., 10:1–4.
12. T[homas] M[iddleton], *The Wisdom of Solomon* (London, 1597) 9:10.
13. The Wisdom of Solomon (Revised Standard Edition) 14:15–31.

14. Ibid., 14:27.
15. Ibid., 15:6.
16. An interpretation of Solomon's fall in a 1532 Latin treatise on the nature of women, by Henry Cornelius Agrippa, receives this seventeenth-century translation: "Who so wise as *Solomon,* who seems to have been Natures Privy-Counsellor, and to have had the honour to behold her *undrest?* yet was not all his wisdome *Amulet* sufficient to guard him against Womens *Charms,* but that he still placed more felicity in their *enjoyment,* than in all the curious Contemplationes and Researches of Philosophy; and even abandon'd the worship of that God, who had bestowed those stupendious parts on him, to wantonize in their Imbraces." Henry Cornelius Agrippa, *Nobilitate & praecellentia foeminei sexus* (Cononiae, 1532), translated by H. C. in *Female Pre-eminence, or the Excellency of that Sex, above the Male* (London, 1670), 37.
17. 1 Corinthians 13.
18. *De Doctrine Christiana* 4:7.11–12.
19. 2 Corinthians 12:9–10 (King James Version).
20. Ibid., 11:17.
21. 1 Corinthians 14:1–5.
22. Ibid., 3:13.
23. Ibid., 9:20, 22.
24. Middleton, *The Wisdom of Solomon,* 8:7.
25. Wallace, *Francis Bacon on Communication and Rhetoric,* passim.
26. Stephens, *Francis Bacon and the Style of Science,* passim.
27. Shakespeare, *Hamlet* II.i.63–66, in *The Riverside Shakespeare,* ed. G. Blackmore Evans (Boston: Houghton Mifflin, 1974).
28. *Odyssea,* trans. Andrea Divo (1537), 34. The parallel passage in the Loeb edition of the *Odyssey,* trans. A. T. Murray (Cambridge, Mass.: Harvard University Press, 1946), is IV.385.
29. *Odyssey* IV.454–55.
30. Natalis Comes (Conti), *Mythologiae* (Venice, 1567), 441. Jean Baudouin's wordy 1627 translation dilutes but does not erase the intellectual and physical import of Comes's verb: "ils le saisissent [seized] et retinssent [held] à toute force" *Mythologie* (Paris, 1627), 866. A later sentence in Baudouin's paragraph, claiming that Proteus' feet were then bound, is an interpolation. Neither Comes nor Homer makes the capture explicitly violent. In Baudouin's case, the verb *garroter* strongly suggests mechanical torture.
31. Virgil, *Georgics,* IV.405, in *Works of Virgil,* trans. John Dryden, 2 vols. (London: Ellerton and Byworth, 1810), I.171.
32. Ibid., IV.399–400.
33. Abraham Fraunce, *The Third Part of the Countesse of Pembrokes Yuychurch: Entituled, "Amintas Dale"* (London, 1592), 22–23.
34. Augustine, *The Confessions,* trans. R. S. Pine-Coffin (Baltimore: Penguin Books, 1961), XI.xi, p. 262.
35. For a study of other interpretations of Proteus' mutability, see A. Bartlett Giamatti, "Proteus Unbound: Some Versions of the Sea God in the Renaissance," in *The Disciplines of Criticism,* eds. P. Demetz, T. Greene, and

L. Nelson, Jr. (New Haven: Yale University Press, 1968). Unfortunately, Giamatti does not discuss the issues raised by the ways of trying to apprehend Proteus.

II. THE TIMAEIC TRADITION

Cosmology and Rhetoric

1. This is Sir Arthur Gorges's more accurate seventeenth-century translation of Bacon's phrase *malitia et impetus* (*SV* VI.639) in *The Wisdome of the Ancients* (London, 1619), 34.
2. See Charles W. Lemmi, *The Classic Deities in Bacon* (Folcroft, Pa.: Folcroft Press, 1969), 55–61.
3. John Calvin, *A Commentarie of John Calvine, upon the first booke of Moses called Genesis,* trans. Thomas Tymme (London, 1578), 26.
4. Ibid., 39–40.
5. Ibid., 40, 58.
6. Ibid., 18.
7. Ibid., 19, 26.
8. Ibid., 20.
9. Augustine, *City of God,* trans. Henry Bettenson (Baltimore: Penguin Books, 1976), 11.10, p. 440.
10. Ibid., 12.26, pp. 505–506.
11. King James Version. See the analysis of the hexaemeral tradition in James Nohrnberg's *The Analogy of "The Faerie Queene"* (Princeton: Princeton University Press, 1980), 519–568. Nohrnberg cites the passage from Augustine on p. 541.
12. Calvin, *A Commentarie of John Calvine,* 27.
13. Ibid., 40.
14. Ibid., 51.
15. Ibid., 19, and Augustine, *City of God,* 11.12, p. 453.
16. Augustine, *City of God,* 11.18, p. 449.
17. Calvin, *A Commentarie of John Calvine,* 19.
18. Ibid., 38.
19. Ibid., 35.
20. Nohrnberg, *The Analogy of "The Faerie Queene,"* 519–568.
21. Augustine, *City of God,* 8.11, p. 315.
22. Ibid., 12.27, p. 507.
23. Ibid., 11.21, pp. 451–453.
24. Bartholomaeus Anglicus, *Batman vppon Bartholome, his Booke,* "De Proprietatibus Rerum" (London: Thomas East, 1582), 118ᵥ.
25. Ibid., 119.
26. Du Bartas, *His First Weeke: Or, Birth of the World,* trans. Joshuah Sylvester in *The Complete Works of Joshuah Sylvester,* ed. A. B. Grosart, 2 vols. (New York: AMS Press, 1967), I.23, lines 456–471.
27. Ibid., line 485.
28. Nathaniel Highmore, *The Historie of Generation* (London, 1651), 3.

29. Ibid., 27.

30. Ibid., 12–13.

31. Ibid., 82.

32. King James I, *Daemonologie,* ed. G. B. Harrison (New York: Barnes and Noble, Inc., 1966), I.vi, p. 22.

33. Ibid., I.vii, p. 25.

34. Although this interpretation is euhemeristic, it is not clearly a reduction of Plutarch's account to natural history. Natural philosophy in the Timaeic tradition seems to have had a suggestive power for poets as well as for philosophers.

35. Plutarch, *Moralia,* trans. Frank Cole Babbitt, 16 vols.(Cambridge, Mass.: Harvard University Press, 1969), V.129.

36. Ibid., 130–131.

37. Ibid., 133.

38. See Lemmi, *The Classic Deities in Bacon,* 126, 162–168. Although in an obscure passage Bacon allows for an association between Typhon and all "vast and strange swelling" (XIII.99), his relegation of Typhon in *De Sapientia Veterum* to the role of a rebel is narrower than any account that Lemmi surveys, including the description of Typhon in Conti's *Mythologiae,* from which Lemmi believes Bacon drew most for his portrait.

39. Plato, *Timaeus,* ed. and trans. R. D. Archer-Hind (New York: Arno Press, 1973), 87B.

40. Plutarch, *Of the Procreation,* trans. John Philips in *Plutarch's Lives and Writings,* ed. A. H. Clough and Wm. H. Goodwin, 10 vols. (Boston: Little, Brown, 1909), VII.331. In the sixteenth century, the text was available in the translation by Loys le Roy, *Le Timée de Platon* (Paris, 1551, 1582).

41. Plato, *Timaeus,* 40A 6–7, 40B 4. My emendations.

42. Ibid., 40B 15–16 and 40A 3–5.

43. Ibid., 47E–48A.

44. Plutarch, *Of the Procreation,* 329.

45. Chalcidius, *Platonis Timaeus, interprete Chalchidio* in J. C. M. Van Winden, *C[h]alcidius on Matter: His Doctrine and Sources* (Leiden: E. J. Brill, 1965), sect. 286, p. 83.

46. Ibid., sect. 278, p. 61.

47. Ibid., sect. 269, p. 33.

48. Frances Yates, *Giordano Bruno and the Hermetic Tradition* (Chicago: University of Chicago Press, 1964), 18.

49. *Asclepius,* in the *Corpus Hermeticum* (II.13–18), ed. A. D. Nock, trans. A. -J. Festugière (Paris: Société D'Edition "Les Belles Lettres," 1960), 299. These translations make use of the modern French version, and occasionally the translations by Frances Yates in *Giordano Bruno.*

50. Ibid., 299.

51. Ibid., 298.

52. Ibid., 316.

53. Ibid., 299.

54. Ibid., 313.

55. Aristotle, *Physics,* 192a.

56. Shakespeare, *King Lear* I.i.90, from *The Riverside Shakespeare*.
57. Aristotle, *Metaphysics*, trans. Richard Hope (Ann Arbor: University of Michigan Press, 1960), 1045B 15–19.
58. Aristotle, *De Generatione et Corruptione*, trans. E. S. Forster (Cambridge, Mass.: Harvard University Press, 1955), 321b 25–35, (1.5), collected with *On Sophistical Refutations* and *On the Cosmos*, trans. D. J. Furley.
59. Ibid., 322a 1–10 (1.5).
60. Aristotle, *On Interpretation*, trans. Harold P. Cooke (Cambridge, Mass.: Harvard University Press, 1973), 16b 6–8.
61. Aristotle, *Topica*, trans. E. S. Forster (Cambridge, Mass.: Harvard University Press, 1976), 101b 18–19.
62. Aristotle, *Categories*, trans. Harold P. Cooke (Cambridge, Mass.: Harvard University Press, 1973), 2b 5, passim.
63. Ibid.
64. Plotinus, *The Enneads*, trans. Stephen Mackenna (London: Faber and Faber, 1956), II.4.
65. Aristotle, *Ethics*, trans. H. Rackham (Cambridge, Mass.: Harvard University Press, 1982), II.i.1–5.
66. Ibid., II.v.4.
67. Ibid., II.iv.3–4.
68. Aristotle, *Poetics*, trans. Ingram Bywater, in *Introduction to Aristotle*, ed. Richard McKeon (New York: Modern Library, 1947), 1448b 14–21.
69. Aristotle, *The Art of Rhetoric*, trans. John Henry Freese (Cambridge, Mass.: Harvard University Press, 1967), I.xi.1, 1369b.
70. Cornelius Agrippa, *De Vanitate*. I am using this seventeenth-century translation of *De Occulta Philosophia Libri Tres* (Cologne, 1533) which seems to be a conscientious rendering of the first complete edition. All quotations are from the rendering by J. F., *Three Books of Occult Philosophy* (London: R. W. for Gregory Moule, 1651). Latin insertions are from the 1533 original. Book and chapter headings are the same in each edition.

   This reference is to J. F.'s page A1, Agrippa's introduction. For a comprehensive summary of Agrippa's treatise, see Charles G. Nauert, Jr., *Agrippa and the Crisis of Renaissance Thought* (Urbana: University of Illinois Press, 1965), 222–259, and Wayne Schumaker, *The Occult Sciences in the Renaissance* (Berkeley: University of California Press, 1972), 134–157.
71. Agrippa, *Three Books of Occult Philosophy*, 328 (I.lv).
72. Ibid., 330 (II.56).
73. Ibid., 30 (I.13).
74. Ibid., 146 (I.65).
75. Ibid., 30–31 (I.13).
76. Ibid., 69 (I.34).
77. Ibid., 34 (I.15).
78. Ibid., 351 (III.iii).
79. Ibid., 34 (I.15). *De Occulta Philosophia Libri Tres*, 20.
80. Ibid., 32 (I.14).
81. Ibid., 26 (I.11).
82. Ibid., 26–27 (I.11). *De Occulta Philosophia Libri Tres*, 15.
83. Ibid., 27 (I.11). *De Occulta Philosophia Libri Tres*, 16.

84. Ibid., 27 (I.11). *De Occulta Philosophia Libri Tres*, 16.
85. Ibid., 148 (I.66).
86. Ibid., 148 (I.66).
87. Ibid., 148 (I.66).
88. Ibid., 72 (I.36).
89. Ibid., 33 (I.14).
90. Ibid., 156 (I.71). *De Occulta Philosophia Libri Tres*, 102. The last part of the passage reads: "per imaginationis impetum, vim maximum conspirant in incantante, atque subinde traiieiunt in rem incantatam ad illam ligandam aut dirigendam, quorum affectus sermonesq; incantantis intenduntur." ([Magicians] inchanting things, are wont to blow, and breath[e] upon them the words of the verse, or to breath[e] in the vertue with the spirit, that so the whole vertue of the soul be directed to the thing inchanted, being disposed for the receiving of the said vertue.) J. F., *Three Books*, 156.
91. Ibid., 153 (I.70).
92. Ibid., 154 (I.70).
93. Ibid., 153 (I.70). *De Occulta Philosophia Libri Tres*, 90.
94. Ibid., 159 (I.73). *De Occulta Philosophia Libri Tres*, 94 (misnumbered 262).
95. Augustine, *The City of God*, 8.23–26, pp. 331–340 .
96. Ibid., 8.26, pp. 338–340. Also see Yates, *Giordano Bruno*, esp. 1–43, 136.
97. Augustine, *The City of God*, 8.24, p. 337.
98. Yates, *Giordano Bruno*, 136.
99. Agrippa, *Three Books of Occult Philosophy*, 316 (II.50). Yates translates *cooperatur* in the active sense (*Giordano Bruno*, 136), whereas the 1651 translation uses the more literal passive.
100. Ibid., 290–291 (II.35).
101. Ibid., 339–340 (II.60).
102. *Asclepius*, 308. ([I]d est curam propriam diligentiae suae, efficit ut sit ipse et mundus uterque ornamento sibi, ut ex hac hominis diuina compositione mundus, Graece rectius *kosmos*, dictus esse uideatur. Is novit se, nouit et mundum, scilicet ut meminerit, quid partibus sibi inseruiendum si, recognoscat, laudes gratesque maximas agens deo, eius imaginem uenerans, non ignarus se etiam secumdum esse imaginem dei, cuius sunt imagines duae mundus et homo.)
103. Genesis 2.1; Thomas Digges, *A Perfit Description of the Celestiall Orbes*, appended to Leonard Digges, *A Prognostication Everlasting* (London: Thomas Marsh, 1585), Nii.
104. Walter Raleigh, *The Historie of the World* (London, 1614), 12, 9.
105. Pliny, *Historia Naturalis*, ed. Jean Beaujeu (Paris: Société D'Edition, 1950), II.4. My translation. *Kosmos*, a variant in line 16, derives from sixteenth-century printed versions. I am taking the Renaissance emendation as my authority for the interpretation of the passage.
106. Augustine, *City of God*, 11.18, p. 449.
107. *Hamlet* III.i.44, II.ii.280, in *The Riverside Shakespeare*.
108. Ibid., III.iv.126–130.
109. Aristotle, *De Anima*, trans. J. B. Smith, in *Introduction to Aristotle*, ed. Richard McKeon, 418a.
110. Henry Peacham, *The Garden of Eloquence* (London: H. Jackson, 1577), Oii.

111. Ibid., Bii$_v$.
112. Aristotle, *De Anima,* 418a 4–7.
113. Stephen Toulmin and June Goodfield, *The Architecture of Matter* (New York: Harper and Row, 1966), 121.
114. Cited in John Arthur Hopkins, *Alchemy, Child of Greek Philosophy* (New York: AMS Press, 1967), 193.
115. Ibid., 74–75.
116. Jean De Meun, *Romance of the Rose,* trans. Harry W. Robbins (New York: E. P. Dutton, 1962), 78.47–48.
117. Shakespeare, Sonnet 33, from *The Riverside Shakespeare.*
118. Stephen Hawes, *The Pastime of Pleasure,* ed. Wm. E. Mead (London: EETS, 1928), lines 909–916.
119. Martinus Rulandus, *Lexicon Alchimiae sive Dictionarium Alchemisticum* (Frankfurt, 1612), 193. I generally rely on the translation of A. E. Waite in *A Lexicon of Alchemy* (London: John M. Watkins, 1964). This reference is on page 132.
120. Rulandus, *Lexicon Alchimiae,* 43; *A Lexicon of Alchemy,* 31.
121. Ibid., 474; 313.
122. Ibid., 474; 318. See also *Lexicon Alchimiae,* 401; *A Lexicon of Alchemy,* 272.
123. Thomas Thomas, *Dictionarium Linguae et Anglicanae* (London, 1587).
124. John Rider, *Bibliothetica Scholastica* (Oxford, 1589).
125. Thomas Elyot, *Dictionary* (London, 1538).
126. Rulandus, *Lexicon Alchimiae,* 7; *A Lexicon of Alchemy,* 5.
127. Elias Ashmole, *Theatrum Chemicum Britannicum* (London, 1652), Ai. A facsimile edition has been published by Georg Olms Verlagsbuchhandlung (Hildesheim, 1968).
128. Frank Sherwood Taylor, *The Alchemists* (London: Heinemann, 1951), 88.
129. Ashmole, *Theatrum Chemicum Britannicum,* 61.
130. Ibid., 61.
131. Ibid., 38.
132. Ibid., 67.
133. Ibid., 82.
134. Ibid., 71–72.
135. Ibid., 92.
136. Ibid., 18.
137. Ibid., 19.
138. Ibid., 189–190.
139. Ibid., 130.
140. Ibid., 142.
141. Ibid., 147.
142. Ibid., 151.
143. Ibid., 151, 144.
144. Ibid., 176.
145. Ibid., 191.
146. Ibid., 178, 180.
147. Ibid., 165.

148. Ibid., 163.
149. Ibid., 129.
150. Ibid., 144, 165.
151. Ibid., 286–287.
152. Ibid., 278–290.
153. Ibid., 288–289.
154. Ibid., 371.
155. Ibid., 200.
156. Ibid., 199.
157. Taylor, *The Alchemists*, 57.
158. Lynn Thorndike, *A History of Magic and Experimental Science*, 18 vols. (New York: Columbia University Press, 1947–58), III.76.
159. Carl Jung, *Psychology and Alchemy*, trans. R. F. C. Hull (New York: Pantheon Books, 1953).
160. Rulandus, *Lexicon Alchimiae*, 324–326; *A Lexicon of Alchemy*, 220–223.
161. Ashmole, *Theatrum Chemicum Britannicum*, 9, 15.
162. Ibid., 18.
163. Ibid., 23.
164. Ibid., 29–30.
165. Ibid., 45.
166. Ibid., 45.
167. Ibid., 444, 446.
168. Ibid., 470.
169. Ibid., 255–256.
170. Cited in Hopkins, *Alchemy, Child of Greek Philosophy*, 193.
171. Taylor, *The Alchemists*, 30.
172. Ibid., 158.
173. Ibid., 31.
174. Rulandus, *Lexicon Alchimiae*, 90; *A Lexicon of Alchemy*, 62.
175. Jean De Meun, *Romance of the Rose*, 78.50.
176. Ibid., 78.109–112.
177. Ibid., 78.109–110.
178. Jean De Meun, *Le Roman de la Rose*, ed. Ernest Langlois, 5 vols. (Paris: Société des anciens textes français, 1914–24), V.135, lines 16142–43.
179. Ibid., 16085–86.
180. Ibid., 16097.
181. Ibid., 16108–12.

II. THE TIMAEIC TRADITION

Persuasion and Ornament

1. Ben Jonson's Dedication to Thomas Wright, *The Passions of the Mind in Generall* (London: V. Sims, 1604), lxv.
2. Cicero, *De Oratore*, trans. E. W. Sutton and H. Rackham, 2 vols. (Cambridge, Mass.: Harvard University Press, 1959), III.i.195.

3. Ibid., II.lxxxvii.356.
4. Ibid., II.li.206.
5. Ibid., II.xlii.178.
6. Ibid., I.xiv.61.
7. Ibid., III.lvi.215.
8. Ibid., III.xxvi.103.
9. Ibid., III.iii.199–200.
10. Ibid., III.liv.207.
11. Ibid., II.lxxviii.317.
12. Ibid., III.v.19.
13. Cicero, *The Orator,* trans. H. E. Hubbell (Cambridge, Mass.: Harvard University Press, 1952), lxviii.227.
14. Cicero, *De Oratore,* III.ix.36.
15. Cicero, *The Orator,* xxi.70.
16. Ibid., xxi.71.
17. Cicero, *De Oratore,* III.xxxvii.150.
18. Ibid., III.xxxviii.157–158.
19. Ibid., III.xxxviii.155.
20. Ibid., III.xlv.178–179.
21. Ibid., III.xlv.180.
22. Ibid., III.xlv.181, 185.
23. Ibid., III.xlv.179.
24. Quintilian, *Institutio Oratoria,* trans. H. E. Butler (Cambridge, Mass.: Harvard University Press, 1953), II.viii.9. My emendations.
25. Ibid., IX.v.5.
26. Ibid., IX.v.7.
27. Ibid., IX.x.7.
28. Ibid., II.xiii.9.
29. George Saintsbury, *A History of Criticism,* 3 vols. (London, 1902), II.45.
30. Girolamo Fracastoro, *Naugerius, Sive De Poetica Dialogus,* trans. Ruth Kelso, in *University of Illinois Studies in Language and Literature* (Urbana: University of Illinois Press, 1924), IX, 3 (August, 1924).
31. Ibid., 69.
32. Ibid., 71.
33. Rosemond Tuve, *Elizabethan and Metaphysical Imagery* (Chicago: University of Chicago Press, 1947), 41–42, 56–57, 152, 195, 387.
34. Thomas Greene, *The Light in Troy: Imitation and Discovery in Renaissance Poetry* (New Haven: Yale University Press, 1982), 78.
35. Ibid., 47.
36. Ibid., 45.
37. Ibid., 43.
38. Richard Lanham, *Motives of Eloquence: Literary Rhetoric in the Renaissance* (New Haven: Yale University Press, 1976), 30.
39. Ibid., 30–31.
40. O. B. Hardison, *The Enduring Monument* (Chapel Hill: University of North Carolina Press, 1962), 66.
41. Ibid., 65–66.

42. John Sturmius, *A ritch storehouse or treasurie called Nobilitas literata,* trans. T. B[rown] (London: H. Denham, 1570), 11ᵥ.

43. Ibid., 32ᵥ.

44. Richard Sherry, *A Treatise of Schemes and Tropes* (London, 1550), Ciiiiᵥ.

45. Ibid., A7.

46. Ibid., Ciiiiᵥ.

47. Ibid., A8–A8ᵥ.

48. Henry Peacham, *The Garden of Eloquence* (London, 1577), Biᵥ.

49. Ibid., Biiᵥ.

50. Ibid., Biiiiᵥ.

51. Ibid., Diii.

52. Ibid., Ciiᵥ.

53. Dudley Fenner, *The Artes of Logicke and Rhetorike* (London, 1584), Diᵥ. See also Abraham Fraunce, *The Arcadian Rhetoric* (London, 1588), A2ᵥ.

54. Ibid., D4.

55. Quintilian, *Institutio Oratoria,* IX.ii.3.

56. Fenner, *The Artes of Logicke and Rhetorike,* Eiiiiᵥ, Hii.

57. Ibid., Ciᵥ.

58. John Hoskins, *Directions for Speech and Style,* ed. H. H. Hudson (Princeton: Princeton University Press, 1935), 12.

59. Peacham, *The Garden of Eloquence,* Kiiii.

60. Ibid., Diiiiᵥ.

61. Ibid., Diiiiᵥ, Ciᵥ.

62. Ibid., Gii.

63. Hoskins, *Directions for Speech and Style,* 8.

64. Peacham, *The Garden of Eloquence,* Aii.

65. Ibid., Fii.

66. Cicero, *De Oratore,* II.xliii.182.

67. *Cleanness,* in *Pearl, Cleanness, Patience, Sir Gawain and the Green Knight,* ed. A. C. Cawley (New York: E. P. Dutton, 1976), 51, lines 1–4.

68. Erasmus, *De duplici copia verborum ac rerum,* in *Collected Works of Erasmus,* ed. Craig R. Thompson (Toronto: University of Toronto Press, 1978), XXIV.299.

69. Ibid., 301.

70. Ibid., 299.

71. Thomas Wilson, *Wilson's Arte of Rhetorique* (London: R. Grafton, 1553), Fol. 92ᵥ.

72. Sherry, *A Treatise of Schemes and Tropes,* Ev–Evᵥ.

73. Cicero, *De Oratore,* III.xxvi.104.

74. Sherry, *A Treatise of Schemes and Tropes,* Eiiiᵥ.

75. Philip Sidney, *Astrophil and Stella,* Sonnets 2 and 100, in *The Poems of Sir Philip Sidney,* ed. Wm. Ringler (Oxford: Oxford University Press, 1962), 165, 231.

76. *The Merchant of Venice,* V.i.108, in *The Riverside Shakespeare.*

77. Wilson, *Wilson's Arte of Rhetorique,* Fol. 88.

78. Ibid., 323.

79. Ibid., 325.

80. George Puttenham, *The Arte of English Poesie,* ed. G. Willcock and A. Walker (Cambridge: Cambridge University Press, 1936), 143.

81. Ibid., 138.

82. Ibid., 142.

83. Thomas Wilson, *The Rule of Reason,* ed. R. Sprague (Northridge: San Fernando Valley State College, 1972), 11.

84. Wilson, *Wilson's Arte of Rhetorique,* Fol. 89v, and Quintilian, *Institutio Oratoria,* VIII.v.34.

85. Quintilian, *Institutio Oratoria,* IX.i.27.

86. John Lydgate, *Courte of Sapyence* (London: W. de Worde, 1510), fi–fii; Hawes, *The Pastime of Pleasure,* 31.

87. Peacham, *The Garden of Eloquence,* Fii.

88. Richard Rainolde, *A booke Called the Foundacion of Rhetorike* (London, 1587), Ai.

89. Thomas Thomas, *Dictionarium Linguae Latinae et Anglicanae.*

90. Puttenham, *The Arte of English Poesie,* 142.

91. Ibid., 162.

92. Ibid., 163.

93. Ibid., 163.

94. Ibid., 163.

95. Ibid., 143.

96. Ibid., 174.

97. Ibid., 179.

98. Ibid., 191.

99. Ibid., 192.

100. Ibid., 180.

101. Ibid., 198.

102. Ibid., 200.

103. Ibid., 204.

104. Ibid., 203 (my italics).

105. Ibid., 203–204.

106. Ibid., 214.

107. Ibid., 226.

108. Quintilian, *Institutio Oratoria,* IX.ii.64.; taken from *The Aeneid* IV.550.

109. Ibid., IX.ii.64.

110. Wilson, *Wilson's Arte of Rhetorique,* Fol. 117 (misnumbered 119).

111. Fraunce, *Arcadian Rhetoric,* H6ᵥ.

112. Ibid., H7.

113. Cicero, *De Oratore,* III.lvi.214, III.lix.220.

114. Ibid., III.lix.221.

115. *Timaeus,* 68A.

116. Fenner, *The Art of Rhetoric,* D3.

117. Puttenham, *The Arte of English Poesie,* 153.

118. Ibid., 174.

119. Aristotle, *Ethics,* IV.iii.16.

120. Aristotle, *Rhetoric* I.ii.5. and III passim.

121. Baldassare Castiglione, *The Book of the Courtier,* trans. Thomas Hoby (London: 1561; repr. London: David Nutt, 1900).

122. Wright, *Passions of the Mind*, 173.
123. *As You Like It*, III.iii.20, in *The Riverside Shakespeare*.
124. Wright, *Passions of the Mind*, 5.
125. *Henry VI, Part 1*, IV.vii.57, in *The Riverside Shakespeare*.
126. *Timon of Athens*, I.ii.214–15, in *The Riverside Shakespeare*.
127. Wright, *Passions of the Mind*, 45.
128. Sherry, *A Treatise of Schemes and Tropes*, Fii.
129. Wright, *Passions of the Mind*, 146.
130. Timothy Bright, *A Treatise of Melancholy* (London: T. Vantrollier, 1586), 221.
131. Ibid., Diii$_v$.
132. Philippe de Mornay, *The True Knowledge of a Mans Owne Selfe*, trans. A. M[unday] (London: J. R. for W. Leake, 1602), 147.
133. Wright, *Passions of the Mind*, 32.
134. Aristotle, *De Anima*, 406a.
135. Bright, *A Treatise of Melancholy*, 87–88.
136. Ibid., 91.
137. Wright, *Passions of the Mind*, 45.
138. Bright, *A Treatise of Melancholy*, 71.
139. Ibid., ii$_v$–iii.
140. John Davies, *Microcosmos*, in *The Complete Poems*, ed. A. B. Grosart, 2 vols. (Hildesheim: Georg Olms Verlagsbuchhandlung, 1968), I.24.
141. Ibid., 25.
142. Ibid.
143. Thomas Elyot, *Castel of Helth* (London, 1541), 87.
144. Bright, *A Treatise of Melancholy*, 195.
145. Aristotle, *Ethics*, I.xiii.11–17.
146. Davies, *Microcosmos*, 27.
147. Wright, *Passions of the Mind*, 17.
148. Ibid., 17–18.
149. Robert Burton, *Anatomy of Melancholy*, ed. Holbrock Jackson (New York: Random House, 1977), 112 (2.2.6.2).
150. Ibid., 378 (3.4.2.1).
151. Ibid., 114 (2.2.6.3).
152. Ibid., 114 (2.2.6.3).
153. Wright, *Passions of the Mind*, 64 (misnumbered 46).
154. Philip Sidney, *A Defence of Poesie*, in *Miscellaneous Prose of Sir Philip Sidney*, ed. Katherine Duncan-Jones and Jan Van Dorsten (Oxford: Oxford University Press, 1973), 73.
155. Ibid.
156. Roger Ascham, *The Scholemaster* (London, 1570), 37–38.
157. John Astley, *The Art of Riding* (London: H. Denham, 1584), 5.
158. Thomas Elyot, *The Book of the Governoure* (London, 1531), 15$_v$.
159. R. S. Crane, "The Houyhnhnms, the Yahoos, and the History of Ideas," in *Reason and the Imagination*, ed. J. A. Mazzeo (New York: Columbia University Press, 1962), 243–253.
160. Quintilian, *Institutio Oratoria*, VII.iii.24, 3.
161. Ibid., II.xvi.16.

162. Marsilio Ficino, commentary on the *Phaedrus* in *Marsilio Ficino and the Phaedrean Charioteer,* ed. and trans. Michael J. B. Allen (Berkeley: University of California Press, 1981).

163. Astley, *The Art of Riding,* 5.

164. Thomas Blundeville, *A New Booke, Containing the Art of Ryding* (London: W. Seres [1560?]), 2.

165. Ibid., 2, 2ᵥ, 12ᵥ.

166. Gervase Markham, *Cavelrice, Or the English Horseman* (London, 1607), 90 (my italics).

167. Ibid., 15.

168. Ibid., 22.

169. Ibid., 98.

170. Ibid., 124.

171. Astley, *The Art of Riding,* 5.

172. Markham, *Cavelrice, Or the English Horseman,* 25.

173. Burton, *Anatomy of Melancholy,* 111 (2.2.6.2).

174. Wright, *Passions of the Mind,* 73.

175. Ibid., 86.

176. Ascham, *The Scholemaster,* 48–49.

177. Blundeville, *A New Booke, Containing the Art of Ryding,* 44.

178. Ibid., 12ᵥ.

179. Ibid., 17ᵥ–18.

180. Ibid., 6.

181. Markham, *Cavelrice, Or the English Horseman,* 47.

182. Ibid., 81.

183. Blundeville, *A New Booke, Containing the Art of Ryding,* 17ᵥ.

184. Markham, *Cavelrice, Or the English Horseman,* 124.

185. Ibid., 80.

186. Phillberte de Vienne, *The Philosopher of the Court,* trans. George North (London, 1575), Aiiiᵥ.

187. Ibid., 23–24.

188. Samuel Daniel, *Musophilus,* in *Poems and A Defense of Rhyme,* ed. A. C. Sprague (Chicago: University of Chicago Press, 1965), p. 96, lines 937–942.

189. Ibid., lines 957–968.

190. Cicero, *De Oratore,* III.ix.36.

191. Sidney, *A Defence,* 78.

192. Ibid.

193. Ibid.

194. Ibid., 79.

195. Ibid., 78–79.

196. Ibid., 130

197. Lewis, *English Literature in the Sixteenth Century,* 321.

198. Ibid.

199. Sidney, *A Defence,* 79.

200. Ibid., 102.

201. Ibid., 81.
202. Ibid., 83.
203. Ibid.
204. Ibid., 84.
205. Ibid., 91.
206. Ibid., 117.
207. Ibid., 86.
208. Ibid.
209. Ibid., 93.
210. Ibid., 96–97.
211. Ibid., 115.
212. Ibid., 102.
213. Ibid., 78.
214. Ibid., 79.
215. Ibid., 102.
216. Ibid., 120.
217. Ibid., 108.
218. Ibid., 78.
219. Ibid., 77.
220. Ibid., 79.
221. Ibid., 83.

II. THE TIMAEIC TRADITION

Nature and Concealment

1. Puttenham, *The Arte of English Poesie,* 160.
2. Ibid., 161.
3. Sidney, *A Defence,* 121.
4. Puttenham, *The Arte of English Poesie,* 183.
5. Ibid., 184.
6. Castiglione, *The Courtier,* 187.
7. Fraunce, *The Arcadian Rhetoric,* A8.
8. Demetrius, *A Greek Critic: Demetrius on Style,* ed. and trans. G. M. A. Grube (Toronto: University of Toronto Press, 1961), p. 85, paragraphs 99–100.
9. Castiglione, *The Courtier,* 116.
10. Ibid., 116.
11. Ibid., 117.
12. Ibid., 111.
13. Ibid., 94.
14. Ibid., 111.
15. Ibid., 80.
16. Ibid.
17. Ibid., 12.

18. Ibid., 7.
19. Ibid., 80.
20. Ibid., 71.
21. Ibid., 60–61.
22. Ibid., 62.
23. Ibid.
24. Ibid., 23.
25. Ibid., 29 (my italics).
26. Ibid., 7.
27. Ibid., 43.
28. Ibid., 44.
29. Ibid., 222.
30. Ibid., 223.
31. Ibid., 301–302.
32. Ibid., 301.
33. Boccaccio, *Geneologia Deorum Gentilium, Books XIV–XV,* in *Boccaccio on Poetry,* ed. and trans. Charles G. Osgood (New York: Bobbs-Merrill, 1956), passim. For a discussion of Boccaccio's bearing on English Renaissance poetics and rhetoric, see Michael Murrin, *The Veil of Allegory* (Chicago: University of Chicago Press, 1969), passim.
34. See below, Chapter IV.
35. Horace, *Ars Poetica,* trans. Ben Jonson, in *The Complete Poetry of Ben Jonson,* ed. W. B. Hunter, Jr. (Garden City: Anchor Books, 1963), lines 183–191.
36. Ibid., lines 455–460.
37. Puttenham, *The Arte of English Poesie,* 191.
38. Ibid., 192.
39. Ibid.
40. Wright, *Passions of the Mind,* 142.
41. Erasmus, *Ciceronianus, or a Dialogue on the Best Style of Speaking,* trans. Izora Scott (New York: Columbia University Press, 1908), 129.
42. Ibid., 123.
43. Ibid.
44. Ibid., 126.
45. Ibid., 127.
46. Ibid., 124.
47. Ibid., 42.
48. Ibid., 127.
49. Ibid., 46.
50. Ibid., 76.
51. Ibid.
52. Ibid., 77.
53. Ibid., 78.
54. Ibid., 31.

III. ADVANCEMENTS AND REFORMULATIONS

Baconian Nature

1. Exodus 16.11–20.
2. Ibid., 4.10.
3. Ibid., 20.4.
4. See the notes in Graham Rees's essay, "Francis Bacon's Semi-Paracelsian Cosmology," *Ambix* 22 (1975), 81–101, esp. 86. Although Rees rejects the idea of a close relation between Bacon's rhetoric and his science, much of his discussion in this section invites speculation on their interaction.
5. Paolo Rossi, *Francis Bacon: From Magic to Science,* trans. Sacha Rabinovitch (London: Routledge and Kegan Paul, 1968), 13–22. Rossi includes extensive notes on the literature of the history of science as it bears upon Bacon's work.
6. A survey of the literature involving some of the issues discussed in this chapter has been collected in Robert E. Larsen's "The Aristotelianism of Bacon's *Novum Organum," Journal of the History of Ideas* 23 (1962), 435–450. Larsen's argument is more general than the one here, but it reaches some roughly similar conclusions about the nature of Bacon's goals for scientific experiment.

III. ADVANCEMENTS AND REFORMULATIONS

Bacon and Rhetoric

1. Alfred North Whitehead, *Science and the Modern World* (New York: Anchor, 1927), 53.
2. Ascham, *The Scholemaster,* 155.

IV. CONTRASTING AND ANTECEDENT TRADITIONS

The Phaedrus *and the* Rhetoric

1. Francis Bacon, *The Works of Francis Bacon,* ed. Basil Montague, 16 vols. (London: Wm. Pickering, 1828), VIII.295.
2. Aristotle, *Rhetoric,* I.i.13.
3. Ibid., I.v.17.
4. Ibid., I.ii.6.
5. Ibid., I.ii.1.
6. Ibid., I.ii.7.
7. Ibid., I.iv.6–7. Here again Freese minimizes Aristotle's meaning.
8. Ibid., I.i.1,12.
9. Ibid., I.ii.7.
10. We know that the *Phaedrus* and the *Rhetoric* were accessible to some six-teenth-century English readers, though the degree of their sophistication and knowledge of the commentaries and the Greek texts is uncertain. In a refutation of one of his critics, Ramus quotes a long passage from the

Phaedrus; see *That There is Only One Method of Establishing a Science,* trans. Eugene J. Barber and Leonard A. Kennedy, in *Renaissance Philosophy: New Translations* (The Hague: Mouton, 1973), 136. Ficino's translations of Plato's works would have opened that dialogue to a host of readers of Latin. Sidney's contemporary John Hoskins makes the notable, though never substantiated, claim that he has seen a portion of Sidney's translation of "the first two books" of the *Rhetoric;* see *Directions for Speech and Style,* ed. Hoyt H. Hudson (Princeton: Princeton University Press, 1935), 41. Ascham quotes from the *Rhetoric,* and tells of its importance to the learned; paraphrases of the work, he says, "shal neuer take Aristotles Rhetoricke . . . out of learned mens handes" (*Scholemaster,* 111). The *Rhetoric* had long been available in translation, included with Aristotle's *Ethics* and *Politics,* which Jardine notes were owned by most students in the four-year arts course at Cambridge ("The Place of Dialectic Teaching in Sixteenth-Century Cambridge," *Studies in the Renaissance,* 27 [1974], 153). Voluminous commentaries attached to Latin translations were available from the Continent, some in multiple editions. Richard Rainolde delivered a course of lectures on the *Rhetoric* at Oxford in the late sixteenth century. Ascham notes that Cicero plainly imitates the *Phaedrus* in *De Oratore,* and takes his matter from Aristotle, as Cicero himself declares in several places (*Elizabethan Critical Essays,* I.11.). My argument in this chapter, however, is not based on studies of influence. It is meant to provide an elucidative contrast between the *Rhetoric,* the *Phaedrus,* and Bacon's own work, including its treatment of Aristotelian and Platonic rhetorical theory and practice.

11. Marsilio Ficino, *Marsilio Ficino and the Phaedrean Charioteer,* trans. Michael J. B. Allen (Berkeley: University of California Press, 1981), 72.

12. Plato, *Phaedrus,* trans. W. C. Hembold (New York: Bobbs-Merrill, 1956), 227 (standard numbering).

13. Ibid., 230.

14. Hesiod, *Theogony,* in *The Poems of Hesiod,* trans. R. M. Frazer (Norman: University of Oklahoma Press, 1983), line 340.

15. Ibid., line 353.

16. J. De Romilly, *Magic and Rhetoric in Ancient Greece* (Cambridge, Mass.: Harvard University Press, 1975), passim.

17. Ronna Burger, *Plato's "Phaedrus": A Defense of a Philosophic Art of Writing* (University: University of Alabama Press, 1980), passim.

18. *Phaedrus,* 231.

19. Ibid., 241.

20. Ibid., 242.

21. Ibid., 243.

22. Ibid., 245.

23. Ibid.

24. Ibid.

25. Ibid., 247.

26. Ibid.

27. Ibid., 253.

28. Ibid., 250.

29. Ibid., 249.
30. Ibid., 254.
31. Ibid.
32. Ibid.
33. Ibid.
34. Ibid., 253.
35. Ibid.
36. Ibid., 249.
37. Ibid., 259.
38. Ibid., 257.
39. Ibid., 261.
40. Richard M. Weaver, *The Ethics of Rhetoric* (Chicago: Henry Regnary, 1953), 3–26.
41. *Phaedrus*, 260.
42. Ibid., 271.
43. Ibid., 276.
44. Ibid., 278.
45. Ibid., 243.
46. Ibid., 278.
47. Ibid., 279.
48. Ibid., 277.
49. Ibid., 260.
50. W. Rhys Roberts, "References to Plato in Aristotle's *Rhetoric*," *Classical Philology*, 19 (1924), 342–346.
51. *Rhetoric* I.ii.6.
52. Edward M. Cope, *The "Rhetoric" of Aristotle with Commentary*, 3 vols., ed. John E. Sandys (Cambridge: Cambridge University Press, 1877); Thomas Hobbes, *Briefe of the Art of Rhetorique* (1637), in *The Rhetorics of Thomas Hobbes and Bernard Lamy*, ed. John T. Harwood (Carbondale and Edwardsville: Southern Illinois University Press, 1986).
53. On Friedrich Solmson's view of the *Rhetoric*, see Carnes Lord, "The Intention of Aristotle's *Rhetoric*," *Hermes* 109 (1981), 328.
54. Lord, "The Intention of Aristotle's *Rhetoric*," 336. Lord elaborates and modifies the work of Wm. M. A. Grimaldi, *Studies in the Philosophy of Aristotle's "Rhetoric*," in HermesEinzelschriften 25 (Wiesbaden: Franz Steiner Verlag, 1972).
55. *Rhetoric* I.i.
56. *Topics* I.i.passim.
57. Ibid., VIII.i., 155b 10.
58. Ibid., I.i, 100b 22–25.
59. *Rhetoric* I.i.11.
60. Cicero, *Orator*, trans. H. M. Hubbell (Cambridge, Mass.: Harvard University Press, 1952), xxxii.114 (my translation).
61. *Rhetoric* I.ii.7.
62. Walter J. Ong, *Ramus, Method and the Decay of Dialogue* (Cambridge, Mass.: Harvard University Press, 1958), passim.
63. *Rhetoric* I.i.22.

64. Ibid.
65. *Phaedrus* 262.
66. *Rhetoric* II.xxii.1.
67. Ibid., II.xxii.3.
68. Ibid., I.i.6.
69. Ibid.
70. Ibid., II.i.6.
71. Ibid., I.ii.4.
72. Ibid., II.i.l., II.xxiv.4.
73. Ibid., I.ii.5.
74. Ibid., II.i.3.
75. Ibid., I.i.10.
76. Ibid., I.i.5.
77. Ibid., I.i.10.
78. Ibid., I.vii.7–11.
79. *Physics* II.7–8.
80. *Rhetoric* II.xxiv.10.
81. Ibid., II.xxiv.11.
82. Ibid., II.vi.8.
83. Ibid., I.ix.28–29 (my emendation of Freese).
84. Ibid., I.ix.29.
85. Ibid., I.i.14.
86. Ibid., I.xi.1.
87. Ibid., II.xxiv.2.
88. Ibid., I.i.12.
89. Ibid.
90. Ibid., I.i.12, III.i.6.
91. Ibid., III.i.5.
92. Ibid., I.ii.8.
93. Ibid., I.i.14.
94. Ibid., I.ii.7.
95. *The Rhetoric of Aristotle,* trans. R. C. Jebb (Cambridge: University of Cambridge Press, 1909), I.ii.7.
96. *Translation of Aristotle's Rhetoric,* W. Rhys Roberts (Oxford: Oxford University Press, 1924), I.ii.7.
97. *Rhetoric,* trans. Freese, III.i.3.
98. Ibid., I.i.3.
99. Ibid., III.ii.9.
100. Ibid., III.i.3.
101. Ibid., III.i.5–6.
102. Ibid., III.i.10.
103. Ibid., III.ii.13.
104. Ibid., III.xix.6.

IV. CONTRASTING AND ANTECEDENT TRADITIONS

Agricola and Ramus

1. Richard W. B. Lewis, "The *De Inventione Dialectica* of Rudolph Agricola and its Sources in Ancient Rhetoric" (MA Thesis, University of Chicago, 1941), passim. See also Richard McKeon, "The Hellenistic and Roman Foundations of the Tradition of Aristotle in the West," *Review of Metaphysics* 32 (1979), 677–715.

2. Lewis, "The *De Inventione Dialectica* of Rudolph Agricola," 47.

3. Jardine, *Francis Bacon: Discovery and the Art of Discourse*, passim.

4. Farrington, *The Philosophy of Francis Bacon*, 63

5. Ong, *Ramus and the Decay of Dialogue*, 160, 195.

6. Ibid., 108.

7. Tuve, *Elizabethan and Metaphysical Imagery*, passim.

8. Fraunce, *Lawyer's Logike*, Biii.

9. Philip Melanchthon, *Reply of Philip Melanchthon in behalf of Ermolao*, in Quirinus Breen, *Christianity and Humanism* (Grand Rapids: W. B. Eerdmans, 1968), 52–68.

10. Ibid., 67.

11. Ibid., 56.

12. Ibid., 66.

13. Rodolphus Agricola, *De Inventione Dialectica Libri Tres*. I use the translation of the 1521 edition *apud Ioannem Knoblouchum*, by J. R. McNally in "Rudolph Agricola's *De Inventione Libri Tres*: A Translation of Selected Chapters," *Speech Monographs* 34 (1967), 393–422.

14. Ibid., 388.

15. Ibid., 402.

16. Ibid., 395.

17. Ibid., 396.

18. Ibid., 399.

19. Ibid., 401–402.

20. Ibid., 396.

21. Ibid., 399.

22. Ibid., 410.

23. Ibid., 411.

24. Ibid., 420.

25. Ibid., 413.

26. Ibid.

27. Ibid., 410.

28. Ibid.

29. Ong, *Ramus and the Decay of Dialogue*, 93 (note).

30. Peter Ramus, *That There is But One Method of Establishing a Science*, ed. Leonard A. Kennedy, trans. Eugene J. Barber and Leonard A. Kennedy (The Hague: Mouton, 1973), 136.

31. Peter Ramus, *Arguments in Rhetoric*, trans. Kevin Roddy (Rheims: Mathew David, 1549), 58 (MS in University of California at Davis translation project

directed by James J. Murphy; page numbers correspond to those in the 1549 edition).

32. Fraunce, *Lawyer's Logike*, 3.
33. Harvey, *Ciceronianus*, 95.
34. Ramus, *Arguments in Rhetoric*, 30.
35. Peter Ramus, *Scholae in Liberales Artes* (Basel: Per Eusebium Episcopium and Nicolai F. Hacredes, 1569; repr. New York: Georg Olms Verlag Hildesheim, 1970), 281.54.
36. Ramus, *Arguments in Rhetoric*, 13.
37. Ibid., 57.
38. Ibid., 38.
39. Ibid., 12.
40. Harvey, *Ciceronianus*, 95.
41. Ramus, *Arguments in Rhetoric*, 28.
42. Ibid., 95, 47.
43. Ramus, *That There is But One Method of Establishing a Science*, 136–137.
44. Ibid., 137.
45. Aristotle, *Topics*, I.i. passim.
46. Aristotle, *Posterior Analytics*, trans. Hugh Tredennick (Cambridge, Mass.: Harvard University Press, 1976), 71b.21–23.
47. Ibid., 71b.34–72a.5.
48. Peter Ramus, *Scholae in Liberales Artes*, 619–620.
49. Peter Ramus, *The Art of Logike of the Most Excellent Philosopher, P. Ramus*, trans. Rolland M'Kilwein (London: Thomas Vautroullier, 1574), 12.
50. Quoted in Jardine, *Francis Bacon*, 53.
51. Aristotle, *Topics*, 159b8–9.
52. Ramus, *That There is But One Method of Establishing a Science*, 117.
53. Fraunce, *Lawyer's Logike*, Civ. In his translation of the key passage in Aristotle, Ramus concedes that "what is known absolutely is perhaps not what is known by all." He concludes, however, that Aristotle means that all definitions must be known "both by nature and to us." The mind will also "understand, by means of the sense, other singulars of the same genus, even though these singulars have never been seen or known before" (*That There is But One Method of Establishing a Science*, 118). In contrast, the line in the Greek text by no means requires the conjunction of both kinds of clarity in all true dialectical definitions: definitions are not good if the definer "happens to have framed his description *neither* from what is more intelligible absolutely *nor* from what is more intelligible to us" [*met' . . . met'*]. (My italics, *Topics*, 142a 15.)
54. Quintilian, *Institutio Oratoria*, VII.i.25.
55. Ibid., VII.i.28.
56. Ibid., VII.i.40–41.
57. Ramus, *Scholae in Liberales Artes*, 551.
58. Aristotle, *Topics*, 155b 29–32.
59. Ramus, *Scholae in Liberales Artes*, 551.
60. Aristotle, *Topics*, 156a 12–14.
61. Ramus, *Scholae in Liberales Artes*, 551.

62. Ibid., 551; Aristotle, *Topics,* 156a 23–24.

63. Ascham, *The Scholemaster,* 93.

V. THE *ESSAYS*

1. Michel de Montaigne, *Essays,* in *Selected Essays of Montaigne,* trans. John Florio, ed. Walter Kaiser (Boston: Houghton Mifflin, 1964), 63–64.

2. Noted in Edward Arber's *A Harmony of the Essays, Etc. of Francis Bacon* (London: English Reprints, 1871), 91 (note).

3. *MS* VII.245.

4. 1 Corinthians 9.19.

5. Ibid., 10.17.

6. Ibid., 9.16.

7. All references to the 1607 edition are to Arber's *A Harmony of the Essays.* The 1607 edition does not appear in Spedding's edition of Bacon's works.

8. *Hamlet,* I.iii.78–80 in *The Riverside Shakespeare.*

9. Arber, *A Harmony of the Essays,* 198, 200.

10. Ibid., 202.

11. Ibid.

12. Ibid., 204.

13. Ibid.

14. Ibid., 266.

15. Ibid., 268.

POSTSCRIPT

1. Flavius Philostratus, *Life and Times of Apollonius of Tyana,* trans. Charles P. Eells (New York: AMS Press, 1967), 292. For further evidence of Bacon's appropriation of magic, see D. P. Walker, *Spiritual and Demonic Magic from Ficino to Campanella* (London: The Warburg Institute, 1958), 199–202.

2. Ibid., 103.

3. Ibid., 219.

4. Ibid., 218.

INDEX

Aaron, 133–134, 136
Abel, 5
Abraham, 91
Achelous, 179
Adam, 5, 8, 16, 43, 250
Agricola, Rodolphus, 199–205, 206, 207, 214
Agrippa, Cornelius: *De Occulta Philosophia Libri Tres*, 59–67; *De Vanitate*, 59, 155; recommended by Bacon, 201
Alexander, 162
Alchemy, 8, 12, 117; Ashmolean, 72–79; Bacon's view of, 79, 148–150, 245
Anaxagoras, 3, 5
Antonius, Marcus, 52, 240
Aphorisms, 6, 17, 218–219
Aphrodite, 187
Apocalypse, 16
Apodeixis. See Aristotle
Apollo, 187
Apollodorus, 1
Apollonius of Tyana, 252–253
Apollonius of Tyra, 63
Apollonius Rhodius, 1
Aquinas, St. Thomas, 65
Areopagites, 119
Argonauts, 1
Aristaeus, 34
Aristotle, 11, 12, 29, 43, 84, 99, 113, 114, 139–140, 151, 152, 154, 155, 156, 169, 202, 204, 207, 210, 213, 247; *apodeixis* as interpreted by Ramus, 208–213; *Analytics*, 206, 209; *De Anima*, 59, 102; *doxa* (opinion), 191, 206; *dunamis* (potentiality), 56–59, 67, 69; *endoxa* (potentially philosophical opinion), 191, 206; *ener-*

geia (actuality), 56–59, 60, 67; *Ethics*, 57–58, 104, 177, 274n10; *Metaphysics*, 56; *On the Generation of Animals*, 114; *Physics*, 56, 195, 209; *Poetics*, 58; *Politics*, 114, 274n10; *Rhetoric*, 58–59, 100, 176–178, 189–199, 204, 206, 274n10; *Topics*, 190–191, 200, 209, 211–212
Arnald of Villanova, 76
Ascham, Roger, 107, 109, 155, 213, 274n10
Asclepius, 55, 67
Ashmole, Elias, 72, 77
Astley, John, 107, 108–109, 110
Astrology, 59–60, 62
Atlantis: old, 19; new, 19, 40, 150, 154, 169–174, 243
Atomism, 36–37, 43–45, 138–142, 147, 148
Augustine, Saint, 9, 22, 27, 35–36, 47, 50, 64–65

Bacon, Francis: *Adv*, 2, 5–8, 15–17, 21, 22, 25–27, 29, 30, 31, 38–40, 77, 134, 137, 139, 148, 151, 152, 153, 156, 157, 161, 163, 164, 166, 167, 176, 193, 201, 230, 243, 247; *CGE*, 110–111, 218; *CNR*, 138, 140, 142, 143, 148, 149; *De Aug*, 20, 22, 24, 25, 27, 29, 37, 41, 42, 44, 132–133, 134, 136, 145, 150, 152, 154, 155, 160, 162, 163, 164, 166, 167, 175, 176, 193, 199, 200, 203, 213; *Essays*, 3, 4, 9, 10, 11, 12, 23, 28, 163; "Of Adversity," 145; "Of Ambition," 239; "Of Beauty," 240–241; "Of Ceremonies and Respectes," 220; "Of Discourse," 219–221; "Of Envy," 251–

Bacon, Francis *(continued)*
252; "Of Expence," 226–227; "Of Faction," 226–228; "Of Followers and Friends," 221–223, 233; "Of Friendship," 223–226, 233; "Of Gardens," 13; "Of Goodness and Goodness of Nature," 234–236; "Of Honour and Reputation," 228, 242; "Of Love," 239–240, 241; "Of Marriage and the Single Life," 236; "Of Masques and Triumphs," 242; "Of Nature in Man," 239; "Of Negociating," 229; "Of Nobility," 243; "Of Praise," 241–242; "Of Regiment of Health," 228; "Of Sutes," 226–227; "Of Simulation and Dissimulation," 31, 37–38, 246–247; "Of Studies," 215–219; "Of the True Greatness of Kingdoms and Estates," 242; "Of Truth," 233, 243–246; "Of [Unity in] Religion," 233, 237–239; "Of Vainglory," 242; "Of Wisdom for a Man's Self," 233–234, 235; *FL*, 8, 14, 137; *HRK*, 26; *HVM*, 134, 145–147, 242, 252; *IM*, 5, 6, 8, 15, 16, 20, 36, 77, 173; *IN*, 9, 159; *ITCM*, 148, 150; *LD*, 201; *LL*, 249; *Masculine Birth of Time*, 201; *MS*, 23, 24, 217–218, 230–233; *NA*, 19, 40, 150, 154, 169–174, 243; *NO*, 4–5, 6, 7, 8, 9, 14, 15, 17, 24, 26, 36, 80, 143, 144, 145, 147, 148, 152, 155, 156, 157, 158, 159, 161, 162, 193; *P*, 36; *PO*, 138, 140, 142, 144, 159; *RCB*, 132, 238; *SS*, 134, 148, 149, 150, 167, 253–254; *SV*, 1–2, 14, 19, 20, 21, 33, 43–45, 135–140, 142, 145, 154, 159–161, 167, 174; *VT*, 176
Barber, Eugene J., 274n10
Basil, Saint, 109
Baudouin, Jean, 259n30
Bembo, 122
Bible: 1 Corinthians, 23–24; Ecclesiastes, 17; Exodus, 132, 134; Genesis, 5–6, 8, 45–48, 59, 60, 139; Hebrews, 46; 1 Kings, 21; Numbers, 133; Proverbs, 17; Psalms, 118; The Wisdom of Solomon, 17, 18, 36
Blundeville, Thomas, 108, 110
Boccaccio, 128
Boetia, Stephen de la, 223
Boreas, 179–180
Bostocke(?), R., 14
Breen, Quirinus, 227n9
Bright, Timothy, 101–106, 108

Bulephorus, 130
Burger, Ronna, 274n17
Burghley, Lord, 5
Burton, Robert, 104–106, 109

Caesar, Augustus, 166
Caesar, Julius, 166
Calvin, John, 46–48, 50
Castiglione, Baldassare, 100, 119, 120–128, 220
Chalcidius: Commentary on the *Timaeus*, 54
Charity, 7–8, 21–25, 165, 232–237, 243, 247–248, 253
Chaucer, Geoffrey, 64, 77
Cicero, 89, 92, 115, 129–131, 151, 154, 155, 156, 169, 176, 177, 202, 213, 274n10; *De Oratore*, 80–82, 90, 99–100, 112, 125; *Orator*, 82; *Rhetorica ad Herrennium*, 130; *Topica*, 200
Claudius, Appias, 240
Cleopatra, 52
Code, 9, 18, 25–29
Coelum, 138–139, 142
Color (tincture), 69–72; alchemical, 72–79, 93; Bacon's view of, 148–151
Columbus, 162
Comes, Natalis, 34
Contemplation: Bacon's defense of, 4–7
Copernicus, 68
Copes, Edward, 189
Cordelia, 56
Cortesi, 130
Crane, R. S., 12, 107–108
Cupid, 44–45, 141, 144
Cyrus, 114, 116

Daedalus, 13, 167–168
Daniel, Samuel, 112
David, 118
Davies, Sir John, 103–104
Delivery, 99–100
Demetrius, 120
Democritus, 138, 139, 141, 142, 160
Demosthenes, 99
Deucalion, 43
Dialectic: in Plato's *Phaedrus*, 186–187; Aristotle's definition of, 190–194; Aristotle's view as interpreted by Ramus, 191–192, 205–213; Ramus's view as interpreted by Bacon, 213–214
Dido, 98
Digges, Thomas, 68

Diogenes, 21
Dis, 145–146
Divo, Andrea, 33–34
Doxa (opinion), 191, 206
Dress, 93–94, 98
DuBartas, Guillaume de Salluste, 49, 50
Dunamis (potentiality), 56–59, 67, 69

Edward VI, 39
Egyptian Learning, 50–55
Elizabeth I, 40, 243
Elyot, Thomas, 72, 104, 107
Energeia, 56–59, 60, 67
Endoxa (potentially philosophical opinion), 191, 206
Erasmus, 151, 201; *Ciceronianus,* 129–131; *De Copia,* 90–91, 203
Eros, 178–189. *See also* Bacon's "Of Love"
Essex, Earl of, 20, 243
Eurydice, 1, 34, 135
Eve, 43

Faerie Queene, 48
Farrington, Benjamin, 10
Feigning, 100, 121
Fenner, Dudley, 88, 99
Ficino, Marsilio, 59, 108, 178, 274n10
Fish, Stanley, 3, 9, 10, 29
Fracastoro, Girolamo, 84–85, 86
Fraunce, Abraham, 34, 88, 99, 120, 203, 206, 210
Freese, J. H., 177, 195, 197
Fridericke, Sir, 120
Funkenstein, Amos, 258n27

Garden of Adonis, 48
Gemma, Cornelius, 34, 261n38
"Georgics of the Mind," 37–38, 167–168
Giamatti, A. Bartlett, 259n35
Golden Fleece, 1
Gorges, Sir Arthur, 260n1
Gorgias, 179
Gower, John, 75–76
Greene, Thomas, 85
Grimaldi, William M. A., 275n54
Gulliver, 108

Hardison, O. B., 86
Harrison, J. L., 10
Harvey, Gabriel, 206, 207
Hawes, Stephen, 71, 94, 95

Helen of Troy, 182
Henry VII, 26, 39, 40, 250
Hercules, 1, 19
Hermes Trismegistus, 55
Hesiod, 179
Hexaemeral Tradition, 46–50
Hieroglyphs, 163–164
Highmore, Nathaniel, 50
Hitchcockes, William, 111–112
Hobbes, Thomas, 189
Hoby, Thomas, 120, 122–123, 124
Homer, 33–35, 259n30
Horace, 115, 116, 120, 128
Horse-training, 100, 106–112; Bacon's view of, 246
Hoskins, John, 88, 89, 274n10

Iago, 97
Instrument, 94. *See Prosthekai*
Isocrates, 187
Isis, 51–52

James I, 39, 40, 152, 243; *Daemonology,* 50–51
Janus, 163
Jardine, Lisa, 4, 10, 11, 201, 202, 274n10
Jason, 1
Jebb, R. C., 197
Jesus, 244
Job, 3, 8, 250
Jonah, 3, 173
Jonson, Ben, 79–80, 92, 128–129
Jung, Carl, 76

Kennedy, Leonard A., 274n10
Kosmos, 99

Lanham, Richard, 85–86
Larsen, Robert E., 273n6
Le Roy, Loys, 52
Lear, 56
Lewis, C. S., 12, 114
Lewis, Richard W. B., 277n1
Limbus, 253–254
Loci, 202–205
Lord, Carnes, 190
Lucretius, 244
Lully, Pseudo Raymond, 71, 78, 79
Lydgate, John, 94
Lysias, 178–189

Machiavelli, 234, 248
Magic, 12, 150, 158, 252–254, 279n1;

Magic *(continued)*
non-goetic, 59–67, 116–117; in the Bible, 132–136
Markham, Gervase, 109–110
Mary I, 40
McKeon, Richard, 277n1
McNally, J. R., 277n13
Melanchthon, Philip, 201, 203
Menelaus, 33–35, 142
Meun, Jean de, 71, 74, 78–79
Midas, 76–77
Middleton, Thomas: *The Wisdom of Solomon*, 20, 28
Minos, 45, 167
Montaigne, 223, 246
More, Sir Thomas, 91
Mornay, Philippe de, 102
Moses, 48, 132–135, 136, 138, 238–239, 243
Murphy, James J., 278n31
Murrin, Michael, 272n33

Nauart Jr., Charles G., 262n70
Noah, 19
Nohrnberg, James, 48
Norton, Thomas, 73, 74, 77
Nosoponus, 130

Oceanus, 179
Oedipus, 13–14, 174, 214
Omnia per Omnia Encryption, 27–28, 42, 232
Ong, Walter, 192, 201, 202
Opinion. See *Doxa* and *Endoxa*
Oriethyia, 179–180
Orpheus, 1–2, 11, 21, 34, 59, 63, 134–136, 139, 141, 146, 176
Osiris, 51–52
Othello, 97
Ovid, 43, 45, 76

Pan, 25, 43–45, 139, 200
Pandarus, 64
Paracelsus, 71, 72, 77
Parmenides, 56
Passions, 100–106. *See also* Eros
Paul, Saint, 15, 21–24, 41, 46, 232
Peacham, Henry, 70, 87–89, 90, 94
Peitho, 179, 186
Penelope: unformed matter, 44, 139–140
Pericles, 3
Phoenix, 43

Pilate, 244
Plato, 9, 12, 19, 30, 43, 62, 64, 84, 113, 114, 139–140, 151, 152, 155, 160, 169, 173, 199, 202, 203, 213; Bacon condemns, 137; myth of the cave as interpreted by Bacon, 175–176; *Phaedrus*, 3, 108, 128, 178–189, 190, 192, 198, 274n10; Ramus's reading of the *Phaedrus*, 206–208; *Timaeus*, 50–55, 57, 60, 99, 172
Pliny, 68
Plotinus, 57
Plutarch: poem as speaking picture, 205; Isis and Osiris in the *Moralia*, 51–53; *Isis and Osiris* condemned by Sidney, 117–118; *Lives*, 52; treatise on cosmology, 52–55, 261n34
Politian, 130
Polonius, 32, 234
Pompey, 89, 166
Potentia (potentiality), 56–59, 67, 69, 76
Pretending, 100
Prometheus, 19
Proserpine, 145–147
Prosthekai, 196–197
Proteus, 32–40, 142–143, 147, 149, 150, 168, 247, 259n30, 259n35
Pugliano, 106–107, 108, 112, 113, 116, 119
Puttenham, George, 93, 95–98, 118–119, 120, 129
Pyrrha, 43
Pythagoras, 160
Pythagoreans, 59

Quintilian, 83–85, 88, 98, 108, 169, 202, 204, 210–211

Rainolde, Richard, 94, 95, 201, 274n10
Raleigh, Sir Walter, 68
Ramus, Peter (Pierre de la Ramée), 189, 191–192, 201, 202, 203, 205–214, 273n10, 278n53; generals, 208, 214
Rawley, William, 132, 238
Rees, Graham, 4, 10
Rhetoric: Bacon's definition of, 29–32; linked with alchemy, 71; as light, 70; *accumulatio*, 69; *adjunctio*, 72; allegory, 120; *anadiplosis*, 97; *anaphora*, 97; *antithesis*, 68; *bomphiologia*, 89; *catachresis*, 97; *corax*, 195; *courtier*, 119; *eclipses*, 95; *ecphonesis*, 89; *enargia*, 96; *energeia*, 56–59,

60, 67, 115; *elaboratio,* 71; *emphasis,* 83–84, 88, 98; *epanados,* 69; *hyperbole,* 89, 96; *hypotiposis,* 70; *imprecatio,* 89; *ironia,* 88, 99; metaphor, 89–90, 96, 99; *metaplasmus,* 88; *paradiastole,* 96; *paralogistikon,* 196; perspecuity, 198; *prosonomasia,* 97; *prozeugma,* 96; *repetitio,* 89; *sinonimia,* 98; *traductio,* 98; *zeugma,* 88, 95

Richter, Ann, 10
Richard III, 26
Rider, John, 72
Ripley, George, 74–75
Roberts, W. Rhys, 189
Roddy, Kevin, 277n31
Romilly, Jacqueline de, 179
Rossi, Paolo, 10, 148
Royal Society, 2

Saint Bartholomew's Day Massacre, 213
Saintsbury, George, 84
Salomon, 170–174
Salomon's House, 170–174
Savill, Sir Henry, 201
Schumaker, Wayne, 262n70
Seminal Forms, 62
Seneca, 19–20
Sewell, Elizabeth, 2, 11
Shakespeare, William: Baconian critics, 28; modern critics, 96–97; *Hamlet,* 32, 69–70, 75, 234; *King Lear,* 56; *Merchant of Venice,* 92; *Othello,* 96–97; *Troilus and Cressida,* 64
Sherry, Richard, 87, 91, 92
Sidney, Sir Philip, 69, 92, 106–107, 108, 112–118, 274n10
Sirens, 137–138
Socrates, 3, 7, 128, 176, 178–189, 199, 207
Solmson, Friedrich, 190
Solomon, 6–9, 16, 17, 18, 20–23, 28–29, 32, 40, 41, 133, 243, 244, 246, 251
Sophists, 7, 151, 189, 190, 195, 198, 212. *See also* Lysias

Sphinx, 14, 160–161, 174, 214, 217
Spirit: Bacon's conception of, 145–147. *See also* Limbus
Sprat, Thomas, 2
Sprezzatura, 100, 119, 122, 124, 130, 220
Stephens, James, 10–11, 29
Stesichorus, 182
Sturmius, John, 86–87
Swift, Jonathan, 107–108
Sylvester, Joshuah, 49
Sylla, Lucius, 166

Taylor, Frank Sherwood, 73, 76, 78
Tethys, 179
Theophrastus, 59
Theseus, 13
Thomas, Thomas, 72, 94, 95
Thorndike, Lynn, 76
Toulmin, Stephen, 70
Trevisa, John de, 48
Tuve, Rosemond, 85
Tyndale, William, 17–18
Typhon, 45, 51, 261n38

Vickers, Brian, 10
Violence, 32–40, 63, 109–112, 142–150; coercion, 94; in Plato's myth of the charioteer, 183–186
Virgil, 33, 37, 167
Vives, Juan Luis, 201

Walker, D. P., 279n1
Wallace, Karl, 10, 29
Weaver, Richard, 186–187
Whitehead, Alfred North, 155
Whitney, Charles, 11, 29
Wilson, Thomas, 91, 92, 93, 98–99
Wright, Thomas, 79–80, 100–106, 108, 129

Xenophon, 108, 116

Zosimus, 71